UNDERSTANDING LEADERSHIP

UNDERSTANDING LEADERSHIP

PARADIGMS AND CASES

GAYLE C. AVERY

With cases contributed by
Andrew Bell, Martin Hilb and
Anne E. Witte

SAGE Publications
London • Thousand Oaks • New Delhi

First published 2004

 SAGE Publications Ltd
1 Olivers Yard
London EC1Y 1SP

SAGE Publications Inc
2455 Teller Road
Thousand Oaks, California 91320

SAGE Publications India Pvt Ltd
B-42, Panchsheel Enclave
Post Box 4109
New Delhi 100 017

British Library Cataloguing in Publication data

A catalogue record for this book is available
from the British Library

ISBN 0 7619 4288 2
ISBN 0 7619 4289 0 (pbk)

Library of Congress Control Number available

Typeset by C&M Digitals (P) Ltd., Chennai, India
Printed in Great Britain by The Cromwell Press Ltd, Trowbridge, Wiltshire

Contents

List of Figures, Tables and Boxes

FIGURES

TABLES

BOXES

Preface

The changing face of leadership in today's increasingly dynamic and dispersed world presents management practitioners and scholars alike with considerable challenges. Are current ways of leading really appropriate for today's organizations, let alone tomorrow's? What kind of leadership is appropriate for different kinds of people and organizations? What are future-thinking organizations doing about developing leadership for tomorrow? How should leadership relate to its context, and is there any one best approach? And how do all those theories and ideas about leadership relate to one another?

To try to answer these and other questions, contemporary case studies from well-known organizations in Europe, Australia and the US are presented to illustrate how diverse leadership can be in 'successful' organizations. In today's interconnected, global world, traditional ideas about leadership are being challenged as both large and small organizations strive to continuously adapt to changing internal and external environments. Future leadership will depend on many factors, some of which most of us probably cannot yet even envision. These research based case studies provide some clues.

This book innovates in various ways in its endeavour to capture the complexity and diversity surrounding leadership. First, it introduces four leadership paradigms to help simplify and clarify the fuzzy, ill-defined field of leadership. The Classical, Transactional, Visionary and Organic paradigms are intended to provide a useful language and set of concepts for understanding leadership theory and practice, as well as to provoke discussion. Many aspects of leadership are integrated in the paradigms in distinguishing them from one another. Some of these differences will undoubtedly be controversial.

In addition, this book covers an extensive range of leadership theories and concepts. Approaches range from getting the every-day front-line managerial work done, to working through emotion, vision, values, and organizational strategy and learning. This eclectic approach contrasts with writings on leadership that adopt a more limited theoretical framework. Rarely have both psychological and strategic approaches to leadership been incorporated in the one book. Traditionally, the study of leadership has tended to focus either on the characteristics of the heroic individual and leader–follower interactions, or else on broad strategic leadership issues.

Understanding Leadership: Paradigms and Cases also departs from many conventional leadership books by approaching leadership at different levels, ranging from the micro-level, through the group and organizational levels, to incorporating considerations beyond the organization itself. This book reflects the fact that, in practice, leadership occurs at different organizational levels, and necessarily encompasses a wide range of issues – including managing knowledge, developing self-managing teams and leadership capability, managing change and innovation, forming partnerships with stakeholders, developing cultures, learning and mentoring, promoting spirituality and meaning in the workplace, and sustaining and growing the organization itself.

Throughout, the book refers to examples derived from the prominent organizations illustrated in Part II. In most of these case studies, the case author worked in or visited the organization in 1999 and 2000, seeking information about the organization at the beginning of the new millennium. The case study organizations are considered leading-edge in their field, and cover both private and government enterprises, and a range of different sizes and industries.

The conceptual tools developed in Part I can be used to understand how leadership operates in the case studies. The reader sees that a best practice company need not always be best practice in every sphere of activity, and that there is no one best way of leading, despite a trend towards more self-leading members in organizations. These living cases depict a palette of leadership approaches, displaying either aspects of excellence in leadership, or raising common leadership issues. Although excellence in leadership is difficult to define, the case study organizations have created, or are adapting, their 'leadership' to fit both their internal and external environments. At the end of each case study, specific questions guide the reader in interpreting and analysing the cases, connecting them to the leadership frameworks and theories in Part I, and challenging the reader to think about the issues raised in each case study.

Acknowledgements

A book like this can only be written over a long time, and with the support of many people around the world. In particular, I would like to thank:

For his on-going criticism, many illustrations and loving patience throughout the drawn-out writing process: Harry Bergsteiner, Australia.

For their invaluable contribution to case study writing: Andrew Bell, Australia; Martin Hilb, Switzerland; Anne Witte, France; and MBA students from Macquarie Graduate School of Management, Australia.

For generously sharing their knowledge and insights about the organizations covered in the case studies with the case authors: Senior executives in the case study organizations.

For an inspiring set of books and personal communication: Wilfred Drath, USA.

For her enthusiastic assistance in editing and production: Gillian Lucas, Australia.

For excellence in obtaining most of the references: Shawkat Alam and Macquarie University Librarians, Australia.

For their critical reading of early manuscripts and valuable feedback: Dr Katarina Hackman, Australia; Dr Sooksan Kantabutra, Thailand; Dr Steven Segal, Australia; my students.

For support in producing the manuscript: Macquarie Graduate School of Management, especially Laura Deverson, TISO, Nick Martorana and their teams.

For background on competencies and Hay-McBer approaches: Wendy Montague, Australia.

For his most valuable assistance in editing the book: Dr Robert Rich, Australia.

For editing and publishing the manuscript: Seth Edwards, Kiren Shoman and the team at Sage Publications, London.

For generously providing stunning environments for writing in Ruhpolding, Bavaria and Roquebrune, France: The Tirichter-Koerner Family, Munich, Germany.

Gayle C. Avery

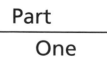

Part

One

Understanding Leadership

What is a leader? Who is one? Could anybody become one? Is the concept outmoded?

Before answering such questions, we need to develop a common language about leadership, which is a complex and confusing field. We can do this using two basic tools presented in Part I of this book. First, a framework organizes ideas of leadership around four *leadership paradigms*. A 'paradigm' is a pattern that serves as an example of a concept. After introducing some fundamental concepts in Chapter 1, Chapters 2 and 3 describe the paradigms so that previous research, which has generally focused on isolated components of leadership, can be better understood and integrated within this framework. This then provides us with a common understanding of the four broad paradigms of leadership.

It is also important to link the many, very different leadership theories to the paradigms. Chapters 4, 5 and 6 summarize a range of leadership theories, concepts and approaches, showing how they find expression at four organizational levels: the individual, dyadic or group, organizational, and external or strategic levels. Chapter 4 covers the micro-level, looking at theories relating to individual leaders, as well as relationships between leaders and followers or teams. Chapter 5 focuses in particular on emotion-based leadership concepts, including emotional intelligence, values, and the visionary, transformational and charismatic components of leadership. More macro-level leadership approaches operating at the organizational level and involving 'external' leadership considerations are covered in Chapter 6. In Chapter 7, leadership theories and concepts are explicitly related to the leadership paradigms, showing that some approaches apply more to certain paradigms than to others.

The chapters in Part One provide a conceptual basis for analysing and understanding the case studies that follow in Part Two, but the text also refers to the case studies to illustrate some of the concepts and theories raised in Part One.

1 The Leadership Scene

Key Points

- Concepts of leadership
- Definitions and ideas of leadership
- Leadership in context
- Leading in changing situations
- Aligning leadership and followership
- Organizational performance and leadership

Leadership has long been a topic of interest in complex civilizations, dating back at least to the beginning of written knowledge. For example, in *The Republic*, Plato distinguished between leaders as men of 'gold', and those not intended to lead as men of 'bronze'. Leadership issues similar to those that people talk about today, such as charisma, leadership as heroic action, the nature of managerial work, organizational equilibrium versus conflict, how to lead through meaning and symbolism, manipulating the truth, and follower participation can be found in Plato's discourse.[1]

The idea of developing leadership capability also stems from antiquity. McCullough's[2] extensive research into ancient Rome, Greece and Troy reveals that many leaders were destined by birth for leadership, and were prepared for this role through their education and experience. Preparing the Pharaohs for leadership was also given considerable thought and attention, while the famous Greek philosopher, Aristotle, was entrusted with the education of Alexander the Great, the future leader of an empire.

Despite literally millennia of interest in the practice and development of leadership, Bennis and Nanus[3] point out that 'leadership is both the most studied and the least understood topic' in the social sciences. The concept of leadership remains elusive and enigmatic, despite years of effort at developing an intellectually and emotionally satisfying understanding. This is probably because people discussing leadership are likely to have different concepts in mind, making communication about leadership rather difficult. Consider which of these examples indicate leadership:

- Julius Caesar, growing up among poor immigrants in the tenement blocks of Rome where mutual learning and exchange of ideas take place.
- Winston Churchill, giving the order to bomb Dresden, after the Second World War had officially ended.
- Hewlett and Packard setting up the HP way.
- The US Supreme court voting 5–4 to give the 2000 presidency to George W. Bush, thereby determining the outcome of the Gore–Bush election.
- Mother Teresa setting up and running her order to treat the poor in India.
- A change of culture in the British Royal Family following Princess Diana's death.
- Firemen ordering people to leave their homes threatened by bushfire.
- A teacher, mentor or coach in action.

Some people may feel that some of these examples stretch the idea of leadership a bit far, while others would argue that despite their differences, the above instances all reflect leadership. Can all these examples possibly refer to the one concept? Answering this question requires an understanding of what leadership is about – a major challenge.

WHAT IS LEADERSHIP?

Understanding leadership is challenging for several reasons:

1 There is *no agreed definition of leadership* or what the concept should embrace. Many definitions are fuzzy and inconsistent, making it extremely difficult to have a sensible conversation about the concept. When discussing leadership some people include:

- what others would term 'management';
- reference to the past, present or future;
- dealing with change or managing stability;
- a figurehead or symbol; or
- a process of influence.

Thus, people may well be talking about very different concepts when using the term 'leadership', as the examples above show. Traditional models of leadership mostly err in assuming that all individuals in a given organization or society share a common experience and understanding of leadership. Even employees within one educational institution hold a range of ideas about what it is to be a leader.[4]

2 *Most ideas about leadership have been intentionally broken down into smaller components* so that scholars can conduct publishable research into them. As a result, much of the work on leadership is currently too simple to reflect the full richness and complexity that practitioners face on the job.

3 *Theories and research into leadership are far from complete.* Individual scholars tend to focus on particular aspects of leadership, with few attempting to build consistent theories. Thus, possibly because of the difficulties in agreeing on what leadership is, leadership research and writings contain many gaps that have not been investigated.

4 The *ideas underlying concepts of leadership have changed over the course of history,* parallelling many social and other changes. Since the end of the twentieth century, society has been undergoing change at an almost breathtaking pace. Some of these changes are affecting leadership concepts and practices, as this book will show. A complete understanding of leadership requires acknowledging that leadership concepts apply within a particular social context, and can vary with place and time. What passes as effective leadership in one context may be seen as ineffective in another. Practitioners are seriously challenged in adjusting to new leadership approaches.

Therefore, common definitions and terms are essential to enable people to discuss leadership in a meaningful way. The chapters in Part One of this book are designed to provide this common platform, illustrated by the case studies in Part Two. This common platform maps out a field in which different definitions are situated in relation to each other.

The available information needs to be organized. This begins in Chapter 2 through the introduction of four fundamentally different ways of looking at leadership: the *Leadership Paradigms.* The paradigms were inspired by four 'phases' of leadership defined by Dr Wilfred Drath and his colleagues[5] at the US Center for Creative Leadership. Although Drath later refined his phases into three, this book expands upon the different ideas of leadership reflected in the four phases.

Ideas of leadership vary, depending on the level of organization to which they are applied. This has led to a range of seemingly unrelated theories. Some focus on the individual leader, others on *leader–follower* relationships, on leadership at the organizational level, or on the influence of external stakeholders and environments. Scholarly tradition has been to separate many of these approaches. This book breaks with this tradition by including and integrating the different perspectives, allowing the understanding of the various theoretical approaches from within a manageable context.

The reader can refine his or her understanding of each leadership paradigm by relating it to other approaches. In addition, readers can focus on the detail in each paradigm while also obtaining a perspective on the relationship between paradigms.

The reader is then invited to apply the leadership paradigms and associated theoretical approaches to case studies from prominent organizations in Part Two of this book. A study of these actual examples will allow you to apply the theoretical concepts of Part One to the full complexity and diversity of leadership, operating in a variety of contexts. You will see that effective organizations exhibit different kinds of leadership, depending on how they approach their environment, structure, core business, culture, people, processes and systems. Further, 'appropriate leadership' depends very much on a very broad range of internal and external factors, particularly the extent to which members of a group share paradigms of leadership in common.

CONTEXT OF LEADERSHIP

Today's organizations operate in a rapidly changing context, which is compounding complexity and uncertainty at all levels of society. Institutions, including business organizations, are changing in paradoxical ways – becoming more complex and yet employing people who work from home, more differentiated and yet more similar globally, more intricately connected both internally and externally, while simultaneously more lonely and isolating for some individuals. Ever-increasing diversity among people, nations and cultures is impacting business organizations in a globalizing world of multicultural workforces. Individuals (at least the better-off ones, mostly from the developed world) now have almost endless choices of lifestyle – they can communicate and work from any location they choose, shop, learn and research on-line, and work hours that suit them. In addition, some of the traditionally most excluded people in society, such as the disabled and the elderly, can become included via the communications revolution.[6]

The 'included' people are forming one intricately connected world, a global village, with complex interrelationships and dependencies among the members. Globally dispersed design teams work around the clock on the same project using virtual technology, for implementation or manufacture in yet other locations. Helpdesks, human resource (HR) functions and other services are becoming centralized in one or two parts of the world to service global operations and customers.[7] Markets are now global, and competitors come from unexpected directions, as do alliance partners. Global information networks are forming both between and within organizations in an effort to create efficiencies, develop markets, and manage knowledge and technology.

Humankind appears to be in the midst of a chaotic transformation on various fronts.[8] Even science is searching for renewal, turning towards the New Sciences of *chaos, complexity* and *self-organization* (described in Chapter 3), with their implications for managing in uncertain times. Major shifts lie ahead in the workplace, where the roles of home and office tend to be reversing. The home is becoming the place of productivity, and the office more like a social hub where people go to meet with others.[9] To maintain human society, people will need to adjust the quality of their relationships by becoming appropriately cooperative and mutually responsible. This is because of the increasing interdependence and connectivity, and because the focus is now on using and developing knowledge (see examples of this in the Gore and Rodenstock case studies).

Although people still need and want products, the old industrial era is no longer sustainable and the emphasis on manufacturing is giving way to, or being expanded to, include knowledge-based service, information, bioscience and new materials economies. For example, EKATO, a case study in Part Two, is moving from merely designing and manufacturing industrial mixing machines, to also becoming a provider of solutions to mixing problems using its employees' and customers' knowledge. Similarly, SAP is shifting from providing software products to solutions.

The speed of change on multiple fronts seems to be pushing humankind to the limits of its adaptability. People have no sooner adapted to one change than the next one is upon them, bringing more uncertainty and complexity. The challenge is for leadership to operate under rapidly mutating circumstances, which requires a rethink of paradigms of leadership both in theory and in practice. For many organizations, this means moving away from the traditional control model towards alternatives that emphasize cultural competence, corporate learning and facilitation skills.[10] The success of new leadership approaches will depend on aligning people, organizational systems, processes and culture with the new conditions. This may well include changing the leadership paradigm(s) prevailing in an organization (see the BMW, Rodenstock and Royal Australian Navy case studies).

DEFINING LEADERSHIP

Before considering how leadership might operate in tomorrow's organizations, it is important to explore what leadership is about. This is not an easy task, given that there are nearly as many definitions of leadership as there are people trying to define it.[11] Broadly-defined concepts such as leadership have the advantage of allowing for innovation and the development of existing ideas, and enabling thinkers from many disciplines to contribute to the field.[12] However, their very broadness makes these concepts highly ambiguous, subject to multiple interpretations and difficult to research.[13] With the scope of leadership virtually endless, it is not surprising that there is little agreement on definitions, measures and other factors necessary to advance the field.

An acceptable definition of leadership needs to be sound both in theory and in practice, able to withstand changing times and circumstances, and be comprehensive and integrative rather than atomistic and narrow in focus. Expecting to find a single definition or approach to a complex concept like leadership is probably rather naïve, for several reasons:

1 *Leadership is not a concrete entity*, but is more appropriately regarded as a social construction that occurs in a historical and cultural context, and within the minds of the people involved.[14] So, to understand how concepts of leadership emerge, it is important to identify how people think about leadership and the mental models they employ.[15] Different people see leadership reflected in different situations, depending on what the perceiver believes leadership is all about, as the examples above illustrate.

2 *Ideas about leadership are affected by concepts of leadership held within a particular culture* or other context in which people find themselves. Box 1.1 illustrates that a person has one idea on leadership in the abstract, but may have another where a particular context is described. Without a context, people tend to hold command-and-control as their basic leadership model.

3 The study of *leadership is replete with myths* bearing little relationship to reality. This does not help advance the field.[16] Leadership myths include the idea of heroic, omnipotent leaders who can solve all organizational problems, often single-handedly. According to other myths, leadership is a rare skill, leaders are born with special characteristics, leadership occurs mainly at the top of an organization, and effective leaders control and command others.[17] Another myth is that leaders work mainly for the good of their organization, but clearly, inept or malicious leaders do not benefit their group. Some leaders work to enhance their own ends. History has judged Hitler as a leader working towards evil outcomes, although he clearly employed many widely used leadership practices.

4 The idea of the *heroic leader* abounds. Intellectually, it is evident that the lone heroic leader cannot continue to exist in today's complex, dynamic organizations, no matter how talented and gifted. Even as founder and major stockholder in Microsoft, Bill Gates does not lead the organization single-handedly, nor can he command people to be creative and committed to the organization. Rather, leadership is a distributed phenomenon, occurring in various parts of an organization, not just emanating from the top (see, for example, the BMW, Gore, Rodenstock and Royal Australian Navy case studies).

Despite these challenges, studying leadership is popular in organizational studies, attracting social scientists from various disciplines, including management, psychology, sociology and politics. These disciplines themselves are continually changing. Some of the changes are reflected in, or impact on, the theory and practice of leadership. In turn, changes to related disciplines influence the study of leadership. For example, developments in the New Sciences have enabled management theorists to move away from viewing organizations as machines to seeing them as complex, self-organizing networks under minimal direct control. This clearly modifies the concept of leadership.

Changing business environments also affect ideas about leadership. Early suggestions that leadership definitions be restricted to leader-attempts to influence followers' behaviour face to face, highlight the importance of adaptability in defining leadership.[18] Clearly, insisting on face-to-face leadership is no longer tenable in an increasingly virtual world, where some leaders and followers interact solely via communication and information technology, and may never meet in person. Therefore, definitions of leadership should be capable of adapting to new ideas and circumstances.

Box 1.1

Mental models of leadership

A mental model is a set of basic assumptions about how the world works. People are generally unaware of the extent to which these assumptions shape their actions.[19] Andrews and Field[20] sought to uncover people's mental models of leadership. To do this, the researchers employed metaphors, that is, linguistic devices in which one object is likened to another by speaking of it as if it were the other. For example, when thinking of an organization as a film, describing the leader as the writer suggests an underlying concept of the leader as the person who creates situations for others to act out, writes the script, and sets the rules of interaction.

The researchers found that the leadership concept that people hold when leadership is not placed in a particular context, is predominantly that of a directive activity. This is rather like the idea of Classical leadership described in Chapter 2. People of all ages, education, work experience and geographic locations held this default model of leadership. A second interesting finding was that vision is not part of the general person's prototype of leadership, despite the popularity of vision in the academic literature. If Classical leadership is a widely held conception of leadership across social and cultural groups, then it appears that the populace has not yet caught up with academic models of leadership.

Since the public tend to populate organizations, this research raises the question of how ready followers are for alternative ideas about leadership. Networked organizations require people to change their established ways of thinking and relating to one another, and to give up some of the traditional notions inherited from hierarchical authority systems.[21] In particular, this mindshift will include abandoning the comforting belief that the leader is in control in this turbulent world.

In addition, research needs to account for leadership occurring at different levels. Most researchers choose to focus on either individual leaders or the broad strategic leadership sphere. A few have attempted to bridge these domains. For example, Boal and Hooijberg[22] propose that the effectiveness of leaders in affecting organizational performance depends in part on individual factors, such as a person's ability to deal with mental and behavioural complexity and social skills. Boal and Hooijberg link organizational performance to *visionary leadership* and leader competencies like *cognitive complexity* and *social intelligence*. They argue that individual leader capabilities, such as possessing managerial wisdom, capacity to change and ability to learn, are critical to this link. However, this and other valiant attempts to consider both micro- and macro-leadership issues are still limited, neglecting many relevant issues.

In trying to understand leadership, scholars have tended to break it down into smaller components, focusing on narrow facets such as decision making.[23] More recent calls are for integrative and holistic approaches.[24] Part of the challenge in defining leadership is that most approaches are based on subjective preferences for including or excluding certain elements or levels of analysis from the concept.[25] This book takes a very broad view of leadership, ranging from the interpersonal level through to the organizational level and beyond. This is done in an attempt to integrate widely diverging theories and approaches to a complex and ill-understood topic.

As Drath[26] points out, effective leadership requires alignment between both leaders' and followers' ideas about leadership. If someone believes that leadership is about leaders telling followers what to do, then a participative approach in which followers are consulted and expected to make decisions will not be interpreted as leadership. It may be seen as the exact opposite of 'proper' leadership – the appointed leader would be regarded as abrogating his or her responsibilities. Similarly, to another person who believes that leadership is all about enticing people to follow grand ideas or visions, using coercion to get people to comply with someone else's command may not be recognized as leadership, but regarded as 'bossing people around'. Effective leadership involves aligning ideas about what leadership is among the members of the affected group or organization.

Researchers also fall prey to social constructions of leadership, as much of the literature shows. For many practitioners and researchers alike, leadership has been raised to an idealistic, lofty status and significance, focused around heroic individuals. This has led to certain approaches, such as *command-and-control* leadership, falling largely out of favour with scholars and no longer being recognized as appropriate within the literature. By contrast, writings on *charismatic* and *transformational* leadership show that scholars typically depict such leaders with almost solely positive attributes, compared with more control-oriented leaders who tend to be accorded negative characteristics.[27] This is reflected in the literature's current favouring of low-control, *visionary* leadership.

Another challenge to a unitary definition of leadership comes from scholars who argue that leadership does not vest in characteristics of leaders, but is attributed to them by followers. Leadership, thus inseparable from the observer, has been defined as the process of being perceived by others as a leader.[28] In other words, leadership 'involves behaviors, traits, characteristics, and outcomes produced by leaders as these elements are interpreted by followers'.[29] In this view, leadership does not exist separately from follower perceptions.

Research suggests that the context influences perceptions of a leader. In one study, participants asked to manage (hypothetically) a troubled group biased their perception of job candidates towards describing them more favourably, making more references to leadership skills and abilities than did those participants given responsibility for a tranquil group.[30] This and other studies suggest that answering the question 'What is leadership?' must therefore look within the mind of the follower; a challenge to any researcher and practitioner.

It is not greatly surprising to find a counter-argument emerging, that leadership is highly romanticized and unnecessary. Advocates of this view even propose abandoning the term altogether.[31] The criticism is certainly justified that the prominence given to leadership as a central organizational process is unrealistic. Whether leaders impact their organizations to the extent many observers claim remains contentious.[32]

However, simply eliminating notions of leadership would leave people without a term to describe the factor that provides direction and cohesion to a group. This factor may not necessarily take human form, but could stem from the culture or interactions between organizational members, a shared set of values and beliefs, or from following long-dead leaders. This book focuses on revealing leadership in its complexity, rather than abandoning the concept.

DOES LEADERSHIP AFFECT PERFORMANCE?

A major consideration before trying to understand more about leadership is whether the effort is likely to be worthwhile. Is leadership important? Does leadership make a difference to organizational performance?

Traditionally, corporate performance has been measured in financial terms, although Kaplan and Norton,[33] in their 'balanced scorecard' approach, and others argue for including non-financial measures as well. These might take the form of employee and customer satisfaction, concern for the environment and other stakeholders, or other measures directly relevant to a particular organization's objectives. However, research studies usually consider performance in terms of tangible factors such as growth and profits.

The very question of whether leadership affects performance reflects a belief that direct cause-and-effect relationships can be observed between a leader and the success of the organization. This assumption is often made, but is difficult to test. Correlations between performance and leader behaviour, even if consistently observed, do not mean that one causes the other, merely that they are associated. For example, the observation that leaders of high-performing units rarely intervene in followers' activities does not mean that the non-intervention is what causes the high performance. Team spirit, incentives and rewards, the interesting nature of the tasks, and working for a well-respected company might be other contributing factors (see the BMW case study). An interventionist approach where these factors are present may also be associated with high performance. Nonetheless, many researchers seek the roots of high performance in leadership, particularly at the upper echelons.

People have difficulty in making judgments about complex phenomena. This complicates observations of cause and effect between leadership and performance, particularly when employees are assessing leadership carried out at a distance from them at top levels.[34] The influence of senior leadership often operates indirectly, making it almost impossible for people to assess its impact. In this case, employees may erroneously assume that the leadership is, or is not, having an effect. Despite many practical and conceptual challenges, the question of whether leadership makes a difference continues to occupy researchers.

Work by Lieberson and O'Connor[35] is generally taken as indicating that top leaders have little impact on organizational performance. The research team obtained external data on 167 major companies across 13 industries, looking at sales, earnings and profit margins, by year, industry, company and leadership. The findings have been widely interpreted as suggesting that overall, leadership does not distinguish between successful and less successful organizations.

Other studies also suggest that change of leadership does not greatly affect organizational performance,[36] with leadership only accounting for 7–15 per cent of changes in city budgets. Collins and Porras, in their study of visionary companies, found no evidence 'that great leadership is the distinguishing variable during the critical, formative stages of the visionary companies ... we had to reject the great leader theory; it simply did not adequately explain the differences between the visionary and comparison companies'.[37]

Pfeffer[38] identifies several reasons why the observed effects of leaders on organizational performance might be small:

1 Those appointed to leadership positions are chosen, and this *process of selection may impose a limited range of behaviour styles*. Therefore, overall, leaders would tend to behave in very similar ways, making it difficult to observe much difference between their leadership effects.
2 Once in the leadership position, *the discretion and behaviour of the leader are constrained* by pressures to conform, play politics and please superiors. In reality, leaders generally do not have as much power and authority as their position might suggest.
3 *Leaders cannot normally affect many of the variables that are likely to impact on organizational performance*, especially external factors. Clearly, the leader's potential lack of influence in some situations further emphasizes the importance of followers in the success of leadership, and the need to understand organizations as broad systems. Thus, leaders' effects might be reduced or enhanced by particular situations.

On the other hand, the Lieberson and O'Connor study and its derivatives may have been misinterpreted. A 1988 analysis across the then published research studies provided consistent and compelling evidence that individual leaders do make a difference.[39] From this critical review of the studies on this topic, Thomas concluded that leadership does make a difference at the level of the individual firm. On an aggregate basis, across industries and firms, other factors such as size and industry can mask leadership effects within a single firm. For example, focusing on large organizations can bias against finding that leadership matters because individual leaders are more likely to have an impact on small organizations.

Hambrick and Mason[40] stress the importance of looking at individual firms to assess the impact of leadership. They take the view that an organization becomes a reflection of its top managers, who act on the basis of their incomplete, filtered understanding of a situation. Hambrick and his colleagues argue that the characteristics of the top team matter far more than those of individual CEOs.[41] Thus, knowledge of the experiences, motives, values and characteristics of *top management groups* would enhance understanding of leadership's effects.

Other writers support the idea of seeking the impact of leadership on performance in individual firms.[42] In one such study, Collins identified a typical pattern of leadership behaviour in those large organizations spectacularly transforming from being good performers to great performers.[43] He terms this 'level 5 leadership', which is described in Chapter 5.

In trying to understand the nature of a leader's influence, Lord and Maher[44] distinguish between a leader's direct and indirect impact on organizational performance. Direct impact refers to a leader's specific influence on followers, decisions or policies in such a way that follower behaviours are changed and substantially impact performance, for example, through feedback or instruction. Direct impacts like these are more likely to occur at lower levels of management than at the top, although they can occur at both levels.

Leaders can also affect followers and organizational performance indirectly – by actions like creating an environment in which subordinates can work effectively, developing an appropriate culture, influencing whether other managers perceive events as challenges or threats, building commitment to organizational goals, and formulating strategy.[45] These mechanisms tend to be diffuse, spread over time and difficult to pinpoint as the direct result of top leadership.

Supporting evidence that leadership operates indirectly on performance comes from the US Malcolm Baldridge National Quality Awards. These awards are based on an assumption that leadership creates results indirectly by driving the organizational system – in terms of financial results, customer focus, process management, human resources, strategic planning and information analysis. A detailed statistical study of this Baldridge assumption concluded that, overall, leadership does drive the system that leads to organizational performance.[46] However, leadership's impact is indirect, ensuring that processes, people, strategy and information are managed appropriately, in turn leading to customer focus and satisfaction, and/or financial results.

Thus, after years of debate, the popular view that leaders impact organizations has received general research support. Now the focus has shifted from whether leaders have impact, to understanding more about leadership.

CONCLUSION

This chapter shows that the notion of leadership is complex, its meaning tending to reflect the social context in which it occurs, and that scholars and practitioners alike disagree over defining the concept. Persistent popular myths and mental models of leadership complicate the picture further. Research suggests that command-and-control leadership prevails as a general mental model, despite a major shift in the management literature towards visionary and emotion-based leadership. Researchers themselves are subject to preconceptions about what leadership is or should be, with many unrealistically ascribing only positive virtues to heroic visionary leaders.

Understanding leadership is challenging because of a lack of agreement as to what leadership is and the tendency for researchers to focus on narrow aspects of the field. Further, theory and research are underdeveloped. Perhaps a search for 'the' definition of leadership is illusory, given the broad range of contexts that the concept has to cover. Not only rapid change, but also increasing diversity, reliance on knowledge, and employing extensive communication networks are complicating the study of leadership. This changing context requires rethinking many ideas about leadership.

An additional challenge comes from the need for leadership theory and research to align with the practice of real-life leaders, particularly given that leadership is essentially an applied concept.

Some scholars argue that, contrary to the prevailing dogma, leadership does not rest in leaders but is attributed to individuals by those who become their followers. Under this view, leadership resides in the minds of followers and other beholders, and is a socially agreed construct. In this case, the proposition that effective leadership stems from aligning ideas of leadership held between leaders and the led is quite compelling.

A radical approach to the confusion surrounding defining leadership is to argue that leadership is an unnecessary concept and should be abandoned altogether. However, increasing evidence that leadership does impact an organization's performance suggests that the concept is worth retaining and researching further.

Rather than either abandoning the concept or proposing a single, necessarily oversimplified definition for leadership, an alternative view is that understanding leadership can be aided by giving the topic more detailed consideration. This is the approach taken in this book. In the next chapters, many ideas underlying leadership and its characteristics are discussed, to help clarify what leadership is all about. Four leadership paradigms are introduced to show how broad concepts of leadership can be identified and used as an aid to discussion on a wide range of complex leadership issues.

NOTES

For full details of these notes, please see the References section at the end of this book.

1 Takala, 1998
2 McCullough, 1998a, 1998b
3 Bennis and Nanus, 1985:20
4 Kezar, 2000
5 Drath, 1998
6 Cairncross, 1997
7 O'Hara-Devereaux and Johansen, 1994
8 Merry, 1995
9 Cairncross, 1997
10 e.g. O'Hara-Devereaux and Johansen, 1994; Kotter, 1985; Krantz, 1990
11 Stogdill, 1948
12 McKinley, Mone and Moon, 1999
13 Weick, 1995
14 Burla, Alioth, Frei and Müller, 1994; Gergen, 1997; Lord and Maher, 1991
15 Andrews and Field, 1998; Drath, 2001
16 Bennis, 1998
17 Bennis and Nanus, 1985.
18 e.g. Campbell, 1977
19 Senge, Kleiner, Roberts, Ross and Smith, 1994
20 Andrews and Field, 1998
21 Hirschhorn, 1988, 1997
22 Boal and Hooijberg, 2001
23 Vroom and Yetton, 1973
24 Cacioppe, 1997; Clegg and Gray, 1996
25 Campbell, 1977; Fairholm, 1998a
26 Drath, 2001
27 Lewis, 1996
28 Andrews and Field, 1998; Lord, 1985; Lord and Maher, 1991; Emrich, 1999
29 Lord and Maher, 1991:11
30 Emrich, 1999
31 e.g. Meindl, Ehrlich and Dukerich, 1985
32 e.g. Pfeffer, 1978; Thomas, 1988
33 Kaplan and Norton, 1992
34 Lord and Maher, 1991
35 Lieberson and O'Connor, 1972

36 Salancik and Pfeffer, 1977
37 Collins and Porras, 1994:32
38 Pfeffer, 1978
39 Thomas, 1988
40 Hambrick and Mason, 1984
41 Cannella, Pettigrew and Hambrick, 2001
42 e.g. Jacobs and Singell, 1993; Miller and Droge, 1986; Norburn and Birley, 1988
43 Collins, 2001
44 Lord and Maher, 1991
45 Lord and Maher, 1991
46 Wilson and Collier, 2000

2 Leadership Paradigms

Key Points

- Establishing a common understanding
- Need for an integrating framework
- The four paradigms explained
- Adopting appropriate elements for the situation

Although there is no shortage of approaches to leadership, the lack of agreement in the field makes discussing, researching and theorizing about leadership difficult, as Chapter 1 highlights. This chapter addresses the problem of confusion over what leadership is about, proposing four leadership paradigms as a device to help establish a common understanding.

The paradigms are intended as a way of tying together a great deal of theorizing and research information into one framework. They attempt to link and differentiate between broadly distinguishable concepts of leadership. Although given the range, variety and fuzzy nature of leadership ideas, no classification system could be comprehensive and contain mutually exclusive categories.

Integrating aspects of leadership ideas and practices has also been attempted elsewhere. For example, Bass[1] proposed that leadership practices fall on a continuum. At one end are *autocratic practices* such as:

- being directive, authoritarian and coercive;
- using leader-based decision-making and power;
- emphasizing goals; and
- adopting a task and performance orientation.

At the other end of Bass' continuum, are *democratic practices*, including:

- consideration for followers;
- consultation;
- consensus;
- developing a people and relationship focus;
- group-based decision making;
- facilitating interactions; and
- sharing power and authority.

In addition, Bass proposed that leadership can range from highly involved to *laissez-faire*, in other words from *active* to *passive*. Stewart and Manz[2] and others have built on Bass' work, for example, by combining the active–passive and autocratic–democratic dimensions.

Broad, holistic approaches such as Bass' provide a valuable starting point for integrating the entire field of leadership. They reverse the trend in most leadership theorizing and research by adopting a more differentiated and yet integrative approach. The tradition of breaking concepts into many smaller components may make researching and theorizing easier and more rigorous, but often results in a superficial and incomplete view of leadership.

One criticism of most attempts at integration is that they still overlook much of the complexity of leadership in their necessarily simplified classifications. Further, adopting an atomistic approach may lead researchers to forget that leadership is 'embedded in a complex of interactions between leaders, followers, colleagues, organizing mode, environmental factors and all those other variables we can handily call context'.[3] The paradigms presented in this book extend, and will hopefully enrich, some of the existing integrative approaches by linking as many relevant findings and approaches from the literature as possible.

The approach adopted here recognizes that in practice, leadership is multifaceted, holistic, spans various organizational levels and spheres, and encompasses many variables including factors both internal and external to the organization.[4] Therefore, the leadership paradigms presented here, and developed further in Chapter 3, include wide-ranging material. The paradigms can be distinguished from one another in terms of various elements derived from the literature. In this way, many theories and research findings are integrated into one framework to reveal much of leadership's complexity.

PARADIGMS

The leadership paradigms are depicted in Table 2.1. They represent four broad sets of ideas, which are termed *Classical*, *Transactional*, *Visionary* and *Organic* leadership. The paradigms are intended as four illustrative points along several continua, rather than as four distinct categories or types.

Table 2.1

Leadership paradigms

Leadership Characteristic	Classical	Transactional	Visionary	Organic
Major era	Antiquity–1970s	1970s–mid-1980s	Mid-1980s–2000	Beyond 2000
Basis of leadership	Leader dominance through respect and/or power to command and control.	Interpersonal influence over and consideration of followers. Creating appropriate management environments.	Emotion – leader inspires followers.	Mutual sense-making within the group. Leaders may emerge rather than be formally appointed.
Source of follower commitment	Fear or respect of leader. Obtaining rewards or avoiding punishment.	Negotiated rewards, agreements and expectations.	Sharing the vision; leader charisma may be involved; individualized consideration.	Buy in to the group's shared values and processes; self-determination.
Vision	Leader's vision is unnecessary for follower compliance.	Vision is not necessary, and may not ever be articulated.	Vision is central. Followers may contribute to leader's vision.	Vision emerges from the group; vision is a strong cultural element.

In Table 2.1, the paradigms are arguably arranged along various continua, which reflect different aspects of leadership. For example, a basic dimension along which the paradigms are arranged is time, reflecting the era of their emergence in the leadership literature. Classical, the oldest paradigm with its origins in antiquity, was the prevailing view until the 1970s, when the human relations movement led to a focus on followers and their environment. This gave rise to the Transactional paradigm. While the Classical paradigm can still be found today, Transactional and other paradigms have emerged to challenge it as the primary one. From the mid-1980s and until about 2000, a major paradigm shift led to the emergence of Visionary leadership with its emphasis on follower commitment to a vision of the future. Finally, the paradigms are shifting again in a distributed, fast-moving, global environment, this time to a paradigm new to many leaders, termed Organic leadership.

The paradigms also differ in their underlying basis of leadership. This ranges from Classical leaders' dominance to a de-emphasis on individual formal leaders under the Organic paradigm. Follower commitment, as opposed to enforced compliance, also increases as the paradigms move from Classical across to Organic leadership. Finally, the paradigms differ in how much they depend on visionary leadership, being arranged in order of increasing dependence on vision. To this extent, the paradigms tend to be arranged along dimensions that reflect Bass' autocratic–democratic and leader-focused versus follower-focused continua.[5]

The leadership paradigms provide a platform for subsequently highlighting broad differences in behaviours, beliefs, power, processes and applications of leadership. The paradigms are largely based on different underlying assumptions. This makes them flexible enough to adapt to different circumstances, and reflects many of the ways that leadership can be understood by different groups of people. The four paradigms are described in more detail below.

Classical leadership

Classical leadership refers to dominance by a pre-eminent person or an 'elite' group of people. This individual or group commands or manoeuvres others to act towards a goal, which may or may not be explicitly stated. The other members of the society or organization typically adhere to the directives of the elite leader(s), do not openly question their directives, and execute orders largely out of fear of the consequences of not doing so, or out of respect for the leader(s), or both. Classical leadership can thus be coercive or benevolent, or a mixture of both.

Examples of Classical leadership abound throughout history, particularly the coercive version. The Egyptian Pharaohs, US slave owners, and European feudal lords were not alone in favouring this style of leadership. More recently, the former Soviet Union, Hitler's Germany, Saddam Hussein's Iraq and other totalitarian societies operated on a version of the Classical leadership paradigm. Germans who disobeyed Hitler risked being sent to concentration camps. Neighbours spied on one another in Communist Eastern Europe. Devotees of admired leaders illustrate the benevolent side of Classical leadership, such as where Lee Kwan Yew turned Singapore from a poor fishing village into a global player. Some entrepreneurs may be followed out of a mixture of respect and fear (see the Bonduelle and Swatch case studies). By the same token, devotees of admired leaders like Hitler also illustrate the non-benevolent side of Classical leadership.

Commanding and controlling people has been a pervasive leadership style in many twentieth-century business organizations, and indications are that it is still popular today. Traditional French leadership operates on dominance and the leader's power, where followers carry out the leader's commands. Many Asian cultures adhere to Classical leadership, where the boss dictates what others have to do.[6] As we have seen, even to many North American people, with their individualistic values, Classical leadership feels right and appears to be basic to people's mental models about leadership.

Classical leadership operates successfully when leaders and followers accept the right or duty of the leader(s) to dictate to the population. This acceptance is often based on beliefs that the leader has this right through:

- birth (kings);
- divine appointment (Catholic Pope, some Egyptian Pharaohs);
- industrial, political or military position (Henry Ford, Singapore's former Prime Minister Lee Kwan Yew, General Patton);
- a particular belief system (cult and sect leaders); or
- cultural norms (tribal chiefs, family heads).

Having others make decisions, give directions and take responsibility has the advantage of freeing followers from these activities.

Irrespective of why Classical leadership is accepted, it lends itself to conditions of stability or slow change,[7] providing that the leader is willing to take charge and accept associated responsibility. Further, both leaders and followers need to believe that the leader knows what is right to achieve specified goals. Classical leadership can also lend itself to rapid change without a consultative process, providing that the followers can and will comply with the leader's requirements and that the followers have the necessary skills.

Evaluating the Classical paradigm

Classical leadership has its limitations. For example, when the Classical leader steps down, succession can precipitate a crisis. Will the successor be able to step into the predecessor's shoes, exercising the required degree of control or attracting the necessary respect (or fear)? Classical leadership is limited where the leader cannot command and control every action, particularly as situations become more complex and beyond the capacity of one person (see the Bonduelle case study). Or when additional commitment from followers is needed to get a job done, such as in reacting to changing circumstances (see the Royal Australian Navy case study). Or when ideas about leadership change and followers no longer accept domination, or follower commitment starts to wane for other reasons.

A further limitation of Classical leadership is that it relies on the idea of a 'great person', implying that only a select few are good enough to exercise initiative. This can encourage followers to de-skill themselves and idealize the leaders.[8] Followers then seek and hold little power, leave the leader accountable for group outcomes, and make relatively little contribution to the enterprise.

Sometimes followers begin to think for themselves and question whether they need this kind of leadership. This was clearly seen in former communist East Germany. Under Classical leadership, East Germany had become the strongest economic power in the communist bloc, but by 1990 times had changed. A new form of leadership was needed. The last major Communist leader, Erik Honecker, lost his control over the population after the people demonstrated on the streets for the fall of the Berlin Wall. East Germans banded together with their new thoughts of freedom and more democratic leadership. The groundswell was too strong for military coercion to be effective (in any case, the soldiers wanted freedom too). External circumstances had also changed when Hungary allowed East Germans to escape though its territory into the West and the Soviet Union signalled its unwillingness to interfere. Hence Honecker's control was undermined. East Germans began to desert their country in droves, and the tide was only stemmed when the leadership and power systems changed.

Transactional leadership

Transactional leaders view followers as individuals, with more focus on their skills, needs and motives than is likely under Classical leadership. The popular definition of leadership as a process in which one individual uses intentional influence to 'guide, structure and facilitate activities and relationships in a group or organization',[9] reflects the basic idea behind the Transactional paradigm.

Transactional leaders and followers interact and negotiate agreements, that is, they engage in 'transactions'. It is thus very important for the leader to have the power to reward followers.[10] Other transactions require correcting followers or only getting involved with issues that need the manager's attention, known as management-by-exception.

Various kinds of Transactional leadership can be identified. Kuhnert[11] distinguishes two types.

- At the minimum level of development, Transactional operators are concerned with achieving their own personal needs, although they can simultaneously serve the interests of individual followers through the agreements they make with staff.
- Other Transactional leaders, whom Kuhnert calls 'team players', are concerned for the welfare of their followers, and for maintaining good interpersonal relationships with individuals and the team as a whole.

In general, Transactional leadership depends heavily on the leader's skills, confidence in his or her chosen direction, and on obtaining some cooperation from the followers. Such leaders attempt to persuade and influence followers to achieve certain ends, taking some account of the followers' points of view as part of the negotiations. Transactional leaders use interpersonal skills to motivate, direct, control, develop, teach and influence followers more than they themselves are influenced.[12] Transactional leaders tend to:

- possess some expertise or knowledge that the group accepts as relevant;
- be skilled at negotiation, persuasion and motivating others; and
- be accepted as the most appropriate person to lead the group at the time.[13]

Although the Transactional leader typically occupies a formal leadership position, who leads a group can even be the subject of negotiation and influence. Sometimes an influential member who does not occupy a formal leader role within the group may emerge as the 'real' leader of a group. A change of leadership can occur when different expertise becomes relevant, or another person becomes more influential than the former leader. However, normally the Transactional leader derives power to reward and influence from holding a formal position.

Influence can work in both directions. By being consulted, followers can influence the leader. A team-player leader, in particular, may be open to a change in direction, just as through consultation followers can be influenced towards the Transactional leader's view. Hearing a range of views also enables this influence-based leader to gather more information, and hence address somewhat more complex situations than under the Classical paradigm. Although a Transactional leader may hold a view of the future, 'selling' this vision is not essential for effective Transactional leadership. The focus tends to be short-term and on maximizing immediate outcomes and rewards.

Typically, the influencing process central to the Transactional paradigm includes using both rewards and incentives. Sometimes the Transactional leader may adopt coercive and dominating behaviour whereby the leader commands followers[14], but consultative decision-making styles are more appropriate to this paradigm.

Stable conditions are likely to provide Transactional leaders with the opportunity to negotiate with followers and act as the situation requires. Suited to managing traditional bureaucratic organizations, Transactional leadership is prevalent in many early twenty-first-century organizations. Considerable leadership/management training focuses on developing a manager's skills in relating to followers.[15]

Evaluating the Transactional paradigm
The Transactional paradigm overcomes some of the limitations of Classical leadership by considering and involving followers. Through this process, the leader gains more information and ideas and followers can be developed and have their individual needs recognized. However, staff can perceive the monitoring typical of Transactional leadership as constraining, reducing their likelihood of contributing to organizational goals. A Transactional leader's corrective interventions and management-by-exception can upset some followers and reduce their performance.[16]

In times of rapid change and uncertainty, Transactional leadership becomes limited, particularly when greater commitment is needed from followers, or if followers need to be willing to make major changes to their mindsets and behaviour.[17] It is unrealistic to expect a Transactional leader to predict and negotiate all the required changes in other than relatively simple situations, and during incremental change.[18] Innovation, much needed for coping with fast-paced complex environments, does not normally flourish under the Transactional paradigm.

Transactional leaders are likely to aim for a united group that heads in the leader's set direction, albeit after the leader has listened to the followers' points of view. As in Classical leadership, where the leader sets direction and gains commitment or compliance, followers of Transactional leaders can become complacent and overly dependent on the leader.[19]

Further, a Transactional leader is likely to approach decisions with a focus largely on short-term payoffs. This means that projects or changes that go beyond the current budget cycle or bring little immediate benefit may not be considered.[20] This does not prepare the organization for change, whereas espousing a view of the future and a longer-term perspective could provide other means of influencing followers. However, adopting such an approach reflects a different leadership paradigm.

Visionary leadership

Both Classical and Transactional leadership suit times of stability or slow change, where the future is relatively predictable, major shifts are not needed in direction or action within the organization, and work processes and markets are known and predictable. Late in the twentieth century, these conditions changed to conditions of increasing turmoil and turbulence, aptly likened to the 'permanent white-water' conditions in river canoeing.[21]

Much of leadership's failure to cope with the new white-water conditions has been attributed to too much management and too little leadership.[22] Trying to influence, control and organize in complex, fast-paced, changing conditions using the Classical or Transactional paradigms was not working. Times of fundamental change were everywhere at the end of the twentieth century, but the way forward was not clear. A different style of leadership was called for.

A popular answer is variously termed 'visionary', 'charismatic', 'inspirational' or 'transformational' leadership, all basically referring to the Visionary paradigm. Employees and shareholders alike often pin their hopes on finding Visionary leadership.

History records numerous leaders who have inspired their followers to work towards a vision. Many have been political leaders such as Martin Luther King or Nelson Mandela, or religious leaders like Jesus Christ, Buddha or Mohammad. Business has also spawned heroic leaders, who seemingly single-handedly turned around collapsing organizations or set up new ventures. For example, Anita Roddick established The Body Shop around environmental and social issues in 1976. Richard Branson of the Virgin Group is another visionary leader. Philip J. Carroll, visionary President and Chief Executive Officer of Shell, inspired staff when he wanted Shell to become the 'premier US company with sustained world-class performance in all aspects of the business'.[23]

Although Visionary leadership can occur at all levels of an enterprise, admirers tend to focus on top leaders who capture the hearts and minds of organizational members with their images of some desired future state. These extraordinary leaders are expected to provide a clear vision of the future, develop a road map for the journey ahead, and motivate followers to realize the vision. This involves the emotional commitment of followers.[24]

It is a mistake to treat Visionary leaders as if they possess superhuman, heroic qualities. Instead, leadership should be regarded as a product of the times, followers, opportunities and the leader's skills.[25] Acclaimed leaders like Iacocca at Chrysler or Jobs at Apple seemed to lose their potency not because the leaders themselves changed, but because the situation and needs of the followers, markets and organization changed, and their visions and skills no longer fitted.

Followers of a Visionary leader are not expected to be passive, but have a responsibility to participate in the group, work towards the vision and make their voices heard in influencing what is accomplished. The many voices contributing to an organization enable the leader to view confusing, complex and ambiguous situations in diverse ways, hence increasing the receptive leader's chances of choosing the 'right' strategy. The Visionary leader tends to consult more widely than the Transactional leader, including voices from outside the immediate group.

Despite being idealized in the literature, Visionary leaders employ coercive tactics at times.[26] For example, Jack Welch purged GE of underperformers on the 'C' team, while he simultaneously inspired followers on the 'A' and 'B' teams through his vision of the future. In transforming organizations, Visionary leaders may employ Classical and Transactional techniques to implement their visions.[27] Even though they may not abandon all the elements of Classical and Transactional paradigms, Visionary leaders work predominantly through inspiration and vision.

Sometimes visions are developed and proclaimed by the leader. At other times, visions emerge from the organizational members. Here the leader's task becomes to listen to the many different views, and then unite the followers behind one inspiring vision. Under the Visionary leadership paradigm, the message is that everyone needs to share the vision and pull in the same direction to implement it.

Interestingly, certain aspects of Visionary leadership appear to be universally recognized, according to the results of a 62-country study.[28] Recognized characteristics of Visionary leadership include:

- being trustworthy, just and honest;
- being charismatic, inspirational, encouraging, positive, motivational, confidence building, dynamic, good with teams, excellence-oriented, decisive, intelligent, a win-win problem solver; and
- exercising foresight.

Not universally recognized as part of Visionary leadership are being:

- a loner,
- non-cooperative,
- ruthless,
- non-explicit,
- irritable, and
- dictatorial.

Evaluating the Visionary paradigm

Like other paradigms, Visionary leadership has its limitations, despite the literature's overwhelmingly positive view of it. Nadler and Tuschman[29] point out the unrealistic expectations followers often place on Visionary leaders, which can create disappointment if things do not work out. Followers can become dependent on Visionary leaders, believing that the leader has everything under control. Further, innovation can be inhibited if people become reluctant to disagree with a Visionary leader.

To overcome these problems, visionary leaders are advised to keep the size of their units as small as they can without compromising the group's goals and activities.[30] The larger the group, the more difficult it is for the leader to take account of individuals' needs and to motivate all the members.

Advocates tend to overlook the fact that leadership involves a political process, which can have both positive and negative effects depending on the observer's viewpoint. Visionary leaders traditionally strive to achieve unity within their organization, rallying the members behind a single vision, set of values, strategy and behaviours. Those members who do not fit typically leave the organization.

The challenge of gaining commitment from followers using a single vision is intensified in a globalizing world, where organizations are increasingly operating within and between different national cultures, with growing diversity in the workforce.[31] More recently, the limitations of unity have been raised and calls made for embracing diversity rather than unity.[32] By recognizing and building on the fact that people in complex organizations hold diverse views, priorities, values, experiences and worldviews, an organization can better meet the needs of local customers and staff in different parts of the world and prepare itself for adapting to unknown changes. This diversity needs to be accommodated in both the content of the vision and in the kind of leadership displayed to ensure that they align.[33]

One of the myths exploded by a study of successful premier companies is that visionary organizations are great places to work for everyone.[34] Only those who fit extremely well with the core ideology and demanding standards of a visionary company find it a great place to work. 'Visionary companies are so clear about what they stand for and what they're trying to achieve that they simply don't have room for those unwilling or unable to fit their exacting standards.'[35]

Despite the management literature's strong favouring of Visionary leadership, Visionary leadership is not necessarily synonymous with good leadership.[36] Effective leaders do not have to be visionary.[37] This paves the way for alternative paradigms of leadership.

Organic leadership

Although management scholars and practitioners have long assumed that the ideal world is one of unity focused around a single leader, emerging forms of networked organizations are making the idea of the single central leader largely irrelevant.[38] According to some writers, the new global firm will employ a process orientation that allows it to innovate and adapt easily to rapid technological change.[39] It will be without boundaries, and increasingly driven by customers' expectations of service. Leaders will operate in a culturally diverse environment in which knowledge is the most critical success factor, along with a well-educated workforce. Multiple perspectives and talents are needed to solve the problems that many organizations face.

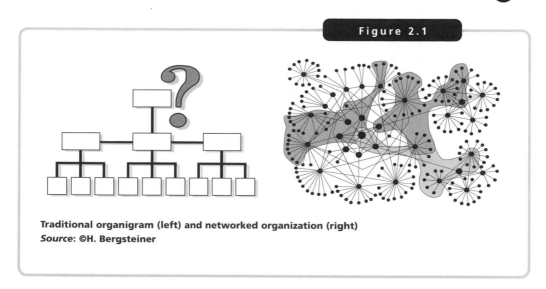

Figure 2.1

Traditional organigram (left) and networked organization (right)
Source: ©H. Bergsteiner

In practice, how can one individual direct or influence the complex, nebulous systems in today's organizations? Figure 2.1 contrasts the oversimplified, idealized, classical organizational charts typically found in company annual reports[40] (left) with the complex linkages between people in a networked organization (right). The right section of Figure 2.1 also shows that many of the interactions in the networked organization bypass the central management and other groups; such organizations are more appropriately depicted as a series of dynamic hubs and nodes, rather than as static boxes joined by horizontal and vertical reporting lines.

Cross-functional work groups, which are often also cross-cultural in composition, are common units within today's organizations. In an organic organization, individual membership of work units may change according to the needs at a particular time (see the EKATO case study), and members may participate in several such groups. Such self-managing, self-optimizing work groups resemble a *'fractal'* organization in which similar units are replicated in various departments.[41] In these self-managing work groups, leadership can change depending on the most appropriate member at the time, rather than being formalized in a permanent, appointed leader.

As more organizations intentionally or otherwise adopt a networked or organic structure, ideas about leadership have to change accordingly. New forms of leadership are needed to take account of the growing fragmentation of workers and of the real complexities and linkages between people in organizations. No single person or group is likely to dominate, influence or even unite networked organizational members through a unified vision.

Instead, leadership will need to operate more through vision and values permeating the entire culture (see the Gore case study), and at many levels in a networked organization. This requires a different concept of leadership for business organizations, although volunteer groups often function in an organic way. Sports and hobby clubs annually elect (coerce into office!) people to positions of responsibility, but decisions are taken as much by shifting subgroups of interested individuals as by the formal committee.

It has long been thought impossible to manage people in a networked organization.[42] Rather, the leader's role in such highly ambiguous contexts is to create enthusiasm and commitment and act as change-agent, cheerleader, coach, teacher and integrator (see the Rodenstock case study). People in leadership roles act more like facilitators than directors. At Gore, bosses are unnecessary and can be replaced by a culture containing a strong shared vision and set of values, supported by 'natural leaders' and sponsors with no directive function. No-one at Gore can tell others what to do.

Complex, global organizations are challenged to simultaneously accommodate diverse ideas about leadership and the future, and yet have all members of the organization working together to achieve common goals. Given the increasing diversity of expertise and culture, it is no longer workable to promote *the* single correct vision or way of doing things. Why should a marketing perspective dominate technical or financial considerations? Or the Chinese way be seen as better or worse than the Japanese or Indian approaches? Increased complexity, ambiguity and uncertainty means that there is no one right answer, and that the entire group needs to contribute to the search for the meanings of the many changes around them, a process often referred to as 'sense-making'.[43] No one person, leader or not, can do this alone.

How contemporary leaders will meet this new challenge is not yet clear. One scenario is that leadership is a process that requires people to constantly examine and redefine their basic assumptions.[44] This includes addressing the fundamental assumption of whether formal leadership is required at all (as at Gore). Another approach invokes Weick's sense-making processes in creating organizational action: processes involving the interconnections of work and people's shared interpretations of events.[45] Widely shared organizational goals, values and work practices emerge from the extensive communication needed to make sense of change (see the BMW case study).

Organic leadership is likely to blur or even eliminate the formal distinction between leaders and followers. Organic leadership will rely on reciprocal actions, where people work together in whatever roles of authority and power they may have, not based on position power.[46] Employees become interacting partners in determining what makes sense, how to adapt to change, and what is a useful direction. The range of partners will extend beyond employees to include stakeholders such as contractors, customers, competitors, suppliers and other alliance partners (see the BMW, Rodenstock and SAP case studies). These interactions form part of the culture and become, or replace, a guiding vision that a Visionary leader or top team was formerly expected to provide.[47]

Rather than relying on one leader, tomorrow's organic organizations are likely to have many leaders – to be '*leaderful*' organizations (see the Gore case study, where about 50 per cent of employees claim that they are leaders). Multiple leaders are valuable because as people cope with heterogeneous and dynamic environments, the knowledge and issues become too complicated for only a few leaders to understand.

Mintzberg[48] proposes the notion of covert leadership, analogous to how a conductor leads an orchestra, with leadership invisibly infused in everything the conductor does. Mintzberg observed that an orchestra's conductor is influenced by all the usual interpersonal concerns – players' sensitivities, union contracts and so on – but leadership is unobtrusive. It is a myth that the conductor is in complete control.

Just as in leading an orchestra, today's management is not about obedience and harmony, but nuances and constraints. Taking the musical analogy further, organizations tend to develop around smaller groups and teams consisting of experts, reminiscent of a jazz or chamber music group. Here, there may be no conductor; rather, leadership is shared as each player's expertise is called upon.[49]

Under Organic leadership, there may even be no formal leaders, possibly because no one individual is recognized as a leader. This might be because different groups of followers cannot agree on what leadership is needed, or because leadership may not be relevant to all the fields in which organizational members are active. Members may all be leaders at different times. Individuals may contribute to the leadership process in different ways, for example, by participating in events that help make sense of changes in competitor or customer behaviour, or by contributing ideas to move the organization forward (see the Novartis case study). Someone may be recognized as the temporary leader because of his or her current expertise, ability to influence others, or willingness to take on the role. Without a formal leader, the interactions of all organizational members can act as a form of leadership, held together by vision, values and a supporting culture (see the Gore case study).

In Organic organizations without a formal leadership structure, an integrator role may emerge to actively link together the many parts of the organization. Integrators can heavily influence decision making based on their unique perspective across the organization. Some integrators will be clearly identified with, and committed to, the success of their product groups, and have the interpersonal skills or credibility needed to resolve difficult conflicts. In the Swatch case, both the Hayek father and son appear to take integrator roles. Interestingly, at BMW the company's brand may well act as a non-human integrator and vision substitute. At Gore, the culture appears to be the integrator.

Evaluating the Organic paradigm

For many people, the Organic paradigm represents a radical change of thinking about leadership, followership and the traditional nature of organizations. It involves letting go of conventional notions of control, order and hierarchy, replacing them with trust and an acceptance of continual change, chaos and respect for diverse members of the organization. In Organic organizations, the members are expected to be self-managing and self-leading.

Other paradigms may enhance a particular organization's productivity, but many organizations today need to continuously self-organize in order to adapt to their internal and external business dynamics and needs.[50] This involves developing a culture and mindset in employees that embrace change as a continual process. In so doing, self-organizing becomes a natural organizational phenomenon incorporating flexible decision-making systems to meet change or anticipated change. In particular, organic forms stimulate creativity and innovation.[51]

Of the case studies in Part Two, Gore reflects the Organic paradigm most closely, but other organizations are tending in this direction. Clearly, although the Organic paradigm is not yet widespread across many organizations as a whole, Organic elements can often be found in self-managing work and project teams (see the BMW case study). Organic leadership is likely to spread as these team subcultures influence the broader organizational culture, starting with 'pockets of excellence' within larger organizations.[52]

It is unlikely that there will be just one form of Organic organization. Rather, leaderful and leaderless organizations may arise, along with hybrid forms in which some parts of the one organization can be termed Organic while others reflect different leadership paradigms. A good example of this is Swatch, where marketing is largely leaderless and Organic, the production arm is systems-driven and Transactional, and the enterprise as a whole can be regarded as the product of a Visionary leader who sometimes adopts elements of Classical leadership. Multiple paradigms are also likely to be found in organizations making the transition to Organic leadership (see the Rodenstock case study).

Organic leadership, with its varied forms, is one response to dynamic, complex, knowledge-based environments, but it is not a universal panacea. Moss Kanter highlights the downside of autonomy, freedom, discretion and authorization, namely loss of control and greatly increased uncertainty.[53] This can be painful and disturbing to some employees, especially managers who have been trained to eliminate 'surprises' or believe that management is about controlling uncertainty. It can also be distressing for followers seeking certainty and predictability.[54]

It is important to recognize that Organic leadership does not mean trading order for disorder. Rather, it is about generating a form of self-control and self-organization, where people have a clear sense of purpose and autonomy within a particular context.[55] An idealized Organic leadership paradigm requires letting go of Classical, Transactional and Visionary leader concepts and trusting in the capacity of the members to solve problems and make decisions in the interests of the organization. Organic leadership clearly relies upon *self-leading* organizational members.

While an increasing trend towards Organic leadership is expected, like all the leadership paradigms Organic leadership will be more easily applied in some cultures and conditions than in others. Importantly, the size of an organization, or its subunits in the case of large organizations, is likely to influence whether Organic leadership can be achieved. Clearly, communication becomes more difficult in large organizations where people may have little contact with one another. One solution is to restrict the size of sub-units within an Organic organization. At Gore, units tend to be split after reaching a maximum of 200 members, although the entire organization employs about 7000 people.

ADOPTING NEW LEADERSHIP PARADIGMS

In practice, leaders are likely to exhibit preferences for a particular paradigm. Rather than fitting one of the paradigms perfectly, they may well use elements of several paradigms. The choice of paradigm is likely to depend on the situation or reflect individual leaders' personal preferences. For example, a Classical leader may choose to consult and convince, even though the system does not require this, just as a Visionary leader may exercise position power to coerce followers at times.

Further, different kinds of leaders may be required in different parts of a complex organization.[56] In innovative and entrepreneurial areas, leaders need to be skilled in dealing with unpredictable and ambiguous knowledge and markets, whereas parts of the organization performing more routine tasks may require leadership that is more consistent and standardized. For example, production departments may accept more Transactional leadership than research and development (R&D) departments (see the Novartis and Swatch case studies).

People's mindsets and beliefs can hinder or facilitate the adoption of new paradigms. Drath[57] argues that recognizing 'leadership' depends on the idea of leadership that people carry around in their heads. Introducing new concepts of leadership, whatever they are, is likely to encounter resistance from deeply held ideologies. For example, followers expecting to be directed by a boss will probably embrace the Classical or Transactional paradigms. Similarly, the common idea of top leadership needing to revolve around one person or select group will hinder the adoption of Organic leadership.

Another example of a mindset that could resist changing paradigms is the belief that traits associated with femininity are not central or important to management. That this is not so is evident in the increasing *feminization* of leadership behaviours – towards more sharing of responsibility and power, helping and developing others, and developing meaningful connections and relationships with a broad network of people.[58] Despite considerable evidence for more 'feminine' trends in management, management writers tend to avoid labelling them as 'feminine'. Fondas[59] has concluded that management culture is ambivalent regarding the question of gender. According to her, most management and organization theory assumes that traits associated with masculinity are 'given' and are essential to organizational life. Such beliefs would probably reinforce Classical and Visionary leadership in particular, and resist Organic paradigms.

Strategy, systems, structure and organizational culture will also restrain the adoption of new leadership models. Systems will need to be aligned with paradigm changes. Examples include continuing to reward individual performance despite the existence of teams in lower and middle management, or retaining hierarchical reporting lines. Achieving alignment between organizational systems and processes and new leadership paradigms is complex and takes time.

Resistance can come from leaders who find giving up control and power difficult, and who still view leadership as a command-and-control function. Having been trained to be in charge, allowing employees to do more may appear to be a personal failure to such managers. Their training and personal managerial style can be an obstacle to implementing necessary changes. Many organizations offer special training and support to supervisors making the transition towards Organic leadership (see the BMW and EKATO case studies).

Sometimes managers are ready to share decision making, but some employees are not willing and able to accept their new roles as partners and decision makers (see the EKATO case study). Some people simply prefer a life of stability and well-defined relationships, disliking the confusion and ambiguities under Organic leadership.

Employees can object to taking on what they consider to be their boss' job, especially in cultures where this represents a major shift from the traditional view of leadership. Even where management is very willing for workers to become self-managing owners of the organization, and provides training and other opportunities to support this move, changing toward an Organic paradigm can prove difficult, as the Columbia Conserve Company case described in Box 2.1 shows.

Box 2.1

Self-managing workers at Columbia Conserve Company

Much of the literature discusses how attempts to allow workers to exercise significant responsibility and control over their work have been blocked by manager resistance. However, sometimes followers resist, as Bussell describes at the Columbia Conserve Company.[60]

The owner, William P. Hapgood, established an early system of worker ownership and management between 1917 and 1943. Columbia Conserve Company became a by-word for enlightened management practices during the 1920s and 1930s. Hapgood believed that industrialism, so successful in generating economic prosperity, had hurt human beings. He wanted to show that a successful organization could honour merit, encourage creativity, and exist without class, social status and wealth distinctions. He strove for governance by and for the workers. Profitable years during the 1920s enabled Hapgood to provide a range of employee benefits and begin promoting a cooperative ethic.

This progressive employer not only guaranteed employment even during slack periods, but also provided free medical, dental and other benefits to workers and their dependents, and pensions to retirees.[61] Being treated as part of the company instead of as part of a machine, employees started to support Hapgood's social experiment. Workers became part of the governing council, which made most decisions by consensus. Hierarchical titles such as 'foreman' and 'supervisor' were abolished in favour of division leader, whom workers were able to elect. In this small company of 150 salaried workers, face-to-face communication was relatively easy, reducing the need for hierarchical and bureaucratic management structures.

Compared with other companies of its era, Columbia Conserve went further than most in addressing workers' needs for material well-being, job security and participation, and managed to sustain that commitment over time. This progressive attitude to the workers was even used in marketing Columbia Conserve's products.

Hapgood believed that for Columbia Conserve to remain competitive and able to afford its social program, employees needed to expend extra effort, work efficiently and maintain a high level of productivity. In an effort to drive efficiency, Hapgood attempted to introduce Taylorist scientific management along with the Columbia Conserve human face. However, most workers resisted attempts to establish formal production standards, complaining that conforming to the standards was stressful and that it seemed as though the company's Standards Department was checking-up on employees. Despite education and training programs to prepare the workers for conducting group discussions and working in a cooperative enterprise, staff mostly remained unable and unwilling to accept the responsibility for making decisions.[62] While this resistance may have been partly due to the low education of the workforce, people tended to defer and respect Hapgood's enthusiasm for the experiment rather than believing in it deeply themselves.

In the end, despite his good intentions, Hapgood may well have been perceived as a meddling patriarch who distrusted worker judgement and claimed to know what was best for them. He looked to the union movement as a possible way of supporting his experiment by having workers represented through external unionists. This led to struggles over control, and eventually Hapgood agreed to recognize the union, subject to salaried employees renouncing their ownership stake in the company and returning to wageworker status. Analysts suggest that what staff really wanted was not control, but good working conditions. Workers did not develop the psychology of ownership that Hapgood had hoped for, but valued instead their family-like culture.[63] They resisted becoming self-managing.

CONCLUSION

The leadership paradigms proposed in this chapter can be broadly distinguished from one another, while acknowledging that they are not four mutually exclusive kinds of leadership. They provide a guide to ideas underlying leadership in both practice and the literature.

Classical leadership is based on the leader's position and power. It extracts follower compliance through high degrees of control and out of respect for, or fear of, the leader. The leader, central to Classical leadership, need not consider or involve followers in decisions.

Transactional leadership is based on influencing followers. It involves followers to the extent that the leader negotiates agreements with them, and attempts to influence them to achieve short-term targets or other concrete outcomes. The Transactional leader typically occupies a formal leadership role with the power to reward and correct followers. However, mutual influencing of leader and followers can occur through the communication process.

Visionary leadership, in which the leader's vision inspires followers to greater achievements, is often praised in the literature as an ideal leadership paradigm, especially for transforming organizations. However, the Visionary paradigm typically focuses heavily on the heroic leader, who creates and shares a vision that appeals to followers' needs and motivations. Workers' commitment and involvement are needed to realize the vision.

In the Organic paradigm, leadership is not necessarily vested in particular individuals, although people might assume leadership roles for a particular purpose. Leadership emerges from the relationships between the members of the organization, who communicate extensively with one another to try to make sense of rapidly changing circumstances. The basis of leadership is communication, often aimed at mutual sense-making, with members creating and sharing vision, values and processes. A leader is no longer the central figure under Organic leadership, instead the entire group becomes key. Group consensus may well determine who should be a leader, if anyone, and for how long. Much of the leadership is through shared vision and core values, extensive communication and aligning supporting systems and processes within the organization.

Within each paradigm, finer distinctions can be made, for example:

- Classical leaders can demonstrate coercive and benign behaviour;
- Transactional leadership can range from *laissez-faire* to proactive;
- Visionary leaders can vary from heroic to coercive; and
- Organic Leadership can encompass leaderful and leaderless organizations.

The paradigms will not necessarily be found in their 'pure' form in a given organization. Rather, elements from different paradigms may occur together, even though one predominates. At Swatch, elements of all four paradigms are evident:

- Classical is reflected in the fear and respect for the founders, and the fear of their autocratic decision-making style;
- Transactional is evident in the process-driven manufacturing areas;
- strong Visionary leadership based around emotion operates at the top of the organization; and
- the Organic paradigm predominates in marketing and R&D, where members communicate extensively as part of making sense of their world and being creative.

No one paradigm offers the perfect leadership solution for all contexts. Each suffers limitations that may make it inappropriate in a given situation. Many factors will influence whether existing paradigms can easily change, including the size of units in an organization, the nature of operations in different parts of an organization, as well as other systems, structural and cultural factors. In particular, the expectations and ideas of leadership embedded in the minds of organizational members can play a significant role in whether a particular paradigm will be recognized as leadership or not. Assumptions about what leaders do may make some managers resist a change from leader-focused paradigms (Classical, Transactional and Visionary) to Organic leadership. Resistance may also operate in the other direction, and stem from employees.

However, a growing trend towards some form of Organic leadership seems inevitable because many organizations are facing dynamic, complex, dispersed environments. This is despite the various factors discussed above that tend to inhibit the change.

In the next section, the characteristics of the four leadership paradigms are discussed in more detail.

NOTES

For full details of these notes, please see the References section at the end of this book.

1 Bass, 1990a
2 Stewart and Manz, 1995
3 Clegg and Gray, 1996:33
4 Freeman, 1984
5 Bass, 1990a
6 Schermerhorn and Bond, 1997
7 Mintzberg, 1979
8 Gemmill and Oakley, 1992
9 Yukl, 1998:3
10 Bass and Avolio, 1994
11 Kuhnert, 1994
12 Drath, 2001
13 ibid.
14 Yukl, 1998
15 e.g. Blanchard and Nelson, 1997
16 Ball, Trevino and Sims, 1992
17 Bass, 1990b; Drath, 2001
18 Bass, 1990b
19 Gemmill and Oakley, 1992
20 Avolio and Bass, 1994
21 Vaill, 1989

22 Kotter, 1990

23 Carroll, 1999

24 Kantabutra, 2003

25 Westley and Mintzberg, 1989

26 Lewis, 1996

27 Dunphy and Stace, 1988, 1990; Kotter, Schlesinger and Sathe, 1979; Nadler and Tushman, 1990

28 den Hartog, House, Hanges, Ruiz-Quintanilla and Dorfman, 1999

29 Nadler and Tuschman, 1990

30 Atwater and Bass, 1994

31 Hofstede, 1991

32 e.g. Drath, 2001

33 Drath, 2001

34 Collins and Porras, 1994

35 Collins and Porras, 1994:9

36 Westley and Mintzberg, 1989

37 Collins, 2001

38 Raelin, 2003

39 Kets de Vries and Florent-Treacy, 1999

40 Mintzberg and van der Heyden, 1999

41 Warnecke, 1993

42 Mintzberg, 1979

43 Weick, 1995

44 Heifetz, 1994

45 Weick 1995

46 Hirschhorn, 1997; Rothschild and Whitt, 1986

47 Drath, 1998

48 Mintzberg, 1998

49 ibid.

50 Brodbeck, 2002

51 Brown and Eisenhardt, 1997

52 Brodbeck, 2002

53 Moss Kanter, 1989

54 Collins and Porras, 1994

55 Meindl, 1998

56 Lawrence and Lorsch, 1967

57 Drath, 2001

58 Fondas, 1997

59 ibid.

60 Bussel, 1997

61 ibid.

62 ibid.

63 ibid.

3 Characteristics of Leadership Paradigms

Key Points

- Identifying key characteristics
- Varying emphasis on leaders and followers
- Knowledge workers
- Types of power
- Styles of decision making
- Changing management thinking
- Culture and diversity
- Adaptability
- Responsibility and accountability
- Matching structure and context

Chapter 2 describes some of the major ideas distinguishing the four leadership paradigms. However, many questions about the paradigms still need clarifying. For example, are the paradigms based on different management philosophies? Do the paradigms suit certain organizational and environmental contexts better than others? How do they relate to power held by leaders and followers?

Based on a range of factors identified in the leadership literature, this chapter proposes that the leadership paradigms lie at different points along a number of broad continua. Each paradigm reflects key characteristics to a greater or lesser extent than others. Often, differing qualities can be more appropriately assigned to the paradigms without specifying amounts.

It is important to point out that given the state of research and theorizing in the field, further research will be needed to refine the factors assigned to each paradigm.

However, the paradigms represent a first step in integrating some otherwise isolated information in describing and differentiating ideas underlying leadership.

DISTINGUISHING CHARACTERISTICS

The elements underlying 13 broad continua for distinguishing the leadership paradigms are summarized in Table 3.1. The continua cover characteristics of the key players, their power, ways of making decisions and being accountable; the management philosophy underlying the paradigms; and organizational considerations such as adaptability, and managing diversity, structure and environmental considerations. Each of the individual factors in Table 3.1 is considered in turn below.

1   Key players

In moving from Classical to Organic leadership, the focus on who is important in the relationship shifts increasingly from the leader to all the members of the organization. The Classical leader is all-important, with followers' ideas, wishes and needs taking very low priority compared with the leader's point of view. Here, both skilled and unskilled followers are expected to follow the directives of their supervisors, and key decisions pass to the leader (see the Bonduelle case study).

Within the Transactional paradigm, followers' significance increases as the leader takes account of workers' skills, needs and motives in the process of influencing them. However, the emphasis is still very much on the leader as the active person in the Transactional relationship (see the Royal Australian Navy case study). Someone is expected to direct, coach, support or otherwise develop followers, who tend to be conceived of as more passive players than the leader.

In a major departure from the Classical and Transactional paradigms – referred to as a 'quantum leap' by Avolio[1] – Visionary leadership adds strong emotional aspects and a view of a desired future to motivate group members (see the Swatch case study). For Visionary leadership, the leader's vision and its emotional impact are central, allowing the leader to take on heroic proportions.[2]

However, the Visionary leader depends on followers who will accept and help execute the vision. Visionary leadership is effective only if the followers become committed to the vision promoted by the leader (see the Rodenstock case study). Therefore, the vision must meet followers' desires, and research has shown that effective Visionary leaders tune in to their followers' needs,[3] making the Visionary leader and followers highly interdependent. Here, the needs and emotions of followers play a larger role than under Classical and Transactional leadership.

Finally, in Organic leadership the focus shifts away from top-down leader(s) to the group, which may have a single leader, multiple leaders, or even no formal leadership

Table 3.1

Comparing the leadership paradigms

Leadership characteristic	Classical	Transactional	Visionary	Organic
1 Key players	Leader.	Leader. Low role for individual followers.	Leader. High role for followers.	Entire group. May be many leaders or no leaders.
2 Followers' knowledge base	Low.	Low to high.	Medium to high.	High.
3 Sources of leader power	Position, reward, coercion, expert, referent, ownership.	Position, reward, coercion, interpersonal skills, negotiated agreements.	Position, referent, expert, personal vision, followers' emotions, charisma.	Group power, expertise, collaboration, sharing power, member attributions.
4 Follower power	Almost zero.	Low.	Medium.	High.
5 Decision making	Leader decides alone.	Leader consults, then makes decision.	Leader collaborates.	Mutual decisions.
6 Management and leadership	Management.	Management.	Leadership.	Distributed leadership.
7 Philosophy of management and complexity	Newtonian, low complexity. High control through leader.	Newtonian, low complexity. High control mostly from leader.	Newtonian and New Science mixed. Medium complexity. Shared control.	New Science, high complexity. Letting go of control. Self-managing members.
8 Cultural dimensions (using Hofstede's national value dimensions)	High on *Power Distance Inequality, Uncertainty Avoidance* and *Masculinity*. Low on *Individualism*.	Low or high *Power Distance Inequality* and *Masculinity*. High on *Uncertainty Avoidance* and *Individualism*.	High or low on *Power Distance Inequality, Uncertainty Avoidance* and *Masculinity*. Medium on *Individualism*.	Low on *Power Distance Inequality, Uncertainty Avoidance, Individualism* and *Masculinity*.

Continued

Comparing the leadership paradigms (Continued)

Leadership characteristic	Classical	Transactional	Visionary	Organic
9 Diversity	Low.	Medium.	Medium.	High.
10 Adaptability	Can be rapid through command, providing followers have necessary new skills. Leader is assumed to know where to go. Better suited to incremental change.	Slow, because followers need to be heard and influenced. Instrumental for aligning processes and systems with new direction. Suits incremental change.	Slow – need to shift mindsets and win people to a new vision. Inspire change. Need to align systems and processes with change. Suits major change.	Can be agile because members are constantly prepared for change but can be slowed by need for extensive consultation. Suits large and small scale change.
11 Responsibility and accountability	Leader high. Followers limited to specific task performance.	Leader high. Followers are accountable to leader for limited outcomes.	Leader high. Followers are accountable to leader for outcomes.	Everyone high. Self-accountability, Self-responsibility by commitment to tasks and to others.
12 Matching structure	Simple, bureaucracy.	Simple, bureaucracy, divisional.	Adhocracy, divisional.	Adhocracy, network.
13 Matching context	Simple, stable.	Simple, stable.	Simple, complex, stable and/or dynamic.	Complex, dynamic.

beyond that emerging from the relationships among the members of an organization or community (see the Gore case study). In such leaderless or leaderful conditions, the emphasis is on the interactions among all organizational members rather than on specific leaders.

2 Followers' knowledge base

Many organizations need to attract and retain top expertise and talent – and yet their key people can walk out the door at any time.[4] The leadership paradigms differ in the extent to which they depend on the skills and knowledge of followers. The paradigms also vary in how well they suit people with high expertise. Essentially, it is proposed that both the need for, and the fit with, knowledge workers increases in moving from Classical to Organic paradigms.

Knowledge workers create new information or knowledge, are skilled in using knowledge, or possess professional expertise of some kind. Increasingly, organizations are becoming dependent on knowledge workers. For example, at Swatch one highly-skilled engineer could manage dozens of automated watchmaking machines in 2000, whereas a much larger number of less-skilled employees was needed to maintain previous generations of machines. At BMW, robots assemble car bodies, while highly-skilled technical staff monitor the machines. High knowledge workers are particularly necessary at firms like EKATO and SAP that sell their employees' knowledge, and at Bonduelle for maintaining quality.

Classical and Transactional leaders tend to be highly directive, enabling them to employ unskilled followers. However, some knowledge workers also typically work under these leadership paradigms. For example, hospital operating theatres traditionally revolve around Classical leadership despite the highly-skilled staff involved. Similarly, airline pilots manage risk by submitting to strict Transactional procedures during their pre-flight checks and at takeoff and landing.

Today's economy is becoming increasingly based on knowledge, and knowledge workers generally prefer inspiration, not supervision.[5] This suggests that Visionary and Organic paradigms would be more appropriate for knowledge workers than Classical or Transactional (see the Novartis case study). Interestingly, the armed forces are conventionally viewed as Classical leadership environments, but today skill, training and following initiative are highly valued (see the Royal Australian Navy case study).

The ability of knowledge workers to navigate and use information, learn new skills and feel comfortable in ambiguous work situations has become as important to success as academic achievement.[6] Visionary leadership could help attract and retain such knowledge workers, providing the leader's vision appeals.

However, Organic leadership seems particularly appropriate for professional and knowledge workers who work in dynamic, chaotic situations. Highly-trained knowledge workers can usually perform many assignments without supervision, and their education often instils a desire for the autonomous, self-controlling behaviour appropriate to the Organic paradigm.[7] In such cases, people may neither need nor willingly accept a leader's direction or vision (see the SAP case study). This shifts the focus away from the leader towards followers under the Organic paradigm. While many unskilled employees would also respond well to such environments, new ways of leading are needed as organizations become increasingly dependent on knowledge workers.

3 Sources of leader power

Leadership and power are closely related concepts. Both are often defined as processes of influence through which others move towards certain behaviours or attitudes.[8] Organizations are highly political places, where members compete for power and scarce resources and pursue their own agendas.[9] Organizational leadership is generally seen as revolving around leader power – in getting others to perform or follow a vision, and in allocating resources, rewards and sanctions.

Not all scholars believe that leadership and power are directly linked, that is, that more senior leadership wields more power. For example, Collins wrote that 'the exercise of true leadership is inversely proportional to the exercise of power … you are a leader if and only if people follow your leadership when they have the freedom not to'[10] (see the Gore case study). Another view is that best innovative efforts come from true commitments freely made between people in a spirit of partnership, not from bosses telling people what to do (see the Gore, Novartis, Rodenstock and Swatch case studies).

Power can stem from various sources in an organization. The organization grants power to people holding certain positions (known as *position power*). Power also stems from a specific individual's characteristics (called *personal power*). French and Raven[11] identified five widely-used kinds of power, namely *legitimate, reward, coercive, expert* and *referent* power. These are described in Box 3.1.

Box 3.1

Types of power

According to French and Raven, five kinds of power can be distinguished:[12]

1 *Legitimate power*   derives from the role or position, rather than from a person's attributes. Organizations usually grant people at the highest levels more power than people below them.

2 *Reward power*   stems from being able to grant rewards to people for achievement.

3 *Coercive power*   is based on fear of punishment, such as a demotion, not receiving a bonus or dismissal for non-performance. Both reward power and coercive power are partly determined by the type and level of a person's position in a traditional organization. Senior people tend to wield more reward and coercion power than junior employees.[13]

4 *Expertise or information power*   stems from a person's knowledge or experience. It is partly a characteristic of the individual (for example, through

having specialized knowledge), but also relates to a person's position (for example, by being in a position to gather and control key information).

5 *Referent power* originates from the attributes of the person. A person with referent power has an ability to influence others by possessing desirable traits, status or reputation. A manager with a strong track record of success would acquire referent power.

Although these five sources of power are widely recognized, they have been criticized.[14] DuBrin points out that power can also stem from other sources,[15] including:

- ownership, for example, being a majority shareholder in an organization (see the SAP, Swatch, EKATO, BMW and Rodenstock case studies);.
- taking advantage of an opportunity, such as being in the right place at the right time (see the Swatch and SAP case studies);
- managing crucial problems, for example, R&D areas in an innovative organization (see the Novartis and EKATO case studies) or marketing at Swatch; and
- being close to others with power (see the Schering-Plough case study).

Multiple forms of power are likely to be associated with each leadership paradigm. However, the paradigms differ in the predominant types of power operating, as well as in where the power lies. Under Classical leadership, all sources of power can operate: legitimate, reward, coercion, expert and referent, along with power stemming from ownership (for example, entrepreneurs as sole or major shareholders). Most power tends to lie at the top. The leader may have acquired power by taking advantage of an opportunity, managing crucial problems or being close to a powerful *mentor*.

Research has identified complex relationships between leader power and Transactional and Visionary leadership.[16] Transactional leadership, being based around agreements and exchanges between leader and followers, relies heavily on position power, particularly reward and coercion power associated with the leader's role. The Transactional leader retains most of the power, as long as the leader is able to deliver rewards and punishments. Followers of passive leaders and those who do very little leading or supervising rarely attribute personal or position power to them.

Leaders who act in a visionary way are more likely to be seen as powerful than Transactional leaders. Visionary leaders who are charismatic, inspiring, intellectually stimulating and considerate of individuals are seen as possessing *referent* and *expert power*, as well as some *reward power*.[17] By definition, Visionary leaders derive much of their power from a vision that followers find attractive.

Under Classical, Transactional and Visionary paradigms, power tends to be centralized. Centralizing power can lead to what Pfeffer identifies as a huge problem in many corporations, namely 'the almost trained or produced incapacity of anyone except the highest level managers to take action and get things accomplished'.[18] A different philosophy is evident at BMW, Novartis and Rodenstock, for example. This involves decentralizing power, because if managers '... empower people with the right information, training, and resources, and combine those with a clear vision and sense of purpose to give them an overall framework and context within which to act ... good things will happen.'[19]

Organic and networked organizations require a major mindshift in how to obtain and manage power. Today's highly dispersed organizations, with distributed teams and remote, global workers, make it much more difficult for top executives to retain control and exercise legitimate power. The keys to success in the new, networked organization are collaboration and sharing power, rather than the traditional centralized, power-based, command leadership.[20]

Authority and power reside in the collectivity of Organic organizations.[21] Thus, under Organic leadership power tends to be distributed throughout the organizational members, rather than being concentrated at the top. Not all members of an organization may seek power to control others, but most would seek to influence decisions affecting their own work and workplace. Interestingly, Organic organizations may be more political than traditional enterprises, because they rely heavily on referent and expertise power to ensure survival of the fittest in political terms.[22]

In summary, the leadership paradigms vary in the kinds of power typically used by the leaders, and where that power lies. Part of a leader's role is often seen as dealing with conflicting interest groups (dispute resolution), fights over scarce resources, and coping with enduring differences in the organization. This perspective tends to generate structures that are excessively centralized, putting and retaining power in the hands of managers. This can arise especially under Classical, Transactional and Visionary leadership where, as already seen, leaders wield considerable power. Power centralized in the hands of the Classical leader shifts towards increasing opportunities for followers to gain power as the paradigms move from Classical and Transactional, through to Visionary and Organic.

4 Follower power

Ironically, a leader's power and influence tend to increase when that power is shared.[23] As team members gain power, they can accomplish more, commitment and accountability increase, and multiple perspectives can be heard on issues. This would normally reflect well on a leader. Distributing power throughout the entire system also provides an organization with agility to adapt, but this can come at the cost of reaching decisions through necessarily extensive communication and negotiation, and in training people to communicate effectively (see the EKATO and Gore case studies). Nonetheless, this cost is partly recouped by speedier execution, increased innovation from sharing knowledge to create new ideas, and widespread buy-in to the decision (see the Gore and Rodenstock case studies).

Where do followers derive power? Even without explicit empowerment or sharing of power, followers wield power at their workplace, starting with the capacity to withdraw their labour or support for a leader. Dispersed followers enjoy the power to seize opportunities at their remote location, either for the organization's benefit or for their own furtherment.

Employees also gain considerable power from their expertise and knowledge, which are core elements of today's knowledge-based organizations. Where an organization depends on specialized knowledge, experts gain several types of power.[24] For example, *informal power* arises through the advice and technical choices experts provide to the organization. This places experts in a position to influence managerial choices before executing them. Another type of power, *expert power merged with formal authority,* comes from such activities as sitting on committees. Here, decision power resides largely with professionals and other experts, whose work is often coordinated by standard skills within a profession. A third form of power, *expert power,* arises when the operators who carry out critical activities themselves are the experts. Thus, considerable power resides in knowledge workers in particular.

The leadership paradigms reflect increasing degrees of *follower power*. Follower power is low with Classical leadership, but increases under Transactional leadership. Here, more two-way negotiation occurs and employees' views can be voiced. Followers can resist being influenced by Transactional leaders and have some power to negotiate and influence outcomes. This includes the power to withdraw or contribute more of their labour.

Compared with Transactional leadership, Visionary leadership allows a medium level of employee power. Employees can refuse to accept and work towards the leader's vision. This power arises because the Visionary leader's power depends on acceptance, sharing and commitment of the vision by the followers.

Under Organic leadership, employee power is high. Through joint sense-making, members influence the direction of the organization and gain power through shared leadership (see the BMW, EKATO and Gore case studies). Sharing work in teams and workgroups also enhances employee power, as does increasing expertise (for example, via multiskilling) and personal effectiveness (for example, through enhanced communication).

Shifting power from managers to employees is not easy, but can be done (see the Rodenstock case study). Nonetheless, fundamental change is unlikely to occur in seeking to empower followers, without examining deeply-held beliefs about leadership, power and authority relationships.[25] Followers may need *intellectual and emotional reskilling* to be able to accept empowerment, Even then, there is no guarantee of success (see the EKATO case study). For effective empowerment, both leaders and followers must hold the same paradigm of leadership. Otherwise, followers may resent taking on part of their leader's role, just as some leaders may dislike giving up power.

In summary, followers gain increased power as leadership paradigms move from Classical to Transactional, Visionary and Organic. Follower power ranges from almost zero under the Classical paradigm to dispersed and strong under Organic leadership.

5　Decision making

Managers can use a variety of techniques for making decisions, and involve their staff to varying degrees. Four basic styles of making decisions can be derived from

Table 3.2

Four basic decision-making styles linked to the paradigms

Style	Decision-making process	Who makes the decision	Paradigm
1 Autocratic	Leader makes the decision mostly alone.	Leader	Classical
2 Consultation	Leader consults individual followers.	Leader	Transactional
3 Consensus	Group involvement, consensus building.	Leader	Visionary
4 Mutual agreement	Decision is delegated to group or individual followers.	Group	Organic

a more detailed range of options in the Normative Decision Model.[26] These are summarized in Table 3.2 and detailed below:

- *Style 1 – Autocratic*   Here the leader makes a decision, with either no, or very little, involvement from followers. This style is appropriate to Classical leadership. The quality of the decision will depend largely on the information and skills of the leader relevant to the issue. Depending on the decision and the circumstances, followers may or may not accept autocratic decisions made without their input.
- *Style 2 – Consultation*   The leader engages in different degrees of consultation with individual followers, but the leader remains the final decision-maker. This is consistent with Transactional leadership. By consulting others, the leader can not only obtain additional information, and so improve the quality of a decision, but may also win supporters for the decision from among those consulted.
- *Style 3 – Consensus*   This method involves extensive group involvement and consensus building. It is quite likely to be found under the Visionary paradigm. During the process, the leader shares the problem with group members and reaches a consensus with them, even though the leader still makes the final decision. This process can improve decision quality because of the input from many people, and can enhance follower interest in, and commitment to, the decision.
- *Style 4 – Mutual agreement*   Here, decision making is dispersed among the followers. This is common in Organic leadership and self-managing work environments (see the BMW and Gore case studies). This method provides maximum follower acceptance of, and commitment to, the decision. However, a Classical, Transactional

or Visionary leader runs the risk of having to accept a group decision that he or she might not agree with.

The appropriateness of each style depends on various factors, such as whether the leader has sufficient information to make a quality decision, the amount of time available for consultation, and whether follower acceptance is crucial to the decision.

Each style broadly matches a leadership paradigm. Moving from Classical to Organic, followers become increasingly more involved in, and responsible for, decision making. The Classical leader would tend to favour autocratic decisions, while the Transactional leader would be expected to consult. The Visionary leader would probably collaborate with the group. Organic, adaptive organizations would tend to enable workers at all levels to exercise judgement on diverse issues, and require their participation in decision making (see the BMW, EKATO, Rodenstock and Royal Australian Navy case studies).

6   Management and leadership

The paradigms can be distinguished by the extent to which they reflect leadership or management. Whether leadership and management refer to similar or different concepts is contentious. Many management thinkers take the view that management and leadership overlap, although the degree of overlap is controversial.[27] Some regard leadership as an aspect of management, somewhat like a 'tool' that managers use when they need to influence people.[28] Mintzberg's taxonomy of managerial roles includes a leader role.[29] Similarly, Bass and Avolio define transformational and transactional leadership largely in terms of managerial practices.[30]

Other management writers distinguish between leadership and management processes. According to Kotter, management is about coping with complexity and bringing order into organizations, particularly in areas like quality and profitability.[31] Leadership is about coping with change towards a desired future. A successful organization needs both management and leadership, but in Kotter's view, many organizations today are 'overmanaged and underled'. Bennis and Nanus distinguish between managers and leaders by saying that managers do things right (for example, organize and create order), while leaders do the right thing (for example, develop vision and strategy, and help the organization adapt to change).[32]

Under a third view, leadership is seen as a 'higher level' activity than management, rather mystical and mysterious, and depending on a leader's charisma for its effectiveness.[33] From this perspective, management tends to over-emphasize control, systems and processes at the expense of fostering creativity, learning and adaptability. Leadership differs from management by inspiring people to aim for a future.[34] Another distinction is based on time, with leadership associated with visions of the future, while management copes with the present or fixing the past. Much of the management literature emphasizes the need for control, and designing systems and structures for a smoothly running organization.[35]

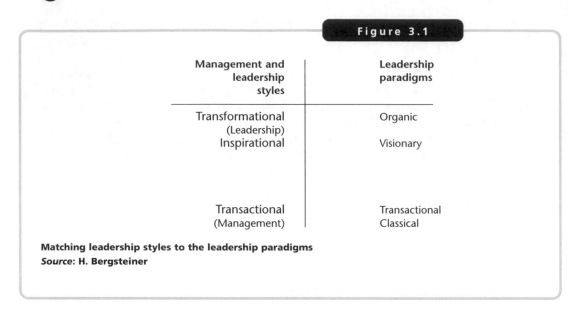

Figure 3.1

Management and leadership styles	Leadership paradigms
Transformational (Leadership) Inspirational	Organic Visionary
Transactional (Management)	Transactional Classical

Matching leadership styles to the leadership paradigms
Source: H. Bergsteiner

These conflicting ideas on management and leadership can be partly resolved by avoiding a sharp dichotomy between them. Instead, as Bass proposed, management (Transactional) and leadership (Transformational) can be regarded as forming two ends of a continuum (see Figure 3.1).[36] In management, the focus is on managing day-to-day systems and processes, with relatively little need for providing a larger vision to inspire workers. In fact, many of the 'workers' can be robots or computer systems.

At the Transformational end of the management–leadership continuum in Figure 3.1, the leaders' main task is to inspire people to work towards a shared vision and strategy rather than managing systems, processes and operations. In between, manager and leader roles involve varying degrees of overlapping activities. The closer to one end or the other, the more dominant that role becomes. In the middle, management and leadership functions are evenly balanced.

To this extent, management and leadership are seen as different activities, carried out in varying mixtures in a particular situation. These roles can coexist in one individual, particularly in small organizations where the entrepreneur may be involved in both management and leadership activities. In larger organizations, the roles of manager and leader are often separated. The Chief Executive Officer (CEO) as leader is often concerned with vision, strategy, internal communication and external relationships, while others manage the day-to-day affairs of the organization. Team leaders both lead and manage, and non-managerial employees might be highly influential leaders (and self-managers).

Therefore, a good working assumption is that leadership and management refer to different but related functions. Different mixes of management and leadership can be seen in the four leadership paradigms. Classical and Transactional leadership lie close to management, both in time (past- or present-oriented) and with their focus on manager control. More future-oriented and emotionally-based leadership emerges with the Visionary and Organic paradigms. Here, follower commitment to a vision of the future predominates over a focus on getting the day-to-day work done (although the work still gets done under all paradigms).

7 Philosophy of management and complexity

Increasingly, organizational scientists are questioning whether the traditional assumptions underlying the dominant mindsets of managers, management researchers and organizational consultants are still relevant.[37] Organizations face a great many uncertainties, paradoxes, confusions, contradictions and messes. Leaders are unable to understand and deal with such complexity using conventional management methods and thinking.[38] This section indicates how new approaches in other areas of science could influence the four leadership paradigms, beginning with the philosophy behind management thinking.

Traditional management thinking
Since the time of Newton in the seventeenth century, many people – in the Western world at least – believed that they inhabited a world of linear order, regularity and stability. Institutions like families, organizations and governments help create order, thus protecting individuals from the anxiety that would otherwise arise from disorder.[39] This desire for order is reflected in the structures people build and the plans and charts they draw up.[40] To create order around them, Western thinking encourages people to conceptually break up the natural interconnectedness of things, giving things different names, categorizing them and looking for certainties, constancies and regularities in relationships.

In organizations, people behave in a similar way. Much of a business manager's task is to predict the future, create order in a small part of the organization and set the system's direction, monitoring it along the way. Diversity and ambiguity are reduced as much as possible, and the manager searches for the one best solution to each problem. Top management assumes that it can take action to steer the organization in the chosen direction by developing rational business plans or visions about the future of the organization.[41] Clearly, this thinking is embedded in the Classical, Transactional and Visionary paradigms.

Believing that management's actions can determine the success or otherwise of an organization is based on several Newtonian assumptions. One is that there is a simple, linear causality between actions and outcomes in an organization. Another is that organizations are stable equilibrium systems in which actions lead to predictable outcomes. Yet another belief is that feedback keeps planning, budgeting and other control and information systems on the correct path.[42] Successful managers are assumed to be those who can form accurate representations of the organization and its environment, and better predict changes. Driven by these assumptions, CEOs come and go because of an assumed correlation between leader actions and organizational performance.

New Sciences and management

While the traditional views may have served management well under stable conditions, it has become evident that social systems, including business organizations, are more complex and less predictable than the machine-like entities that the Newtonian approach assumed. The so-called 'New Sciences' offer promising insights that radically challenge conventional views of how organizations work. Box 3.2 shows how chaos theory could apply to management.

The New Sciences employ a range of theories relating to complexity, self-organizing entities, fractals, chaos and complex adaptive systems. They contrast with the Newtonian approach in important ways. Novel for many managers is the New Science focus on the whole system, rather than just on its parts. The whole becomes more than the sum of the individual components. Further, ideas about simple cause-and-effect have little relevance to social systems if these systems are thought of as complex, interacting entities. Practitioners have known this for a long time, but for many management scientists, it was 'simpler' to assume direct causality and seek order.

Linking to the paradigms

The leadership paradigms reflect different understandings of management science. Classical and Transactional leadership imply a Newtonian, mechanistic view of the world in which outcomes are predictable, and in which leaders can impact events by setting goals, controlling execution and monitoring outcomes. In general, Classical and Transactional paradigms lend themselves to environments of low complexity, where the leader can know what is happening, and to processes that can be mechanized. The technical system becomes more regulating, operations become more routine and predictable. Control can become more impersonal and pass from people to technology. Even now, many of the functions of Classical and Transactional leadership are being automated, with computers monitoring and controlling employees and automated HR systems replacing some managerial functions.

Box 3.2

Managing in chaos

Chaos is one potentially useful New Science concept for management theory. Probably the most commonly held misconception about chaos theory is that it is about disorder. In fact, chaos theory asserts that while it is impossible to predict the state of a system exactly, it is generally quite possible, even easy, to model the overall behaviour of a system.

Chaos theory does not emphasize the disorder of the system that makes it inherently unpredictable, but rather, the order inherent in the system – the universal behaviour of similar systems.[43] Surprisingly, chaos theory suggests that order can spontaneously emerge from chaos, even though the origin of the order is unknown.[44]

Many complex modern organizations resemble a chaotic system, and in uncertain conditions people try to make sense of what is going on.[45] With a lack of information, or where there is some ambiguity and it is hard to distinguish between conflicting interpretations, people seek order. One way to do this is to rely on a sense-maker, such as a leader. Whether leaders in fact bring any order or not, their function may simply be to create the illusion of order among their followers.

In complexity science, disorder plays a vital role, providing tension that leads people to self-organize as they discover and create a new future. Creativity is only possible at the edge of chaos, but tolerating chaos is incompatible with Newtonian beliefs of order and control.[46] However, many people intuitively feel that too much chaos is problematic for healthy organizational functioning. Indeed, so-called 'deep chaos' can be dangerous.

However, people rarely consider that too much order can also be unhealthy. For example, too much order leads to rigidity. Allowance must be made for novelty, discontinuous change, innovation, experimentation, development, entrepreneurship and self-organization.[47] Too much order can prevent systems from adapting to changing circumstances. Yet, in times of chaos and uncertainty, many managers and employees tend to become more controlling rather than letting go of control, promoting self-management and empowering employees.[48] Here, relaxation of control could be more effective.

Abandoning the idea of mastering order does not necessarily leave people facing a disordered world. Rather, it reminds people of how to survive in an avalanche or in high surf. Managers are advised to 'ride the wave' and not attempt the impossible, namely trying to stay in total control of the situation.[49] Within a world focused on abolishing, or at worst managing, disorder, accepting disorder and giving up the sense of control takes courage. Doing so represents a new challenge for future leaders.

Visionary leadership could operate within either a Newtonian or a New Science view of management. Under the Newtonian perspective, the leader strives to organize systems and staff to implement the vision, based on the assumption that these rational actions largely determine the organization's future. As a result, many Visionary leaders take the consequences of their failed visions (but often leave with a handsome compensation package, a cynic might say).

However, Visionary leadership can also be consistent with a New Science view of unpredictability and uncertainty. The leader tries to steer a general course into the future, but is willing to change as necessary and recognizes that mistakes may well occur given the complex situation. Visionary leadership guided by New Science philosophy enables leaders to operate in more complex environments, providing that followers share the vision and willingly work towards it.

Organic leadership is based around the New Science perspectives of unpredictability, self-organizing systems, complexity and uncertainty. Organic leadership allows order to emerge from chaos, as described in Box 3.2. Here the advice is to let go of control, not try to create order, and to share information. Rather than bringing order and control, an Organic leader's role is to 'contain the anxiety of its

Table 3.3

Defining national value dimensions, based on Hofstede[55]

Dimension	Power Distance Inequality	Uncertainty Avoidance	Individualism/ Collectivism	Masculinity/ Femininity
Description	Extent to which a culture accepts unequal distribution of power.	Extent to which a cultural group finds ambiguity stressful, preferring certainty and predictability.	Extent to which a culture values a strong collective identity versus individual identity and personal choice.	Extent to which assertiveness, challenge and ambition are valued (masculine) compared with cooperation and good working relationships (feminine).

members as they operate at the edge of chaos where they are creating and discovering a new future that none could possibly foresee'.[50] These concepts present new challenges to many leaders and followers alike.

In a rapidly changing world, traditional Classical and Transactional managers have a greatly reduced place. Even leaders with a vision can only hope that they have chosen wisely. Of the four paradigms, Organic leadership lends itself most to operating within complex systems, where what the various members do now influences where the system or organization will go in the future.[51] By enabling members to interact freely, share ideas, experiment with new strategies and learn from the outcomes, Organic leadership promotes creativity and develops members' agility in responding in a changing environment. Further, Organic leadership encourages and values diverse views, which develops the variety needed for the next adaptation.

8 Cultural dimensions

A major proposition underlying the four leadership paradigms concerns whether organizational members recognize some of the paradigms as constituting 'leadership'. This will depend on their ideas, expectations and experiences with leadership. For example, considerable evidence suggests that women think and behave differently from the traditional images of leadership based on the experiences of white men in the same society.[52] Similarly, different ideas of leadership can be seen in different countries, fields or generations.[53]

Understanding how the paradigms relate to national culture is critical, because many organizations operate in different parts of the world and encounter cross-national and regional cultures within their workforce, customers or governmental influences. Further, by fostering diversity, organizations position themselves to adapt to change. At least some of their diverse members may have the know-how, skills, insights, values or other capacities needed to succeed under changed conditions.

Geert Hofstede's groundbreaking work into different values held by people of different nations shows how national culture can influence concepts of leadership.[54] Hofstede originally identified four broad dimensions to describe national values, which are summarized in Table 3.3.

Hofstede's four cultural dimensions are briefly described from a management perspective[56] :

1 *Power distance inequality* Power distance deals directly with people's expectations of, and relationships to, authority. In particular, it refers to the extent to which a culture accepts unequal distribution of power. In low power distance inequality cultures, leader–follower relationships are theoretically close and less formal (compatible with a consultative and approachable management culture). In high power distance inequality cultures, these relationships are more distant, hierarchically ordered and reserved (leading to a preference for autocratic and Classical leadership).

2 *Uncertainty avoidance* Uncertainty avoidance is the extent to which people in a culture prefer certainty and predictability, finding ambiguity stressful. In high uncertainty avoidance cultures, members prefer rules and stable jobs with long-term employers. This compares with the greater risk-taking and tolerance of organizational ambiguity and change found in low uncertainty avoidance cultures. Leaders in high uncertainty avoidance cultures would be expected to find ways of exerting and keeping control (certainty) within their work units.

3 *Individualism/collectivism* Individualism/collectivism refers to the extent to which a culture focuses on individual identity and personal choice, as opposed to valuing a strong collective identity. Individualistic cultures emphasize individual goals, whereas the collective culture emphasizes the welfare of the 'in-group'. One could predict, for example, that managers from individualistic cultures would be perceived by their subordinates as promoting team building more than managers from collectivistic cultures, whose subordinates are probably already group-oriented.

4 *Masculinity/femininity* Masculinity/femininity classifies cultures into those in which assertiveness, challenge and ambition are valued (masculine cultures), and others where greater emphasis is placed on cooperation and good working relationships (feminine cultures). Hofstede argues that both masculine and feminine values are needed in managerial jobs.[57]

Although additional dimensions for differentiating between national cultures have been proposed – by Hofstede and others – the four dimensions described above

Table 3.4

Cultural dimensions hypothesized to match the leadership paradigms

Cultural dimensions	Classical paradigm	Transactional paradigm	Visionary paradigm	Organic paradigm
Power Distance Inequality	High	Low or high	Low or high	Low
Uncertainty Avoidance	High	High	Low or high	Low
Individualism	Low	High	Medium	Low
Masculinity	High	Low or high	Low or high	Low

provide some indication of potential national cultural differences in the leadership paradigms (summarized in Table 3.4). Using dimensions such as these allows predictions to be made about the broad patterns of leadership expected in a given nation.

For example, the directive Classical leader is likely to fit well with national cultures characterized by high power distance, uncertainty avoidance and masculinity, and with low individualism. Here the necessary respect for the leader, tolerance for assertiveness and a collective orientation would be found. The case study on Bonduelle, the family-owned French company, provides an example.

Transactional leadership could operate in a range of cultural values, including with either low or high power distance inequality and masculinity/femininity, but presumably with high uncertainty avoidance and individualism. The latter two values would encourage followers to appreciate the structured transactional environment the leader creates, as well as the individual focus of the Transactional paradigm (see the Royal Australian Navy case study).

Visionary leadership could accommodate high or low preferences on power distance, uncertainty avoidance and masculinity/femininity, depending on the circumstances. It may well operate better under medium individualism, bringing more of a balanced focus on the collective in pursuit of the leader's overall vision (see the Swatch case study).

Finally, Organic leadership would be expected to operate under conditions of low power distance inequality, uncertainty avoidance, individualism and masculinity. Here, low power distance and a collective focus would be reinforced by a tolerance for ambiguity and focus on cooperation and good working relationships (for example, at BMW and Gore).

Relating Hofstede's four dimensions to specific leadership situations can be very complex. In Japan, where power distance is high, the culture emphasizes conformity, consensus and collectivity at the expense of individual goals.[58] The result is that the Japanese collectivist culture supports participative management, in spite of high power distance. By contrast, the cultural values can suggest that participative management is likely to be more difficult to introduce in individualistic cultures with high power distance, such as in France. A traditional French leader possesses great authority and is expected to be very knowledgeable, having attended elite schools (see the Bonduelle case study). Consulting subordinates could easily be perceived as a weakness and evidence of poor leadership ability. More egalitarian countries like the US and Australia, being relatively low in power distance, would allow for follower participation. However, the US and Australia are highly individualistic cultures, which could pose an obstacle to working in a team environment. Box 3.3 illustrates some opposing ways of thinking about cultural diversity in transnational organizations, where both local and global forces operate.

Box 3.3

Organizational versus national culture

No one national leader profile has emerged, according to an analysis of 64 Hay/McBer leadership studies worldwide.[59] Rather, understanding and using both organizational and national culture is essential. For example, building business relations through mutual respect and trust is important in Asian countries, while emphasizing participation and sharing decisions is important in the American context.

Whether globalization forces are leading national cultures to adopt similar organizational philosophies and practices is particularly of interest in the European Union (EU), where an increasing number of transnational institutions are emerging. Two opposing views arise. Under the 'process of convergence' argument, national differences are shrinking and more standardization is emerging as a result of globalization. For example, many multinationals are standardizing their HR and other policies around the world. This seems to be reducing their capacity to deal with diversity.

An alternative view proposes that national cultures continue to dictate different ways of managing at the local level, which is referred to as a 'process of divergence'.[60] Both convergence and divergence are probably operating simultaneously, with certain universal aspects of leadership developing while other culturally specific aspects are retained.[61] Further research is clearly needed into the impact of national culture on leadership, and the extent to which convergence and divergence are taking place as a result of globalization.

---

9 Diversity

Following on from the above discussion of cultural diversity, the leadership paradigms suggest another progression from Classical through Organic paradigms. This is along the dimension of increasing capacity to deal with diversity arising from differences other than those arising from cultural values. Differences can stem from the roles of different stakeholders and values held by diverse interest groups. A further difference seems to arise in the way men and women manage organizations, as Box 3.4 illustrates. Much of the literature on management stems from the male perspective, and Helgesen has shown that female managers often take a different approach.

Box 3.4

Women's way of leading through inclusion

Helgesen questioned many of the myths about how universal management behaviours actually are, especially between men and women.[62] About 20 years earlier, Mintzberg had published observations of seven male managers, from which he concluded that men often worked at an unrelenting pace, with no breaks taken during the day.[63] Male executives experienced many interruptions and spared little time for activities unrelated to their work. The men felt that their identity was directly tied to their job, and that they derived considerable prestige sitting atop the hierarchical pyramid. Immersed in the day-to-day need to keep the company going, managers often reported feeling isolated, with no time left to reflect and plan. The men generally had difficulty in sharing information with others, but their own access to information provided these male executives with their chief source of power. With information so bound up with their power, the men also became reluctant to share information. The males reported having a complex network of colleagues outside of work, and preferring face-to-face interaction to all other means of communication.

Helgesen's findings from a similar study of five female managers were rather different. The only thing in common with Mintzberg's findings about males was that managers of both genders prefer live encounters via phone or face to face to written communications, and have a complex network of colleagues outside work.

On Mintzberg's other findings, Helgesen's female executives differed quite remarkably. The women reported working at a calm steady pace, with frequent small breaks taken during the day 'to sit and catch my breath'.[64] Female managers did not consider unscheduled events to be interruptions, but saw them as a normal part of their work. Dealing with unscheduled interruptions was seen as being caring, involved, helping and responsible. All the women reported having a number of non-work-related activities, and that they made time for these family and personal activities. The female executives did not feel intellectually isolated as Mintzberg's men reported, but found themselves having time to read and reflect on the 'big picture'. Helgesen points out that this difference may have arisen because of the 20-year time difference between the two studies, and a shift to more Visionary leadership in Helgesen's era.

The women did not identify exclusively with their jobs as the men did, but rather saw their own identities as complex and multifaceted. This may have been because other aspects of their lives simply took up too much time to permit total identification with their careers. Additionally, the female executives scheduled time to share information with both their colleagues and their subordinates, and did not tend to hoard information like the men. Helgesen argues that this impulse to share information probably derives from the women's concern with relationships. The sharing was facilitated by the women perceiving themselves as being in the centre of things, rather than at the top. It was more natural for the women to reach out rather than down.

Although the studies were 20 years apart, Helgesen's identification of a 'female' leadership style, which she calls' the web', is supported by a number of other studies. Helgesen's *web of inclusion* is defined as a circle with the manager in the centre and interconnected to all other parts of the department or organization. This view differs sharply with the traditional pyramid structure that was common in many organizations, especially at the time of Mintzberg's study.

The circular web-like structure, and the female's position within it, allows the leaders to be both accessible and informed. This structure sends out signals that the concern is the group as a whole, one of inclusion. Leaders at the centre of the web have direct access to all others in the organization and their employees have access to them. As a result, the web of inclusion prevents people from feeling isolated and out of touch with the needs of their subordinates and their organization. In today's era of rapid change, businesses would do well to look at such alternative structures.

How the potential conflicts within a diverse set of constituents are dealt with is likely to differ between the leadership paradigms. Under Classical leadership the leader's view is likely to predominate, without considering the views of diverse followers unless they are very powerful. Transactional and Visionary leaders consult and consider others to varying degrees, but the leader's role is to decide which of the many voices will prevail over the others. Those whose views have not 'won the day' are still expected to work towards a unitary vision, often determined by the leader under a Visionary paradigm.

By contrast, Organic leadership hears and holds a wide range of views as valuable. Under Organic leadership, conflicting voices tend to be accepted and ways found to accommodate them wherever possible (see the BMW case study). Diverse ways of doing things may be acceptable in different contexts under the Organic paradigm.

10 Adaptability

The paradigms can also be distinguished in terms of the support they tend to provide for change. Operating conditions must become significantly dynamic before an organization will change, because even in turbulent times a growing organization cannot realistically change its structure every month.[65] Therefore, organizational change is likely to be characterized by periods of dramatic revolution, rather than incremental change.[66]

This is partly because the organization's entire systems, processes and culture may be destroyed and have to be rebuilt as the organization tries to realign itself with new realities. For example, a bureaucratic organization seeking to become organic will need to convert its formal processes, management layers, blame and control culture, and members' mental models for a more agile, organic structure to succeed (see the BMW, Rodenstock and Royal Australian Navy case studies). Similarly, entrepreneurial organizations often need to adopt more formal management processes and procedures as they grow or face stiff competition. These changes and their consequences are evident in larger organizations that were once entrepreneurial start-ups, such as SAP.

Since it is too costly for many organizations to destroy the old order for small benefits, organizations tend to be slow to change. The price for this slowness may be the occasional revolutionary period of major upheaval with its attendant costs and confusion, when organizations have to make major adaptations (see the Rodenstock case study). In continually changing environments, Classical and Transactional leadership tend to become dysfunctional, being suited to more placid and predictable operating environments.[67] One of the costs of Classical and Transactional leadership is that employees may be distracted from the outside world by their internal systems and procedures and have neither incentive nor motivation to seek out emerging opportunities or pursue innovative ideas.[68] Thus, Classical and Transactional paradigms are likely to be suited to conditions of incremental change, where small changes occur slowly, unless the Classical leader can coerce fast change.

Many theorists argue that Visionary leaders are required to manage and inspire the change process, and make the difference between success and failure in change.[69] Organizations undergoing major change need more than transactional behaviours like the exchange of material, social and personal benefits for services satisfactorily rendered. Commitment and flexibility become critical. Bass pointed out that in uncertain, dynamic environments a firm needs to foster Visionary leadership at all levels.[70] Such leadership provides the firm with much-needed flexibility to forecast and meet new demands and changes as they occur.

Bass' idea of distributed Visionary leadership seems somewhat similar to an Organic paradigm. However, Visionary leadership focused on a central leader seems less adaptive than Organic leadership. This is because change requires this leader to shift the hearts, minds and behaviours of followers away from an existing vision towards a different future. In some cases the Visionary leader may succeed, but over time too many changes may lead to cynicism, with followers abandoning the leader. Some followers may not accept the new vision.

Other observers note that Visionary leadership alone is insufficient for successful major change. A more down to earth 'instrumental' style of leadership is also essential for transforming organizations.[71] Instrumental leadership includes activities associated with building teams, clarifying required behaviours, and instituting appropriate measures, rewards and sanctions to support the desired new behaviours.[72] Many of these activities occur under the Transactional paradigm. In other words, Visionary leadership needs some instrumental/Transactional management to align systems and processes for effective transformation.

Under more chaotic Organic leadership conditions, the entire organization can be constantly prepared for change, with everyone understanding the need for continuous adaptation to an ever-changing environment. Long-term viability requires organizations to harness the knowledge, commitment and value added by all the members in adapting to change.[73] This may eliminate the need for occasional cataclysmic changes. Members assist in the change process as they help each other make sense of chaotic circumstances. While adaptability can be impeded to some extent by the extensive communication process necessary under an Organic paradigm, once a new order emerges it is more likely to be readily implementable and accepted. Simultaneously, the organization is ready for the next set of changes.

11   Responsibility and accountability

Responsibility and accountability are key factors in organizing.[74] Responsibility and accountability refer to that part of a system intended to ensure that people behave in a particular manner. Behaviour should be at least consistent with specified standards and expectations, and preferably exceed a personal or organizational vision. The literature on responsibility and accountability tends to confuse the two terms, but a distinction can be drawn:[75]

- *Responsibilities* of various kinds that the literature distinguishes (role/task responsibility, legal/ethical responsibility, moral responsibility, causal responsibility, felt responsibility and judged responsibility) relate to tasks or events. People are given role/task responsibilities to make decisions and act in the light of legal, ethical and moral constraints. Their actions lead to *consequences* that the actors may or may not feel responsible for, but upon which they generally will be judged.
- *Accountability* has to do with determining *whether, to what extent*, and *how* a person's contribution to a consequence should be responded to. Options include a reward, feedback, counselling or punishment. *Whether* a person can be held accountable will depend on facts such as whether the person was capable of rational behaviour or whether the consequence could possibly have been foreseen. Asking '*To what extent?*' is important because the person's action may not have been entirely volitional. '*How?*' becomes significant since the response to past behaviour will influence future behaviour in a particular direction.

The paradigms can be distinguished in terms of where responsibility and accountability tend to rest. In Classical leadership, the leader is generally responsible and accountable for all aspects of the enterprise, since followers are largely disempowered and their voices seldom heard. Followers are held accountable for any disobedience and dissent, and for not achieving specific tasks they have been assigned.

Responsibility appears more distributed in Transactional and Visionary leadership than in Classical, because people lower down the line take on more of a decision-making role. People no longer blindly follow the leader's instructions to the best of their ability, but are empowered to make decisions and act with a degree of autonomy. This wider range of responsibilities brings with it new accountabilities. In some circumstances, agreements may be negotiated under Classical and Transactional leadership that make followers responsible, and hence accountable, for specific outcomes within their sphere of influence (see the Bonduelle case study). The leader is still accountable for larger outcomes. Given the essential role that followers under Visionary leadership play in implementing the vision, they would be expected to take increased responsibility and accountability over that of the Transactional leader's followers. Furthermore, as one moves from the Classical to the Organic paradigm, there is a shift towards people assuming more responsibility for decisions (instead of simply completing tasks, with the attendant accountability).

Followers of Organic leadership are likely to make mutual commitments to accept individual and shared responsibility for particular projects or tasks. Hence, accountability would be more widely shared across the team or organizational members (see the BMW and Gore case studies). Individuals are expected to hold themselves accountable for specific commitments and are likely to be held jointly accountable for the success or failure of the entire team or other enterprise.

In summary, leader accountability remains high under Classical, Transactional and Visionary paradigms, but can be diluted where leadership is shared, as is characteristic of the Organic paradigm. On the other hand, follower responsibility and accountability tend to increase from Classical to Transactional, Visionary and Organic leadership.

12 Matching structure

Management strategists propose that appropriate leadership styles vary depending on the structure of a given organization. While many different structures can be identified in practice, four basic organizational forms are:

- *simple form*;
- *bureaucracy (machine bureaucracy* and *professional bureaucracy)*;
- *adhocracy (flexible, self-renewing organic structure)*; and
- *divisionalized form.*[76]

The *simple form* allows direct centralized supervision, as occurs in new or small businesses. A *bureaucratic configuration* tends to move the firm increasingly toward more stability, regularity and standardization.[77] McDonald's is an example of a *machine bureaucracy*, where processes and systems are heavily standardized to ensure consistency in products worldwide. A *professional bureaucracy*, such as a university or hospital, relies on the professional training and skills of its members (see the Novartis case study). The *divisionalized form* is found in larger organizations, such as BMW, Novartis and the Royal Australian Navy. Here, decision making is traditionally delegated to semi-autonomous managers heading specialized units.[78] The *adhocracy* resembles many of today's networked organizations, although it has been popular in the literature for several decades.[79] Adhocracies move organizations in the direction of innovation, flexibility, informality and customization.[80]

Adhocracies, with their emphasis on external relationships with the environment, appear to support more open systems than bureaucracies, which tend to be more inwardly focused. In the case studies presented in Part Two, a general tendency away from bureaucracy towards adhocracy is evident, making many parts of the organizations more adaptive. However, different structures are evident in different parts of some organizations. For example, production at Swatch tends to exhibit a more bureaucratic structure, while the marketing department resembles an adhocracy.

The leadership paradigms fit with some structures better than others. The idea that leadership emanates from the top is easy to maintain in simple and centralized bureaucracies where control can be imposed from the top down (see the Bonduelle case study). This is consistent with the Classical and Transactional paradigms. Transactional leadership also lends itself to managing the divisional form.

Visionary leadership could be used in all four organizational configurations, but is most likely to fit with simple, bureaucratic and divisional forms. While vision is important to an adhocracy, the vision need not emanate from a central Visionary leader.

Organic leadership fits well with adhocracy or networked organizations. This is because adhocracies require organizations to decentralize decision making and power to managers and specialists, yet provide ways for them to interact flexibly so that they can respond to unpredictable changes (for example, see the BMW, EKATO and Gore case studies). Mutual adjustment, which coordinates work through informal communication, becomes the main coordinating mechanism in the Organic paradigm.[81] However, the ability of people to communicate effectively depends partly on organizational size. Gore prefers to keep groups below about 200 members, in order to facilitate communication needed for mutual adjustment. However, others have concluded that there is no optimal size for the Organic organization to function at, just diminishing returns on communication as size increases.[82] Thus, the paradigms can be broadly associated with different organizational structures. However, appropriate structures also relate to the operating context.

13 Matching context

The operating environment can impact leadership as well as other elements in an organizational system. Even within the one organization, structure and the required leadership can vary with changes in the operating environment. For example, military organizations tend to be very bureaucratic in peacetime, with an emphasis on planning, drilling and discipline, and exhibiting a clear chain of command. However, in battle the environment becomes more dynamic and haphazard, and so the structure needs to be more flexible.[83] This tends to be accompanied by more flexible Organic leadership in battle that empowers the people on the ground to decide how to act.

The paradigms suit different operating environments. In stable environments, an organization can set more standardized rules, formalize work, and plan actions to become an undisturbed system with standard procedures operating from top to bottom (see the Royal Australian Navy case study). The simple form has also been found to perform best of Mintzberg's structures in terms of return on sales – in stable environments.[84] In essence, the Classical and Transactional paradigms fit simple, stable conditions.

Visionary and Organic paradigms lend themselves to more complex, chaotic, dynamic environments. Here, problems and requirements cannot be broken down into specialist tasks within a clearly defined hierarchy (see the BMW, Novartis and Swatch case studies). While the Visionary and Organic paradigms could also function in simple environments, they shine in more uncertain complexity. Forcing Organic leadership on a simple, stable environment could be as inappropriate as forcing a machine bureaucracy on a complex, dynamic situation, according to Mintzberg.[85]

The general message has long been: 'the more dynamic the environment, the more organic the structure'.[86] This is despite major opposing forces, such as organizational size, that might otherwise drive an organization towards more bureaucracy. The implication is that for most organizations today, an Organic structure matched with Organic leadership is increasingly necessary in today's dynamic contexts. Yet most organizations have not adopted the Organic paradigm. Does this mean that hierarchies fill deep human needs, as Leavitt[87] suggests?

CONCLUSION

The leadership paradigms exhibit broadly distinguishable characteristics, making them appropriate for different contexts. These distinguishing factors appear to fit along a set of broad continua, generally changing across the paradigms. Further research is clearly needed to define and measure the changes along the hypothesized continua. However, the intention here is to stimulate discussion about the differences between the paradigms.

Classical leadership revolves around a powerful leader, with followers having very little power beyond the power to withdraw their labour in some cases, and assuming limited responsibility and accountability for outcomes. Diverse views go largely unheard as the Classical leader's view predominates. Newtonian management thinking underlies Classical leadership, which can be effective in stable, simple or bureaucratic environments, and with low-knowledge workers. However, Classical leadership appears generally limited in complex, dynamic situations and where follower input, knowledge and commitment are needed.

Followers are involved more under Transactional leadership than in the Classical paradigm. The Transactional leader consults and influences followers to achieve set goals. Despite any mutual influencing, the Transactional leader retains more power than followers, deriving power largely from reward and coercion, personal characteristics, and interpersonal and influencing skills. Followers have low power on a day-to-day basis, but can withdraw their support for the leader, exit agreements and band together to influence the leader. However, most control resides with the leader.

Newtonian management ideas of creating order, searching for cause and effect, predictability and valuing control underlie Transactional leadership, limiting this style to situations of relatively low complexity. That followers are able to voice opinions is a first step to managing diversity within the organization or group, even though the leader's final view is expected to prevail. Adaptiveness is slowed down compared with the Classical paradigm, because followers need to be heard and negotiated with. Leader responsibility and accountability for outcomes are high, with followers taking responsibility and accountability on a limited basis only. Transactional leadership can operate in simple, bureaucratic and divisional structures, but may not always be appropriate for self-managing knowledge workers.

Scholars and practitioners often regard Visionary leadership, where the leader's vision inspires followers to greater achievements, as the ideal paradigm, particularly when organizations need to be transformed. Research suggests that performance is enhanced under Visionary leadership, possibly because the successful Visionary leader employs a vision that appeals to followers' needs and motivations. Followers are then expected to play a substantial role in executing the vision to create a desired future, thereby enhancing their power above that typical of followers under Classical and Transactional paradigms. Visionary leader power comes from a wide range of sources, including position, reference power, their vision, sometimes personal charisma, and followers' emotional attachments. While belief in the efficacy of the leader's actions is strong, and thereby consistent with a Newtonian management philosophy, Visionary leadership also allows the more adaptive New Sciences view to emerge, including dealing with unpredictability and complexity.

Although the Visionary leader listens to and considers followers' views, this leader's role is to meld the group into one entity, united behind one of the visions and views raised. Providing the leader can shift the followers away from the current vision to some new vision, adaptiveness can be more substantial than under the Classical and Transactional paradigms. However, adherence to a strongly held vision and values can reduce the organization's ability to change, particularly when organizational structures and systems have been aligned to achieve a particular vision. Responsibility and accountability for outcomes under Visionary leadership still reside with the leader. Visionary leadership appears to fit primarily with divisional and organic structures, in both dynamic and stable environments.

Organic leadership allows for both leaderless and leaderful organizations to emerge. Leadership is not necessarily vested in particular individuals, although people might assume leadership roles for a time. Rather, the relationships between the members of the organization give rise to leadership, through extensive communication as members make sense of rapidly changing circumstances. Organic leadership is based on processes of mutual sense-making.

The entire group membership becomes key to the Organic paradigm, rather than a designated leader. Leadership is often determined by group consensus. Much of the leadership emanates from a shared vision and core values embedded within the organizational culture, and supporting systems and processes need to be aligned within the organization. Management philosophy underlying Organic leadership derives from the New Sciences, and places the organization in a state to deal with high levels of complexity and adaptation (although the need for extensive communication may initially appear to slow change).

Organic leader control is typically minimal. Followers are encouraged to be self-leading and self-organizing, thereby acquiring high levels of power from expertise, personal and information sources. To achieve this, extensive information needs to be available to all members. Power tends to be shared across the members rather than vested in specific leaders.

Communication and sharing information occupy considerable time in an organic organization. Diverse views and values are accepted and accorded equitable treatment. There is a high level of self-accountability and commitment (see the Gore case study). Responsibility and accountability are shared, with individuals or teams making commitments that they will complete specific tasks. Organic leadership lends itself to adhocracies and networked structures, as well as to complex dynamic environments.

The appropriate paradigm for any given enterprise will depend on many factors, including the organizational structure, stability of the operating environment, aspects of national or regional cultures, and whether followers are expected to be professionally educated or creative. Given that many organizations are facing dynamic, complex environments, a trend towards Organic leadership seems inevitable. However, other factors pull an organization away from an Organic paradigm. For example, large organizations or those with a traditional Classical culture, may find it very difficult to move to an Organic paradigm (see the EKATO and Royal Australian Navy case studies).

Successful leadership in a given context results from a combination of factors, including whether followers and other stakeholders can buy into the prevailing leadership paradigm; leadership behaviours are consistent with the enacted paradigm; and organizational systems, processes, structure, environment and culture are appropriate to that paradigm.

Mental models of leadership held by organizational members will determine whether particular paradigms are recognized as 'leadership'. For any of the paradigms to be effective, the beliefs and behaviours of both leaders and followers within a particular organization will need to align with a given paradigm, as will the organizational systems and culture. Thus, shifting paradigms is not a simple matter.

At this stage, it is important to point out that multiple paradigms may be operating in any given organization or its parts. This will be the case particularly where an organization is undergoing major change. Nonetheless, the paradigms are intended to clarify communication about the nature of leadership observed in today's organizations, and so help people develop their ideas about the practice of leadership.

Some formal theories of leadership are examined in the next chapters, and linked to the leadership paradigms outlined here.

NOTES

For full details of these notes, please see the References section at the end of this book.

1   Avolio, 1996
2   Maccoby, 2000

3 e.g. Gilmore and Shea, 1997; Shamir, House and Arthur, 1993
4 Bennis, 1998
5 Mintzberg, 1998
6 Abell, 2000
7 Howell, Bowen, Dorfman, Kerr and Podsakoff, 1990
8 e.g. DuBrin, 1998; Steers, Porter and Bigley, 1996; Yukl, Kim and Falbe, 1996
9 Bolman and Deal, 1997
10 Collins, 1999:25
11 French and Raven, 1959
12 ibid.
13 DuBrin, 1998
14 Spillane and Spillane, 1998
15 DuBrin, 1998
16 Atwater and Yammarino, 1996
17 ibid.
18 Pfeffer, 1992:281
19 Meindl, 1998:21
20 Hirschhorn, 1997
21 Rothschild and Whitt, 1986
22 Mintzberg, 1979
23 DuBrin, 1998
24 Mintzberg, 1979
25 Gemmill and Oakley, 1992
26 Vroom and Jago, 1988; Vroom and Yetton, 1973
27 Yukl, 1998
28 e.g. Fayol, 1949; Schriesheim and Neider, 1989;
    Tannenbaum and Schmidt, 1973
29 Mintzberg, 1973a
30 Bass and Avolio, 1994
31 Kotter, 1990
32 Bennis and Nanus, 1985
33 Bass 1990b; Bennis, 1983; Zaleznik, 1989
34 Bennis and Nanus, 1985; Sashkin, 1988
35 Mintzberg, 1998
36 Bass, 1990a
37 e.g. Complexity and Management Centre, 2000; Merry, 1995; Stacey, 2000;
    Vaill, 1989; Wheatley, 1992
38 Bennis and Nanus, 1985
39 Merry, 1995
40 Wheatley, 1999
41 Stacey, 2000
42 Complexity and Management Centre, 2000
43 Gleick, 1987
44 Wheatley, 1999

45   Weick, 1995
46   Stacey, 2000
47   Complexity and Management Centre, 2000; Merry, 1999
48   Cameron, Whetten and Kim, 1987
49   Weick, 1991
50   Complexity and Management Centre, 2000:12
51   e.g. Holt, 1999
52   Kezar, 2000
53   Ichikawa, 1996
54   Hofstede, 1984
55   ibid.
56   ibid.
57   Hofstede, 1991
58   ibid.
59   Hay-McBer, 1995
60   Communal and Senior, 1999
61   Hilb, 1999
62   Helgesen, 1990
63   Mintzberg, 1973a
64   Helgesen, 1990:20
65   Mintzberg, 1979
66   Miller and Friesen, 1980
67   Emery and Trist, 1973
68   Ghoshal and Bartlett, 1998
69   Bass, 1990b
70   ibid.
71   e.g. Kets de Vries, 1994; Vaill, 1989
72   Nadler and Tushman, 1990
73   Ghoshal and Bartlett, 1998; Hesselbein, Goldsmith and Somerville, 1997
74   Frink and Klimoski, 1998
75   Bergsteiner and Avery, 2003
76   Miller, 1990; Mintzberg, 1979
77   Miller, 1990
78   Mintzberg, 1993
79   Mintzberg, 1979
80   Brodbeck, 2002
81   Mintzberg, 1979
82   Rothschild and Whitt, 1986
83   Mintzberg, 1979
84   Drago, 1998
85   Mintzberg, 1979
86   Mintzberg, 1979:270
87   Leavitt, 2003

4 Micro-level Leadership Theories

Key Points

- Understanding leadership theories and models
- Traits and behaviours of the individual leader
- Influencing skills
- Leader-follower relations
- Situational influences
- Linking theories to the paradigms

How do the paradigms relate to the many leadership theories and concepts? Over the next three chapters, major leadership theories and ideas are discussed in relation to the paradigms. This chapter describes the evolution of leadership theories and approaches, particularly as they apply to individual leaders and their relationships with their followers.

Most formal leadership theories were developed in the twentieth century, although many of the underlying ideas about leadership are much older. These theories tend to deal with specific facets of leadership or leadership at particular levels breaking the concept into simpler components for ease of study or in order to develop particular leadership tools. Few writers address leadership in its complexity or try to link their theories to one another. None addresses the full range of leadership ideas and levels, although Bass and Yukl have made major attempts to do so.[1]

Most theorists ignore the fact that national and dynamic corporate cultures, different political contexts and multiple stakeholders affect leadership. A comprehensive view of leadership will not just be internally-focused, but will place leadership in an operating context. This will allow for interactions with the external world, including with competitors, governments and politicians, suppliers and alliance partners.

Thus, the leadership field consists of the writings of groups of relatively isolated scholars. Adopting a broad approach to leadership as advocated in this book requires integrating many theoretical approaches. Any theory or model that encompassed the full range of internal and external leadership issues would be very broad, and so probably not detailed or predictive enough to be useful for empirical researchers. However, writers and practitioners are calling for a multilevel framework that incorporates leadership effects at individual, group and organizational levels.[2]

The question is, at which organizational levels should leadership be discussed?[3] A common recommendation is to use different management levels: higher levels (executive or upper echelon management), middle management and lower levels (front-line or entry-level). One difficulty with this approach is determining the comparability of levels in various organizations, especially in networked organizations. Yammarino proposes focusing on four 'groups' to understand leadership theories and models, namely the *individual*, *dyad* (two person, one-on-one interactions), *subgroup* and *whole group* levels.[4] However, these levels tend to be focused internally on the organization and need expanding to include the external leadership environment.

Ideally, the many facets of leadership should be integrated and viewed holistically, as part of a dynamic process. However, the linear nature of a book requires this complex set of issues to be split into smaller elements. Therefore the discussion in the following chapters is structured around levels of leadership similar to those defined by Yammarino. The micro-level is covered in this chapter, starting with the individual and proceeding through dyadic to larger group levels. These theories are sometimes referred to as 'supervisory theories'. Chapter 5 bridges the micro- and organizational-levels by discussing emotion-based approaches to leadership that typically emphasize the role of a vision, shared values and other emotional bases underpinning leadership. In Chapter 6, macro-level approaches focused at higher organizational levels and on the broader external environment are introduced. The leadership paradigms relevant to each of the theories are also indicated during the discussion, and each chapter concludes by integrating its content into the paradigms.

INDIVIDUAL LEVEL

The belief that individuals are distinguished as leaders by virtue of their birth, traits or behaviours places a strong focus on the leader as a special kind of person. This section considers the characteristics and behaviours associated with these individuals.

Great men

Great Men ideas, based largely on class and birth, were very popular during the nineteenth and early twentieth centuries. Great Men views propose that people from the upper classes inherit desirable leadership qualities and the right to lead.[5] This applied particularly to men (see Box 4.1 for challenges facing *Great Women*).

Under the Great Men view, everyone inherited a place in society and expectations or opportunities rarely change this. Reflecting society at the time, the nineteenth and early twentieth century business world was also divided into classes, with leaders considered born to the role, not made. People tended to accept the world as being divided into leaders and followers. Max Weber's observations about the civil service, with his ideal bureaucratic ways, reinforced this class division. Those who understood how to manage directed the lesser classes.[6]

Early in the twentieth century, 'the successful executive was generally pictured as possessing intelligence, imagination, initiative, the capacity to make rapid (and generally wise) decisions, and the ability to inspire subordinates.'[7] Even today, children from certain dynasties, family business people and royalty are considered, by some, born to rule.

The belief that birth determines a person's fitness to lead may have diminished over time, but the often-related notion of the heroic leader, with a strong focus on one key person, still pervades leadership theory and practice. Attributing the outcome of events to actions of heroic leaders is common in many cultures, where the fates of organizations, empires, armies or their followers are attributed to these leaders. This attribution can become extreme when people hold unrealistic expectations about a leader's abilities, and leaders can seldom live up to these high hopes.[8]

Box 4.1

Where are the great women leaders?

Compared with 'Great Men', the emergence of the 'Great Woman' leader was traditionally much more difficult unless she was born into a leader role. Alternatively, she could marry into a family from which leaders traditionally come, or take over from her husband, like the Ghandis in India.

Mary Kay Ash was an exception. Disappointed at how she was treated by a previous employer, she resolved to build an organization that provides women with opportunities to excel. In doing so, she created the largest direct seller of skin care products and the best-selling brand of colour cosmetics in the US.[9] Mary Kay Inc. employs more than 500 000 independent beauty consultants in 29 markets worldwide, and has been featured among the *100 Best Companies to Work for in America* three times since the list began in 1984 (see URL: http://www.marykay.com/).

Ash is obviously not alone in her success, but even today relatively few women are in senior leadership positions in business. Various explanations have been advanced for this, including that men have an advantage over women in leadership positions because the business context is male-oriented. 'Concepts of leadership ... are gendered, embedded inside assumptions, practices, norms, belief systems that make men normal.'[10] Men define leadership and organizations in terms that are appropriate to men, so that when women enter the leadership arena, they do so within men's cultural norms.[11] In this context, some people are bemused at Mary Kay Ash's extravagant and emotional award ceremonies, at which her top sales-women receive pink Cadillacs or pink fur coats, where she calls her saleswomen 'daughter', and where women's business suits are colour-coded to indicate rank.

Research into the scarcity of women in leadership roles shows that being a leader makes men feel masculine, whereas for women being a leader does not make them feel feminine. Instead, women leaders often try to deny their sexuality and gender.[12] These strategies tend to be self-defeating, especially when women are accused of 'trying too hard to be one of the boys'. This constant attempt at concealment deprives women of an important part of their identity and feeling of self, which men derive from traditional styles of leadership. Thus, given the male culture in many organizations, and the potential conflict between a woman's iden-tity and leadership, it is not surprising that relatively few women are in leadership positions. Nor is it surprising that Mary Kay Ash 'feminized' her organization.

It will become evident that the notion of the heroic leader continues to per-meate many leadership theories and approaches. In terms of the leadership para-digms, the 'Great Man' approach fits well with the Classical, Transactional and Visionary leadership ideas, but not with the distributed leadership behind the Organic paradigm.

Traits

Some researchers argue that regardless of whether leaders are born or made, they are different from other people.[13] Leaders need to have the 'right stuff', which not every-one has. Identifying this 'stuff' could help in the search for individuals with leader-ship potential.

Early attempts to find the essence of leadership were disappointing, as Stogdill's famous review of trait studies showed.[14] Only two characteristics seemed to help dis-tinguish leaders from non-leaders with any degree of consistency: leaders were slightly taller and slightly more intelligent than non-leaders. Of course, Hitler and Napoleon provide examples of men of short stature who acquired considerable power, as do the Prime Ministers John Howard (Australia) and Silvio Berlusconi (Italy).

Nearly half a century later, researchers resumed the search for leader traits using improved measures and looking for traits linked more closely to leadership activities than height.[15] While exceptions can always be found, the six traits described in Table 4.1 have been found to distinguish leaders from non-leaders, at least under the US business model:

Table 4.1

Six leader traits

Drive	Desire to lead
Leaders exhibit achievement, motivation, ambition, energy, initiative and tenacity.	Leaders want to lead, and are willing to exercise some power over, and to discipline, others
Being honest/having integrity	**Self-confidence**
This characteristic enables leaders to form trusting relationships with followers, and not violate promises or confidences.	Others' perceptions of the leader's self-confidence are important, as is displaying emtional stability, being even-tempered and able to deal with stress.
Knowing the business	**High-level intelligence**
Knowledge of the business enables informed decisions to be made and promotes understanding of the implications of those decisions.	Leaders need to be able to gather and process considerable information, formulate strategies, and solve problems. A high '*g*' (general intelligence) level is important.

Source: Adapted from Kirkpatrick and Locke[16]

- drive,
- honesty and integrity,
- knowing the business,
- wanting to lead,
- having self-confidence, and
- being intelligent.[17]

A more complex approach to understanding and measuring leader traits comes from the competency movement begun by David McClelland.[18] The *competency approach* searches for the underlying characteristic(s) of an individual related to effective or superior performance.[19] Clearly, what constitutes superior performance can be difficult to define, especially for senior executives, but researchers are attempting to develop appropriate measures.[20]

Many organizations are seeking leaders able to function globally. Increasingly, senior managers are agreeing that tomorrow's leaders will operate in a global context, and that different capabilities will be required of global leaders.[21] In research into effective global leaders, Gregersen and his colleagues identified the necessary characteristics as being partly specific to the global context, and partly generic to leaders generally.[22] They concluded that about one-third of a global leader's success comes from having the knowledge and skills for specific contexts, such as industry knowledge and understanding the corporate culture. The remaining characteristics apply to leaders generally, including:

- being able to affect others emotionally
- being ethical and inquisitive
- managing uncertainty, and
- developing 'savvy'.

Being inquisitive, adventuresome, curious and open-minded were considered particularly important in successful global leaders.

However, even if currently-known traits and competencies were accepted as those necessary for leadership, especially for the single leader-based Classical, Transactional and Visionary paradigms, it is still not clear how much of each trait is needed in particular leadership situations. It is also hard to accept that possessing special traits propels so many people into leadership roles in organizations where leadership is widely distributed.

Further, merely possessing certain traits is probably not sufficient to distinguish leaders from non-leaders. Leaders also need to display evidence of their traits by behaving 'appropriately', as discussed below.

Leader behaviour

Focusing on leader behaviours broadens the concept of leadership beyond birth or personality. Leadership becomes increasingly democratic, being seen as a more general capability that many people could potentially achieve. If leaders can be identified by their actions, then more people could be trained to act like leaders.

Researchers, disappointed in the results of the search for leader traits, began to look at the behaviours leaders display. Their observations resulted in two broad categories of leader behaviours: *task-related* behaviours (concerned with the job to be done), and *relationship* behaviours (people-oriented behaviours, such as being supportive and providing feedback).

Studying relationship behaviours was an important development in leadership theory, because until this time, most of the focus in organizations had been on making tasks as efficient as possible, with individual workers being considered rather irrelevant. For instance, Taylor's scientific management and engineering model had looked at ways of making work more efficient through his famous time-and-motion studies.[23] Although Taylor's approach started to focus a little more on workers and followers, as well as the context in which people were operating, the emphasis was primarily on improving processes and systems. It has long been known that a focus on people enhances productivity.[24] Henry Ford was one of the earliest industrialists to recognize this, when he stemmed the tide of worker attrition by introducing the then generous $5 per day minimum wage, profit sharing, and reducing the working day from nine to eight hours.[25]

In more recent research, a leader's focus on relationships has been found to be effective in the workplace.[26] Good relationships result in more satisfied workers.[27] Increasingly, social science research indicated that leaders should also consider human relations among the members of workgroups, and the image of an effective leader began to change from that of an *autocrat* to someone who was more *democratic*.

Identifying appropriate leader behaviours led to the production of management guidelines. Yukl, for example, provides guidelines for a range of managerial practices significant to effective leadership.[28] These practices include familiar management actions with an emphasis on getting the job done, such as planning, organizing, problem solving, monitoring and setting objectives.

Other guidelines cover behaviours often associated with managing relationships, such as motivating, inspiring, consulting, delegating, supporting, developing and mentoring staff, rewarding, managing conflict, networking and team building. Behavioural guidelines like these can be of great assistance to Transactional leaders seeking to enhance their interpersonal and influence skills. See Box 4.2 for some guidelines on influencing.

Yukl proposes that modern leader behaviours should encompass a third category in addition to task and relationship behaviours, namely behaviours related to *change*.[29] Change-oriented behaviour includes activities such as improving decisions, innovating, adapting strategy to suit the environment and making major transformations.

Clearly, the appropriate blend of task, relationship and change-oriented behaviours will depend on environmental factors, such as how stable or dynamic the organization's marketplace, industry and operating environment are. In stable environments, change can be incremental, with most emphasis on managing the task and relationships. In times of turbulence, more radical change-oriented behaviour is often needed, accompanied by a shift to more Visionary leadership.[30]

Box 4.2

Guidelines for influencing

The following tactics for influencing others are based on Yukl's recommendations:[31]

- *Rational persuasion*: use logical arguments and factual evidence to persuade the target person to your position.

- *Inspiration*: make a request or proposal that excites the target person by appealing to that person's values, ideals or aspirations, or by increasing the target's self-confidence.

- *Consultation*: seek the target person's participation, for example, in planning a strategy, activity or change, or be willing to modify your proposal to address the other person's suggestions and concerns.

- *Ingratiation*: use praise, flattery, friendly or helpful behaviour to put the target person in a good mood or think favourably about you before asking for something. For example, compliment them on past achievements, or be sympathetic about problems your request may cause.

- *Personal appeals*: appeal to the target's feelings of loyalty and friendship toward you when asking for something, for example, by appealing to friendship, explaining why the request is important to you, beginning the requests with 'I need a favour ...' before stating what it is.

> - **Exchange**: offer an exchange of favours, indicate your willingness to reciprocate later, or promise a share of benefits if the target person helps you accomplish the task.
> - **Coalition tactics**: seek others' aid to persuade the target person to do something, or use the support of others as a reason for the target to agree. For example, mention credible people who support the proposal; bring someone along to help influence the target; provide evidence or an endorsement; or solicit the help of someone with higher authority.
> - **Legitimating tactics:** try to establish the legitimacy of a request by claiming the authority or right to make it, verifying that it is consistent with organizational policies, rules, practices or traditions, or refer to some precedent.
> - **Pressure**: use demands, threats, frequent checking, or persistent reminders to influence the target person to do what you want them to do.

One of the strengths of behaviour-based approaches is that leaders can develop their skills by identifying effective behaviours, for instance:

- Classical leaders can acquire monitoring and controlling behaviour;
- Transactional leaders can learn to influence others;
- Visionary leaders can adopt techniques for honing and communicating visions; and
- Organic leadership can enhance team and communication skills.

Where leader behaviours can be learned, the base of leadership can be broadened as more people acquire the desired behaviours.

While the behavioural approach has provided valuable guidelines for enhancing some leader behaviours, it has been criticized for a variety of reasons. Some authors regard the fundamental division into relationship and task behaviours as too broad and unspecific. Further, the categories are not mutually exclusive.[32] What is the difference between the two categories, especially when a task-related action like monitoring also includes communication, feedback and elements of supportive behaviour? Similarly, an informal chat can be about job-related issues as well as making the employee feel good. Change-oriented behaviour may involve both task and relationship elements in implementing a vision.

Finally, in behavioural theories, the person being managed is usually assigned a passive role in the leadership process, although some writers also provide guidelines for followers.[33]

Evaluating individual approaches

Clearly, leadership approaches that focus on an individual's leadership characteristics, whether traits or behaviours, reflect the view that the leader is central to understanding leadership. Sometimes leaders are born to their role, but often they are appointed or achieve leadership in some other way.

Understanding the traits and behaviours that distinguish better from worse leaders would enhance the quality of leadership appointments. It would also allow appropriate leadership development. Unfortunately, the traits and behaviours that differentiate between effective and less effective leaders mostly elude researchers. This is no doubt partly due to the difficulties of identifying effective leadership, and possibly because researchers have focused on narrow populations rather than taking broad examples.

Probably the biggest shortcoming of all the theories to date is that they focus on the individual leader and do not take very much account of the follower or the context in which leadership takes place. An exception is Yukl's inclusion of change-oriented behaviours. The next section presents approaches that investigate the follower's role as well.

DYADIC AND GROUP LEVEL: INTERACTING WITH OTHERS

The notion of a leader without followers is a contradiction in terms. Leadership implies some relationship between leader and followers. This relationship can occur between a leader and a single follower (known as a dyad), or between leaders and multiple followers (groups or teams). This section discusses some theories relating to a leader's relationship with individuals and groups.

Leader–member exchange theory

The *Leader–Member Exchange* (LMX) approach is based on the observation that followers form relationships of varying intensity and quality with their leader,[34] and that leaders do not treat all followers equally, but establish close relationships with subordinates regarded as part of the *in-group*.

Members of the in-group experience a rich exchange, enjoying relationships with their leader that are characterized by trust, loyalty and a sense of common fate. In-group members tend to receive better assignments, more freedom and greater opportunities to work with the leader, and come to function as the leader's assistants or advisers. Members of the *out-group* do not have such close relationships with the leader, are likely to be assigned less desirable jobs, have few opportunities to interact with the leader, and are often excluded from important decisions or activities.

Many factors influence the leader–member exchange relationship, including similarity in values between leader and followers, demographic characteristics and follower competence.[35] National cultural factors may also impact in-group and out-group membership. From Hofstede's work showing that cultures differ in how individualistic or collective they are, it is evident that individualist cultures such as the US and Australia value individual performance.[36] In these countries, leaders are expected to select their own in-groups based on the members' competence and contribution to the organization. Appointing family and friends would be regarded as exhibiting favouritism or nepotism.

On the other hand, leaders in many Asian countries would be reluctant to allow strangers into the in-group. In Japan and certain other parts of Asia, leaders generally prefer to surround themselves with family members because family is considered a comfortable and loyal choice.[37] Outsiders are hired to help the organization, but access to the in-group is based on community factors in collectivist societies. In Hong Kong and Malaysia, what others might regard as nepotism and showing favouritism would seem very normal, because loyalty to one's village, clan or family is of primary concern.[38] In these countries, managers prefer to employ people whom they know and/or who are referred to them by people they know.

Irrespective of how in- and out-groups are formed, relationships between leaders and individual workers have traditionally been at the core of many organizations, although the nature of the leader–follower relationship may be changing as more global enterprises organize around teams, particularly virtual teams. The LMX model has been extensively researched, but many questions remain unanswered, such as how in- and out-groups form and whether people can move from one group to another. LMX theory also does not prescribe which patterns of exchange enhance the leader's effectiveness. Further, the long-term relationships between supervisor–subordinates upon which the LMX theory has been based are becoming less prevalent in an increasingly mobile workforce.[39]

Since the LMX theory focuses on leadership emerging from the relationships between people in an organization, the theory could apply to all four leadership paradigms. Given the emphasis on the leader's relationship with individual followers who form the in- and out-groups, the theory is particularly applicable to Classical, Transactional and Visionary leadership. The LMX theory seems less applicable to Organic leadership, where more fluid in- and out-groups shift as the leadership or project changes, and the membership of groups continually changes.

Socio-cognitive approach

According to the socio-cognitive view, leadership is in the eye of the beholder. Leader actions and behaviours, and not hierarchical positions, underlie whether people *attribute* leadership to them. Follower perceptions are thus central to acknowledging leadership under this approach, rather than the characteristics or actions of the leader *per se*.

Socio-cognitive researchers explain perceptions of leadership using one of two different processes: *recognition* or *inference*.[40] People form leadership perceptions by observing someone's daily interactions with others. Observers may well conclude that leaders are intelligent, decisive individuals who can communicate effectively. This *recognition* stems from the observer's past experience with leaders, and whether the current person matches the leader criteria the observer has developed from those past experiences. Recognition-based perception is assumed to be largely automatic, that is, it can happen without being consciously thought about.[41] Clearly, what individual observers recognize as leader behaviour will depend on their past experiences and cultural background. For example, those who regard leadership as a shared group experience may well not recognize Classical or Transformational acts as 'leadership', classifying them as non-leadership behaviour instead.

Inference is the second process through which leadership can be identified. Attributing leadership to someone is *inferred* from the outcomes of significant events, such as enhanced performance or someone's promotion. Although inferred leadership is frequently a controlled mental process, it can be influenced by the stereotypes or prototypes individuals hold about leadership.[42] For example, improvements in profits or share prices might be attributed to the collective efforts of followers under Organic leadership, or to the leader's personal efforts in the Classical paradigm.

Recognition and inferential perception processes probably dominate at different levels of an organization.[43] At lower levels, where direct relationships between leader and followers play an important role, leadership perceptions will tend to be more automatic and recognition-based. Rewards and sanctions can be used directly and immediately to influence followers, and it is relatively easy to note some link between leader behaviour and performance. For example, people can recognize that in rewarding high performance, a leader directly influences how followers behave.

Most employees do not experience a senior executive's influence directly, and so draw conclusions about top leadership from indirect evidence. Observers outside the top team may have trouble accurately assessing what the leader does and establishing links between those actions and organizational performance. Exceptions arise where senior management's actions directly affect the organization, such as introducing new technology or downsizing. However, in general, top-level executives operate through indirect influence on the organization. These people may experience difficulty in being perceived as leaders because they do not fit the prototypical ideas of leadership that individuals hold.[44]

If they do not directly experience the effects of a leader's actions, people tend to rely on cultural stereotypes or beliefs to form perceptions of leadership.[45] For example, the comforting myth that leaders should be able to control everything that affects an organization's performance can form the basis for leader perceptions. Using this belief, when an organization is performing well, the leader is accorded the credit for the success, but when organizations are performing poorly, responsibility for the failure is also attributed to the leader.

Socio-cognitive approaches are well linked to extensive research into cognition. However, focusing on the follower's mental processes to determine leadership represents a major departure from conventional approaches that emphasize the characteristics and role of the leader. The socio-cognitive approach also contributes a valuable distinction between perceptions of leadership at different organizational levels.

Since perceiving leadership depends on the stereotypes or beliefs that a person holds about the concept, the socio-cognitive approach applies to each leadership paradigm.

Evaluating dyadic approaches

A major contribution of the dyadic and group approaches is that they recognize that leadership emerges from interactions between leaders and followers. The LMX theory acknowledges that these interactions are not all equal, and that this impacts leadership relationships. The socio-cognitive approach attributes the major role in leadership to followers and their perceptions of leadership.

However, the theories considered so far tend to be acontextual, that is, they do not focus on the context in which leadership is occurring. The socio-cognitive approach does recognize that leadership can differ at various levels within an organization, depending on how close the attributing follower is to the leader concerned. However, the focus of the dyadic approaches tends to be at the micro-level, independent of the broader situation. The next section considers theories that involve the context very strongly.

CONTINGENCY THEORIES: SITUATIONS MATTER

Most of the approaches covered so far have dealt only peripherally, if at all, with the context in which leader-follower relationships take place. This section introduces views that focus more on the situation. These approaches, which trace their origins back to the two-dimensional behaviour theories, are often called 'contingency' theories because they prescribe that leader behaviour should depend, or be contingent, on the situation.

Situational leadership

Hersey and Blanchard made a major contribution to leadership theory by extending the early two-dimensional behavioural models based on task and relationship behaviours to include a third dimension.[46] This dimension, akin to individual or group *psychological maturity* or follower development level, attempts to take into account the human environment in which a manager operates. This model evolved into a highly popular approach known as Situational Leadership (SL), of which there are now several versions in use in addition to those developed by the original proponents.[47] This book adopts Blanchard's terminology in describing SL.

SL models propose that effective managers provide individual followers with differing amounts of direction and support on performing tasks and achieving goals, depending on each person's *developmental level.*[48] The combination of a person's *commitment* and *competence* constitutes that individual's developmental level on a given task or goal.[49] *Competence* refers to the person's knowledge and skills relating to the task, as well as to their transferable skills. *Commitment* refers to an individual's motivation and confidence for undertaking that task or goal.

Effective SL derives from an appropriate combination of *Supporting* ('relationship behaviours', such as listening, recognizing, communicating and encouraging) and *Directing* ('task-related behaviours' such as providing instructions and monitoring how closely they are followed). Combining *Supporting* and *Directing* behaviours forms four key SL behaviour categories or styles:

- S1 *Directing* (high directing, low supporting);
- S2 *Coaching* (high directing, high supporting);
- S3 *Supporting* (low directing, high supporting); and
- S4 *Delegating* (low directing, low supporting).

The idea is that managers should begin with Directing, move to Coaching, then on to Supporting and finally to Delegating as the follower develops on a given task.

Corresponding to the S1 to S4 styles are team member developmental levels of D1 to D4 respectively.[50] Blanchard describes the four developmental levels as:[51]

- D1 – enthusiastic beginner, low on competence and high on commitment;
- D2 – disillusioned learner, with increasing competence and low commitment;
- D3 – capable but cautious contributor, with moderate-to-high competence and variable commitment; and
- D4 – self-reliant achiever, high on both competence and commitment.

SL prescribes that leaders should match the style they use to an individual follower's developmental level, striving to develop staff as they move through Directing, Coaching, Supporting to Delegating (see Figure 4.1). The model can also be applied to developing and managing teams, with the SL style related to the team's developmental level.

An intuitively appealing leadership model for practitioners, particularly Transactional leaders, SL emphasizes the importance of adjusting leader behaviour to follower needs. Upon closer evaluation, many theoretical and consistency flaws have been identified in SL theory and the accompanying questionnaires. For example, how to define and assess development levels is unclear, and how to match leader behaviours is not defined consistently from one situation to the next.[52]

The model has received relatively little academic and research attention.[53] Some see this as rather alarming, given SL's extensive use as a training tool.[54] Since several SL models exist that vary in definitions, terminology and even fundamental concepts, it is not surprising that the little research conducted into SL has failed to produce clear-cut outcomes.[55]

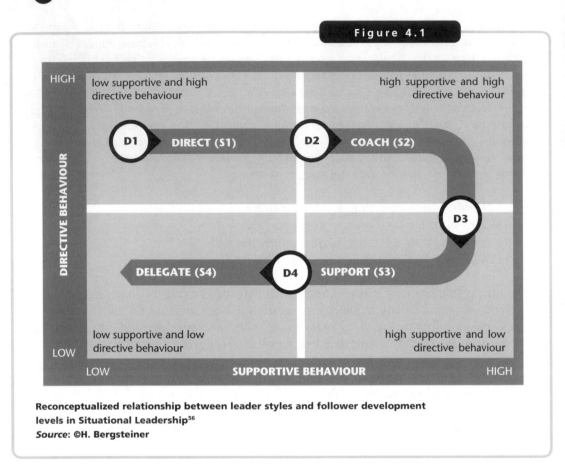

Figure 4.1

Reconceptualized relationship between leader styles and follower development levels in Situational Leadership[56]
Source: ©H. Bergsteiner

Despite its theoretical shortcomings, SL has impacted practice probably more than any other management tool, with over three million managers trained in it.[57] Research among practitioners suggests that SL is popular for a variety of reasons. Its concepts are intuitively appealing, the model is easy to understand and apply, SL fits comfortably with the role of the Transactional leader/manager, and has a wide range of uses on-the-job.[58] How much managers actually apply the model is questioned in Box 4.3.

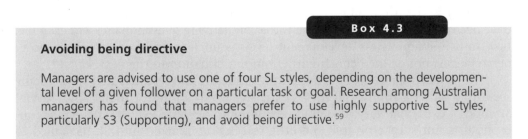

Box 4.3

Avoiding being directive

Managers are advised to use one of four SL styles, depending on the developmental level of a given follower on a particular task or goal. Research among Australian managers has found that managers prefer to use highly supportive SL styles, particularly S3 (Supporting), and avoid being directive.[59]

These preferences persist even after training.[60] In interviews with practising managers trained in SL who claimed to apply the model at work, some managers expressed shame because they did not follow the model and apply all four styles. Respondents often acknowledged their preferences for supportive styles and that they struggle to use the low-supporting S1 (Directing) and S4 (Delegating) styles. The researchers cite a respondent who, after using SL for two years, said: 'I prefer the coaching and supporting styles. But since the course, I've been more of a delegator.' Another manager reported: 'My comfort zone is coaching and my non-comfort zone is directing, but I'm having to use all four because it's required now.'

Such was the general dislike for directing that one person described it as 'tiresome and boring', another as 'I hate having to stand there and ... get forceful'. Respondents described strategies that they had developed to avoid being directive, such as trying to employ people who do not need directing or delegating any directing tasks to others. As one manager said: 'A lot of the work – the S1 stuff, I actually delegate that. When we get new employees in who are ... D1s, raw ... I really don't have the time to go up there and S1 them. So I get guys like my equipment manager (to undertake the directing role) ...'[61]

This bias towards relationship behaviour has been attributed partly to a strong 'mateship' culture in Australia, where telling another person what to do is considered unfriendly. Certainly, to increase worker satisfaction and leadership 'success', research indicates that Australian managers need to relate more individually to their followers compared with managers elsewhere.[62] However, research generally suggests that establishing and maintaining harmonious relationships with supporters is advantageous for leaders.[63] Researchers have found that subordinates generally need large amounts of supportive behaviour, regardless of their developmental level, and some argue that if one element of SL behaviour were to be perceived as 'best', that element would involve high supportive behaviour.[64]

Thus, the extent to which SL is actually applied, in that all four styles are used as prescribed, remains doubtful, at least among Australian managers. This may well be different among managers from other cultures.

Fiedler's contingency model

Fiedler's model proposes that leadership effectiveness is a function of the match between a leader's style and the leadership situation.[65] If the style matches the situation, the leader will be effective; if not, the leader will not be effective.

Fiedler distinguishes between *task-motivated* leaders and *relationship-motivated* leaders. He proposes that task-motivated leaders draw their self-esteem from accomplishing tasks, whereas relationship-motivated leaders draw their self-esteem from interpersonal relations. To a relationship-oriented person, relationships appear more important than accomplishing a task. The opposite is true for those who are task-motivated.

Fiedler describes a *leadership situation* in terms of three factors:

- the relationship between leader and followers;
- how structured the task is; and
- the leader's position power.

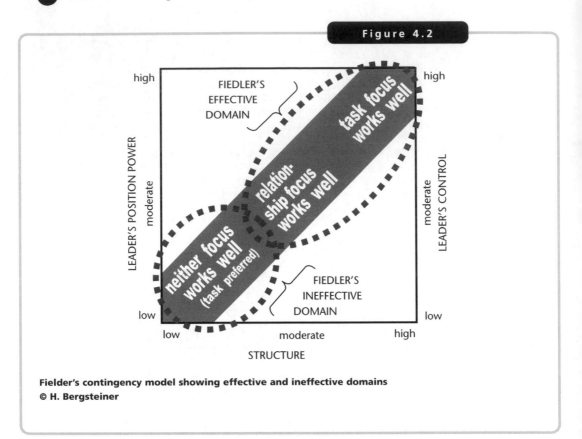

Figure 4.2

Fielder's contingency model showing effective and ineffective domains
© H. Bergsteiner

Combining these three elements describes the amount of control the leader has over a particular situation (see Figure 4.2). A good leader–follower(s) relationship, a highly structured task and a leader with high position power form one end of the control continuum. This provides the leader with high control over the situation. Conditions like these appear to favour the Classical and Transactional paradigms.

In the middle of the continuum lie situations where the task is unstructured or the leader and followers do not get along very well. Here, the leader cannot exert full control over the situation, which makes the leadership environment difficult for the task-oriented leader. At the lower end of the situational control continuum, the task is highly unstructured, leader–follower relations are poor and the leader has very little power. This creates challenging conditions for Classical and Transactional leadership.

Central to Fiedler's contingency model is the *match* between the leader's style and the situation. As the situation changes, so does the leader's effectiveness, because the leader finds himself or herself in and out of match. Overall, the model predicts that task-motivated leaders will be more effective than relationship-oriented leaders where there is either high or low control over the situation. Relationship-motivated leaders will be effective under conditions of moderate situational control.

Looking at each of these situations in turn:

1 *High control situations*: According to Fiedler's model, task-motivated leaders perform well in high control situations. Here, their self-esteem is not threatened, so they can provide resources to help the group perform. In the same situation, relationship-motivated leaders are likely to be bored, as leaders, and may feel that there is nothing for them to do. If the group is cohesive and the task is clear, the leader's role becomes taking care of details and removing obstacles. This tends not to appeal to relationship-oriented leaders, who prefer to work with people.

2 *Moderate-control situations*: Moderate control can arise where either group cohesiveness or task structure is lacking. Here, the situation becomes ambiguous, and completing the task is uncertain. The relationship-motivated leader's interpersonal skills and participative style suit this situation, because this leader can rally the group to work together to define and clarify the unclear task. Under these conditions, the relationship-motivated leader feels comfortable, and helps the group be productive by using the group as a resource.

   Moderate-control conditions can threaten the task-motivated leader, who may become concerned that lack of group support or ambiguity in the task could jeopardize completing the job. Striving to get the job done, a task-oriented leader will probably attempt to hurry things along, and may become autocratic in order to gain a sense of accomplishment. Typically, task-motivated leaders do not use their groups well, preferring to rely on their own skills and experience, and so the task-motivated leader's group performs poorly under moderate control conditions.

3 *Low-control situations*: Low-control situations can become chaotic and reach a crisis point at which they offer no group cohesion, no task structure and no strong position power. Neither task nor relationship leaders function particularly well under these conditions. The task-motivated leader's focus on completing the task tends to lead to an attempt at taking over, controlling the group, and making autocratic decisions without worrying about the group members. Although the resulting performance is not high, task-motivated leaders can achieve some outcomes in low-control situations.

   The same low-control situation tends to reduce the relationship-motivated leader's effectiveness when the group's lack of cohesion prevents it from progressing on the task, and the group's disarray interferes with efforts at reconciling the members. Relationship-motivated leaders often withdraw from these situations ceasing to prove any leadership.

A major assumption behind Fiedler's model is that the leader's style is long lasting and stable. Another is that although everyone can exhibit behaviours typically associated with the other style, people's fundamental motivational basis does not change quickly. However, in practice, the situations that leaders face are often dynamic, making a leader move rapidly from *in-match* to *out-of-match*. Fiedler does not advocate changing the leader's style to match the situation. Rather, the leader should learn how to diagnose and modify situational control. This should allow an optimal match between leadership style and the changing situation to be maintained.

Several extensive research reviews support Fiedler's hypotheses, including in applied settings.[66] Overall, in-match leaders perform better than out-of-match leaders. Despite this being one of the more reliable and predictive leadership models, strong criticisms have been voiced about it.[67] Criticisms relate to the distinction between task- and relationship-motivated leaders and whether the model can predict successful leadership.

Being able to control a situation is probably a vain hope in today's turbulent environments, making the Fiedler theory less relevant in dynamic organizations than under stable conditions. Therefore, Fiedler's theory would be more applicable to Classical and Transactional leadership than to Organic and Visionary paradigms. In chaotic or low control situations, where Visionary and Organic leadership prevail, neither task- nor relationship-oriented leadership is likely to be very effective. As already discussed, the New Science advice is for leadership to let go of control in chaotic times.

House's path-goal theory

House and his associates propose a third contingency approach in which the key role of a leader is to clear the way for others to accomplish goals.[68] The leader reaches personal goals by allowing followers to fulfil their needs. At the heart of the model is the idea of an implicit or explicit exchange between leaders and followers. Leaders and followers establish a transactional relationship that revolves around the exchange of the leader's guidance or support for the followers' productivity and satisfaction.

Path-goal theory is based on the Porter-Lawler expectancy model of motivation.[69] This model assumes that people make rational choices about their behaviour, based on individuals' perceptions of the extent to which their own effort and performance produce outcomes that they value. Under expectancy theory, the key to motivation is to remove obstacles that may weaken follower perceptions of the linkages between effort and performance. Similarly, under *path-goal theory*, the role of the leader is to help strengthen linkages between effort, performance and outcome, and to remove obstacles to followers' performance, thereby allowing them to do their jobs.

Again, the situation plays a role. The nature of the task, coupled with characteristics of the followers, determines which leadership behaviour contributes to subordinate satisfaction. On a new, unstructured and unclear task, followers are likely to waste their efforts through inexperience, and so may feel unmotivated and frustrated. In this situation, the path-goal leader needs to be task-focused in providing instructions and training, thereby removing major obstacles to employee satisfaction and motivation.

After mastering a routine task, followers sometimes start to lose interest. This situation requires the leader to show empathy, consideration and understanding – behaviours designed to remove the blocks to satisfaction in these cases. Which behaviours the leader uses to motivate employees will depend on the needs of each follower, requiring the leader to consider each individual. Some followers may prefer guidance and clear instructions, while others may seek challenges and autonomy to solve their own problems. A follower who likes challenges and values autonomy will not need the leader to be directive and structuring, even on an unstructured task. Here, being directive may be detrimental by reducing the follower's satisfaction.

Parallels with SL can be seen here, in terms of matching leader behaviours to the needs of the follower. Like SL, the path-goal approach foresees that not all leader behaviours will be successful with all employees. However, path-goal theory differs from SL in that it derives its rationale for when a leader should be directive and supportive explicitly from motivation theory, whereas the basis for SL assumptions is unclear.

Does path-goal theory work? In a review of contingency theories, Schriescheim and Kerr concluded that the path-goal theory appears internally consistent, but needs testing in practice.[70] Since then, mixed empirical support has emerged for the theory. For example, while letting followers who like to be challenged solve problems themselves makes intuitive sense, researchers have found that exhibiting relationship behaviours leads to higher employee satisfaction regardless of the kind of task.[71] In other tests of the theory, leaders successfully used structuring behaviour in structured situations.[72]

On the one hand, the path-goal theory is transactionally based and therefore could apply well to Transactional leadership. Interestingly, the role of the leader in path-goal theory is that of an obstacle remover, a role similar to that ascribed to modern team leaders. Removing obstacles is also an essential empowering activity of a Visionary leader to enable followers to achieve a vision (see the Novartis and Rodenstock case studies). In self-managing Organic environments, followers may not require leaders to remove obstacles because the followers themselves take on this role, as at Gore or BMW.

Evaluating contingency theories

The contingency theories reviewed here focus on the context beyond the individual leader and his or her transactions with followers. They represented a major advance in the 1960s and 1970s beyond theories limited to leader traits and behaviours. All the theories have their critics, and some have been far better conceptualized, researched and supported than others. For example, SL, while less well conceptualized and researched than the others, has been widely adopted in practice, prescribing how managers should vary their leadership style to suit the developmental level of each follower (or team). By contrast, Fieldler's contingency model has been relatively widely researched, but criticized on conceptual grounds. House's path-goal theory, which proposes that a leader's role is to remove obstacles for others to accomplish their tasks, appears theoretically consistent, but needs more testing in practice.

The three theories – SL, Fieldler's contingency model and House's path-goal theory – tend to adopt a leader-centric focus despite some consideration for followers and the situation. Essentially, these contingency theories fit within the Transactional paradigm, although path-goal theory with its focus on goals and motivation could also apply to Visionary leadership.

CONCLUSION

This chapter has covered a range of theories and models applying to the micro-levels of organizational leadership – those theories that focus primarily on the characteristics of a particular leader or on interactions between leaders and individual or group followers. Certain people may be destined to lead by virtue of being born into royal or industrial dynasties, but many business leaders need to acquire appropriate leader characteristics. There is debate over what those characteristics should be.

Some theories predict that leaders will differ from others by virtue of possessing special traits. Modern research suggests that these traits could include displaying drive, desire to lead, integrity, self-confidence, knowledge of the business and high-level intelligence. In looking at behaviour that distinguishes leaders from others, most theorists have focused on task and relationship behaviours, although Yukl specifies other behaviours such as influencing, planning, inspiring and dealing with change.[73]

While many theories take the leader as the unit of study, clearly leadership requires followers and a comprehensive understanding of leadership would encompass the interactions between leaders and followers. Accordingly, various leadership theories and models apply to the dyadic and group levels within an organization. These approaches include the LMX theory, which examines the quality of the relationship between leader and individual followers. A quite different approach is evident under the socio-cognitive approach, which essentially argues that leadership stems from follower perceptions rather than residing inevitably in leader traits or behaviours.

Table 4.2

Linking micro-level theories to the leadership paradigms

Classical	Transactional	Visionary	Organic
Great Men	Great Men	Great Men	
Traits	Traits	Traits	
Behaviour	Behaviour	Behaviour	
LMX	LMX	LMX	
Socio-cognitive	Socio-cognitive	Socio-cognitive	Socio-cognitive
	Situational Leadership		
Fiedler's	Fiedler's		
Contingency Model	Contingency Model		
	House's Path-goal	House's Path-goal	

Contingency theories posit that the context in which leadership takes place is essential. Situational leadership is based on the assumption that leaders will develop their followers, and provides a four-quadrant tool for assisting managers in this process. Depending on each follower's developmental level on a given task, the leader is advised to use a different leadership style. Fiedler's contingency theory proposes that a leader's effectiveness depends on the match between the leader's style and the given situation. Fiedler predicts that task-motivated leaders will be more effective than relationship-oriented leaders when the situation allows high or low control by the leader. Under conditions of moderate control of the situation, relationship-oriented leaders are expected to be more effective (essentially because they can use their interpersonal skills in involving their group). House's path-goal theory emphasizes that a leader's role is to clear the way for followers to accomplish tasks and to strengthen linkages between perceived effort, performance and outcome.

Throughout the discussion in this chapter, the micro-level theories have been linked to the leadership paradigms. Table 4.2 summarizes how these theories seem to relate to the paradigms. The Great Men, Traits, Behaviour, LMX, Socio-cognitive and Fiedler's contingency model approaches seem most appropriate to Classical leadership. For Transactional leadership, all those theories applying to Classical leadership would also apply, plus the Situational Leadership Model and House's Path-goal theory. Theories particularly relevant to the Visionary paradigm are the Great Men, Traits, Behaviour, LMX, Socio-cognitive and Path-goal approaches. Most of the micro-level leadership theories and models are not considered relevant to the Organic paradigm, except for the Socio-cognitive approach.

The theories discussed in this chapter tend to be rationality-based, implying that managing others does not necessarily involve emotion. Another group of theories, described in the next chapter, focuses on the emotional connection between leaders and followers.

NOTES

For full details of these notes, please see the References section at the end of this book.

1   Bass, 1985; Yukl, 1998
2   e.g. Tracey and Hinkin, 1998
3   Lord and Maher, 1991; Waldman and Yammarino, 1999
4   Yammarino, 1997
5   Kirkpatrick and Locke, 1991
6   Weber, 1978
7   Tannenbaum and Schmidt, 1973:162
8   Bradford and Cohen, 1984
9   Farnham, 1993
10 Duerst-Lahti and Kelly, 1995:19
11 Duerst-Lahti and Kelly, 1995; Sinclair, 1998
12 Sinclair, 1998
13 e.g. DuBrin, 1998; Kirkpatrick and Locke, 1991
14 Stogdill, 1948
15 Yukl, 1994
16 Kirkpatrick and Locke, 1991
17 ibid.
18 McClelland, 1973
19 Briscoe and Hall, 1998
20 Pierce, 1994
21 Gregersen, Morrison and Black, 1998
22 ibid.
23 Taylor, 1911
24 e.g. Roethlisberger and Dickson, 1939
25 King and Fine, 2000
26 Cairns, Hollenback, Preziosi and Snow, 1998; Goodson, McGee and Cashman, 1989; Vecchio, 1987; Wexley, Alexander, Greenwalt and Couch, 1980; Yukl, 1981
27 Fleischman and Harris, 1962

28 Yukl, 1998
29 ibid.
30 Bass, 1990b
31 Yukl, 1998
32 Kerr, Schriesheim, Murphy and Stogdill, 1974
33 Chalef, 1995; Yukl, 1994
34 Dansereau, Graen and Haga, 1975; Graen and Cashman, 1975
35 Ashkanasy and Weierter, 1996
36 Hofstede, 1984
37 Ichikawa, 1996
38 Nahavandi, 1997
39 Rousseau, 1997
40 Lord and Maher, 1991
41 ibid.
42 ibid.
43 ibid.
44 ibid.
45 ibid.
46 Hersey and Blanchard, 1969
47 Hersey and Blanchard, 1969, 1982, 1996
48 Blanchard and Nelson, 1997
49 Blanchard, Zigarmi and Nelson, 1993
50 Blanchard, Zigarmi and Zigarmi, 1985
51 Blanchard and Nelson, 1997; Blanchard, Zigarmi and Nelson, 1993
52 Graeff, 1983
53 Blank, Weitzel and Green, 1990; Graeff, 1983, 1997; Vecchio 1987
54 Goodson, McGee and Cashman, 1989
55 e.g. Cairns, Hallenback, Preziosi and Snow, 1998
56 The SL model shown here differs substantially from the original Hersey and Blanchard version. Bell curves, as used in the original model, usually refer to data sets and the use of such a curve is therefore incompatible with the 2×2 matrix structure of the SL model, which implies no continuous data set. Furthermore, in modelling theory, an almost universally accepted convention is that temporal sequences go from left to right (Britt, 1997), which the original model also violated.
57 Blanchard and Nelson, 1997
58 Avery and Ryan, 2002
59 Avery, 2001
60 Avery and Ryan, 2002
61 ibid.
62 Parry and Sarros, 1996
63 Duchon, Green and Tabor, 1986; Steiner, 1988; Wexley, Alexander, Greenwalt and Couch, 1980; Yukl, 1981

64   Goodson, McGee and Cashman, 1989
65   Fiedler, 1997
66   e.g. Ayman, Chemers and Fiedler, 1995; Peters, Hartke and Pohlmann, 1985; Strube and Garcia, 1981
67   Nahavandi, 1997
68   House, 1971; House and Dessler, 1974; House and Mitchell, 1974
69   Porter and Lawler, 1968; Vroom, 1964
70   Schriescheim and Kerr, 1977
71   e.g. Johns, 1978
72   e.g. Bass, Valenzi, Farrow and Solomon, 1975
73   Yukl, 1998

5 Emotion in Leadership

Key Points

- Understanding emotional intelligence and maturity
- Role of charisma
- Level 5 leadership
- Transformational and inspirational leadership
- Leading through vision and values
- Meaningful workplaces

The approaches to leadership discussed so far have been concerned with the leader's traits; leader behaviour, especially task and relationship behaviours; follower matches and perceptions; and situational variables. Most of these views have been limited to rational, objective ideas about leadership, which are presumed to be separable from emotions. By contrast, ideas considered in this chapter emphasize the emotional relationship between leaders and followers.

Emotions and their expression are often controlled and managed in organizations.[1] Certain emotions are expressed, while others are suppressed; some emotions can be contagious, spreading throughout an organization. The Newtonian and Taylorist legacies in organization theory and managerial practice are increasingly becoming a liability with their emphasis on relating ends and means in a rational way. This devalues the irrational and emotional aspects of organizations.

Emotions cannot be excluded from the workplace, and some organizations thrive on emotion (see the Swatch case study). This chapter emphasizes approaches concerned with emotion in leadership, as increasing prominence is given to non-rationality in organizations. The first part starts with emotional intelligence, followed by the emotion-based notion of charisma in leadership, emotion-based leadership theories, vision, values and spirituality in organizations.

EMOTIONAL INTELLIGENCE

Currently popular is the idea that effective leaders should possess high *emotional intelligence*, often referred to as 'EI' or measured by 'EQ' (emotional quotient). Salovey and Mayer first coined the term 'emotional intelligence',[2] but the concept was later popularized by Daniel Goleman.[3] Although the basic idea behind emotional intelligence, namely relating well to others, is not new, there is much controversy and disagreement as to exactly what emotional intelligence is (see Box 5.1).

Emotional intelligence is variously defined as a set of behaviours or as a capacity to use emotional information. Illustrating the former, Goleman proposes that EI consists of skills, attitudes, abilities and competencies that determine an individual's behaviour, reactions, state of mind and communication style.[4] On the other hand, Salovey and Mayer define emotional intelligence as 'the ability to monitor one's own and others' feelings and emotions, to discriminate among them and to use this information to guide one's thinking and actions.'[5]

Both definitions can probably be regarded as akin to emotional maturity, in which an individual displays control over personal emotions and empathizes with others' feelings. Some authors argue that most employees know how to behave on the job, but their personality – which includes *emotional maturity* – can prevent them from behaving as required.[6]

Box 5.1

What is emotional intelligence?

In 1995, Daniel Goleman popularized the concept of emotional intelligence in his book *Emotional Intelligence: Why It Can Matter More Than IQ*. Goleman's work led many others to write about emotional intelligence in the popular press, although some scientists had already been researching the issue. One benefit from a focus on emotional intelligence is that it broadens the general understanding of what it means to be clever, allowing emotional information processing a new place in science and popular thinking.

Emotional intelligence has been defined in various ways. For example, Salovey and Mayer regard emotional intelligence as the capacity to reason with emotion in four areas:

- to perceive emotion;
- to integrate emotion into thought;
- to understand emotion; and
- to manage emotion.[7]

These researchers claim to have developed reliable scales to measure emotional intelligence as a unitary ability related to, but independent of, cognitive intelligence.

Under his version of emotional intelligence, Goleman refers to similar ideas of knowing and managing one's own emotions, and recognizing emotions in others. He also includes handling relationships with others, empathy and warmth. Where Goleman's concept departs from Salovey and Mayer's is that Goleman includes factors not normally associated with emotion and intelligence as most people would understand them, such as motivation and persistence. Emotional and general intelligence are not opposing competencies, according to Goleman. Rather, people tend to mix and use them different in different amounts. Instead people can enhance their emotional intelligence through training and experience.[8]

Leaders with high emotional maturity are considered more capable of maintaining cooperative relationships with subordinates, peers and superiors than people with low emotional maturity.[9] The scant research available suggests that key components of emotional maturity are associated with managerial effectiveness and advancement.[10] Some of these components include self-awareness, understanding one's strengths and weaknesses, and an orientation toward self-improvement.[11] It is likely that these aspects of emotional maturity would underlie inspiring followers, mentoring and the ability to learn from mistakes, and so would be essential in Visionary and Organic leadership.

The popular literature suggests that the emotionally intelligent person has a major advantage in life, but these claims appear somewhat excessive according to emotional intelligence research.[12]

CHARISMA

Exceptional leaders who have extraordinary emotional effects on their followers, and often positively impact on their organizations (or other social systems), are sometimes said to have *charisma*. Such leaders are believed to transform the needs, values, preferences and aspirations of their followers from self-interest to collective interest.[13] Clearly, this notion is also very close to the concept of the heroic leader, discussed earlier, since it is the leader who influences the followers in working towards this transformation. The source of the influence is often attributed to the leader's charisma.

Weber had recognized charisma as a source of a leader's authority based on followers' perceptions of the leader's strength of character and inspiration.[14] Bass referred to Weber's idea of the charismatic leader as that of a mystical and personally magnetic saviour who promoted a doctrine or vision.[15] Bass proposed that this kind of leader arises in times of crisis.

However appealing, the nature of charisma in leadership is highly disputed. Contrary to the common view of charisma, where the focus is still overwhelmingly placed on the person of the leader, many researchers consider that charismatic leadership does not emanate from the leader's traits or behaviour *per se*. Instead, charisma is seen as an emotional interaction between a leader and followers.[16] Socio-cognitive researchers and others argue that charisma is essentially an attribution of the followers to the leader.[17] An alternative view is that charisma is merely a social delusion or fiction that allows followers to escape responsibility for their own actions or inactions by relying on the leader.[18]

Nonetheless, many people associate charisma with leadership, so how does charisma affect leaders and followers?

First, what makes a charismatic leader? This question has occupied several researchers who have identified sets of traits and behaviours characteristic of charismatic leaders.[19] Charismatic leaders have been found to:

- manage impressions to increase followers' trust;
- articulate an appealing vision of the future that becomes the basis for the cause;
- role model desirable behaviour that followers admire and identify with;
- communicate high expectations that induce followers to become committed to higher performance; and
- introduce challenging goals.[20]

Charismatic leaders also display high levels of energy and enthusiasm and possess excellent communication skills, which they use to mobilize followers.[21] In addition, charismatic leaders need to be able to manage and integrate complex information, find and structure relevant data from the environment around them, and make it relevant to their followers.[22]

Given that charisma stems from an interaction between followers and leaders, the next question is whether followers of such leaders exhibit particular characteristics. Bass concluded that followers of the charismatic leader:[23]

- exhibit a high degree of respect and esteem for the leader;
- display loyalty and devotion to the leader;
- show affection for the leader;
- hold high performance expectations of leader and group; and
- offer unquestioning obedience to the leader.

It appears that charisma is not necessarily a permanent characteristic. Roberts cites the case of an executive who became regarded as charismatic only after successfully helping an organization out of a crisis.[24] The executive had not been considered charismatic beforehand, and was not regarded as charismatic in subsequent positions. This and other evidence suggests that charisma is not only dependent on followers' perceptions, but also on the context.

Some writers suggest that for charismatic leaders to prevail, followers need to find the current state of affairs unacceptable and perceive that a crisis is looming.[25] The group then searches for new solutions to the crisis. An individual able to capture and represent the needs and aspirations of the group is likely to become the group leader. In addition, those individuals who demonstrate competence and loyalty to a group and its goals are provided with a kind of 'credit' that can be spent to assume leadership roles. This process allows these individuals to emerge as leaders and change the direction of the group.[26]

Charisma is not essential to successful leadership, according to the researchers cited in Box 5.2. Although charismatic leaders could arise under all four leadership paradigms, they are often particularly associated with Visionary leadership. Organic leadership is least likely to revolve around charisma, given the lack of emphasis on formal or heroic leaders.

Box 5.2

Beyond charismatic leadership – Level 5 leadership

Level 5 leadership is counter-intuitive because these leaders are not larger-than-life heroes. Instead, they are humble, modest and shy, as well as fearless and strong-willed.[27] In researching how good companies become great companies, Collins and his team found that great companies were distinguished from good companies by Level 5 leadership, which is leadership beyond Visionary leadership. Level 5 leaders build greatness through a paradoxical combination of personal humility and an unwavering resolve.

Personal humility is evident in not being boastful, shunning public adulation, acting with quiet, calm determination, and not inspiring charisma to motivate followers. Ambition is channelled into the enterprise instead of the self, and these leaders set up their successors to achieve even more greatness in the future. The leader shoulders the responsibility for poor results, never blaming others, external factors or bad luck. Professional will shows in an unwavering resolve to do whatever needs to be done to produce the best long-term results, and an unwillingness to settle for anything less than the standards required to build a great company. However, the credit for success is attributed to other people, external factors and good luck.

Level 5 leaders are very rare, with only 11 being identified in a study of 1435 companies that appeared on the *Fortune 500* list since 1965.[28] All 11 companies had Level 5 leaders in position at a pivotal time of transition, leading Collins to conclude that Level 5 leadership is not the only factor driving successful change, but is an essential component in successful transformation.

Collins concluded that great performance is based on combining a culture of discipline with an ethic of entrepreneurship (see the Gore and Novartis case studies) Level 5 leaders appear to do six major things:

1   They get the *right people* in place, rather than starting with vision and strategy.
2   *Facts and faith* co-exist – these leaders confront the brutal facts of their current reality, while maintaining absolute faith that they will prevail in the end.
3   By being persistent in pursuing their goals, Level 5 leaders patiently build up *breakthrough momentum*, rather than lurching back and forth trying various radical change programs and restructurings.
4   Breakthroughs happen when the leader *focuses on three 'best' questions*, eliminating distractions that do not fit with the answers: What can this company be the best in the world at? How do its economics work best? What best ignites the passions of its people?
5   The companies making the transition from good-to-great did not jump on technology bandwagons, but made bold investments in *carefully selected technologies* linked to achieving their goals.
6   Good-to-great companies were characterized by *discipline*: disciplined people, disciplined thought and disciplined action. Disciplined people meant hierarchy was unnecessary, disciplined thought removed bureaucracy, and disciplined action reduced excessive controls.

EMOTION-BASED LEADERSHIP THEORIES

In the 1990s, a group of emotion-based theories became prominent. They were variously referred to as charismatic, inspirational, visionary or transformational. These approaches were similar in that they shifted the focus of leadership to the emotional reaction of the follower.[29] Leaders who breathe life into a vision (= *inspire*) by using powerful language and positive communication can be said to be *inspirational*.[30] Leaders who change their group's direction are often known as *transformational*. Bernard Bass is credited with initiating the focus on transformational leadership in management science, and this section outlines his concept of transformational leadership.

Transformational leadership
Transformational leaders are characterized by four 'I' behaviours, according to Bass and his colleagues.[31] These characteristics are:

*   *Idealized influence*: equivalent to charisma.
*   *Individualized consideration*: providing followers with support, encouragement, praise and coaching.
*   *Inspirational motivation*: espousing an appealing vision and using symbols to focus subordinate effort.
*   *Intellectual stimulation*: involving followers in viewing problems from new perspectives.

In his transformational theory, Bass incorporates many of the visionary, inspirational and charismatic elements of other emotion-based leadership theories, but he argues that the four 'I' elements interact to produce changes in followers' level of awareness (for example, of the challenges facing the business).[32] These elements affect follower motivation to solve business issues and pursue the vision. Transformational leaders appeal to followers' 'better selves' and even forego selfish goals for the sake of the group. They attempt to transform their followers by serving as coach, mentor or teacher.

Transformational leaders appear to make the difference between success and failure. Employees not only perform better when they believe their leaders are transformational, but also are much more satisfied with the organization's performance appraisal system.[33] Studies have compared the effects on group performance of transformational leadership with transactional leadership, finding increasing empirical support for Bass' concept. For example, transformational leadership was found to be effective in managing technology change[34] and positively related to subordinate ratings of leader effectiveness.[35]

Bass attributes the success of some of Fortune's toughest bosses to the transformational qualities these leaders display.[36] Although these leaders may at times exhibit tough Transactional or even Classical authoritarian behaviours, they basically succeed through transformational factors such as charisma, treating individual subordinates differently and providing intellectual stimulation. These transformational leaders frequently raise standards, take calculated risks, and get others to join them in their vision of the future. They challenge and change the culture of the organization, even when things already appear to be successful. Characterized by self-determination and self-confidence, these leaders succeed because of their transformational behaviours (see the Rodenstock case study).

For Bass, transformational leadership can occur at all levels of the organization. Mass communications directed toward individual employees are much more likely to have an impact if the messages are reinforced face-to-face by their supervisors at all organization levels.

Nonetheless, Bass points out that transformational leadership is not a panacea, and in certain situations transactional processes are indicated, especially for firms that are functioning in stable markets.[37] If the technology, workforce and environment are also stable, then an organization is likely to perform well with managers who simply promise and deliver rewards to employees for carrying out assignments. However, when faced with turbulent conditions, transformational leadership needs to be fostered at all levels in the firm. This kind of Visionary leadership provides the firm with the flexibility to forecast and meet new demands and changes as they occur, while members work towards the envisioned future.

Having a vision and arousing an emotional response in followers are not part of the Classical and Transactional paradigms. The heavy focus on the heroic leader in the Visionary paradigm also makes emotion-based leadership in this sense not relevant to Organic organizations. However, this is not to claim that Organic leadership is without strong emotional components attaching its members to the organization (see the Gore case study).

As currently formulated, transformational/charismatic/Visionary approaches tend to be based on the idea of relatively simple Newtonian causality between leader and follower behaviour and organizational performance. These leaders tend to be seen in heroic terms, and this can be dangerous as Box 5.3 illustrates. Whether a leader is transformational or not appears to be an individual matter, and team members seldom agree on their leader's transformational characteristics.[38]

Emotion-based theories still need developing to uncover many of the other factors that influence organizational performance, including Level 5 leadership. Nonetheless, transformational leaders focus on the needs of, and emotional connections to, their followers, through visions and values and by creating more 'spirituality' in the workplace, as discussed in the next sections.

Box 5.3

Narcissistic potential in heroic visionary leaders

Psychoanalyst Michael Maccoby looks at the pros and cons of heroic Visionary leaders, whom he calls narcissistic leaders.[39] He reminds us that CEOs of large companies between the 1950s and 1980s typically shunned the media and avoided the limelight. By contrast, at the end of the twentieth century, corporate superstars had acquired high profiles. They hired their own publicists, wrote books, granted interviews and were generally in the public eye – nearly everyone knows in this way of Bill Gates, Steve Jobs and Jack Welch from the US, and Richard Branson from the UK.

Maccoby believes that leaders who thrive in chaotic times resemble the personality type that Sigmund Freud called 'narcissistic', the kind of individuals who impress others as being 'personalities'. Kets de Vries distinguishes between two types of narcissistic leaders[40]: The first are guided by a kind of *reactive* narcissism, driven by a need to get even and come to grips with their past; the second, *constructive* narcissistic individuals, are well-balanced, have a positive self-regard and a secure sense of self-esteem. These two kinds of narcissists deal with the world differently. Constructive narcissists have the capacity for introspection; they radiate a sense of positive vitality and are capable of empathic feelings. This contrasts with the reactive narcissists, who are continually trying to boost a defective sense of self-esteem and are preoccupied with emotions such as envy, spite, revenge or vindictive triumph over others. (Some reactive narcissists, however, eventually overcome their original feelings of bitterness and are motivated by reparation: that is, trying to prevent others from suffering as they have.

On the plus side, narcissistic personalities have transformed society, organizations and other groups. Henry Ford exploited new technologies and restructured the American car industry. Bill Gates exploits new technologies to alter how people live and work in profound ways. Pierre Cardin democratized haute couture in building his fashion empire as a reaction to teasing and sufferings during his childhood.[41]

Narcissists can be dubbed 'productive' or 'unproductive' narcissists. Jack Welch and George Soros are examples of productive narcissists. Gifted and creative strategists, they tend to see the big picture and face the risky challenge of changing their world and leaving behind a legacy. Unproductive narcissists lack self-knowledge, according to Maccoby, and become unrealistic dreamers, harbouring the illusion that only circumstances or enemies block their success. This becomes the dark side of narcissistic personalities.

While narcissists achieve great things, their dark side leads them often to being emotionally isolated and highly distrustful. A narcissist's achievements can trigger feelings of grandeur and a need to achieve some grand vision at almost any cost (to self and others). This means that narcissistic leadership does not always mean successful leadership, particularly if the dark side dominates.

Maccoby[42] concludes that the dark side dominated with Jan Carlzon, a former CEO of SAS, the Scandinavian airline. Carlzon allegedly stopped listening to alternate views – he followed his grand vision but isolated himself from the people around him who might have held him closer to reality. Like many narcissistic leaders, Carlzon's success led to an inflated self-image and drove him to expand the organization rather than to develop it, to the detriment of both himself and the organization.

In 2000, Maccoby was warning that narcissistic Visionary leaders could self-destruct and lead their organization astray. He worried that increasing numbers of narcissists were being placed at the head of corporations that needed leaders who could create the future, develop a vision and realize it. To avoid derailing, narcissistic leaders need to recognize their own limitations and take steps to overcome them, for example, by surrounding themselves with, and listening to, supporters who operationalize the vision and keep the leader rooted in reality.[43]

VISION

The central requirement of emotion-based leadership is providing an inspiring *vision* around which followers can coalesce and direct their productive energies, a vision that followers can relate to emotionally.[44] Many writers see vision as a core component of leadership.[45] Management researchers often view using a vision either as a form of leadership[46], or at least as one of the essential tasks for senior organizational leadership.[47] Either way, vision is regarded as central to leadership in inducing others to take action toward a common goal.[48]

Like many organizational terms, *vision* is used in different ways, but is intended to provide an organization with clarity about its direction. Poorly defined and often confusing, vision has various synonyms including purpose, mission, goal, legacy, calling, personal agenda and looking ahead. Kouzes and Posner prefer the term 'vision' because it relates to seeing the future, is an image of what could be and an ideal, and can be made unique to an organization.[49]

Traditionally, vision is seen as a destination for an organization, but New Science approaches regard vision as a force field in which people create a power to move the organization forward, not as a place.[50] Vision becomes more of an influence than a destination. Kouzes and Posner believe that leaders enact the meaning of the organization in every decision they make and in every step they take toward the envisioned future.[51] This is consistent with the Visionary paradigm, where the leader strives to get organizational members to commit to a common goal.

Weick emphasizes the importance of sense-making processes like visions and stories in creating organizational action, particularly processes involving people's mutual interpretations of events.[52] Under Organic leadership, the sense-making process, including the vision, lies with the members, not just with the leaders.

Leaders, or multiple leaders in the case of an Organic organization, also need to develop a strategy for achieving the vision, thereby turning it into what is sometimes known as a *strategic vision*. Strategy researchers have proposed that an organization with a well-articulated strategic vision can achieve sustained competitive advantage over those organizations lacking such a vision.[53] This is partly because a strategic vision provides a cognitive map that underpins how resources are used and combined within the organization. To that extent, the vision channels organizational competencies in the direction of the organization's goals.

Can visions be effective? Bennis and Nanus found that attention to vision was a key strategy employed by the 90 leaders they studied.[54] These leaders enlisted others in a common vision by appealing to their values, interests, hopes and dreams. Senior management in unsuccessful organizations that had 'surrendered' tended to lack the courage to commit their companies to heroic goals, creating a lack of confidence in top management's ability to revitalize the whole organization.[55]

What makes a vision effective? Not a great deal is known about the elements of an effective vision, but some characteristics are discussed in Box 5.4. Seven attributes appear to distinguish visions of successful and less successful organizations. These are that the vision should be:

- brief, that is, concise;
- clear;
- have a future orientation;

- remain stable for some time;
- offer challenge;
- be abstract rather than concrete; and
- be inspiring to followers.[56]

These attributes have been found to combine in contributing to an employee's emotional commitment to a manager's vision. For example, a vision's desirability, or capability to inspire followers, is where part of the emotional connection occurs, but clear visions have also been found to enhance employee emotional commitment by clarifying where people need to head.[57]

For implementing a vision, followers obviously need to learn about the vision. This can be achieved through devices such as:

- inspirational speeches;
- written and electronic messages;
- appeals to shared values;
- role modelling;
- rewarding; and
- behaving consistently with the vision.[58]

Is Visionary leadership worth the effort? Although the concept of vision has its detractors, research suggests that in practice effective visions do make a positive difference to performance, both directly and indirectly.[59] Lack of vision appears to be associated with failed attempts to manage change.[60] An effective vision not only underpins Visionary leadership and greatly assists in binding people together and setting direction under Organic leadership (see the Gore, Rodenstock and Swatch case studies), but is aligned with follower and organizational values.[61]

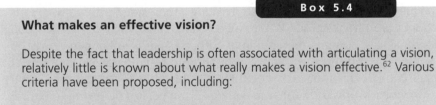

Box 5.4

What makes an effective vision?

Despite the fact that leadership is often associated with articulating a vision, relatively little is known about what really makes a vision effective.[62] Various criteria have been proposed, including:

- being *inspiring, abstract, brief, stable* and *motivating*;[63]
- *widely accepted* and *integrated with the visions of others*;[64]
- *strategic* and *well-communicated*;[65] and
- *long-term* and *focused*.[66]

Further, an effective vision should be *understandable* so that it can be communicated to followers, and should *direct effort*.[67] Research indicates that the more salient top management's vision is to followers, the more effective it is.[68]

In practice, seven attributes distinguish visions of successful entrepreneurial enterprises from less successful ones:

- brevity;
- clarity;
- having a future orientation;
- remaining stable;
- offering challenge,
- abstractness; and
- being capable of inspiring followers.[69]

Similar findings occurred among retail apparel stores, with store managers whose visions scored highly on these seven attributes also being associated with increased satisfaction among staff and customers.[70]

Little is known about the content or core message of effective visions, but because it indicates a future direction, the content is likely to be important. This assumption is supported by research showing that vision content is directly related to the growth of entrepreneurial firms[71] and managing change.[72] Some guidelines recommend that a successful strategic vision takes into account the industry, customers and competitive environment in order to focus on a specific competitive position.[73]

VALUES

Appealing to follower values through the vision and associated actions for implementing it is an important component of emotion-based leadership. *Values* refer to enduring beliefs that provide the common standard by which people can calibrate their decisions and actions.[74]

Values help people determine what to do and what not to do. People can hold several different values simultaneously, creating a *value system*, the components of which set a person's priorities. While value systems can change over time through social influences, personal maturation or both, this tends to happen slowly.[75]

Some writers distinguish between public and private values – arguing that people's public behaviour can belie their private values.[76] An example is when an anti-smoker works for a tobacco company or a person believing in euthanasia works as a geriatric nurse.

Three types of values can be identified in an organizational context:

- personal values;
- those values shared with others; and
- values core to the organization.

Each individual in an organization, including leaders, holds *personal* values, and the challenge, for Visionary and Organic leadership in particular, is to channel these individual values towards achieving desired outcomes.

One foundation for unifying personal values is through forging *shared values* (without necessarily demanding conformity in personal values). Values shared by leaders and other organizational stakeholders guide mutual action, with Classical, Transactional and Visionary leaders in particular acting as setters and champions for those values. Shared values can serve as the primary organizing principle for action under various leadership paradigms, as for example, at Gore (Organic), the Royal Australian Navy (Classical) and Rodenstock (Visionary).

Shared values can make a positive difference to work attitudes and performance.[77] Leadership can benefit in various ways when individual employees' values align with organizational values. For example, a necessary condition for a leader's messages to have charismatic effects is for the message to be congruent with the existing values and identities of potential followers.[78] To achieve this alignment, leaders are advised not to impose decreed values on employees, but to be proactive in obtaining ownership of the values and involving people in the process of creating the values: 'Unity is forged, not forced'.[79]

Aligning a leader's vision and actions with shared organizational values is one way of creating a unique identity for the organization, which can promote competitive advantage.[80] Similarly, shared values appear fundamental in managing change. 'Unless we are prepared to explore our values, and question the world-view and assumptions that lie behind them, we are not really serious about change. No real change is possible without a shift in value priorities and the development of new skills and behaviours to live them.'[81] Values-driven leadership is about moving people from how they view the world now to some other view of the world.

However, if Rokeach's assertion that personal values change slowly[82] also holds for shared values, then deep-level changes in values may be difficult to achieve. This is especially so, given the short time-frames available for making most adaptations before the next organizational change arrives. Members who hold multiple values can assist an organization in making major adaptations, since some values will be carried forward into the new environment, bringing the members holding those values along with them. Often different values will require different skills to realize them, so that organizational members will generally need new skills when new values become important in the organization. For example, staff may need retraining when shared values shift towards a customer-focus.

Core values form a solid, enduring foundation for an organization and do not drift with the trends and fashions of the day. The importance of enduring core values has been emphasized by research into excellent organizations. Collins and Porras concluded: 'The basic elements that distinguish the visionary companies usually appeared in the companies long before they became hugely successful premier institutions.'[83] While keeping their core values fixed, these companies strive for progress that enables them to change and adapt, using the diversity that they encourage around their core ideals. In Organic conditions, shared values often hold the organization together.[84]

Interestingly, visionary companies are six times as likely to promote insiders to chief executive officer as comparison companies.[85] The *continuity* of quality leadership tends to distinguish the visionary companies from the comparison ones more than the quality of leadership – this continuity serves to preserve the organization's core values. GE's Jack Welch was not an aberration, but was the continuation of a GE leadership tradition in which leaders have been appointed from within for the past 100 years. Hiring top management from outside the organization makes it hard to become and remain a highly visionary organization, and external appointees may not fully share the core values.

Certainly, fostering enduring core values would not weaken the position of any of the leadership paradigms. Under Classical leadership, individual follower values may be suppressed as people obey the leader's instructions. Transactional leadership could involve attempts to influence others to adopt certain public values, but most likely any private conflicting values would be suppressed once people enter agreements with a Transactional leader. Alignment of follower and leader values is central to emotion-based leadership, such as transformational, inspirational and charismatic forms of Visionary leadership. Given the minimal controls under Organic leadership, the importance of shared and core organizational values is heightened in 'gluing' members of these organizations together.[86] A challenge resides in how to accommodate diversity in personal values within organizations bound by strong values, and how to align workplace activities and employee values.

SPIRITUALITY

Many employees' priorities are changing. Possibly in reaction to a strong focus on management and obedience, a movement towards increasing *spirituality*, or seeking meaningfulness in the workplace, has emerged in some parts of the world, particularly in the US. In addition, issues of work/life balance, concern for environmentally and socially dangerous or damaging products, and disengagement at work from the final product or service contribute to feelings of a lack of connectedness with many workplaces. Spirituality emphasizes the human and emotional side of organizations. Fairholm writes that in too many organizations '... the manager predominates to the virtual exclusion of leadership. The cause can be traced to the simplicity and comfort of measurement and control, the central facets of management today.'[87] In many of the case studies in Part Two, the organization is striving to provide meaningful, self-managing work for staff, for example, EKATO, Novartis, and Swatch.

Another factor driving spirituality is that people in organizations are noticing increased pressure to work fast, driven and enabled by, but not necessarily caused by, modern technology.[88] Not only does this pressure impact the workplace, it enters the home, blurring the boundaries between home and work and even bringing management techniques into the home in its wake.[89] At home, people manage time by setting aside 'quality' time for the children, holding family meetings and bringing work into the domestic sphere. How much longer the pressure and pace of contemporary work patterns can be sustained is questionable (see Box 5.5). People are calling for more meaningful, balanced work places.

Box 5.5

Sustainabililty of overwork

Work occupies a major portion of people's lives in many parts of the world. A five-year UK study found that over 42 per cent of managers reported always working beyond their contract hours, with 78 per cent of them always working more than a 40-hour week.[90] The more senior the manager, the greater the number of hours worked, with 25 per cent of CEOs and Managing Directors working over 60 hours per week. The study found that weekend and evening work was the norm for many managers. Not only do long working hours endanger family life and relationships with partners and children, but managers reported adverse effects on health (59 per cent), morale (56 per cent), and productivity (53 per cent). About 20 per cent of managers said that working long hours is unacceptable, but the pressure of work in modern organizations appears to be driving people to work excessively long hours.

Long hours are not just a phenomenon for managers. In Australia, long working hours are impacting employees as well. Some 71 per cent of employees and 75 per cent of owner managers usually work more than 35 hours a week in their main job, and similar proportions of employees and owner managers (22 per cent) worked between 41 and 50 hours a week.[91] Approximately 11 per cent of employees worked more than 50 hours a week, as did 36 per cent of managers. Just over 60 per cent of employees said they had done some work on weekends or at night in the previous four weeks.

About 30 per cent of people working over 50 hours per week said that they would prefer to work shorter hours. Much of this extra work is not compensated. Around 21 per cent of employees reported that they had worked extra hours in the previous four weeks but had not been compensated in the same period of time at all, whether by pay, time off in lieu of the extra hours worked, through their work agreement or salary package, or by any other type of benefit.[92]

Even if workers do continue to accept the long hours, can human beings sustain this pressure? Is work meaningful enough to occupy the central place in so many employees' lives?

When asked what 'spirituality' means to them, people from various organizations reported that if a single word could capture the meaning of spirituality and the role it plays in people's lives, that word was 'interconnectedness'.[93] Spirituality in the workplace is based on a foundation of meaning and values.[94] People want to be able to bring more of their complete selves to work and use more of their creativity, emotions and intelligence in the workplace. The spirituality movement entreats organizations to place a higher value on creativity, intelligence and integrity. Organizational members seek interesting, exciting, challenging work and want leaders who can make work seem worth their personal time and identity. Increasing the meaning of work can be done under all four paradigms. For example, the Royal Australian Navy provides a strong vision to its employees and opportunities for self-development within a fairly Classical paradigm.

Spirituality is particularly compatible with the Visionary and Organic paradigms. In a spiritual organizational culture, humanistic practices and policies are an integral part of an organization's daily operations. Each worker is viewed as a whole person with varied skills, knowledge and abilities that extend beyond the confines of job needs. Managers recognize that it is difficult for people to separate work from other parts of their lives. At BMW, for instance, a wide range of flexitime models and training options allow individuals to pursue their interests.

As a focus for Visionary and Organic leadership, spirituality makes sense intellectually, but problems may arise unless an organization's core values support more humane workplaces. Spirituality runs counter to traditional management and leadership ideology, under which many business executives are trained to objectify their professional lives, not to personalize them. It is contrary to viewing employees as resources or contractors who can be called in when needed and discarded in between jobs. Lack of life-long security and employment prospects is leading people to seek meaning outside work. Here, long-term employment at companies like Bonduelle, EKATO and Gore, coupled with interesting work provide the basis for spirituality in the workplace. Spirituality's hope lies in the changing nature of work with movement to teams and knowledge work and away from meaningless repetitive tasks to innovative ones.

What can leaders do? Leaders could make spiritual needs part of the vision for the organization or team, enhance personal liberty and give people purpose. Shifts to meaningful work, tolerance for diversity, consideration for life/work balance and increasing interconnectedness in networked organizations reflect enhanced spirituality. This is typically more consistent with Organic leadership than the other paradigms, but leaders from all paradigms could implement some aspects of spirituality.

Spirituality is an emerging movement, particularly strong in the US, but is not widely recognized as an organizational or leadership theory or model. It brings an important focus on the emotional, holistic nature of working and the need to balance both social and economic factors in the workplace. However, spirituality's effectiveness in improving happiness and efficiency still needs to be demonstrated.

How widespread the striving for spirituality is outside the US is also not known. Nor is whether workplace values such as 'mateship' in Australia can act as substitutes for spirituality. However, many people in the English-speaking world appear to be seeking more emotionally satisfying, balanced and less rational work environments, thereby reflecting the emotion-based paradigms of Visionary and Organic leadership.

In parts of Europe, spirituality seems strongly built into many workplaces because of the prevailing view that a 'company is a true community that offers a lasting place for each of its members'. This is sharply different from the Anglo-Saxon model, in which the company is often no more than the sum of a series of contractual arrangements between temporarily convergent interests: in short, a cash-flow machine, a collection of assets. The Rhine company is a living institution to be guarded and nurtured through work. In return, the company pledges to protect its own members through numerous social benefits...' (Albert, 1992:22).

The Rhine company that Albert refers to is built around ideas of being fair to a range of stakeholders, including employees, the environment and local communities. Working under conditions offered by the Rhine model may well provide employees with feelings of more spirituality, meaning and connectedness than are typically available in US or Australian companies.[95]

Evaluating emotional approaches

Overall, emotion-based approaches represent an advance on earlier theories by including the non-rational side of leadership. They also allow for understanding the collective actions of, and bonding between, members in some organizations. Both of these elements have been missing from most earlier theories.

Emotion-based approaches are often criticized for being generally very leader-focused, reflecting heroic notions of leadership that focus heavily on the person at the top.[97] However, emotion-based leadership can be distinguished from 'Great Men' heroic theories in not being restricted to paternalistic or elite leaders, particular genders or social-classes, or depending on exaggerated claims about the leader's power and influence.[98]

It is difficult to evaluate emotion-based concepts until more research has been conducted, a challenging task because these relatively new approaches are complex and often conflicting and ill-defined.[99] For example, the distinction between Bass' concepts of transformational and transactional leadership is conceptually unclear.[100] Originally, Bass had proposed that these were contrasting styles, claiming that transformational leaders are more effective than transactional leaders.[101] Later, Bass and his colleagues viewed transformational leadership as necessarily building on a transactional basis rather than being qualitatively different, and argued that transformational leadership is not effective when standing alone.[102]

Researchers also have difficulty in identifying charismatic persons and events, and defining and measuring inspiration and other associated emotional components. This is not surprising if charisma is indeed 'in the eye of the beholder'. However, the organization may suffer when a charismatic leader has to be replaced, unless the leader has groomed a successor in the same mould (see the Swatch case study).

The basic belief that a transformational/Visionary leader can shape people's feelings, beliefs and values and lead them to greater heights and self-awareness may well be unrealistic. Newer approaches are beginning to allow for the possibility of strategies other than charisma, inspiration and employee participation to effect culture change in organizations.[103] This is wise, because Collins and Porras concluded that a charismatic/Visionary leader is not required for a company to be successful, and may in fact be detrimental to a company's long-term prospects.[104] Less-intensively leader-focused approaches appear to be successful as well, such as Level 5 leadership described in Box 5.2.

CONCLUSION

The concepts described in this chapter take a very different emphasis from the predominantly rational trait, behavioural and contingency theories by bringing in emotion. Individual leaders are said to gain substantially by possessing traits of emotional intelligence and having charismatic qualities attributed to them. Further research is needed into developing both these concepts.

Inspirational, visionary and charismatic theories rely on leaders forming an emotional connection with their followers, usually by espousing an appealing and motivating vision, and often by using language and positive communication. Emotion-based approaches are considered powerful for transforming organizations and leading them to a desired future state. Whether charisma is an essential leader characteristic or just an attribution to the leader by the followers is not yet resolved, but emotion-based approaches begin to provide explanations for larger collective actions, beyond small-scale group leadership.

Vision is often regarded as central to leadership, primarily because it provides an organization with clarity about its purpose and direction. A well-articulated strategic vision has been found to bring sustainable competitive advantage to an organization. Current indications are that an effective vision displays characteristics of brevity, clarity, future-orientation, remaining stable over time, offering challenge, being abstract and inspiring followers. However, further research is needed into what distinguishes effective from less effective visions, particularly regarding a vision's content.

Aligning the values of organizational members with the vision is another major part of emotion-based leadership. Personal, shared and core values can be distinguished. Personal values are individual, whereas shared values are common to a group of people or organization. Personal and shared values can

Table 5.1

Emotion-based approaches and the leadership paradigms

Classical	Transactional	Visionary	Organic
		Emotional intelligence	Emotional intelligence
		Emotion	Emotion
		Values	Values
		Vision	Vision
		Spirituality	Spirituality
		Charisma	

change, albeit slowly. Core values endure and provide competitive advantage to an organization. Organizations with enduring, core values appear to perform better than those without. Shared values are also important because they can make a positive difference to work attitudes and performance. Part of a Visionary leader's task is to align individual and organizational values when creating unity, while leaving room for diverse personal values. In achieving this alignment, leaders are advised to forge, not force, unity.

Spiritual approaches also focus on the human and emotional elements in the workplace, and call for workplaces where employees find meaning in their work. Spiritual workplaces take a holistic view of the organizational members, recognizing that people cannot separate their personal and work selves. Part of enhancing the spirituality in an organization may involve reviewing the vision and values prevailing in the workplace and corporate attitudes towards social and environmental issues.

Table 5.1 summarizes how the ideas described in this chapter relate to the leadership paradigms. Emotion-based approaches are not seen as essential to Classical leadership, although undoubtedly emotions such as love or fear play a major role in this kind of leadership. For the Transactional leader, possessing emotional intelligence should be an advantage in influencing followers, but is not essential to this paradigm. However, emotion-based approaches apply substantially to both Visionary and Organic paradigms. All approaches discussed in this chapter would be expected to relate to Visionary leadership – emotional intelligence, emotion, values, vision, charisma and spirituality. All the preceding concepts would be central to Organic leadership, except leader charisma, which is not core to a leadership paradigm that de-emphasizes individual leaders.

In this chapter, the focus started on the individual leader's emotional intelligence and charisma and then moved to broader organizational considerations of emotion-based leadership, vision, values and spirituality. The next chapter continues and develops this broadening, considering organization wide and external leadership factors.

NOTES

For full details of these notes, Please see the References section at the end of this book.

 1 Mann, 1997
 2 Salovey and Mayer, 1990
 3 Goleman, 1995
 4 ibid.
 5 Salovey and Mayer, 1990:189
 6 Grensing-Pophal, 1998
 7 Mayer, 1999
 8 Goleman, 1995
 9 Yukl, 1998
10 Bass, 1990a
11 Howard and Bray, 1988; McCauley and Lombardo, 1990; Tichy and Devanna, 1986
12 Mayer, 1999
13 Shamir, House and Arthur, 1993
14 Weber, 1947
15 Bass, 1990a
16 e.g. Wasielewski, 1985
17 Conger and Kanungo, 1987
18 Gemmill and Oakley, 1992
19 House, 1977
20 ibid.
21 Bass, 1985
22 Kets de Vries, 1994
23 Bass, 1985
24 Roberts, 1985
25 Hede and Wear, 1996; House, 1977; Shamir, 1991; Trice and Beyer, 1993
26 Hollander, 1979
27 Collins, 2001
28 ibid.
29 e.g. Avolio and Bass, 1991; Bass, 1988; Carless, Mann and Wearing, 1996; Conger and Kanungo, 1988, 1994; House and Shamir, 1993
30 Kouzes and Posner, 1995
31 e.g. Bass and Avolio, 1990

32 Bass, 1985
33 Bass, 1990b
34 Brown, 1994
35 Lim, 1997
36 Bass, 1990
37 ibid.
38 Yammarino and Dubinsky, 1994
39 Maccoby, 2000
40 Kets de Vries, 1994
41 ibid.
42 Maccoby, 2000
43 ibid.
44 e.g. Bennis, 1989; Burns, 1978; Krantz, 1990
45 e.g. Hamel and Prahalad, 1989; Kirkpatrick and Locke, 1991; Meindl, 1998; Senge, 1990a
46 Hunt, 1991; Sashkin, 1988
47 Pearson, 1989; Phillips and Hunt, 1992
48 Locke, Kirkpatrick, Wheeler, Schneider, Niles, Goldstein, Welsh and Chah, 1991
49 Kouzes and Posner, 1995
50 Wheatley, 1999
51 Kouzes and Posner, 1995
52 Weick, 1995
53 e.g. Hamel and Prahalad, 1989
54 Bennis and Nanus, 1985
55 Hamel and Prahalad, 1989
56 Baum, Locke and Kirkpatrick, 1998
57 Kantabutra, 2003
58 Kirkpatrick and Locke, 1991
59 Baum, Locke and Kirkpatrick, 1998; Oswald, Stanwick and LaTour, 1997
60 Coulson-Thomas, 1992
61 e.g. Kets de Vries, 1994; Shamir, House and Authur 1993
62 Kantabutra and Avery, 2002a, 2002b
63 Locke, Kirkpatrick, Wheeler, Schmeider, Niles, Goldstein, Welsh and Chah, 1991
64 Sashkin, 1988; Sims and Lorenzi, 1992
65 Conger, 1989
66 Jacobs and Jaques, 1990; Kouzes and Posner, 1987
67 Nanus, 1992
68 Oswald, Mossholder and Harris, 1994
69 Baum, Locke and Kirkpatrick, 1998
70 Kantabutra, 2003
71 Baum, Locke and Kirkpatrick, 1998
72 Larwood, Falbe, Kriger and Miesling, 1995

73   Pearson, 1989
74   Rokeach, 1973
75   ibid.
76   Schein, 1992
77   Kouzes and Posner, 1995
78   Shamir, House and Authur 1993
79   Kouzes and Posner, 1995:217
80   Intagliata, Ulrich and Smallwood, 2000
81   Colins and Chippendale, 1991:144
82   Rokeach, 1973
83   Collins and Porras, 1994:235
84   Rothschild and Whitt, 1986
85   Collins and Porras, 1994
86   Rothschild and Whitt, 1986
87   Fairholm, 1998a:115
88   e.g. Hochschild, 1997; Perlow, 1999
89   Hochschild, 1997
90   Worrall and Cooper, 1999
91   Australian Bureau of Statistics, 2001
92   ibid.
93   Mitroff and Denton, 1999
94   Fairholm, 1998b; Turner, 1999
95   Avery, 2004
96   Meindl and Ehrlich, 1987; Meindi, Ehrlich and Dukerich, 1985
97   Gronn, 1995
98   Masi and Cooke, 2000
99   Bass, 1985
100   ibid.
101   Avolio and Bass, 1988; Yammarino, Spangler and Bass, 1993
102   Lewis, 1996
103   Collins, 2001: Collins and Porras, 1994

6 Macro-level Leadership

Key Points

- Leadership on an organizational level
- Leadership as part of a system
- Self-leadership
- Substitutes for leadership
- Organizational culture
- External influences
- Considering stakeholders
- Creating a learning organization

The approaches discussed in the preceding chapters tend to focus on aspects of the leader's person or role relating to followers in specific contexts. In particular, the leader is typically viewed as prime mover and motivator, whether through fear, rewards, influence, vision, inspiration, charisma or emotion. Most leadership theories ignore the relationship between broader aspects of organizations and leadership,[1] tending to focus on either individual leaders or groups of leader–followers. Only a few scholars prefer to disregard individuals altogether, assuming that situational variables provide sufficient explanation for leadership effects.[2]

Clearly, leadership issues arise at the broader organizational level and are impacted by events and considerations beyond the organization itself. While member interactions and relationships form the centre of an organization's leadership capacity, the overall context in which these relationships take place cannot be disregarded.[3]

The first part of this chapter looks at organization-wide leadership, while the second part discusses external influences. In each case, the topics are related back to the leadership paradigms.

ORGANIZATIONAL LEVEL

Being embedded in often contradictory and certainly complex organizations, leaders and their groups need to be studied within these broader settings. Structures, systems, culture and operating circumstances create a framework for action and *sense-making* in an organization – they support or hamper change, creativity and other initiatives. Explanations without reference to people, like those without reference to the context, are incomplete for understanding leadership.

This section discusses organizational systems, leader substitutes, self-management and self-leadership and organizational culture. While some of these elements can apply at divisional and team levels in an organization, they are of particular significance when applied at the organizational level.

Systems approaches

Most of the leadership approaches covered so far assume that a leader initiates and largely controls leadership interactions, especially under the Classical, Transactional and Visionary paradigms. However, from a systems perspective, leadership is the property of an overall system, stemming from the ongoing process of interaction among the important elements of an organization.[4] Leaders and followers are clearly important elements, but organizations and other social systems develop their own logic and rules, making it essential to look beyond the individual leader and focus on specific systems.[5]

For some writers, leadership is understood as beginning and ending in the system, that is, in the interrelations of people working and sharing together.[6] Sharing is where the leadership process itself comes from – from what goes on between people and when they make promises and commitments, and share interpretations and agreements in working together.[7] This is reflected in the Organic paradigm.

Leadership arises when people work together in reciprocal relationships – a distributed process shared by many ordinary people, rather than the result of a single extraordinary person.[8] This notion, consistent with the Organic leadership paradigm, goes well beyond the idea that leadership is a personal trait or set of behaviours vested in special people. It goes beyond the idea that anyone can be a leader, and beyond the idea that leadership can and should be shared between leader and followers.[9]

Instead, what leaders do is not independent of, but is interdependent with, follower actions and organizational processes. Leadership is thus related to a complex system that contains various subsystems, including:

- members' personalities;
- intergroup processes;
- tasks;
- work processes and practices;
- accountability systems;
- policies; and
- administrative structures.

These sub-systems need to fit together within the overall system in order for leadership to be effective.

Sometimes organizational systems impede or prevent the introduction of new practices such as sharing information, knowledge, power and rewards. For example, certain groups may refuse to provide the business results essential to sharing information, a team culture might be hampered by a reward system based on individual performance, or restrictive policies or procedures might inhibit innovation or sharing customer information. An appropriate relationship between the administrative structure and the task, or the reward system and work processes, is therefore needed.

This fit reflects an organization's leadership capacity, with the various subsystems dynamically related to one another in creating the overall leadership capacity of an enterprise. Commonsense suggests that an organization's systems and processes also need to align with the vision, values and strategic direction.[10] At BMW, for example, the performance management system rewards the all-pervasive teamwork, which is in turn supported by extensive training opportunities.

Viewing leadership from a systemic perspective raises new challenges for researchers seeking to study this complex phenomenon. Traditional social science methods are poorly suited to studying dynamic social systems in a way that preserves their configuration and deals with complexity and uncertainty. By breaking a social system into small parts, people are destroying the very thing they are attempting to understand.[11]

Clearly, without overall systems support, it is difficult to maintain a particular leadership paradigm. Vision, values, systems, rewards, processes and culture need to be aligned with the chosen leadership paradigm as part of the overall context. Specific systemic approaches to leadership, starting with substitutes for leaders and self-leadership, are discussed below.

Substitutes for leaders

Since heroic leadership is not the panacea for organizations that people once assumed, how can complex organizations function? One suggestion is that *substitutes for leadership* will predominate. That is, various elements of the system or environment will operate in place of a leader.[12] Where leader substitutes are operating, employees may neither need, nor willingly accept, a leader's direction because the system, including such elements as core values, provides the necessary leadership.

Substitutes for leadership are plentiful.[13] For example, developing closely-knit teams of highly-trained individuals can minimize a leader's work because team dynamics take over in controlling members' behaviour (see the BMW and EKATO case studies). Providing people with work that they find intrinsically satisfying reduces the need to motivate followers, who will tend to get on with the job for its own sake (see the EKATO and Novartis case studies). Professionally educated and otherwise highly skilled workers can perform most assignments without relying upon technical guidance from their manager, with their professionalism acting as a leader substitute (for example, the Novartis, Royal Australian Navy, SAP and Schering-Plough case studies). Direct client, peer and task feedback serve functions formerly undertaken by managers. Computer technology, as in some call centres, is increasingly performing many management functions, providing task guidance, control, direction and incentives that are not supplied by a manager. Detailed workbooks, guidelines, policies and procedures provide important non-leader guidance. Emerging expert and knowledge management systems can also substitute for leadership.

In effect, internal and external substitutes for leadership are set up using a combination of job design techniques, developing a team culture, recruiting and training staff appropriately and introducing proper performance management. The right job design and team can act as substitutes for external leadership (see the BMW case study). Employees' skills and internal motivation serve as substitutes for the presence and guidance of a leader.

Creating substitutes does not necessarily imply abolishing the leadership function; rather, it is in itself an act of leadership.[14] Gore, for example, regards itself as a *leaderful* organization, although there are no ranks and titles, or lines of formal authority. However, the challenge is often to design an organization with a large range of leader substitutes (see examples in the BMW and Rodenstock case studies).

Formal research into substitutes for leadership has led to disappointing results, with relatively few supporting studies to date. One reason for this might be that followers' differing needs for supervision have not been taken into account.[15] A concept like *need for supervision* might help distinguish between situations in which leaders do and do not affect follower behaviour. A leader has a large opportunity to influence followers with a strong need for supervision, but little opportunity to affect those with a low need for supervision. Situational factors influence the need for supervision, moderating the relationship between leadership styles and outcomes.[16] For example, employees with considerable work experience, engaged in tasks that offer plenty of feedback and working in a strongly cohesive team are not likely to be greatly influenced by a leader, irrespective of the follower's need for supervision. However, followers' need for supervision will affect the extent to which a leader's style influences staff behaviour in a given situation, and may affect how well leader substitutes work.

Although the concept of substitutes for leaders has not been tested extensively, it is intuitively appealing and incorporates organizational processes that other models do not. It is hard to envisage effective Organic leadership operating without substitutes for leadership. Although Classical, Transactional and Visionary leaders may choose not to actively employ substitutes for leadership, doing so would still enable these leadership paradigms to operate. However, implementing leader substitutes may pose threats to those leaders who perceive the substitutes as a loss of managerial control and authority. More enlightened leaders will see substitutes as freeing them from micro-level tasks, making their people more self-managing.

Identifying substitutes for leadership operating in different environments provides insight into how different kinds of leadership styles might be made effective. With today's networked and dispersed global organizations, there may be no option but to focus on leadership substitutes when leaders are increasingly unavailable in person, representing a shift to self-leadership.

Self-leadership

Changes in how organizations operate are leading to a focus away from leaders to self-leading workers.[17] In creating a self-leading environment, leaders can help others to lead themselves by acting as teacher or coach, and not as director. *Self-leadership* can therefore be regarded as a kind of leader substitute. In organizations like GE, the CEO is personally involved in teaching other leaders, who in turn are expected to pass on the learnings to their own people. At both GE and in the case of Schering-Plough, it is interesting to note that the top leaders release employees to become self-leading. By contrast, at Gore each associate is paired with one or more sponsors to guide the associate's development, but the sponsors' role is not one of a leader who can transfer power to the associate.

Self-leading can be distinguished from self-managing. For example, Manz views *self-management* as 'a set of strategies for managing one's own behavior to reduce discrepancies from existing work standards.'[18] The focus is on behaviour that helps meet the demands of the surrounding system, as appropriate under a Transactional paradigm. Self-leaders seek to influence the overall purpose behind the system, thereby serving higher-level organizational goals. Self-management focuses on short-run deviations from standards, but does not question the appropriateness of those standards. Self-managing employees generally lack influence over what should be done and why, which is another difference from self-leading. Self-management is typically sustained by extrinsic rewards, whereas internal motivation and rewards tend to maintain self-leading.[19]

Organic leadership rests heavily on self-leading members, while Transactional and Visionary leadership can probably accommodate self-managing followers more easily than self-leaders (see the BMW, EKATO and Royal Australian Navy case studies). Conditions can be created under which self-leading team members require very little external leadership, such as in a strong team culture where team norms and other substitutes for leadership can intervene. To be successful, self-leadership requires employees to be empowered and to align with an organization's culture and values. Self-leaders do not require organizing, controlling and monitoring from Transactional leaders or directing under the Classical paradigm. Self-leadership implies redefining the concepts of both leadership and followership more towards Organic leadership.

The role of self-leadership and other leader substitutes is primarily that of helping others to lead themselves, in contrast to heroic leadership, where the leader is expected to provide answers and guide, protect and rescue subordinates. Self-leading staff free managers for other activities and still allow the organization to achieve its objectives. The organizational culture, processes and systems need to align to support self-leading employees, including reporting and accountability systems.

Organizational culture

Creating, maintaining and developing a culture and atmosphere suited to a group or organization is considered to be a major leadership task.[20] Despite the importance that the leadership literature often gives to managing the organizational culture, there is little agreement on how to define *corporate culture* and what it should encompass. *Culture* basically refers to certain ideas or things that groups share or hold in common, which can include:

- observed behaviours;
- special competencies that group members display;
- shared values, assumptions, norms, philosophies and meanings;
- the implicit rules for getting along in the organization;
- organizational climate;
- habits of thinking and mental models; and
- certain symbols.[21]

The concept of organizational culture is fuzzy and incorporates contradictions, paradoxes, ambiguity and confusion. However, it provides the overall shared rules that guide members of an organization. Culture also provides shared meaning and symbolism, where meaning refers to how a group tends to interpret what is said or done, and symbols stand for something special to organizational members.[22]

Culture covers the behavioural, emotional and mental elements of group members' functioning, and reflects the group's striving towards integration. The result of this striving provides some *structural stability* in the group, and a *pattern* of values, rituals and behaviours that tend to bind the group into a coherent whole.[23] Clearly, subcultures can exist within an organization, for example, between marketing and production at Swatch, and between the 'old' and 'new' employees at Rodenstock. Less obvious are subcultures that impact leaders at different levels, such as where middle managers are 'caught' between the culture stemming from the manager above and the norms among his or her followers.

Organizational culture can vary in strength and cohesiveness, as organizations struggle with common issues that they need to reconcile. These issues include:

- deciding on the group's boundaries so people know who is in and who is outside the group;
- how power and influence are to be distributed among the members, which is not always refected in allocated formal positions;

- how to develop workable relationships among the members;
- which behaviours are to be rewarded and punished, and how; and
- the stories and myths that the members will use for explaining 'mysterious' events.[24]

As a result, strong and weak cultures develop, depending on how widely shared the responses to these key issues are among the members of an organization. Most of the case organizations in Part Two exhibit strong cultures that influence people's behaviour and beliefs, and many have experienced the challenges of trying to change their strong culture (see the Bonduelle and Rodenstock case studies).

While culture reflects a group's shared learning, leaders, particularly founders, often leave a deep impression on the assumptions that are passed down from one generation to another within an organization (see the Bonduelle, EKATO, Gore, Rodenstock and Swatch case studies). Leaders act as role models for other organizational members, and stories and legends can perpetuate this influence after the individual has left. What people within the organization do, value and believe can be modelled on the leader, particularly under the Classical, Transactional and Visionary paradigms. Followers can take their cues from leaders on which behaviours are and are not acceptable, as well as what constitutes status symbols within the culture.

However, culture is not always influenced by leaders. The extent to which leadership is determined by the organizational culture is particularly evident where managers have moved from a culture where one leadership paradigm has prevailed to another – the same person acting under different paradigms in different organizational cultures. Clearly, where a strong culture permeates the organization, as at Bonduelle and BMW, new leaders did not create the culture but have had to adjust to the existing culture themselves, and find it very hard to change the prevailing culture.

In addition, it is helpful to realize that what happens in the world is a social construction, based on shared agreements.[25] People often underestimate the extent to which situations, and the expectations of others via the organizational culture, can constrain and shape behaviour.[26] For example, culture is critical in developing and maintaining levels of intensity and dedication among employees in successful firms.[27] Organizational commitment is generally thought of as an individual's psychological bond to the organization, including a sense of job involvement and belonging to the culture. For Visionary and Organic leadership in particular, obtaining organizational commitment is essential. At Gore, the organizational culture, including its core values, provides the 'glue' that binds this organization together.

The culture created by people's expectations and behaviours may or may not be desirable. It depends on the critical tasks to be accomplished, and whether the organizational system provides sufficient opportunities to complete the tasks. The existing organizational culture can also constrain leaders, or their emergence. For instance, an adaptive organizational culture will tend to encourage and enable leaders with visionary qualities to emerge.[28] Paradoxically, at SAP, which had a Visionary co-leader, an adaptive culture that needed to meet a rapidly changing market and industry was constrained by multiple layers of management.

Cultures that enable organizations to anticipate and adapt to environmental change have been found to be associated with high levels of performance over time.[29] Such adaptive cultures tend ultimately to enhance performance by fostering Visionary or Organic leadership. On the other hand, charismatic and Visionary leaders are likely to be prevented from emerging in cultures averse to change, innovation and risk taking. Organic leadership is suited to adaptive cultures, particularly where the organizational culture is strong and organizational commitment is high (see the Gore and BMW case studies).

Summary

An organization-wide perspective has been taken in considering leadership issues. This includes viewing leadership itself as a phenomenon that can arise from organizational systems, rather than from qualities associated with particular individuals. It is possible to design organizations in such a way that many facets of leadership are built into the system, thereby supplying substitutes for leaders. The effectiveness of leader substitutes may be related to followers' need for supervision, but further research is required into the extent and ways characteristics of systems, tasks, teams and individual worker skills can reduce the need for leaders and managers.

Many organizations seek to develop self-managing and self-leading staff. Self-managing employees try to reduce discrepancies in their behaviour from set standards, whereas self-leading people seek to influence the purpose behind their workplace.

A major component in an organizational system is the culture, and managing culture is often seen as part of a leader's role. Strong cultures may be difficult to change by individuals, but decisions about organizational strategy and structure can help shape the culture, thereby aligning this part of the system with the organizational vision. Adaptive cultures that allow organizations to anticipate and adapt to environmental change tend to be associated with high levels of performance.

THE BROADER ENVIRONMENT

Discussion so far has covered theories and concepts relating to the organization as an isolated entity. However, a comprehensive understanding of leadership needs to consider influences coming from the environment outside the unit, team or organization. Ideally, an organizational system should be internally consistent, while adapting to the external situation the organization faces. In the interests of its own future and survival, an organization will normally put one or more of its members in a leadership role, charged with worrying about the organization's external boundaries, survival and growth.[30] In Organic organizations like Gore, one or more associates may make a commitment to take on this role, and remain in the role as long as they are supported in doing so by the rest of the organization. In leader-led organizations the CEO is normally expected take this formal role, although responsibility may be shared among a top team.

Determining what is external can be difficult because the boundaries between what is inside and what is outside an organization are blurring:

- suppliers work on production lines within manufacturing plants and stock supermarket shelves;
- competitors enter into strategic alliances or joint ventures;
- customers advise product developers; and
- employees work at customers' premises or from home.

The question becomes: Which roles and people fall inside the organization? Or are some players part of a broader organizational system extending beyond traditional boundaries? Where should the boundary be drawn, if at all?

Factors relating to the external environment are considered below. These are strategic planning, stakeholders and organizational learning, including knowledge management, teaching and mentoring.

Strategic planning

A core role, typically assigned to leadership, is developing and implementing a strategy. Strategic management specialists traditionally argue that an organization needs to develop plans for the future, despite facing considerable uncertainty. This involves making important decisions about the future and linking them together to form strategies.[31] Part of a traditional leader's role is to develop a strategy, taking into account external factors as well as internal capabilities, and to ensure that the structure, culture and systems within the organization are appropriate to realizing the strategy. In Organic organizations, this may occur through mutual adjustment or agreement, and people beyond top management may be involved in formulating the strategy under any of the paradigms. In any case, the organization is continuously monitoring an ever-changing environment and aligning the organization's structure, capabilities and strategies with it,[32] making strategic management important to all four leadership paradigms.

Some writers argue that strategic management is more about managing a cultural change within an organization than formulating objective, rational plans for the future.[33] Indeed, the process of formulating strategy is itself part of the organizational culture, or is at least influenced by it. Although some writers believe that leadership plays an insignificant role in organizational performance,[34] others disagree, calling for leadership to be explicitly linked to, and aligned with, business results and strategy.[35] In this way, leadership takes on a distinctive form in each organization – referred to as *branded leadership*.[36] A branded leadership culture can permeate an organization, creating a form of competitive advantage if this culture is aligned with the business strategy and linked to results (see the BMW case study).

The following subsection covers issues relating to strategic planning and the resulting need for alignment with organizational systems as part of effective leadership.

Planning

Different organizational environments appear to require different degrees of strategic planning formality, which in turn impacts a leader's role and behaviour. Terminology is somewhat confused in the literature, particularly about terms like strategic thinking, planning and management:[37]

- *Strategic thinking* involves appreciating how the organization creates its value, and how to solve problems.
- *Strategic planning* involves ways of converting the strategies that have been thought up into action, whereby thinking and planning mutually influence one another.
- *Strategic management* refers to managing these thinking and planning processes, and their implementation.[38]

Traditionally, the strategy process has been thought of as a top-down, rational activity. For example, Mintzberg describes three broad ways in which strategy could be made in organizations, although these modes can also be combined (see Table 6.1):[39]

- The *entrepreneurial mode* of strategy making is dominated by the active search for new opportunities. Power is centralized in the hands of the chief executive, growth is the dominant organizational goal, and strategy making is characterized by dramatic leaps forward in the face of uncertainty. This mode would sit well with Classical and Visionary paradigms.
- The *adaptive mode* accepts the status quo, clear objectives do not exist, and strategy tends to be reactive. The disjointed decisions that are taken in the adaptive mode are made in incremental, serial steps. Strategy making reflects a division of power among members of a complex coalition. The Transactional paradigm would suit this mode, rather than Classical leadership where power resides with the leader, or Visionary leadership that pursues a particular direction.
- In the *planning mode*, the analyst plays a major role in strategy making, with a focus on rational, systematic analysis and the costs and benefits of competing proposals. The planning mode attempts to integrate decisions and strategies into one coherent whole. This method could be used under all of the four leadership paradigms, but with its integrative, systemic and holistic approach it seems an appropriate match for Organic.

Some writers question the wisdom of expecting the CEO to be responsible for formulating strategy, and argue for involving the entire organization in the process. This concept would be compatible with Organic leadership, in particular. The capacity

Table 6.1

Strategic planning modes linked to the leadership paradigms[40]

Strategy mode	Who plans?	Paradigm	Focus
Entrepreneurial	CEO	Classical Visionary	Searches for new opportunities, moves in dramatic leaps.
Adaptive	Complex powerful coalition	Transactional	Status quo, moves in incremental, disjointed steps.
Planning	Analysts	All paradigms could use this mode, focus seems to fit with Organic.	Seeks integrative, systemic, integrated, holistic approach.

for strategic thinking is not just restricted to senior managers, but all staff can be expected to think, analyse and act spontaneously to serve customers and markets.[41]

Others have questioned the extent to which traditional, formal strategic planning is useful in today's fast-paced environments.[42] Advocates of New Science approaches emphasize that organizational planning is based on false assumptions.[43] First, the idea that management's actions determine the success or otherwise of an organization is based on Newtonian assumptions of simple, linear causality between actions and outcomes in an organization. This leads to the second assumption that organizations are essentially stable systems in which actions lead to predictable outcomes, whereas almost all organizations today are in a state of change. A third questionable assumption is that feedback keeps planning, budgeting and other control and information systems on the correct path, particularly negative feedback. If this were the case, plans would need to be constantly changing, so why bother creating firm plans? Environmental conditions will almost certainly have changed before the completion of a formal plan, and the result is more likely to constrain than assist an agile, adaptive organization.

Thus, while intuitively appealing, the practicality of planning for organizational fit with the environment and internal elements has been challenged, because environments are constantly changing and therefore the organization will continually go in and out of fit. This leads us to a discussion of the concept of alignment within organizational systems.

Alignment

Implementing strategy involves the whole organizational system, only part of which is the configuration or structure. An organization can be viewed as an open system in which members' behaviours are interrelated, and these behaviours in turn interrelate with the task, rewards and controls and corporate culture.[44] Each business unit or function needs to fit with various environmental variables, the predispositions of its members and with the overall organizational structure. This fit is known as *alignment*.

It is difficult to separate elements like strategy, structure, processes and culture within an organizational system because these facets become tightly interwoven over time, that is, they become aligned. These elements become increasingly homogeneous, and the system starts to conform to one central 'theme'.[45] Themes establish a process that brings corporate culture, strategies and infrastructures into alignment.

Masi and Cooke show how the existing structure, processes and regulations can hamper a change of leadership style within a bureaucracy.[46] In the military, for example, these researchers show that leadership does not appear to be as important to organizational effectiveness as other organizational factors. Therefore, impediments need to be identified, and realigned with the strategy, structure and culture (see the Rodenstock case study). A major challenge in doing so arises because alignment between the elements in an organization is dynamic, that is, constantly changing.[47]

Is the effort of seeking alignment even worth the result? For many years strategic management theorists have proposed a connection between organizational alignment and performance.[48] Various researchers have found improved organizational performance, including financial performance, when there is a good fit between various environmental variables and the structure and orientation of the organization.[49]

Summary

Although more research into the relationship between strategy, structure, alignment, planning and leadership is required, it appears that appropriate leadership will involve different amounts of formal strategy, depending on the kind of organization and the context in which it operates. The degree of planning and alignment possible will vary with the situation, and the range of organizational members involved in formulating strategy will depend on whether the CEO is perceived as being solely the creator of strategy or whether other employees should be involved.

We have seen that Classical and Transactional leadership will generally thrive in bureaucratic, slow-change situations and therefore will have time to create and execute detailed plans and achieve alignment. Heroes can lead simple, stable organizations, but complex, dynamic organizations can rarely rely on heroes. More dynamic conditions shift the required leadership paradigms towards Visionary and Organic, accompanied by more fluid networked or adhocracy structures. As people cope with heterogeneous and dynamic environments, the knowledge needed to deal with diverse issues becomes too complicated for only a few leaders to understand. A demand for fast responsiveness and the need for on-going sense-making to understand ambiguous environmental changes are likely to render formal planning and aligning the organization unrealistic in practice. Therefore, widespread leadership and considerable agility are needed in today's increasingly complex organizations. This again shifts leadership towards the Organic paradigm.

Stakeholders

Leaders are often exhorted to serve the interests of company *shareholders* by maximizing traditional performance measures such as profits, shareholder value and returns on investment. This focus on shareholders, that is, on the investors in an enterprise, is surprising in the light of analyses showing that shareholders of large organizations are unimportant and powerless. On average, only about 4 per cent of an established company's funds come from equities, and shareholders are traditionally kept at bay using various tactics to minimize their power in influencing a business.[50]

Yet senior managers frequently claim to be operating in the interests of their shareholders. Doing so usually overlooks the interests of many other parties affected by the organization's activities, known as *stakeholders*. This includes subordinating the interests of stakeholders such as employees, suppliers, the environment, society at large and local communities. Although for a long time customers were also relegated to a secondary place, it is now widely accepted that to serve shareholder interests, customers' interests must be given priority.[51]

The range of other potential stakeholders is wide. Given the practical realities of limited resources, the question of who are relevant stakeholders becomes important.[52] One very broad view of what a stakeholder is includes nearly every combination of people, from a single individual to groups of individuals and subsets of identifiable groups like unionized employees and baby boomers.[53] Others narrow the concept of stakeholders to embrace employees, customers, suppliers, managers, patrons and board members, and all those with expectations of gain from the organization's success.[54]

Alliance partners are considered as stakeholders in some organizations, leading to a growing emphasis on inter-organizational networking and collaboration (see the Novartis, Rodenstock and SAP case studies). Strong ties to other organizations can help reduce uncertainty by increasing communication and information sharing, and gaining ideas for change.[55] By maintaining a wide range of alliances, an organization gains access to different kinds of information, which can affect its ability to identify and respond to threats coming from the business environment. In the process, the partners develop an interest in each other, thereby becoming stakeholders.

Another set of stakeholders includes governments and politicians, because of the significant effects they can have on the business context in which organizations operate.[56] As a result, corporations try to manage these external political relationships, even forming alliances with competitors to collaborate in government lobbying, thereby increasing the complexity of managing stakeholder relationships.

Similarly, community groups and others representing community stakeholders can mobilize opinion for or against a corporation's environmental and social performance, and should therefore be included among the stakeholders.[57] BMW, EKATO, Gore and Novartis do this, for example.

Increasingly, US companies are recognizing a wider set of stakeholders, as many German and other European organizations have long done.[58] This is occurring for various reasons, including trying to improve organizational performance,[59] and in the belief that many parties have legitimate and intrinsically worthwhile claims. An additional incentive to consider diverse stakeholders is that appropriately juggling competing demands from multiple stakeholder groups appears to be a key to organizational success.[60] The *balanced scorecard* approach to tracking and guiding strategic efforts assists in the process of addressing the financial and non-financial interests of multiple stakeholders.[61] Some of the cases in Part Two explicitly aim their activities at multiple stakeholders (for example, BMW, Gore, Rodenstock and the Royal Australian Navy).

At first glance, it might look as if attending to the interests of stakeholders could disadvantage shareholders, for example, through spending potential profits on environmental protection measures. However, it may well be that by protecting the interests of the ecology, shareholders' interests are really being considered. This can happen by making products more attractive to customers, attracting higher quality staff to work for an environmentally-friendly company, appealing to investors in *green shares*, preventing legal suits for damaging the environment, or generating positive publicity for the company (see the BMW and Novartis case studies). Furthermore, shareholders are as susceptible to the adverse effects of poor environmental action as anyone else.

One advantage of listening to diverse stakeholders is that an organization can use the information acquired in shaping its own future, a hallmark of a learning organization. Another reason for doing so is because it is the 'right thing to do'. Moral philosophers would challenge using a stakeholder approach merely to serve shareholders' interests, arguing that a stakeholder approach should genuinely transcend maximizing shareholder profits. Further, a study of successful US companies concluded that visionary companies do not have maximizing shareholder value as their driving force, rather they pursue a cluster of objectives of which making money is only one.[62]

Clearly, leaders from all four leadership paradigms can choose to focus on a range of stakeholders. However, this perspective appears particularly appropriate to Visionary and Organic paradigms in their dynamic business environments. Classical leaders are least likely to consider stakeholders given the low participation rate that major stakeholders, namely employees, tend to be permitted.

Learning organizations

A strongly emerging view is that leadership's role is to create a *learning organization,* where people are continually expanding their capabilities to shape their own future. This enables the organization to adapt to new contexts as markets, competitors, technologies and other factors change. A leader's job is often seen as helping build systems and communities of practice that produce a more reliable transformation of knowledge into action,[63] while attempting to harness the brainpower and knowledge of internal and external stakeholders. This is no easy task (see Box 6.1). In leaderful Organic organizations, like Gore and BMW, learning comes as people communicate as part of the sense-making processes within such organizations. Innovative organizations are likely to provide both formal and informal learning opportunities for their employees (see the Novartis case study, for example).

Box 6.1

Managing knowledge

According to W. Edwards Deming,[72] there is no substitute for knowledge. Warren Bennis,[73] Peter Senge[74] and others believe that the key to competitive advantage in the future lies in the capacity of leadership to create the social environment that produces intellectual capital.

Knowledge management (KM) is currently regarded as a major challenge in organizations, as they struggle to find competitive advantage in a rapidly changing world. Part of the difficulty is that many people falsely conceptualize knowledge as something tangible and explicit that is independent of organizational culture or values. The popular approach of capturing knowledge in a fancy IT system is insufficient,[75] and many corporations, like Novartis, realize that they need to create environments that enable all people to create knowledge. This means making people the core of value creation, instead of IT systems.[76]

Managing and sharing knowledge often means changing existing organizational cultures and values that implicitly discourage sharing ideas and know-how.[77] For example, employees are seldom rewarded for sharing knowledge or teaching others if it is not part of their defined duties, and some may be reluctant to share information that provides part of their power-base in traditional organizations. Knowledge-focused leaders create environments that reinforce norms of sharing information, and set expectations through their actions as well as their words.[78] Communication is at the heart of the knowledge management environment,[79] along with the communication skills needed to influence, persuade, negotiate and share knowledge (see the Gore and Schering-Plough case studies).

Many definitions of organizational learning have been proffered, but it can be seen as a process by which individuals and the organization as a whole develop and use their store of knowledge.[64] Learning can be an internal process, but it can also involve influences from customers, suppliers and other groups external to the organization.

Inside the enterprise, members need to convey their learning to one another, and develop shared understandings about how to apply knowledge.[65] This requires an environment conducive to learning, referred to as an *organizational learning culture*, allowing both learning by individuals and learning by the group as a whole.[66] At BMW the entire organization attends training courses in small groups over a three-year period, and uses quality circles and many other devices to foster learning, in addition to undertaking extensive education courses. Further, BMW's manufacturing plants are arranged into teams, so that learning and sharing information occurs across these boundaries.

Knowledge management and organizational learning are linked in that organizational learning can be considered as the development of an organization's memory,[67] or as its ability to store accumulated knowledge.[68] While originally regarded as an internal issue, knowledge management is now being viewed as both internal and external. Many organizations regard knowledge management as a key source of competitive advantage by sharing industry-wide knowledge with a network of competitors and suppliers.[69] The network provides more diversity of knowledge than is available within a single firm (see the Rodenstock and SAP case studies). Toyota, for example, has developed coordinating principles to effectively create and manage network-level knowledge sharing with its suppliers and competitors. In doing so, Toyota resolved three major dilemmas for knowledge sharing, namely how to:

- motivate members to participate and openly share knowledge;
- prevent members from free riding, that is, gaining but not contributing; and
- efficiently transfer various kinds of knowledge.

Organizational learning processes need to be extended well beyond the organization itself, to include learning from outside. At Novartis, networks have been developed among its people and universities, customers and other groups in order to learn and share knowledge. Through employee turnover, joint ventures, outsourcing among organizational networks, virtual collaborations and other forms of flexible organization, learning inevitably occurs across organizational boundaries.[70] For example, SAP has instituted formal processes to enable staff to learn from customers and alliance partners.

However, employee turnover, outsourcing, subcontracting and converting employees into subcontractors also endangers organizational memory as individuals retain their knowledge outside the firm. Therefore it is vital that today's organizations provide environments to attract and retain staff and external contractors. 'The knowledge-focused manager creates learning opportunities, encourages knowledge sharing, sees staff turnover as loss and considers recruitment too important to be delegated to the HR department.'[71] Clearly, SAP lost considerable knowledge during the period when many managers left the organization.

Klimecki and Lassleben[80] identified two basic modes of organizational learning: structural and strategic. *Structural learning* pushes people to find cures for problems, while *strategic learning* pulls and inspires people to realize visions. Organizations facing serious problems are more likely to adopt the structural learning mode, whereas the strategic learning mode is likely to arise in the presence of an attractive vision.[81] A further difference between the two modes is that structural learning tends to emphasize a production-orientation, whereas strategic learning modes profit from a customer-orientation. Further links between organizational structure and knowledge are described in Box 6.2.

Box 6.2

Knowledge and structure

Lam[85] has linked different kinds of knowledge to organizational structure, including professional bureaucracies, machine bureaucracies and adhocracies.

According to Lam, professional bureaucracies, such as universities, derive their capacity from formal knowledge held by highly-trained individual experts. Coordination is achieved largely via standardization of knowledge and skills through the individuals' formal training and education. Formal knowledge tends to form the boundary of internal work rules, jobs and status. The learning focus tends to be narrow and constrained within the boundary of formal specialist knowledge.

In a machine bureaucracy, knowledge is heavily encoded through specialization (sharp division of labour), standardization and control because the aim is to achieve efficiency and stability.[86] Here the knowledge agents are not the individuals directly engaged in operations. Rather, the management hierarchy is responsible for formalizing operating skills and experience, thereby reducing uncertainty in the operating tasks. This clear dichotomy between the application and generation of knowledge is seen in the standardization at McDonald's.

By contrast, in an adhocracy like a professional partnership or consultancy, Lam points out that there is little standardization of knowledge or work process. The adhocracy relies on the formal knowledge of its members, as well as the diverse know-how and practical problem-solving skills embodied in individual experts (see the Gore case study). Administration tends to be fused with the operating task, providing individual experts with a high degree of autonomy and discretion in their work. In this way, adhocracies generate tacit knowledge through considerable experimentation and interactive problem solving. This is essential in organizations engaged in providing non-standard, creative and problem-solving services directly to clients. Formal professional knowledge may play only a limited role, hence the importance of embodied skills and know-how competencies. The knowledge structure of an operating adhocracy is both individualistic and collaborative. The downside is that frequent restructuring of teams may hinder the transfer of learning.

Structural learning would be expected to operate in Classical and Transactional environments, whereas a *strategic learning* organization would fit a leadership paradigm that embraces continuous adaptive change, such as Organic leadership, and one that pulls people to work for a desired future like Visionary leadership. In a learning organization, leaders' roles differ dramatically from that of the traditional decision-maker, becoming more subtly that of designers, teachers and stewards (see Box 6.3). Thus, leaders in learning organizations are responsible for learning and for building a climate in which people are continually expanding their capabilities to shape their future. This involves both teaching and mentoring.

Teaching organizations

Teaching organizations are even more agile than learning organizations, tending to come up with better strategies and implementing them better.[82] Well-known examples of teaching leaders are Andy Grove (Intel), Jacques Nasser (Ford), Roger Enrico (PepsiCo) and Jack Welch (GE).

Box 6.3

Emerging roles for leaders

Eminent management writers state that the role of leaders is changing to becoming designers, teachers and stewards/servants.[87] Briefly, these new roles are:

- *Leader as designer*: The leader designs and aligns the organization's structures and processes, in particular the institutional learning processes. As part of these activities, management teams and other organizational members share and question their mental models or fundamental assumptions about the company, markets and competitors.[88]
- *Leader as teacher*: Tichy strongly encourages top leaders to develop the organization's leaders in formal programs, for three main reasons:[89]

    i   Top leaders set a direction for everyone in the organization, and hearing about new directions from the top provides power, support and understanding about the new directions and required behaviours.
    ii Through teaching, senior leaders obtain feedback from people in the organization, and so can amend ideas where necessary to make them more relevant to the current environment and focus on ideas that add significant value.
    iii By teaching, senior leaders provide frameworks for the decisions of managers at all levels, including common goals and actions that can be implemented back in the work environment.

    Specifically, the leader can influence people to view reality at three distinct levels: events, patterns of behaviour and system structure. Critical is where leaders predominantly focus their own and their organization's attention. Senge argues that unfortunately most leaders focus attention on events, and only occasionally consider the more informative patterns or trends, or search for systemic and structural explanations of what causes the patterns of behaviour.[90]
- *Leader as steward*: This is the subtlest role of leadership, according to Senge.[91] The leader as steward role is largely a matter of attitude, but an attitude critical to learning organizations. Greenleaf's explanation of stewardship is where the leader is servant first.[92] Stewardship begins with feeling that one wants to serve above all else, and this conscious choice brings one to aspire to lead. That person is sharply different from someone who is leader first, perhaps because of the need for power, status or material possessions. A leader's sense of stewardship operates on two levels: stewardship for the followers, and stewardship of the mission or purpose that underlies the enterprise. Overall, the Visionary and Organic paradigms would be expected to be most consistent with servant or steward leadership.

Teaching leaders project the ideas that propel people towards a common goal, live the values that define acceptable behaviours within the organization, and tell stories over and over to describe the winning future.[83] In particular, they participate in teaching other leaders how to lead, and are encouraged to spend up to one third of their time developing the organization's leaders in formal programs.[84]

While all leadership paradigms could accommodate teaching, it is expected to be found more often in Visionary and Organic organizations as people try to make sense of turbulent and uncertain futures. Another characteristic of teaching and learning organizations is that they often rely on mentoring to develop leadership, discussed below.

Mentoring

Mentoring is a learning/teaching approach that is gaining increasing recognition. *Mentoring* is basically a process in which one member of an organization or network guides another.[93] Hilb traces the origin of the term 'mentoring' to the Greek legend of King Odysseus, who charged a trusted person called Mentor with the upbringing of his son, Telemachus, while Odysseus was away. During Odysseus' absence, Mentor took over the roles of father figure, confidant, teacher and counsellor for Telemachus.[94]

Although the classic case of mentoring involves an older person *counselling* a newer or younger person, *reverse mentoring* can also occur, in which younger people share their wisdom with older people, for example, in the use of new technology at GE. While frequently confined to relationships within an organization, mentoring can also extend to relationships beyond. For example, *mentors* or *mentees* can come from outside a formal organization. An extended view of mentoring can arise when an organization solicits on-going customer advice and guidance in developing new products (see the SAP case study). Related to mentoring is the concept of *sponsoring*, in which the sponsor actively guides and champions another person (see the Gore case study).

Mentoring is perhaps the most widely used developmental relationship within organizations.[95] It may take different forms. *Informal mentorships* tend to occur spontaneously without formally involving the organization. *Formal mentorships*, on the other hand, are managed by an organization that might adopt a mentoring policy, decide who is to be mentored and by whom, provide guidelines for mentors, and evaluate the process. The literature frequently mentions the importance of top management support in the success of mentoring programs.[96]

The *mentor's* role is as coach, counsellor, evaluator and promoter. At the same time, the *mentee* actively cooperates in this process by working with the mentor, thereby developing himself or herself. In what is often thought of as an intense interpersonal exchange, the mentor traditionally provides advice, support, direction and feedback on both career plans and personal development:[97]

- The mentor's *career role* facilitates and advances the mentee's career, and typically provides the mentee with sponsorship, exposure and visibility, coaching, protection and challenging assignments.
- The personal development *role* serves to enhance the mentee's sense of competence, identity and work-role effectiveness. Here, the mentor provides role

modelling, acceptance and confirmation, counselling and friendship, in an effort to promote the mentee's self-image and competence.[98]

Is mentoring effective? The Schering-Plough case study suggests that it can be. Many other reports also indicate positive outcomes from mentoring for mentees, mentors and organizations.[99] A consistent finding is that mentees reap significant benefits, such as:

- higher overall compensation and accelerated career mobility;[100]
- increased self-esteem;[101] and
- reduced role stress and role conflict.[102]

Mentoring is particularly important for women, and Sinclair found that the few women who achieve formal leadership positions value mentoring received from older male managers.[103] This is because, typically, men define for women their eligibility for leadership. Women tend not to think of themselves in these terms until an older male recognizes ability and demonstrates confidence.[104]

Mentors also derive benefits from the mentoring process, including:

- job satisfaction, fulfilment and a personal sense of accomplishment frequently grow as a result of the mentoring relationship;[105]
- often explaining something to someone else can help the mentor better understand the topic;
- mentors may also benefit from the creativity and energy of the mentee[106] and remain up to date; and
- enhanced esteem among the mentor's peers and supervisors.[107]

Organizations themselves receive long-term benefits from mentoring.[108] Benefits can stem from increased employee productivity,[109] enhanced organizational commitment,[110] and lower levels of turnover.[111] A study of the effects of mentoring over a five-year period found support for differences between mentored and non-mentored individuals.[112]

An organization's structure, culture and processes can potentially promote or hinder mentoring. An *adaptive* culture that encourages frequent and open communication across hierarchical levels appears to encourage the formation of mentoring relationships more effectively than where communication across levels is rigid and discouraged.[113] Management systems in which power is centralized and communication is limited to supervisors and subordinates do not support widespread mentorships, suggesting that mentoring would most likely suit shared Visionary and Organic leadership rather than Classical leadership. The role of mentoring in Transactional leadership would depend on the extent to which power and communication extend beyond the managers.

Mentoring tends to be associated with *soft human resource systems* and management styles, and with organizations that seek to develop abilities, competencies and concepts in people and facilitate and encourage their use (see the BMW case study). This contrasts with systems of control and extrinsic motivation, the latter being seen as *hard human resource systems*. Thus, provision of mentoring opportunities is likely to be most consistent with Visionary and Organic leadership paradigms and adaptive organizations, but mentoring on tasks would also be compatible with Transactional leadership where the manager seeks to develop the followers.

CONCLUSION

This chapter has focused on approaches to leadership at the organizational and external levels, essential because understanding of leadership is limited if it concentrates merely on leader–follower relationships. An alternative approach involves discarding the individual perspective to focus on leadership as emerging from complex organizational systems. Here, leadership is not a property of individuals, but more of the interactions between people and between people and systems. Leadership arises as people work together, share information and tasks, and make commitments to each other in reciprocal relationships.

Related to the systems view of leadership is the concept of substitutes for leaders. This refers to how elements of the system, culture or operating environment can replace the need for supervision or other traditional leader roles. Substitutes for leaders are many and varied but include professional education for employees, closely knit teams, computer monitoring systems and guidelines. Another form of leader substitute is creating self-leading members in an organization.

Organizational culture reflects a group's striving towards integrating and creating shared patterns in the members' behavioural, emotional and cognitive functioning. This integration and patterning is achieved to varying extents in different groups and subgroups in an enterprise. Leaders are influential in creating and maintaining culture through the decisions they make and how they allocate resources. Leaders are often advised to manage or change an organization's culture to suit their objectives and/or vision. In strong cultures, in particular, this is very difficult to do and leadership may instead be more influenced by the organizational culture.

In addition to internal influences, leadership needs to take account of the external environment and consider the enterprise's future position. Organizations typically seek to develop a strategy to take account of external factors as well as internal capacity, striving to achieve an appropriate alignment between internal and external elements. Leadership occurs within a complex system comprising various subsystems that need to be aligned so that they fit together. This alignment creates the leadership capability of the entire organization. Aligning organizational processes, systems, culture and structure often enhances performance, but achieving alignment can be difficult in turbulent times as elements go in and out of fit. Different organizational environments lend themselves to varying degrees of planning formality, but detailed planning in today's fast-paced environments can be challenging, if not a waste of time. Smaller business units may need to develop their own strategies in keeping with the overall vision, strategy and organizational structure.

Another issue facing organizational leadership is whether to focus on shareholders or consider a broader range of stakeholders in pursuing shareholder value. Increasingly, successful organizations appear to be listening to a wide range of voices both within and outside the organization.

In responding to external changes, many organizations are striving to become learning organizations, to change into open systems that respond to feedback from both internal and external sources. Learning organizations evolve continuously, and systems of practice are needed that enable organizational members to acquire and transform their knowledge into action.

Two kinds of organizational learning have been identified: structural organizational learning focuses on problem solving, as opposed to achieving a vision under strategic organizational learning. These two kinds of organizational learning have been related to different organizational structures, and hence would relate to different leadership paradigms. Structural organizational learning, with its production focus, is probably more applicable to Classical and Transactional leadership, whereas strategic learning seems suited to Visionary and Organic paradigms.

Even more adaptive than learning organizations are teaching organizations, where executives participate in developing other leaders. Through this process, vision and values are discussed, feedback is two-way, and both teacher and learners benefit. A commonly used developmental tool is mentoring or sponsoring, whereby a more experienced individual or group helps develop a less experienced person or group.

The leader's role is changing from designer of structure, strategy and process to teacher and steward, where the leader as steward serves stakeholders and the overall mission underlying the enterprise.

How do these approaches to leadership relate to the leadership paradigms? Table 6.2 summarizes these relationships. Under Classical leadership, most macro-level approaches are not expected to be particularly relevant, although individual leaders may employ strategic tools like planning and aligning systems, and create or work with a particular organizational culture. However, learning is likely to take a structural form under the Classical Paradigm. For Transactional leaders, mentoring and substitutes for leadership can be used to create an appropriate environment for followers to work in, but again, learning would be more structural and related to solving problems than aimed at achieving a strategic vision.

By contrast, Visionary and Organic paradigms would relate more strongly to the approaches outlined in this chapter. Both paradigms are consistent with substitutes for leaders, working with culture, strategy, adopting a stakeholder focus, strategic learning and teaching, knowledge management, mentoring and servant leadership.

Table 6.2

Broad macro-level approaches related to the leadership paradigms

Classical	Transactional	Visionary	Organic
			Systemic focus
	Substitutes for leaders	Substitutes for leaders	Substitutes for leaders
		Self-management Culture Strategic planning Stakeholder focus	Self-leadership culture Strategic planning Stakeholder focus
Learning (structural)	Learning (structural)	Learning (strategic)	Learning (strategic)
	Mentoring	Knowledge management Teaching organization Mentoring Servant leader (steward)	Knowledge management Teaching organization Mentoring Servant leader (steward)

Visionary leadership would value self-managing followers to implement the common vision, whereas self-leading people would be more compatible with Organic leadership, where they can influence the organization's purpose. Organic leadership would recognize that leadership stems from elements in an organizational system and so would be expected to adopt a more systemic focus than the other paradigms. Nonetheless, all organizations operate within their own systems, which leadership needs to take account of.

In the next chapter, the theories and concepts covered in Chapters 4, 5 and 6 are integrated into the leadership paradigms in more detail.

NOTES

For full details of these notes, please see the References section at the end of this book.

1 Grendstad and Strand, 1999
2 e.g. Pfeffer, 1998
3 Bennis, 1989
4 Krantz, 1990
5 Mayrhofer, 1997

6 Lambert, 1995
7 Drath, 1998
8 Drath, 1998, 2001; Rost, 1991
9 Drath, 1998
10 Lawler and Mohrman, 1989
11 Mitroff and Pondy, 1978
12 Howell, Bowen, Dorfman, Kerr and Podsakoff, 1990
13 ibid.
14 ibid.
15 De Vries, Roe and Taillieu, 1998
16 ibid.
17 Manz, 1990; Manz and Sims, 1991
18 Manz, 1996:581–2
19 Manz, 1986
20 Schein, 1985
21 ibid.
22 Alvesson, 2002
23 Schein, 1992
24 ibid.
25 Gergen, 1997
26 O'Reilly, 1996
27 ibid.
28 e.g. Kotter and Heskett, 1992; Waldman and Yammarino, 1999
29 Kotter and Heskett, 1992
30 Schein, 1992
31 Mintzberg, 1973b
32 Tvorik and McGivern, 1997
33 Alvesson, 2002
34 e.g. Pfeffer, 1978
35 e.g. Intagliata, Ulrich and Smallwood, 2000
36 ibid.
37 O'Shannassy, 2003
38 ibid.
39 Mintzberg, 1973b
40 Adapted from Mintzberg, 1973b
41 O'Shannassy, 2003
42 e.g. Mintzberg, 1994; O'Shannassy, 2003; Zaheer, Albert and Zaheer, 1999
43 Complexity and Management Centre, 2000
44 Lawrence and Lorsch, 1967
45 Miller and Friesen, 1980
47 Masi and Cooke, 2000
46 Miller, 1990
48 e.g. Miles and Snow, 1978; Mintzberg, 1979
49 Geletkanycz and Hambrick, 1997; Lawrence and Lorsch, 1967

50 Estes, 1996
51 Ogden and Watson, 1999
52 Mitchell, Agle and Wood, 1997
53 Jones, 1995
54 Donaldson and Preston, 1995; Scott and Lane, 2000
55 Kraatz, 1998
56 Hillman and Hitt, 1999
57 Henriques and Sadorsky, 1999
58 Freeman, 1984
59 Donaldson, 1999
60 Collins and Porras, 1994; Judge, 1999
61 Kaplan and Norton, 1992
62 Collins and Porras, 1994
63 Pfeffer and Sutton, 1999
64 Herbert, 2000
65 Rousseau, 1997
66 Bechtold, 2000
67 Cross and Baird, 2000
68 Herbert, 2000
69 Dyer and Nobeoka, 2000
70 Rousseau, 1997
71 Sveiby, 2000
72 Deming, 1993
73 Bennis, 1998
74 Senge, 1990a
75 Pfeffer and Sutton, 1999
76 Sveiby, 2000
77 Tan, 2000
78 Pfeffer and Sutton, 1999
79 Abell, 2000
80 Klimecki and Lassleben, 1998
81 ibid.
82 Cohen and Tichy, 1997; Wolff, 1999
83 Cacioppe, 1998
84 Tichy, 1997
85 Lam, 2000
86 ibid.
87 Greenleaf, 1977; Senge, 1990b
88 Senge, 1990b
89 Tichy, 1997
90 Senge, 1990b
91 ibid.
92 Greenleaf, 1977
93 Aryee, Chay and Chew, 1996; Bernardin and Russell, 1993

94 Hilb, 1997

95 McCauley and Young, 1993

96 Berstein and Kaye, 1986; Douglas and McCauley, 1999; Noe, 1991; Rosenbach, 1993; Zey, 1991

97 e.g. Dreher and Ash, 1990; Kram, 1983

98 Kram, 1985

99 Burke and McKeen, 1997

100 Dreher and Ash, 1990; Fagenson, 1989

101 Chao, Walz and Gardner, 1991; Dreher and Ash, 1990

102 Wilson and Elmann, 1990

103 Sinclair, 1998

104 ibid.

105 Ragins and Scandura, 1994

106 Kram, 1985

107 Hunt and Michael, 1983

108 Noe, 1988; Wilson and Elman, 1990

109 Silverhart, 1994

110 Aryee, Chag and Chow, 1996

111 Scandura and Viator, 1994

112 Chao, 1997

113 Douglas and McCauley, 1999; Ragins, 1990

7 Integrating Theories and Paradigms

Key Points

- Theories and paradigms reviewed
- Linking theories and approaches with paradigm characteristics
- Pressure to change in the new environment
- Resistance to change
- Tomorrow's leadership

Leadership is a wide-ranging concept, which has been defined and approached in many different ways as scholars and practitioners seek to understand more about this elusive phenomenon. This is an important quest because leadership appears to impact organizational performance.

This book has introduced a framework based on four leadership paradigms: Classical, Transactional, Visionary and Organic. Some very diverse leadership theories and approaches have been structured around these paradigms in the preceding chapters, divided according to whether they affect the micro-level, macro-level or emotional aspects of leadership. This chapter integrates all the previous approaches into the paradigms, showing which theories and concepts appear to underlie which paradigms.

Trying to integrate so many important leadership ideas to the leadership paradigms is challenging for several reasons. First, there is no agreed definition of leadership or what the concept should embrace, leading to fuzzy and overlapping ideas throughout the literature. Different scholars have chosen particular facets of leadership to study according to their own interests, rather than building on each other's work to create definitions and theories that apply across different situations and organizational levels.

A second challenge in taking an integrative approach is that leadership research and writings still contain many gaps, making current knowledge far from complete. Some might say that the present attempt to integrate the pieces and take a broad view of leadership in the absence of a comprehensive and sound theoretical framework is foolhardy. No doubt, this attempt to graft inexact leadership concepts and approaches at poorly defined organizational levels onto four leadership paradigms will be enhanced and expanded as knowledge and theorizing become more complete. It is hoped that management scientists and practitioners alike will find the paradigms a useful starting point for their work.

Before integrating the theories and paradigms, the major approaches and paradigms are briefly reviewed, beginning with the theoretical approaches.

REVISITING THE THEORIES

Both micro- and macro-level approaches to leadership have been canvassed in Chapters 4, 5 and 6 to illustrate the multifaceted nature of leadership. Micro-level theories are concerned with an individual leader's characteristics, such as traits and behaviours. Dyadic and group-based approaches emphasize that leadership is not a solo endeavour on the part of designated heroic leaders, but involves interactions between leaders and followers. One emerging perspective is that perhaps leadership does not exist outside the perceptions of those observing it, typically the followers. This makes leadership an attribution of observers, rather than a characteristic of leaders themselves. Box 7.1 illustrates how vice presidents perceive their presidents differently in successful and unsuccessful organizations.

By adding a focus on how leadership differs with the situation, contingency theories take account of a broader context than just relationships between leaders and their followers. Situational Leadership, Fiedler's contingency model and House's Path-goal model emphasize situational factors such as the developmental level of the follower, the power and control a leader has in a given situation, and the need to clear obstacles from followers' paths in achieving goals.

Emotion, once excluded from leadership studies, has been fashionable in leadership theory since the mid-1980s. Concepts of emotional intelligence and charisma relate largely to the individual leader's characteristics, and his or her impact on individuals and groups. Calls for increased meaning and humanity in the workplace come from spiritual approaches, which generally promote a holistic and interconnected view of organizational members and their work and private lives.

Major emotion-based theories focus on inspirational and transformational leadership through which visionary leaders revolutionize the enterprises they lead.

Proponents claim that Visionary leadership enhances organizational performance over non-emotional leadership. The management literature appears to have 'fallen in love' with visionary approaches, attributing largely positive outcomes to such leaders and rarely recognizing the negative potential. The Visionary leader represents a return to the heroic Great Men theories in the larger-than-life portrayal of some of these leaders and their deeds, contrasting with the humility attributed to the Level 5 leader.

Other leadership issues become relevant as the level of analysis widens to consider the organizational and broader strategic impacts. A current view is that leadership does not vest in individual leaders or followers, but emerges from the interactions, commitments and other relationships between the members of an organization. Certainly, leadership occurs within a complex system and any comprehensive and useful theory needs to take account of the broader context.

The concept of alignment becomes important as people's activities need to be consistent with where the organization is going; the skills, needs and values of the members; and the demands of the external operating environment. With appropriate alignment, substitutes for leadership can reduce the need for leader involvement in many areas of the organization's activities. Systems can be developed to enhance substitutes for leadership, thereby freeing leaders for strategic and other activities, rather than controlling internal operations.

The organizational culture is clearly important, and many writers see managing the culture as a key leader activity. Organizational practices, behaviours and beliefs form part of the culture, as do values. Behaviour, beliefs and practices tend to be amenable to change. However, major organizational change often involves attempting to shift shared and even core values in an organization. While shared values might be changed with some difficulty, core values by definition are deep-seated and enduring.

Part of a leader's role at the macro-level includes formulating strategies for the future, along with plans to achieve them. In dynamic contexts, planning might be a rather futile activity, given that operating environments can change rapidly and make plans go out of date very quickly. A major debate concerns the extent to which an organization should consider stakeholders beyond shareholders, with many advantages derived from adopting the stakeholder model.

Similarly, an organization's systems, processes and people can go in and out of fit with the current strategy. Changing and realigning the structure and systems creates a major upheaval for affected organizations, representing heavy costs – particularly for tightly structured organizations with fixed processes and systems. Therefore, considerable misalignment within an organization tends to be tolerated for some time, until circumstances force the organization to undergo change.

On the other hand, an organization that constantly scans its environment and is ready for continual adaptation may not need to experience major upheaval. Instead it can shape its own future. Such adaptive enterprises are often called learning organizations. Members of learning organizations learn from customers, suppliers, formal training, discussions, mentoring, explicit teaching and many other sources. Knowledge is shared among the members in both formal and informal ways, so that even when members leave, the organization itself retains much of the knowledge. Two types of organizational learning are distinguished: *structural learning* drives people to find solutions to problems, whereas *strategic learning* pulls people to realize visions.

Box 7.1

How do presidents rate in the eyes of their VPs?

A study of 204 presidents of large US corporations, from leading manufacturers, service businesses and utilities, was conducted in 1989. Vice presidents were asked to rate their presidents on a range of factors.[1] The five areas investigated included leadership performance criteria, personal characteristics, leadership skills (technical, interpersonal and conceptual), personal traits and leadership behaviours. The findings are summarized for each of the five areas below.

- *Leadership performance criteria:* Most presidents were rated as strong on leadership performance. Only 3–4 per cent of presidents were rated as weak, while between 72–77 per cent were rated as strong on the four factors of general leadership, company knowledge, industry knowledge and their own reputation/track record.

- *Personal characteristics:* The vice presidents were asked to select five characteristics that best described their president. They chose the following five top characteristics: intelligent (66 per cent), determined (55 per cent), honest (39 per cent), forward-looking (38 per cent) and straightforward (37 per cent). The least chosen labels were cooperative (4 per cent), mature (8 per cent), broad-minded (8 per cent), loyal (9 per cent) and caring (12 per cent).

- *Leadership skills*: Presidents were seen overall as multiskilled individuals, strong in analytical and conceptual skills with persuasiveness ranking third (74 per cent, 71 per cent and 69 per cent respectively). Major weaknesses were seen as lack of tactfulness (7 per cent), poor self-planning (7 per cent) and poor group planning (8 per cent).

- *Personal traits:* The top five personal traits were energetic (83 per cent), self-confident (80 per cent), assertive (75 per cent), achieving (73 per cent) and ambitious (70 per cent). Truskie notes that both 'visionary' and 'participatory' traits were well down the list.[2]

- *Leadership behaviours:* Based on Kouzes and Posner's work, vice presidents ascribed the following five leadership behaviours to their presidents.[3] A majority of presidents challenge the process (64 per cent), encourage performance (61 per cent), model the way (58 per cent), and to some extent enable others to act (51 per cent). The lowest ranking behaviour was 'inspires a shared vision' (46 per cent).

Truskie then compared the more successful enterprises with the less successful ones, as indicated by the company's listing in *The Corporate 1000*. Both groups of presidents were similarly rated as intelligent, determined, honest and straightforward. Both groups tended to be adaptive rather than rigid, participative rather than authoritative, relaxed versus tense, warm and not cool, self-critical versus defensive, sensitive instead of insensitive, and conservative rather than liberal.

The two sets of leaders were also found to differ in various ways. For example, leaders of the more successful companies were seen by their executives as having a stronger reputation and track record, and as demonstrating their abilities more in activities such as strong leadership, business acumen and industry knowledge. They also tended to be more forward-looking, imaginative and inspiring than their counterparts, although the latter were seen as being more ambitious and independent.

Leaders of the more successful companies were rated higher on each of the leadership skill areas, particularly on persuasiveness (85 per cent, compared with 30 per cent of the other leaders). Presidents from less successful companies were rated strongly on leadership skills overall, but not as strongly as presidents from the more successful companies.

The most telling differences between the two groups emerged from the leadership behaviours, which the leaders of the more successful companies displayed more frequently than the other presidents. In particular, leaders of the less successful companies rarely or never displayed 'inspiring a shared vision' and 'enabling others to act'.

REVISITING THE LEADERSHIP PARADIGMS

The leadership paradigms differ in many characteristics. It is proposed that most of the distinguishing features tend to lie along a broad continuum, generally changing as one moves from the Classical through to the Organic paradigm. While further research is clearly needed to define and measure the changes along the proposed continua, the paradigms are provided as a useful framework for understanding many leadership issues.

Classical leadership

Classical leadership revolves around a powerful leader or elite group, who derive(s) power largely from fear or respect. This command-and-control style represents a pervasive stereotype of what leadership is about for many people. Followers have very low power in the Classical paradigm, beyond the power to withdraw their labour in some cases (but death awaited slaves who did not perform in ancient Egypt). On the other hand, followers are expected to assume little or no responsibility and accountability for outcomes, most of this falling to the leaders. Newtonian management thinking of cause and effect, and predictability, tends to underpin this paradigm. Diversity is largely ignored because the Classical leader's view predominates. Classical leadership lends itself to stable, simple or bureaucratic environments, and where high knowledge workers are not required to innovate. However, Classical leadership appears generally ineffective in dynamic situations requiring follower input, knowledge and commitment.

Transactional leadership

Followers are involved more under Transactional leadership than under the Classical paradigm. The Transactional leader consults and influences followers to achieve set goals. Although some mutual influencing occurs, the leader retains more power than followers. Leaders tend to base their power largely on reward and coercion, personal characteristics, and their interpersonal and influencing skills. Followers may have low power on a day-to-day basis, but can increase their power by withdrawing their support from the leader and previous agreements. Further, followers may band together to try to influence the leader.

Newtonian management ideas of creating order, searching for cause and effect relationships, predictability and valuing control underlie Transactional leadership, making this paradigm suitable for situations of low complexity. Leader responsibility and accountability for outcomes are high, with followers taking responsibility and accountability on a limited basis only. Diversity is dealt with in the organization or group where followers can voice opinions during consultation, but the leader's final view is expected to prevail after listening to the group. Transactional leadership can operate in simple, bureaucratic and divisional structures, but is not well-suited to self-managing knowledge workers. Adaptiveness is slowed down where followers need to participate and be influenced.

Visionary leadership

Visionary leadership is often praised as the ideal paradigm, especially in making major change to organizations. Here, the leader's vision inspires followers to greater achievements, with some research suggesting that performance is enhanced under Visionary leadership, compared with the Classical and Transactional paradigms. Followers need to play a substantial role in executing the vision to create a desired future, and self-managing knowledge workers are vital for realizing the vision. However, responsibility and accountability for outcomes reside with the leader.

The Visionary leader is dependent on followers to implement the vision, which enhances follower power above that typical of Classical and Transactional followers. Visionary leaders obtain their considerable power from various sources, including position, reference power, their vision (which should appeal to followers' needs and values), expertise and followers' emotional attachments to the cause. Whether charisma is essential to effective Visionary leadership is not clear. Bass indicates that charisma is an important component of his concept of Transformational leadership, while various other authors have found that charisma is not essential to effective leadership.

The management philosophy underlying the Visionary paradigm spans both Newtonian and New Science perspectives. Belief in the effects stemming from the leader's actions is typically strong, reflecting a Newtonian approach. However, Visionary leadership also lends itself to the more adaptive New Sciences view when leading change in chaotic environments, and hence in dealing with unpredictability and complexity. Visionary leadership appears to fit primarily with divisional and adaptive structures, and to operate in both dynamic and stable environments.

The Visionary leader's role is to meld the many views among group members into one shared vision. However, adherence to a strongly held vision and values can reduce the organization's agility and ability to change, particularly when organizational structures and systems have been aligned to achieve a particular vision. If the leader can inspire followers to align behind a new vision, adaptiveness can be more substantial than under the Classical and Transactional paradigms. This is because followers are ready to implement the new vision. They do not have to be coerced or otherwise influenced to go in the new direction.

Organic leadership

Under Organic leadership, leaders cease to be central because Organic leadership is based on processes of mutual sense-making. This paradigm encompasses both leader-less and leaderful organizations. Here, leadership is not necessarily vested in particular individuals, although people assume leadership roles for a time. Leadership is often determined by group consensus. More generally, the relationships between the members of the organization give rise to leadership, through the extensive communication processes that occur as members make sense of rapidly changing circumstances.

The entire group membership becomes key to Organic leadership, rather than any particular designated leader. Much of the leadership emanates from a shared vision and core values embedded within the organizational culture, and from aligning the supporting systems and processes within the organization. Management philosophy underlying Organic leadership derives from the New Sciences, and enables the organization to deal with high levels of complexity and adaptation (although the need for wide-ranging communication may initially slow change). Organic organizations tend to be continuously poised for change.

Organic leader control is typically minimal, with followers encouraged to be self-leading and self-organizing. Responsibility and accountability are shared, relying on self-accountability as individuals make commitments to complete specific tasks. Organic followers acquire high levels of power from expertise, personal, interpersonal and information sources. However, power tends to be shared across the members, rather than vested in leaders.

Mutual adjustment is a critical organizational principle. In other words, communication and information-sharing occupy considerable time in an Organically-led organization. Communication allows diverse views and values to be heard, accepted and accorded equitable treatment. Organic leadership lends itself to adhocracies and networked organizational structures, and to complex dynamic environments.

Although the paradigms have been distinguished in various ways, they cannot be assigned to watertight categories. Rather, they are intended to provide broad concepts for further discussion about, and understanding of, leadership's many facets. In practice, multiple paradigms are likely to be found in a given enterprise, particularly in large organizations.

Table 7.1

Linking theories and approaches to leadership paradigms

Classical	Transactional	Visionary	Organic
Behaviour	Behaviour	Behaviour	
Great Men	Great Men	Great Men	
Traits	Traits	Traits	
LMX	LMX	LMX	
Socio-cognitive	Socio-cognitive	Socio-cognitive	Socio-cognitive
Fiedler's model	Fiedler's model		
	Situational leadership		
	House's Path-goal	House's Path-goal	
		Emotional intelligence	Emotional intelligence
		Emotion	Emotion
		Charisma	
		Culture	Culture
		Knowledge management	Knowledge management
Learning (structural)	Learning (structural)	Learning (strategic)	Learning (strategic)
		Mentoring	Mentoring
		Self-management	Self-leadership
		Servant leader (steward)	Servant leader (steward)
		Spirituality	Spirituality
		Stakeholder focus	Stakeholder focus
		Strategic planning	Strategic planning
	Substitutes for leaders	Substitutes for leaders	Substitutes for leaders
		Teaching organization	Teaching organization
		Values	Values
		Vision	Vision
			Systemic leadership

INTEGRATING THEORIES AND PARADIGMS

In deepening an understanding of the many components of leadership, it is useful to summarize how the various approaches to leadership link to the Classical, Transactional, Visionary and Organic paradigms (see Table 7.1). These linkages are based on broad characteristics of the leadership paradigms. Not all theories are likely to fit perfectly into the four paradigms, but a surprising number do. Further, individual leaders classified under a particular paradigm may from time to time display characteristics attributed to other paradigms, rather than conforming to all aspects of a 'pure' paradigm. However, Table 7.1 is intended as a tool to indicate how the existing theories of leadership could broadly relate to the paradigms.

Basically, the Great Men, traits, behaviour, Leader Member Exchange, and socio-cognitive theories are compatible with the Classical paradigm. While it does not render a Classical leader ineffective to use strategy, emotional intelligence, vision, core values and tools such as mentoring, knowledge management and substitutes for leadership, these are not regarded as essential to Classical leadership. Classical leadership can be effective under stable conditions, as long as leaders and followers share this view of leadership, the leader's right to lead is accepted and conditions are not complex.

Contingency models apply partially to the Classical paradigm. Classical leadership relates to the high structure, high power and high control conditions of Fiedler's model (see Box 7.2, where Fiedler's model is more closely linked to the paradigms). Similarly, Situational Leadership's directing style fits Classical leadership, and Classical leaders can also remove obstacles to enable followers to see the relationships between their actions and set goals, as House's theory advocates. However, the latter two contingency approaches have not been listed in Table 7.1 because they apply only partially, and presume a stronger focus on followers than the Classical paradigm postulates. If organizational learning occurs, it is expected to be structural, that is, aimed at problem solving and operations.

Theories applying particularly to Transactional leadership include Great Men, traits, behaviour, socio-cognitive, Situational Leadership, Fiedler's model, Leader Member Exchange, Path-goal and substitutes for leadership. To the extent that Transactional leadership involves becoming a teaching/learning organization, structural organizational learning would be expected to prevail, with its focus on operations rather than on strategy or a vision. Although not central to this style, there is also no reason why Transactional leadership could not embrace mentoring, managing knowledge and knowledge workers and limited strategic planning, use emotional intelligence in relating to followers, and work through the organizational culture. Transactional leaders can also adopt servant leadership within their paradigm and encourage followers to become self-managing. However, while these approaches could work within a Transactional paradigm, they are not essential in

Box 7.2

Linking the leadership paradigms to Fiedler's model

Fiedler's contingency model relates fairly directly to Classical and Transactional leadership, as Figure 7.1 shows. Under conditions of high leader control and power, and structured task conditions, Classical leadership would be expected to operate with minimal relationship behaviour. Moderate-control conditions require more relationship behaviours, thereby favouring the Transactional paradigm over Classical leadership. In low control, or potentially chaotic conditions lacking group cohesion, Fiedler proposes that leadership becomes ineffective, favouring if anything, task focused leaders.

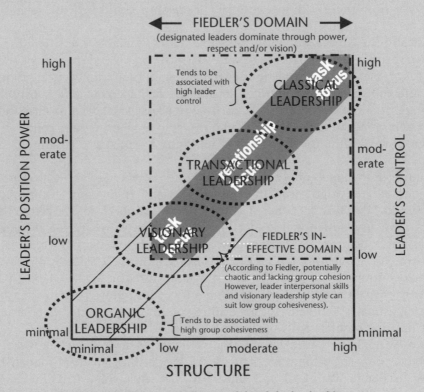

Figure 7.1   Potential links between Fiedler's model and the leadership paradigms © Harald Bergsteiner

However, an alternative view is that Fiedler's model could be extended to incorporate Visionary and Organic paradigms under conditions of low leader control and power, and poor task structure. This is illustrated in Figure 7.1. A relationship focus and low control by a designated leader (Visionary leadership), or the absence of control by a designated leader (Organic leadership), coupled with high group cohesiveness, could be effective.

characterizing that paradigm. Therefore, the less central theories have not been included in Table 7.1, which focuses on the approaches applying most generally to the paradigm.

Nearly all the theoretical concepts and techniques covered in this chapter are likely to be employed under Visionary leadership. These include Great Men, traits, behaviour, socio-cognitive, strategic planning, Leader Member Exchange, emotion, emotional intelligence, working with the organizational culture, Path-goal theory, substitutes for leadership, charisma, vision, values, self-management, learning organization (strategic emphasis), teaching and mentoring, servant leader, knowledge management and promoting spirituality. Tools like Situational Leadership and Fiedler's model, while not central to this style of leadership, may be instrumental in managing day-to-day operations, but have been omitted from this paradigm in Table 7.1.

Finally, Organic leadership, in not relying on an individual leader, would encompass only a selection of the leadership approaches. The following are most likely to be emphasized: emotion, emotional intelligence, spirituality, systemic leadership, vision, values-based leadership, substitutes for leadership, fostering self-leading employees, using the organizational culture, strategic planning, (through the group's sense-making activities), servant leader, socio-cognitive attributions, strategic learning, teaching, mentoring, and managing knowledge. While various other tools and techniques could be employed on occasion, they are not seen as core to Organic leadership.

Theoretically, all four leadership paradigms could include a focus on stakeholders, providing that leaders are prepared to recognize multiple views from both within and outside the enterprise. This recognition is likely to increase as more voices are heard within the organization. Therefore, given the increasing role of followers across the paradigms, the likelihood of a broad focus on stakeholders being adopted is probably lowest under Classical and Transactional leadership, increases under Visionary leadership, and has the greatest chances under Organic leadership.

Examining Table 7.1 suggests that very few approaches span all four paradigms. One that does is socio-cognitive theory, with its emphasis on leadership being a follower attribution based around particular stereotypes or schemata. The stereotypes associated with each of the paradigms enable the paradigms to be recognized as leadership by observers, especially followers. Learning is also attributed to each paradigm, although the nature and extent of learning are expected to vary. Problem-focused structural learning is likely to concern Classical and Transactional leaders, while strategic learning aligned to a vision is more appropriate to Visionary and Organic paradigms. In addition, Organic leadership is expected to be the paradigm most concerned about creating teaching and mentoring organizations.

To the extent that all enterprises need a means of moving towards some future state, strategic-level approaches are relevant to all paradigms. Planning, aligning processes, systems, people and culture, are fundamental to organizing. However, the paradigms most focused on adapting to the future, namely Visionary and Organic, are likely to be most concerned with strategy for achieving that future, even if plans are loose rather than tight for maximum flexibility.

WHERE TO NEXT?

Although one of the four paradigms can usually be seen to prevail in organizations, or parts of an organization, there is no doubt that many external pressures are driving fundamental change. At the Royal Australian Navy and Bonduelle, competition for attracting talent, increasing demand for retaining knowledge workers, and changing technology are among the factors pressuring these organizations to change from Classical leadership. EKATO and Rodenstock expended considerable resources in moving from Classical towards Organic leadership and self-managing employees. For EKATO, this was a question of survival, and for Rodenstock speed is part of their core business. SAP has had to become more customer focused and remove many of its Transactional management constraints to survive in the fast-paced IT industry and stop its managers from leaving. Innovation is driving Swatch, Novartis and BMW to focus on promoting self-leadership as they strive to become more organic and thus competitive in fast-paced markets.

In short, although four paradigms can be distinguished, external factors are driving many organizations towards Organic leadership, as most of the case studies in Part Two show. The question becomes, what form of Organic leadership will different organizations adopt? All Gore's departments, from R&D to manufacturing and sales, function under the Organic model. Other organizations subject to heavy regulations or unable to sustain failure, such as airlines or hospitals, may be reluctant to become Organically-led across the entire organization, preferring to retain different paradigms in different parts of the organization. In individual departments that need high levels of creativity, such as marketing or R&D, Organic leadership could prevail, while the more regulated areas function under Transactional leadership (see the Swatch case study). However, even in manufacturing and regulated areas, the input from all employees is needed for continuous improvement and adapting to change.

Moving to Organic leadership from the other paradigms is not likely to be easy. For many organizations this would involve cataclysmic change and disruption, requiring them to totally reinvent themselves – which would only be entertained for very compelling reasons. A fundamental consideration is that individual members of the organization hold schemas of what leadership is, and that these schemas influence their comfort with particular paradigms.[4] This can be a challenge for global organizations where cultural differences affect what is seen as constituting leadership (see Chapter 3), making it potentially difficult to find followers comfortable with the other paradigms in some locations. For example, in some cultures, models of leadership similar to the Classical paradigm prevail, where followers expect leaders to make decisions without consulting them, be highly directive, shoulder all responsibility, and be accountable for outcomes (see the Bonduelle case study). In this context, a leader espousing a vision, inviting follower participation, involving followers in decision making and expecting followers to operate as self-managing individuals may not even be recognized as exhibiting leadership and may be seen instead as a leader trying to pass on his or her responsibilities to followers.[5] In this case, followers and leaders would be operating on different stereotypes or schemas for what constitutes 'leadership'. However, for most organizations, the twenty-first century business environment will inevitably involve change, requiring leaders and followers alike to adjust their leadership paradigms accordingly.

Achieving alignment between the leadership schemas held by a particular set of leaders and followers will often be a challenge. Organic leadership at Gore may dismay prospective associates used to being directed, and such people may avoid the organization. On the other hand, self-leading followers tend to find the Classical and Transactional styles a poor match for their needs. Call centres operating along Transactional lines can expect high turnover among their professionally-educated staff, for whom automated monitoring and directing may be too constraining. Attracting and retaining knowledge workers, and those seeking more spirituality in the workplace, is an increasing challenge for organizations operating under Classical and Transactional paradigms. A radical change of paradigm might well involve losing staff who preferred the previous leadership culture, and this loss can be costly for an organization. But then so can continuing to operate under an inappropriate paradigm.

What about people who resist paradigm changes? Clearly, support is needed to help managers used to supervising and directing others to change to a more collaborative style, and to train employees generally in possibly unfamiliar work processes like communication, problem solving, working in teams, conflict resolution and self-management and self-leading. Companies like EKATO and BMW invest heavily in on-going training to help team leaders adjust to their new role, and train all members to ensure smoothly running teams. At Gore, communication is a major focus of workplace training. Thus, extensive training and support will be needed in adapting to a new paradigm.

The leadership paradigms can be used to challenge stereotypical views of leadership and help people accept that leadership is complex, encompassing multiple dimensions. The paradigms can clarify that employees from diverse backgrounds will have different ways of understanding leadership, whether the diversity stems from gender or national culture, education or field of expertise. If people can be helped to see where others are coming from, they can appreciate the differences rather than dismissing them. Further, the paradigms can help in the change process by highlighting the current paradigm(s) prevailing in an organization, showing where the people need to move to and why.

A serious incentive for Transactional leaders, and to some extent Classical leaders, to make the transition to more emotion-based and follower-based paradigms is that the future of their very role could be limited. Many aspects of Transactional leadership are being automated, with computer systems increasingly supervising and monitoring employees' behaviour in the workplace, assigning work tasks, providing on-line help and delivering e-learning packages. Even HR functions, so recently devolved to the line-manager, are now being centrally automated via on-line and call systems, taking much of the HR management away from managers.

As knowledge work increases and computer technology takes over management functions, fewer Transactional managers will be needed in the workplace.

The leader-centric Visionary paradigm is also limited in the new century because a singular vision can be wrong, and followers may become cynical and uncooperative if the vision keeps changing. Questions of succession arise with an all-pervasive leader, particularly whether successors can maintain the emotional link to followers necessary for Visionary leadership. In its extreme form, Visionary leaders may not accept the vital checks and balances coming from close associates needed to anchor their behaviour in reality, as narcissistic leaders have shown. An alternative form of leadership may stem from the unassuming, non-heroic Level 5 leader who shares the credit, does not profile him or herself and yet achieves high levels of organizational performance.

Since organizations have to be agile and innovative to survive and thrive in fast-moving environments, thus experiencing pressure to move towards an Organic paradigm, organizations would be wise to de-emphasize the heroic leader. Instead, they should focus on becoming leaderful, where leadership resides in different people depending on the situation and expertise required. Some outsiders have difficulty conceiving how Gore can successfully operate manufacturing, sales, R&D and other functions based in many countries using an Organic model. It is probably less difficult to accept the more limited idea of different paradigms suiting different parts of an organization. This would be a step in what appears to be a sustainable and inevitable direction for many enterprises.

CONCLUSION

From Part One of this book, it is evident that the concept of leadership is very broad and takes a variety of different meanings, which are often confusing and limited in scope. In seeking to capture the complexity and richness of organizational leadership, this book has used two frameworks that integrate and distinguish characteristics of different leadership concepts. The first framework identifies four leadership paradigms or fundamental approaches that leaders and followers take to leadership. The leadership paradigms are distinguished from one another using a range of academic and practical knowledge. This allows readers to view the depth of each paradigm while relating it to the other paradigms. Building on this, a second framework summarizes scholarly approaches taken to leadership, showing how they apply to the four paradigms.

By integrating many facets and levels of leadership in the leadership paradigms, this book attempts to reflect the complexity of leadership in practice. It draws on diverse ideas, theories and research findings relating to leadership from various fields, including the behavioural sciences, sociology, strategic planning, management and the physical sciences. Issues covered range from looking at the individual leader through to systemic and organic concepts of leadership; from the micro-level focus on follower and frontline manager through to strategic leadership; and from classical ideas to suggesting approaches to tomorrow's leadership. This book highlights more than the importance of aligning organizational systems and processes with different kinds of leadership. It also shows the need for congruence between the kind of leadership used and the often-unverbalized beliefs of the organization's diverse members.

The specific intention of this book has been to develop a theoretical framework that allows a more differentiated and yet focused discussion of leadership issues raised by the case studies in Part Two. That such an analytical discussion is likely to be important and worthwhile is reinforced by research indicating that leadership has an impact on a firm's performance. In other words, since leadership does appear to make a difference, it is valuable to analyse the key factors that underlie its effects.

Part Two contains ten case studies illustrating many aspects of leadership in different contexts. The leadership paradigms are intended as tools for examining how different kinds of leadership operate within diverse organizations and contexts. The reader now has the opportunity to apply to these case studies the ideas, paradigms, theories and approaches to leadership discussed in Part One of this book. It is hoped that this will continue the process of understanding where leadership is headed in the future.

NOTES

For full details of these notes, please see the References section at the end of this book.
1   Truskie, 1990
2   ibid.
3   Kouzes and Posner, 1987
4   Lord and Maher, 1991
5   ibid.

Part Two

Case Studies

The purpose of the following case studies is to show how successful organizations are approaching leadership at the beginning of the twenty-first century, a period characterized by great turbulence. The case studies, which generally represent a snapshot in time between 1999–2001, were written by people with first-hand knowledge of each organization, gained either from working in the organization or from researching, visiting and speaking with senior management and other people there. This information was supplemented by data from the web, media and information supplied by the organizations themselves. The selected organizations come from a range of industries and leadership contexts, including manufacturing, service and knowledge-based industries.

All organizations in the case studies are trying to adapt themselves to changing environments to ensure their sustainability, requiring them to take a variety of approaches to leadership. The case studies illustrate many different forms of leadership ranging from Classical, through Transactional and Visionary to Organic paradigms. Most exhibit mixtures of different leadership styles. Critical is the alignment between ideas of leadership held by leaders and followers with the organization's systems, processes, culture, structure and strategic intent.

The case studies are described using a variety of formats, and vary in length depending on the amount of information available to the writers. Some of the information is in the public domain, but most of the insights into the intangible field of leadership could only emerge from the inside knowledge provided by each organization. The author is immensely grateful to the executives who gave of their time and wisdom for this project.

At the beginning of each case study is a key insight from a senior organizational representative. They each end with issues for discussion that link the case study back to the leadership paradigms and the theoretical approaches to leadership outlined in Part One. A summary of key issues follows the description of each case study, to provide a guide to answering the discussion questions.

One **BMW: Sheer Driving Pleasure**[1]

GAYLE C. AVERY

BMW Group products are in greater demand worldwide than ever before. Fiscal 2000 was a year of records, with deliveries, sales, and profits reaching a new all-time high. This is the result of our brand strength, our product substance, and our decision to reorient the BMW Group along new strategic lines.[2]

Joachim Milberg, CEO

Bayerische Motoren Werke's (BMW) long, proud history starts with its founding in 1916 by Gustav Otto, the son of the inventor of the internal combustion engine. The company began by producing aeroplane engines, shifting to automobile production in the late 1920s. Today, the Munich-based Quandt family owns over 48 per cent of this publicly-listed company with its worldwide reputation for highly engineered cars. At the beginning of the new millennium, more than 5 million BMWs were on the road in over 130 countries.[3]

One of the world's 12 largest car manufacturers,[4] BMW remains an independent automobile manufacturer in an industry that *The Economist* describes as being in a 'fever of consolidation'. Headquartered in Munich, BMW employed over 97 000 people in 2001, operating at sales and distribution locations in 26 countries, and at 15 production sites and 8 plants.[5] The company has so far resisted takeover and hostile consolidation attempts. However, the leadership faces many challenges, including a worldwide oversupply of cars, with the car industry as a whole capable of producing millions more cars than it is likely to sell.[6]

In trying to survive by growing, BMW had acquired British Rover in 1994. However, this acquisition was unsuccessful, and Rover was sold off in 2001 after creating heavy losses for BMW and leading to the dramatic departure of the responsible CEO, Bernd Pischetsrieder. Pischetsrieder moved to Volkswagen, leaving his successor to build a new strategy for BMW under difficult conditions.

Joachim Milberg had taken over from Pischetsrieder as CEO and Chairman of the Board of Management in 1999.[7] Milberg had previously been on the Management Board, responsible for production, since 1993 before becoming CEO. After his retirement in 2002, Milberg was to become a Member of the Supervisory Board at BMW. According to the Chairman of the Supervisory Board, Volker Doppelfeld, 'under Milberg, the enterprise experienced the most successful period in its history'.[8] Dr Helmut Panke was appointed successor to Milberg as CEO and Chairman of the Board of Management.[9]

Car production steadily increased between 1997 and 2001 from 672 238 to a record 904 335 BMWs in 2001.[10] In addition, over 42 000 MINIs were produced in 2001, along with 100 213 motorcycles.

Commanding a premium price for its cars, BMW recorded a net loss in 1999, but was already back in profit in 2000. The difficulties encountered by BMW are not surprising, given the challenges of market downturns, overcapacity and increasing competition from Ford, Daimler-Chrysler and other major car manufacturers. More informed consumers also pose challenges because of their expectations of increased product options and better service. BMW's then Chief Financial Officer, and current CEO, Helmut Panke (see Box CS1.1), was able to present a record profit in 2000 of €1209 million. In 2001, BMW's net profit was even larger, at €1866 million.[11] The BMW Group managed to increase retail sales by more than 10 per cent in 2001, in a world market that is stagnating.

Box CS1.1

Portrait of CEO Helmut Panke

Trained as a physicist, Helmut Panke has been with BMW for about 20 years, taking over the helm in 2002. Panke's varied background includes experience abroad and across different areas of the organization, in addition to having worked in various industrial sectors. Born in 1946, Panke spent one year studying in the US before completing his doctorate at Munich University. He worked as a nuclear researcher at a Swiss institute and taught at Munich University before moving to the private sector in 1978.[30]

From then until 1982, Panke was a consultant at McKinsey in Dusseldorf and Munich, and then joined BMW. He headed the planning and controlling department within the R&D division, becoming responsible for the important areas of organization and strategic planning. In 1993 he was appointed head of BMW Holding in the US. A member of the Management Board since 1996, Panke was initially responsible for HR and IT, but in 1999 he took over responsibility for finance following the personnel changes resulting from the Rover crisis.

At BMW, production is customer driven, with pressure for made-to-order vehicles being assembled in hours rather than weeks. This is a problem throughout the industry. At BMW these processes are being continually improved, managed by a centralized Logistics Group, whose objective is to achieve punctual delivery and acceptable completion times (known as 'time quality' at BMW).

THE 'PREMIUM' BRAND STRATEGY

BMW's slogan of 'sheer driving pleasure' aims to attract car owners around the world who enjoy high-performance, innovative, luxury vehicles. The company claims that its brand profile has developed over many years into being synonymous with energy, performance and sheer driving pleasure.[12] The BMW brand also stands for determination and high standards, with professionalism defining every element. This gives the brand a strong and consistent position, defined by its clearly profiled identity.

BMW protects its valuable brand, building its growth strategy on maintaining the brand at a 'premium' level in every market sector. The BMW Group, a multi-brand automobile manufacturer, pursues a consistent, pure premium brand strategy ranging from the smallest car all the way to the top segment. The intention is that BMW products and the image presented to customers make the premium strategy of the organization clear and tangible in all areas, creating an obvious distinction from most of the competition.[13] Even the new MINI brand, in production in Oxford since April 2001, is positioned as a premium product in the rapidly growing small car segment. As of 2003, BMW rounded off its brand spectrum with Rolls-Royce cars.

ORGANIZATION

Publicly-listed German companies are structured with a Supervisory Board and a Board of Management. At BMW, the Supervisory Board consists of 21 members. The Quandt family appoints the Chairman, and has two direct representatives on the Supervisory Board: Stefan Quandt and Susanne Klatten (née Quandt). Approximately half the Supervisory Board consists of BMW employees, while other members represent various internal business units and external partners.[14]

BMW is structured around teams. The ten-member Board of Management forms the highly-qualified executive management team. The next level of management comprises a complex network of interrelated, multi-skilled teams that extend vertically and horizontally throughout the organization, from middle management all the way to the factory floor.[15] In 1997, self-organizing teams of 8–15 people were set up in the production areas, and subsequently extended to design, engineering and administration. These highly-skilled employees, or 'associates' in the BMW culture, are empowered to self-organize, make decisions, solve problems and operate under a working structure that blends satisfaction with efficiency to suit BMW conditions and culture. The team decides how tasks are rotated within the team and across team products. Not only do employees work in teams, but individual production plants form a comprehensive production network.

The performance management system supports the team-based organization and rewards individuals for their contribution to the team. Training helps group members move smoothly from working under supervision to working in a self-managing group.

In addition, BMW has moved away from the classic division of labour to integrating the functions of workers and managers, reflecting a new way of thinking about manager–worker relationships, and providing workers with a greater understanding of how the company operates. Employees at all levels are expected to think in business terms, and BMW's work structures are designed to support responsible, business-focused workers. Self-managing teams make their own decisions and carry responsibility for quality assurance, logistics, production and maintenance, which had all previously been the responsibility of various departments external to the teams.[16]

BMW teams enjoy a high degree of autonomy as well as group responsibility and provide a forum for continuous improvement. Each group has a spokesperson who works as a member of the group as well as coordinating its activities, chairing discussions and representing the group to the company as a whole. Elected by the group, this person does not have the power to give orders or take disciplinary action, but needs to influence others.[17]

INNOVATION IS FUNDAMENTAL

'Innovation is a state of mind', according to former BMW Board Member, Dr W. Reitzle, and every customer needs to be guaranteed the highest possible engineering and technology.[18] 'Thinking along new lines is the prerequisite for progress. What is needed are innovations that provide benefit and pleasure to our customers,' wrote Milberg in the 2001 annual report. True to its philosophy, BMW has created a Research and Engineering centre in Munich with about 6000 engineers, designers, model builders, information technologists and scientists, along with purchasing staff and supplier specialists. BMW in

Japan also assesses design and technology advances in Asia, while BMW's Technology Office in California liaises with US electronic, telecommunications and new materials companies.

Innovations in the pipeline at BMW include headlights that know when the next bend is approaching, traffic jam warnings that sense a traffic jam, steering that shortens stopping distances, and engines able to breathe more freely.

QUALITY

Quality is a key concern at BMW and underpins the value of the brand. Each self-managing work team is customer focused, passing superb quality along to the next production team (their internal 'customers'). BMW has developed a range of quality management tools, which suppliers also use. These include quality function deployment, cross-functional teams, statistical process control, as well as risk analysis and process optimization. Quality control is tracked internally at each stage of production, and audits are conducted throughout the manufacturing process. This focus on quality has reduced the number of suppliers, and the remaining suppliers conform to the quality standards in ISO/DIN 9000 as well as undergoing regular audits.

All employees participate in Quality Circles. The production line is stopped twice each month for at least one hour per shop for team discussions. Problems, solutions, ideas and learning programs form the focus of these meetings. Groups have a choice of about 35 training modules covering a range of topics, including quality. Learnings from the chosen programs are followed up at the next month's discussion.

PARTNERS

Cooperation with suppliers is extensive to ensure that suppliers know of BMW's requirements, and allows BMW to take account of supplier limitations and future developments. For example, suppliers are involved in processes aimed at continuous improvement at the early stages of production and are linked together through an electronic data network. This ensures that production costs are kept as low as possible, and helps produce optimal designs. Suppliers also receive extensive feedback about BMW's production processes to assist them in improving their own processes.

SUSTAINABILITY

The principle of sustainable business development is based on the belief that no generation should live at the expense of successive generations. BMW's corporate responsibility encompasses not only the needs of employees, but also those of the environment and society as a whole, showing a more human face within the global economic system. Like other companies that are committed to sustainability, BMW places equal importance on economic, ecological and social concerns in the formulation of their business strategies. Safeguarding and creating jobs, and commitment to the environment, are considered just as important as innovative, problem-solving expertise and open dialog.[19] Every individual within BMW is called upon to actively implement these objectives in their individual sphere of influence. BMW plants fulfil tasks and duties to the community beyond the provision of jobs by opening their plants to visitors daily, seeking to be a good neighbour and partner for the local region, and actively sponsoring cultural and sporting events.

Taking care of the environment is also important at BMW – beyond government requirements. BMW operates under the added pressure of occupying a manufacturing location in Munich's central area surrounded by people's homes, in addition to greenfield sites. In 1973, the company appointed its first Environmental Commissioner at the same time as it started experimenting with the hydrogen-powered car. In 1989, BMW introduced water-based paints into the paint shops, and by 1997 paints were powder-based and solvent-free. In 1990, BMW opened its own car dismantling and recycling plant, and now the 3 series is almost completely recyclable, while the 5 series is about 85 per cent recyclable. Not only have BMW cars been designed to reduce fuel consumption, but the amount of water required to produce a car is continually being reduced. Other ways of protecting the environment include transporting components and finished products by rail wherever possible, and creating flexible work schedules that permit BMW employees to travel outside peak hours.

The annual sustainability-rating index produced by the Swiss investment and ratings agency, SAM Sustainability Group, attests to the BMW Group's success. This index is based on an assessment of around 2000 of the world's largest companies in 64 sectors and 36 countries. In two consecutive years, BMW has been nominated the worldwide leader in the automobile industry by demonstrating high achievements in economic, ecological and social spheres. Its listing in the *Dow Jones Sustainability Group Index* also shows that companies can reap financial benefits through active involvement in social and environmental issues.[20]

KNOWLEDGE MANAGEMENT

The BMW Knowledge Management Division aims to motivate employees to acquire and exchange knowledge. One way BMW does this is through its on-line learning market, using its Intranet as an 'electronic marketplace' to provide learning services for a growing number of users. In 1999, BMW organized almost 7000 training events for over 40 000 employees. In that year alone, the BMW Group spent almost €90 million on the training and development of its employees – about the equivalent of the annual budget of an average-sized German university.

BMW captures its employees' experience through the i-motion suggestion program, under which employees continuously improve the firm's performance. I-motion enables and encourages associates to influence the workplace and receive rewards (up to about €15 000) for good ideas reflecting engagement, quality and cost savings. Team leaders score ideas with points reflecting how much value the idea adds to the workplace in what is intended to be a rapid, direct and non-bureaucratic decision-making process. During the trial run in 1998/99, around one suggestion for every second employee was submitted, resulting in direct cost savings of €50 million.[21]

HUMAN RESOURCES POLICY

Considerable value is placed on people at BMW. According to the BMW Group website, the human factor is the number one criterion in determining a company's relative success, and BMW associates are thus an essential performance factor. The BMW HR policy is an integral feature of overall corporate policy in both strategic and operational decisions, although its shape has changed over time.[22] In 1983, a value-oriented staff policy was introduced to secure the people side of the business operations. Here people were no longer viewed as a cost, but as an investment. By 1989, major changes taking place in Germany following the fall of the Berlin Wall meant that BMW needed to attract the highest-potential employees. By 1994, BMW had developed a long-term HR policy aimed at increasing its international competitiveness through both cost efficiencies and performance improvement. Optimizing expenditure on staff enhanced performance and reduced costs in three main ways:

- by enhancing staff ability (thereby securing staff potential);
- willingness (through leadership and cooperation); and
- staff opportunities (through HR systems, compensation and flexible working systems).[23]

Associates and employer enjoy an explicitly symbiotic relationship in which the organization makes demands on its employees – who in turn make demands on the BMW Group.[24] As a future-oriented company, BMW seeks to pursue a creative and associate-oriented HR policy, making significant contributions to business success through their HR activities. As part of this process, every two years management and others rotate jobs within their areas. People apply for open positions or are nominated for them.[25]

Training is very strong at BMW, including group training. Shop floor staff attend special training weekends, designed to promote teamwork on the line. Over three years, every team attends a three-day workshop, allowing the company to enter the next phase of teamwork training. Learning is regarded as lifelong at BMW, enabling employees to keep up to date, contribute to the process of change, and capitalize on opportunities. The company offers a wide range of training in different professions and trades, using varied learning and teaching methods.[26]

BMW has hundreds of flexible working time models, driven partly by the need for efficiency in managing expensive German labour and seasonally-induced short working times, while running the expensive production machines for longer. Separating human and machine operating times achieves considerable flexibility through a variety of plant-specific working time models and regulations.[27] For example, at the Munich plant, associates work four days per week, while in Regensburg employees enjoy five consecutive days off every three weeks to compensate for working nine-hour shifts at other times. The Berlin motorcycle plant irons out peaks and troughs in demand for its products by employees working longer hours in summer and fewer in winter. At the Dingolfing Plant located in a rural community, BMW normally closes in August to enable its employees to join in the harvest on their family farms. Working hours and operating times are oriented on market demand in order to quickly meet customers' needs, and to also enhance employees' work/life balance.[28]

LEADERSHIP

A major challenge for BMW as a large, distributed manufacturing organization is how to be innovative and agile in responding to the fierce pressures in a rapidly changing and highly competitive global environment. When asked about his aims for the company, Milberg said that '… the most important thing is that … [the CEO] … must be someone with vision and the ability to turn his vision into reality together with his team.'[29] Milberg continued by saying, 'it's important for a company to have a culture of openness and the courage of one's convictions.' When asked how he intended to implement that at BMW, he replied, 'I work according to it. It's part of the leadership style to point out perspectives, define tasks, and then agree on objectives. That also includes reporting back if agreed targets are not met, which demands a certain amount of courage. Employees must not withdraw into passive roles.'

One way of achieving this is through collaboration between workforce and management, based on mutual trust and a mature partnership. This culture of trust demands individual responsibility, self-organization and flexibility – with maximum continuity.

Leadership is highly valued at BMW, although the firm does not publicly display its mission, vision or values. Instead, its key message of enjoyment, quality and high performance seems to apply to employees as much as to products. As visitors to the BMW site wrote, 'During the site visit we were witness to and accepted that every worker in BMW lives and breathes BMW. Perhaps the very name BMW, and all that it symbolizes, has previously represented the vision of the company. From this perspective, perhaps BMW had cultured a sense of vision and mission without ever needing to put it to print ...'[31] This form of vision appears distributed throughout the organization, encouraged through the BMW Associate and Leadership Model.

BMW's Associate and Leadership Model, driven by Chairman Milberg, forms the cornerstone of the leadership process, both in setting out requirements and providing direction. This model, designed to support team and process-oriented cooperation, is a long-term leadership strategy aimed at creating a culture of 'We at BMW'. Personal responsibility, self-reliance and approaching change as a form of opportunity are encouraged.

The Associate and Leadership Model comprises two main parts: the associate model and the leadership model. The associate model sets individual goals and expectations throughout the workforce, while the leadership component challenges management to view its actions and activities within a culture of proactive leadership and development. Criteria for evaluating leadership include:

- achieving business goals (both hard and soft goals);
- displaying corporate thinking and acting;
- possessing technical and professional competency;
- showing leadership and team behaviour; and
- holding personal qualities.

Using these criteria, both high- and underperforming leaders can be identified.

The core philosophy behind the overall model is to:

- generate a culture of trust;
- provide orientation;
- promote cooperation; and
- realize responsibility (especially self-responsibility and self-organization).

The model is based on ten leadership principles:

1 Increasing risk-taking
2 Role modelling
3 Agreed objectives
4 Fun
5 Efficient teams
6 Realistic visions
7 Achieving business goals
8 Communication
9 Building trust and confidence
10 Diversity

The Associate and Leadership Model aims at developing a distributed 'leaderful' organization. Leadership is benchmarked internally via employee surveys and through a feedback process involving subordinates. This supplements a top-down annual performance management process. As part of this annual review, an individual's potential as a manager is assessed and compared with that of other managers. All first-line managers review and discuss the second-line managers as part of the benchmarking process, comparing 'my best manager against your best manager.'[32] This initiative provides the template for managing the performance and potential of every individual within BMW.

BMW rarely hires top executives from outside, preferring to 'grow their own lifelong managers' from within the organization, unless a critical skill gap cannot be filled internally. BMW's active management development process involves three components:

1 corporate development programs (for example, on culture and e-commerce);
2 professional development programs (for example, skills such as conflict management); and
3 dialog (for example, communication skills, working cross-functionally).

These processes are managed through customized in-house training, typically undertaken through alliances with freelance trainers and business schools.

In addition, special programs help develop future leaders, such as providing global managers with opportunities to spend three to five years abroad, after which employees are required to return home. The leadership part of the Associate and Leadership Model is aligned with the 'Drive' management development program, intended to 'strengthen, broaden and accelerate the specialist and management potential of junior personnel, in a consistent and progressive way.'[33] In 2000, 1000 young BMW associates participated in the Drive program, with a view to the most promising forming the basis for BMW's future management.[34] The Drive program aims to develop qualified graduates and doctoral students.

The name 'Drive' is rich in symbolism, suggesting energy, mobility, ambition, being active and thinking and acting in an entrepreneurial way. The Drive program seeks to deploy new, well-trained employees in a rational way, supporting their enthusiasm and promoting the overall quality of their performance. Each Drive participant is provided with a mentor for the 18–24 month duration of their contract, and at various stages during the program assessment and reviews are undertaken for each candidate, including evaluating their performance, personality and potential for further development. After the Drive program, the participants may or may not be taken on as permanent employees.

DISCUSSION ISSUES

1 Which paradigm(s) of leadership can you see operating at BMW? What is the leaders' view and expectation of followers? Are the systems, processes, and leadership and followership ideas aligned appropriately?

2 Where is leadership located at BMW? Does the structure support this kind of leadership appropriately? Can you identify any substitutes for leadership?

3 BMW has no explicit vision or values statement. Is this a failing or are there possible substitutes for vision and values operating at BMW? What might they be?

4 Can you comment on the challenges in a large organization like BMW becoming an agile, market-responsive, innovative company that uses the potential of its employees? Is there evidence of empowerment, personal development, opportunities for self-actualization and self-development at BMW?

5 Is BMW developing spirituality in the workplace? Can you see evidence of emotion?

6 What does BMW do that would attract and retain the kinds of workers it seeks? What is the role of the HR department in developing leadership?

7 Do you find evidence that BMW is a learning or teaching organization? Is it a knowledge-based organization? If so, where is the evidence?

8 How is leadership developed and spread in the company? What roles do mentoring and training play at BMW?

9 Who are the stakeholders at BMW? How are they taken into account as part of the firm's sustainability philosophy?

10 What role do the major shareholders, the Quandt family, seem to play in the company's leadership?

KEY ISSUES

- BMW's size could drive it to being bureaucratic and divisional, yet it is trying to operate in a collaborative and organic way.
- Culture of trust.

- Self-managing teams, empowered workers, self-organizing employees.
- Management is primarily by self-managing teams.
- BMW's brand appears to provide the vision internally, as well as drive the growth strategy.
- Considerable evidence for training, for example, capturing knowledge through the Intranet, quality circles, i-motion and other programs.
- As a global company, BMW has strategies for developing global managers.
- Innovation is a state of mind.
- Corporate intelligence is evident in the technology centres, plus close liaison with suppliers.
- Cross-functional teams, quality circles and other modern quality management tools are employed.
- Close cooperation with suppliers brings them into the web of management too, for example, BMW audits suppliers and liaises closely with them to obtain extensive feedback.
- Sustainability and giving back to society is a value, as is protecting the environment.
- Highly rated company on sustainability indexes.
- Extensive training and development for associates.
- Advanced HR policies, for example, bank of hours, flexible work times.
- The Quandt family appears powerful as the major shareholder, for example, they appoint the Chairman of the Supervisory Board and have two family members on this Board.
- Employees at all levels are expected to think in business terms.
- Associate and Leadership (not leader!) Model aims at creating trust, orientation, cooperation and responsibility in the culture.
- Strong Drive program to develop future leaders and personnel generally.
- Seek to develop people from within but also recruit new skills from outside.
- Aim is to develop well-trained employees.
- Some degree of spirituality is evident, for example, in expecting workers to think and understand how the company works, providing for their needs through flexible conditions, and probably in the emotional tie to the brand.

NOTES

1 The author is indebted to the many people at BMW who generously gave of their knowledge and time for this project.
2 BMW (2000) *Annual Report*, Munich. Accessed on-line on 10 July 2001 at http://www.bmw.com/
3 BMW (undated), BMW AG, Dingolfing Plant.

4   Tierney, C. and Schmidt, K. (2001) 'Will this man drive Volkswagen?', *Business Week*, 19 February, p. 53.
5   BMW (2001) *Annual Report*, Munich.
6   'The car industry: Barbarians at Bavarians' gates', *Economist*, 13 February 1999.
7   Gibson, I. (2002) *Report of Automotive Innovation and Growth Team (AIGT)*, URL: http://www.autoindustry.co.uk/companies/aigt/index. html accessed 27 July 2003.
8   'BMW: Milberg kündigt Rücktritt an' *Wirtschaftswoche*, 4 December 2001.
9   BMW Group (2001) *Annual Report*, Munich.
10 ibid.
11 ibid.
12 http://www.bmwgroup.com/ accessed 10 July 2001.
13 BMW Group (2001) *Annual Report*, Munich.
14 http://www.bmwgroup.com/ accessed 10 July 2001.
15 *BMW Presentation* from Mr Wachter and Mr Hartmann, Munich during site visit in 1999.
16 BMW (1998) *New work structures at BMW*. BMW Factbook.
17 ibid.
18 Reitzle, W. (1998) 'The driving force, Gernot Brauer', *BMW Australia Magazine*, 2.
19 http://www.bmwgroup.com/ accessed 10 July 2001.
20 ibid.
21 BMW (1999/1998) *Annual Report*, Munich. Accessed on-line on 10 July 2001 at http://www.bmw.com/.
22 http://www.bmwgroup.com/ accessed 10 July 2001.
23 BMW (1996) *Long-term personnel policy in the BMW Group*. BMW Factbook.
24 http://www.bmwgroup.com/ accessed 10 July 2001.
25 Personal communication during visit to the BMW Dingolfing Plant, 28 July 2000.
26 BMW AG undated, Dingolfing Plant, BMW AG.
27 BMW (1998) *Flexible working times at BMW*. BMW Factbook.
28 BMW (2002) *Flexible working hours at the BMW Group*. Munich.
29 'We've never been stronger', *BMW Magazine*, April 1999.
30 'Portrait des neuen Konzernchefs: Helmut Panke' *Wirtschaftswoche*, 4 December 2001.
31 Burdock, R., Holy, R., McPherson, R., Ng, J., Vankadara, M., and Vigilante, N. (2000) *Briefing report on BMW*. Macquarie University, unpublished report.
32 Presentation from HR department during visit to BMW at Dingolfing, 28 June 2000.
33 BMW (2000) *Information Department Publication*. Personal – und Sozialwesen, PZ-3.
34 BMW (undated) *Drive*. Personal–und Sozialwesen, BMW AG, PZ-3.

Two **W.L. Gore & Associates, Inc:**
Natural Leadership

ANDREW BELL[1]

> **Grow an enterprise with great opportunity for all who will join in it, a virile**
> **organization that will foster self-fulfilment and which will multiply the capabilities**
> **of the individuals comprising it, beyond their mere sum.**
>
> Bill Gore, Founder, 1961

Bill Gore believed that people have limitless potential, which is almost completely under utilized by business organizations. So he set about creating an
organization where people could come together to unleash that potential. This
philosophical approach to organization and management has been the foundation of the enormous success of W.L. Gore & Associates, ranked in the top
200 of the Forbes top 500 privately held companies for 2000. Its history of
product innovation and consistent profitable growth is a remarkable story.

BACKGROUND

Wilbert (Bill) L. and his wife Genevieve (Vieve) Gore founded W.L. Gore &
Associates, Inc. on 1 January 1958 in Newark, Delaware. Bill was already 45 at
the time and had spent the previous 17 years working at DuPont, mostly as a
research chemist. In particular, he had explored commercial applications for
the newly discovered Teflon (polytetrafluoro-ethylene – PTFE).

Bill Gore constantly suggested new possibilities for applications of this new, inert polymer to DuPont. He became particularly excited, however, by one use. Tinkering in the basement of his home one evening, Bill discovered a new way to make computer ribbon-cable insulation using Teflon. Convinced that this product had real commercial opportunities and having failed to convince DuPont to invest in the idea, he left DuPont to form W.L. Gore & Associates in that same basement of his home – a basement that continued to have great significance in the organization for many years.

Stories of the early years of the organization abound at Gore. One example is about the first time Bill and Vieve received an order for a length of twisted cable, longer than could be assembled in the basement, and how the twisting process was moved to the freshly-mown front lawn. That resulted in the Gore family spending most of the entire night picking grass clippings out of the cable so that it could be shipped off to the customer on time the next day.

Vieve would regularly tell the story to associates of how her kitchen oven was destroyed by Bill trying to heat Teflon to high temperatures for long periods. Another story relates to how Vieve's brand new pressure cooker was converted into a new tool to manufacture a particular process. These stories subsequently became an important part of an organizational culture that has made Gore extremely successful.

The business started with virtually no capital, and with no infrastructure or customers – just with a patent on Bill's ribbon-cable process filed by his son, Bob Gore, and Bill's determination that commercial applications for Teflon presented large opportunities. Gradually the business grew from these small beginnings as the ribbon-cable became popular with engineers designing the third generation of computers, like IBM's 360.

In 1969, Bob discovered that rapidly stretching PTFE created a very strong, microporous material – expanded PTFE known as GORE-TEX® ePTFE – which offered a range of new, desirable properties. This discovery and its patent led to a major source of new ideas and products. Gore now holds approximately 650 US patents, and thousands more worldwide.

All Gore products are backed by the strongest guarantees, based on one of Bill's earliest declarations that 'we won't ever sell a product if we can't warrant it. Our products will do what we say they will do.'

Gore has numerous competitors in each of its businesses, but no single competitor that operates across the diverse scope of opportunities that Gore pursues. The focus of the organization is to develop, make and sell the very best products in each of its markets. The company has regularly withdrawn from sale products that it no longer believes are the very best available. This demanding standard helps to create a strong momentum for innovation throughout the businesses, and a relatively large percentage of revenues are re-invested each year directly in research and development.

ORGANIZATION

Gore was quick to pursue global opportunities, commencing manufacturing operations in Germany in 1968, and forming a joint venture in Japan in 1974. In 2000, around 7000 Gore Associates worked in about 45 locations, including Argentina, Australia, Austria, Chile, China, Finland, France, Germany, Greece, Hong Kong, India, Italy, Japan, Korea, Malaysia, The Netherlands, New Zealand, Scotland, Singapore, Spain, Sweden, Switzerland, Taiwan and the US. Manufacturing facilities are predominantly clustered in several major locations around Newark, Delaware and Flagstaff, Arizona but also in Japan, China, Germany and the UK.

By the beginning of the twenty-first century, the business was structured into five major operating divisions:

- the original Electronic Products Division, which manufactures high-specification wire, cable and signal insulation, packaging and interconnect devices;
- Industrial Products, which specializes in both industrial filtration and sealant applications, also produces the fibre used to make astronauts' space suits;
- Medical Products where GORE-TEX® ePTFE is used in applications such as cardio-vascular bypass grafts and patches to repair membranes around the brain or holes in human hearts;
- GORE-TEX® Fabrics products are probably best known to consumers such as skiers, adventurers, fire fighters and the military (among many others) for providing comfort and protection from the elements; and
- Consumer Products, where a huge variety of products all based on GORE-TEX® ePTFE are sold direct to consumers. These products range from dental floss to guitar strings and footwear to satellite dish covers.

From the outset, Bill and Vieve were very clear about the type of organization they wanted to build. Bill had been happiest and, he believed, able to make the most contribution during his time at DuPont, when he was working in small teams of people who had come together to focus on achieving a particular outcome. In these situations there tended to be fewer rules, greater appreciation of the strengths and expertise of each person on the team, quicker decision making and greater clarity of focus on a particular outcome. Bill thought that it should be possible to transfer this experience to the organization of the whole company.

The Gores were also influenced by Douglas McGregor's book, *The Human Side of Enterprise*, in which McGregor expounded a continuum of management behaviour ranging from Theory X to Theory Y. Theory X practices are hierarchical, controlling and directive and lead, in McGregor's view, to employees who are unable to reach their full potential. On the other hand, Theory Y postulates a management approach involving high empowerment of employees, and this certainly reinforced Bill and Vieve's own thinking.

The Gore organization lacks a traditional hierarchy. Instead, the highly team-based environment encourages direct, person-to-person communication among all 'associates', as employees are known. This structure emerged from Bill Gore's philosophy and has been continued after Bill's death in 1988 by his successor, his son Bob.

Bill Gore's definite ideas about the nature of groups underpinned his thinking about how 'the Associates' (as he frequently called the company) should be organized. Groups of people come together voluntarily, he believed, when the needs of the members are better satisfied by participation.[2] When these people have come together in business, Bill argued, the key considerations should be 'efficiency of cooperation, magnitude of synergism, and utilization of individual human resources'.[3] He believed that 150 people was the point at which groups began to lose these benefits.

As the number of people in a group increases, the possibility for synergy increases while communication becomes more complex and inefficient, and barriers start to appear that impede the type of communication that is possible. Bill Gore believed that a noticeable drop in cooperation occurs when a group becomes so large that everyone no longer knows each other. When this is the case, even the language being used in the group changes from 'we decided (or did, believed and so on)' to 'they decided'. In these circumstances, rules, regulations and procedures become necessary to govern the cooperation process. In order for individuals to have the opportunity to maximize their accomplishments and realize their potential, Bill believed that each group in the organization should be no larger than about 150 people.

This belief has spawned 'clusters' of plants around Gore, where few individual buildings house more than 150–200 people, but many plants are located near each other so that expensive resources can be shared and functional groups of people can come together easily to share knowledge, expertise and experience between plants.

A business unit, or division, then, may consist of several manufacturing plants clustered together in different parts of the world, combined with sales offices all drawing upon some central shared resources. An extraordinarily high degree of autonomy rests at the individual plant level.

THE LATTICE

There are no organizational charts at Gore and job descriptions exist only at a very high level – more a list of the kinds of performance expectations that would be expected from a series of commitments that one might make. The organization is described as a 'lattice' – a non-hierarchical matrix with no bosses. Associates make voluntary commitments to achieve certain outcomes as part of a team.

Each person in the lattice is encouraged to interact directly with any other person, as and when necessary. This direct person-to-person communication without intermediaries or approval-seeking is a hallmark of the Gore environment. It quickly becomes evident that open and direct communication is a key to the success of the organization.

Bill Gore defined a number of attributes of his lattice organization:

- No fixed or assigned authority
- Sponsors, not bosses
- Natural leadership defined by followership
- Person-to-person communication
- Objectives set by those who must make them happen
- Tasks and functions organized through voluntary commitments

Bill Gore stated that 'the simplicity and order of an authoritarian organization make it an almost irresistible temptation. Yet it is counter to the principles of individual freedom and smothers the creative growth of man. Freedom requires orderly restraint. The restraints imposed by the need for cooperation are minimized with a lattice organization.'[4]

Gore's structure is founded on a single common objective and a set of core principles that govern the operation of the whole organization.

OBJECTIVE AND PRINCIPLES

Bill Gore stated that the objective of his new enterprise was 'to make money and have fun'. Like many of his simple, but profound, statements this one endures today as the core objective of the business. Making money is critical to run the business, invest in R&D and provide financial security to associates. Fun comes through enjoyable working relationships, social activities and celebrations and the conviction that what you're engaged in is meaningful and worthwhile.

From the very beginning, four operating principles at Gore have supported the objective. These principles have become known as Fairness, Freedom, Commitment and Waterline. The principles are taken very seriously at Gore, and provide the 'orderly restraint' Bill called for. He believed that these four principles were the necessary and sufficient conditions for organizational success.

The principles are deliberately not black-and-white statements that tell people what they may or may not do. Rather, the language encourages interpretation, experimentation and evolution, just as Bill intended the organization itself to evolve.

- *Fairness*: Try to be fair. Sincerely strive to be fair with each other, our suppliers, our customers and all persons with whom we carry out transactions. Striving to be fair in interactions with others is the hallmark of a civilized organization, Bill believed. Deliberate or careless unfairness erodes trust between people, creates anger and resentment, and this destroys both the communication and the cooperation between people that is so necessary for an organization to be creative, non-hierarchical and successful.
- *Freedom*: Allow, help and encourage associates to grow in knowledge, skill, scope of responsibility and range of activities. This 'freedom' principle is the well-spring of the creativity and innovation that the organization has enjoyed. In many ways, this principle is the engine that drives organizational growth. It holds all associates to account for learning, personal growth and taking on increased responsibilities and different roles. This encourages creativity and innovation throughout the organization.
- *Commitment*: Make our own commitments – and keep them. Working hand-in-hand with the freedom principle, commitment is the glue that holds the lattice together. With no positional authority and power at Gore, there is no one to tell anyone what to do. associates make voluntary commitments to tasks and are relied upon by their other associates to keep their commitments. Making a commitment at Gore is like making a sacred trust with the organization. The worst thing an associate can do is to make a number of commitments and fail to keep them.

An important interrelationship exists between the principles of freedom and commitment. An associate earns credibility and respect from other associates by making and keeping commitments. The more commitments that an associate can keep, the more freedom this associate earns to try new things, take on responsibility and grow a career.

- *Waterline*: Consult with other associates before taking actions that might be 'below the waterline' and cause serious damage to the enterprise. The waterline principle is based on the analogy that the organization is like a ship that all the associates are on together. Decisions might be categorized as being above or below the waterline of the ship. If an associate makes a mistake above the waterline, it is akin to making a hole in the ship that will not have a terribly adverse effect on the ship overall. However, a decision below the waterline that goes wrong would be like making a hole that might sink the ship. Gore wants all associates to make the decisions that they need to make to meet their commitments ('we don't tax creativity with bureaucracy'). So the waterline principle states that when an associate is confronted with a waterline decision (any action that could harm the financial resources, reputation or future opportunities), they are obliged to consult with other knowledgeable associates. Importantly, the waterline principle is not about command and control. Rather, it is about consultation and sharing the burden of risk.

  The longer associates are with the organization, the clearer they are about where the waterline is – and indeed, over time, where the waterline is will be different for different associates with different levels of skill, experience and knowledge. Two questions are often used to assess whether a decision is above or below the waterline:

- If I try and succeed, will it have been worth the effort?
- If I try and fail, can I/we stand it?

A 'yes' answer to both questions usually means above the waterline and go ahead. Answering 'no' to the first question usually puts a stop to the idea as effort and resources will be better used elsewhere. 'Yes' to the first and 'no' to the second indicates a below-the-waterline situation, and the need for consultation.

FINANCIAL SUCCESS

With total annual revenues in the vicinity of US$1.5 billion, Gore remains privately held by the Gore family and associates of the organization. Both Bill and Bob Gore have refused many offers to sell the company. The Gore family believes that private ownership allows the organization to make long-term investments in businesses and ideas that the quarterly reporting regimen of public ownership can discourage.

Gore measures itself first at the organizational level, aggregating the business results from all units. Using economic value added (EVA) as its primary financial metric has allowed high-performing divisions to 'carry' the investment in poorer performing divisions during different economic cycles. This is vital, given the huge diversity of markets into which the company sells.

The organization has a long history of pursuing both short- and long-term profitability very successfully, with some investments not delivering a return for many years. Gore has at times 'carried' business divisions through periods of unprofitability, betting on strong future returns which have invariably been delivered. The company uses a very structured and rigorous approach to this decision-making process, and applies the process to all project reviews and new product development decisions. These are waterline decisions, and are always made by assembling a group of knowledgeable associates to work through a particular process to reach a decision together.

PRACTICES DRIVING SUCCESS

Gore is regarded as successful not only financially and in terms of innovation, but also for its culture. Gore is one of only a handful of companies that have been recognized in every one of the *100 Best Companies To Work For in America* lists, beginning with its inclusion in the original Levering and Moskowitz book in the early 1980s. Fortune magazine's 2001 ranking of *100 Best Companies To Work For in America* placed Gore at number 35 on the list, although previously Gore has been ranked in the top ten. Awards such as this help Gore be as well known for its unique corporate culture as for its innovative products.

Comparing Gore with studies of successful companies,[5] several common characteristics stand out:

- the visionary way in which Bill Gore built a business through his organizational architecture;
- the passion people have for the organizational culture;
- an environment of entrapreneuring and experimentation;
- bold goal setting;
- developing leaders from within the organization; and
- a ruthless focus on preserving the core elements of the culture, combined with an ability to flexibly adapt individual practices to meet changing organizational circumstances.

LEADERSHIP

'Leadership is a verb, not a noun. It is defined by what you do, not who you are,' said Bill Gore. W.L. Gore & Associates has sometimes been called a leaderless organization, but that description is a strong misrepresentation. In 1982, *INC* magazine described Bill Gore as 'the Un-Manager', partly based on his own comment that 'we don't manage people here, people manage themselves'. For some people over the years, this has led to a view of Gore as a 'do-as-you-please' organization where anything goes. This is not the case. Rather, Gore should be described as a leaderful organization where hierarchy and titles are avoided and authority derives from respect, credibility and followership rather than position and rank.

Leadership at Gore is defined by followership, and evolves naturally in the lattice organization. A leader emerges as his or her contributions and abilities are recognized by other associates. Leaders are rarely appointed and do not hold rank or title. Opportunities for leadership abound throughout the organization. Leaders emerge in functional teams, on new product teams, for special projects, or to lead a global business division or a plant. In recent years, when asked to respond to the question 'Do you consider yourself as a leader?' in the annual employee survey, close to 50 per cent of associates typically answered 'yes'.

Leadership can be quite fluid at Gore. The associate with the spark of an idea for a new waste reduction project may initially lead that project and gain followers who make a commitment to work on it. As this team-building and visioning phase concludes and the detailed work of the project team commences, a different set of skills and experience may be required from the leader. It is no longer necessary to sell the project and convince others to join, for what is required now is a detailed focus on process re-engineering and resource allocation. A different leader may well emerge to see the team through this new stage. The leader who established the project may stay involved or may have moved on to other commitments. Consequently, the make-up of the team and its leadership continually evolve.

Associates follow leaders at Gore for their ability to set direction around a business opportunity. The main task of leaders is to align the members of the team to the business goal. This is not a democratic process, leaders are not voted for, rather they emerge through a consensus of followership. Everyone on the team (or in the business group) does not individually have control over who their leader is (although on small project teams this is more likely).

The process of leadership emergence is somewhat mystical and subtle, and is quite difficult to understand from outside the organization. It is a function of the growth of the individual concerned, this person's passion for the opportunity or task at hand, a past history of successfully resolving difficult issues, strength of interpersonal relationships with other associates, personal style and the satisfaction of team members.

The process can be likened to planting a seed in fertile soil. That seed, when watered and nurtured, will germinate and start to grow, at first slowly beneath the ground until one day it will break through the soil and grow stronger and taller, eventually bearing fruit. At Gore, associates join an organization that encourages them to reach their potential, to grow and be creative. They are given a broad scope of responsibility by their leaders and are nurtured and encouraged by a sponsor. As they build credibility and a track record in the organization, other associates begin to seek them out to ask for their advice and guidance. When those associates follow that advice and guidance, a new leader has emerged.

There is no standard leadership profile for a plant, sales office or country. Some facilities support a single business leader for that location, while a very similar facility may choose to follow a group of leaders and some facilities have, over quite short periods, fluctuated between different leadership models as their particular needs and aspirations dictated. The Australian sales office is a good example of how this can occur when, after the retirement of the first Australian associate and subsequent business leader for many years, a group of three associates emerged from different businesses and functional areas to assume the leadership of this office.

The relationship between associates and leaders is very important at Gore, along with another very important relationship that is at the heart of the organization: sponsorship.

SPONSORSHIP

One rarely hears the words 'performance management' at Gore. That is not to say that there is no performance management process, rather that performance management is so embedded in the fabric of the organization through sponsorship that it does not become defined as a unique process. While leadership is a group or team relationship, one to many, sponsorship is a relationship between two individuals – the sponsor and sponsored. Every associate at Gore has one or more kinds of sponsors.

Bill Gore defined a sponsor as 'one who, by mutual agreement, accepts a responsibility to help another associate improve his or her contribution to the success of our enterprise and to assure that the person being sponsored is treated fairly.'

- **Starting sponsors:** A starting sponsor is assigned to a newly recruited associate. The sponsor helps the new person to settle into the organization, and quickly achieve success. The starting sponsor helps the new associate become comfortable operating in the Gore culture, identifies high impact commitments for the new associate to make and keep, and provides constant feedback on how the new associate is performing and fitting into the organization. The focus of this relationship is for the new associate to become successful quickly, to get some 'quick wins' under the belt, and to become an advocate for the Gore culture.

At some stage the new associate is no longer new. The timing of this differs, but sometime after about 6–12 months the starting sponsor and associate will have a conversation about future sponsorship. Future sponsorship is likely to involve different kinds of sponsors, particularly a contribution sponsor and a compensation sponsor.

- **Contribution sponsors:** Any associate can choose an ongoing contribution sponsor (and, of course, may elect to stay with the current starting sponsor). The contribution sponsor makes a commitment to those they sponsor to help them increase their contribution to the organization. Contribution sponsors act as sounding board, mentor, coach and positive advocate for the associates, making sure that associates being sponsored get credit and recognition for their contributions and accomplishments.

  The contribution sponsor's role is to provide continual open and honest feedback about performance, and what the associate can do to be ever more successful in the organization. A contribution sponsor helps associates plan their development, and supports them in seeking out new commitments and roles. These sponsors will also play a mediating role in conflicts between an associate they sponsor and another Gore associate. Sponsors are close to those that they sponsor, meet with them regularly, and typically go through a biannual goal-setting and review process to provide input into the pay review process.

- **Compensation sponsors:** Every associate also has a compensation sponsor. This role is to ensure that the sponsor's protégés are fairly paid for their contribution to the enterprise. The compensation sponsor represents the associate at pay review discussions and will speak positively on the associate's behalf. In many instances, the contribution and compensation sponsors are the same person. Due to the dynamics of the compensation process, sometimes a team or functional leader may assume the role of compensation sponsor. Compensation sponsors represent groups of associates to a Compensation Committee, which will usually consist of a team of four to six experienced associates. It is this Compensation Committee that actually sets an associate's pay, so in no way can compensation sponsors be seen as a different label for a 'boss'.

Sponsorship is a very serious commitment at Gore and is a key system to ensure the continued functioning of the culture and success of the business. Sponsorship training and development activities are offered continually to support sponsors in their role. Although there are no written rules, the sponsorship system can fall down when one person is sponsoring too many associates and so, generally, sponsors are limited to eight–ten associates.

PEOPLE

Maintaining the Gore culture begins with the recruitment and selection process. Some people are likely to find the unstructured Gore culture a poor fit for their style and work preferences. However, the organization prides itself on its ability to select people for their suitability for the culture, and has developed interviewing processes over time to achieve this. Mistakes occur, but are the exception.

The search for a new associate begins with the commitment of a starting sponsor to work with the new person immediately upon arrival. Clear starting commitments will also have been defined for the new associate. The sponsor, having received particular training in effective interviewing techniques, will be heavily involved in the interview process, whose primary focus is the new associate's ability to work effectively within the Gore culture. During this recruitment and selection process, the new associate will meet not only the starting sponsor but also other associates who are likely to be close contacts. All associates involved in the process have input into the final selection decision, and agree to take some responsibility to ensure that the new associate is welcomed and supported appropriately during entry to the organization.

Orientation

Upon arrival, the orientation process is intensive. All new associates, no matter where they are, are immersed heavily in Gore culture, tools and processes in a consistent four-day program. The focus of orientation is very heavily on helping new associates gain the cultural familiarity to become successful quickly. The intent of the orientation program is to create a cohort of cultural champions who are imbued with the corporate philosophy and way of doing things from day one.

Story-telling is a key element of these orientation sessions. A frequently used tool is a video of Bill and Vieve Gore and many of the 'legendary' early associates, discussing the first years of the company and its humble beginnings, as well as the importance of the culture and how to be successful.

All associates at Gore know the stories of the Gore's basement, Bob's discovery of GORE-TEX® ePTFE, and how Howard Arnold, the first associate Bill employed, boarded with the Gores, made machinery from scraps he found at the tip and took shares in the fledgling company in lieu of pay, which the Gores could not afford. These stories act as cultural glue in the organization and are regularly re-told by sponsors and leaders to illustrate a Gore point of view about a particular practice or approach. This is a very powerful element in the maintenance of the culture – a culture that values today the same elements that form the foundation – the teachable point of view – of these stories: innovation, ownership, experimentation and wise investment.

Many stories reflect Bill's willingness 'to bet on people' – to put his faith in the ability of an associate or team of associates to rise to the challenge of a particular goal and be successful. This practice continues in the company. Associates at Gore regularly commit to bold goals, both short- and long-term. These goals have resulted in Gore regularly bringing new products to market at incredible speed, inventing products with features and benefits that many had thought impossible to achieve, and growing revenues and profits at consistently high rates. Associates have not been afraid to invest in long-term projects – projects where the profit horizon may be five or ten, or even more years away.

Learning and development

The success of Gore's team-based, non-hierarchical culture relies fundamentally on the interpersonal communication skills of the associates, and Gore makes a significant investment in development programs to support this. A core development curriculum for all associates stresses communication, feedback and cultural behaviours. Each year, most associates participate in a 'people' skills development program, which represents a significant investment of time and resources. Functional curricula support and build technical expertise for each area in the organization.

Traditional career development does not happen at Gore. Instead, associates build a career by the commitments they choose to make. Sponsorship is a key element of this process and sponsors work with their associates to help them make decisions about their development plans and commitment choices, and act as advocates for their participation in learning programs.

COMPENSATION

Gore associates receive fixed pay, a share of the profits and share ownership. EVA targets are used to trigger profit-sharing. Global EVA targets are set, and as soon as the target is reached, a profit-share is apportioned across the entire organization. This profit-share is based on the same formula for all associates, and does not occur at any set time other than every time the new EVA target is reached. This practice not only acts as a performance incentive for both revenue growth and critical review of expenses and investments, but also sends a powerful bonding message to all associates that they are a part of one global organization: they share in the plan in the same way, irrespective of the individual performance of their business group, plant or location.

Somewhat unusual today is Gore's continued practice of no variable pay for any associates, even its sales teams. No-one at Gore receives performance bonuses, incentive pay or commissions of any kind outside the profit-sharing plan described above. Over the years, there has been considerable pressure at times to introduce incentive plans, at least for salespeople, where it is extremely rare not to have performance pay. However, Bill Gore always claimed that he failed to understand why a sales person should be rewarded any more for his or her efforts in closing a sale than the efforts of the people who made the product or designed or arranged for its shipping. That philosophy remains today, and underlies the reason why all associates share in profits.

Fixed pay is reviewed twice a year. All roles are externally benchmarked to ensure external competitiveness. Peers, sponsors and leaders rank all associates internally relative to each associate's perceived contribution to the success of the business. These 'contribution lists' and sponsor feedback are reviewed by committees of compensation sponsors, HR specialists and leaders (Compensation Committees) to determine pay increases for all associates. The principle is that people who contribute the most should be paid the most. Associates who are consistently at the top of contribution lists can find that their fixed pay moves quickly and significantly.

Theoretically, associates who found themselves sliding backwards in their position on a contribution list over a number of cycles might face a reduction in pay, but this has rarely, if ever, happened. More likely is that the pay of such associates' would stagnate and a serious conversation with their sponsor would take place about their future in the organization.

Gore is jointly owned by the Gore family and Gore associates, and the organization operates a phantom stock plan as the vehicle for associate ownership. Once an associate has been with the company for more than one year, the company contributes 15 per cent of the associate's salary into the ownership plan each year. This happens for each and every associate. This is a significant contribution and is a major reason that Gore ranks among the most generous providers of benefits in the US. The share price is set by external financial advisors, who compare each of Gore's operating divisions with a basket of high-performing industry companies each quarter. Over the life of the organization, the share price has experienced consistent high growth, delivering very strong returns to shareholders. Associates thus are significant owners of the business, and are not only encouraged to behave like owners of the business, but also are empowered to do so.

DISCUSSION ISSUES

1   Where is the leadership to be found at Gore? Which leadership paradigms can you identify? How does Gore ensure alignment between leaders and followers, and its organizational processes? Is Bill Gore still part of leadership at Gore today?

2   What is the function of the objective and principles in the Gore culture? How have the principles and objective been able to be preserved for about half a century? Will they endure sufficiently to take Gore into the future?

3   There is no doubt that Gore is a different organization and has been enormously successful over time. What is Gore's core competence that competitors cannot copy? Does the difference in the organization drive the successful performance? What is likely to happen if Gore were to strike difficult times?

4   To what extent is Gore a fractal organization relying on self-managing, self-optimizing and self-leading teams? Is it realistic for Gore to aim to become even more fractal? Could the employees be empowered further?

5   What evidence is there that Gore is a learning organization? Which elements in the culture drive and foster innovation? How does Gore manage knowledge and intellectual property? What forms of mentoring can you find and how seriously does the organization promote mentoring?

6   Could the successful principles and processes employed at Gore be transferred to other organizations seeking to be successful? Could most organizations revert from a hierarchical to a completely non-hierarchical structure like Gore's? If so, how should this process be managed? If not, what would hinder this transfer?

7   How can Gore ensure its sustainability? How does it deal with shareholders and other stakeholders? Would moving out of family ownership necessarily disrupt the Gore culture?

8   What kinds of people would be attracted to, and thrive in, the Gore culture? Who would be unlikely to thrive at Gore?

9   Which substitutes for leadership can you see operating at Gore? What role(s) would management play in this organization and how would you recommend that managers and leaders behave towards Gore employees?

10   What is the role of emotion at Gore? Would you regard Gore as offering spirituality?

KEY ISSUES

- Privately owned, US$1.5 billion turnover.
- Based around Teflon products.
- Heavily international organization.
- Financially and culturally successful, as well as highly innovative.
- 650 US patents, thousands more worldwide.
- Gore withdraws products that are not the best in their field, a strict quality criterion.
- Stories of struggle and success abound in the organization.
- No single competitor for the entire business, different competitors in each market.
- Strong focus on small teams to enhance innovation and fast decision making.
- Few rules and little bureaucracy.
- Based on groups of people coming together to work on projects voluntarily.
- Maximum group size at Gore is 150–200 people, although such groups often form co-located clusters to provide efficiencies of scale.
- Lattice structure – no organizational chart or detailed job descriptions.
- Direct person-to-person communication without intermediaries.
- No one tells anyone else what to do at Gore.
- Sponsors, not bosses, provide guidance.
- Various kinds of sponsors: starting, contribution and compensation sponsors.
- High empowerment of associates.
- Organizing is based on the voluntary commitment of associates.
- Objective is 'to make money and have fun'.
- Four principles provide 'order by restraint':
  - Fairness – with all.
  - Freedom – wellspring of creativity and innovation as people develop.
  - Commitment – the glue that holds the lattice together.
  - Waterline – decision-making principle.
- Consistently on the 'best company to work for' list.
- Leadership is defined by what people do.
- Leaders emerge when others follow them, principle of 'natural leadership'.
- Gore is a leaderful organization, not leaderless.
- No ranks, no titles, no hierarchy, no bosses.
- Leaders can easily change in functional teams.
- Teams are fractal – self-managing, self-optimizing, composition can easily change.

- Recruitment and selection maintain the culture, with intensive orientation for new people.
- Associates enter with starting sponsor and other associates making commitments to support the new person.
- Learning and development – strong focus on communication and soft skills.
- Associates receive fixed pay based on the principle of whoever contributes the most gets paid the most.
- Profit sharing is across the board whenever set targets are achieved at the organizational level, using the same formula for all associates.
- No variable bonus or commissions for anyone, including the sales team.
- Phantom stock plan is the vehicle for associate stock ownership.
- Associates are significant owners of the business and are encouraged and empowered to behave like owners of the business.

NOTES

1   Andrew Bell was an associate at Gore from 1992 until 1999. Then he joined Hewitt and Associates, being based in Sydney, until he moved to Hong Kong in mid-2003 to take up the position of Head of Research, Capability and Talent for the Asia-Pacific region.
2   Gore, W.L. (1976) The Lattice Organization – A Philosophy of Enterprise. Unpublished paper, W.L. Gore Associates, p. 3.
3   Gore, W.L. (1976) The Lattice Organization – A Philosophy of Enterprise. Unpublished paper, W.L. Gore Associates, p. 3.
4   Gore, W.L. (1976) The Lattice Organization – A Philosophy of Enterprise. Unpublished paper, W.L. Gore Associates, p. 8.
5   Such as James C. Collins and Jerry I. Porras (1994) *Built To Last: Successful Habits of Visionary Companies*, New York: HarperBusiness, a study of visionary corporations with outstanding long-term financial success. Or Charles A. O'Reilly and Jeffrey Pfeffer (2000) *Hidden Value: How Great Companies Achieve Extraordinary Results with Ordinary People*, Boston: Harvard Business School Press, describing the people practices of a cohort of successful companies.

Three **Novartis: People Chemistry**[1]

GAYLE C. AVERY

Winning through people.[2]

Daniel Vasella, Chairman

Novartis was formed in 1996 from the merger between pharmaceutical giants Ciba-Geigy and Sandoz, and has become a leading international pharmaceutical company. The name, derived from the Latin *novae artes* meaning 'new skills', is intended to reflect Novartis' commitment to research and development in bringing innovative new products to the communities it serves. At one stage, Novartis was number nine in its field worldwide, but in 2001 was ranked number 40 among healthcare organizations because of consolidations within the industry.[3]

Based in Switzerland and operating through 275 affiliates in 140 countries, Novartis originally offered its products and services through six legally autonomous sectors: Pharmaceuticals, Consumer Health, Generics, Animal Health, CIBA Vision and Agribusiness.[4] Each sector has its own vision (see Box CS3.1).

Box CS3.1

Divisional visions at Novartis

- *Pharmaceuticals*: committed to improving health and quality of life by focusing on the discovery, development, manufacture and marketing of innovative prescription medications.
- *Consumer Health*: dedicated to maintaining and improving the health and wellbeing of consumers and patients – at home or in hospitals – by fulfilling their nutritional and self-medication needs.
- *Generics*: a global business comprised of companies that provide high-quality, off-patent pharmaceutical products and substances at competitive prices.

- *Animal Health*: focuses on the wellbeing of companion animals and on the health and productivity of farm animals, seeking to lead the market with continuous innovation and services for pet owners and farmers.
- *CIBA Vision*: works to improve, protect and preserve people's eyesight through products and services for vision correction and ocular health.
- *Agribusiness*: provides products and services that support sustainable agriculture and enhance the production of safe, healthy and high-quality foods, food ingredients, feed, plants and plant derivatives.

During its first four years, Novartis was a broadly diverse pharmaceutical company (see Figure CS3.1). In 1999, Novartis decided to focus exclusively on the healthcare business, taking account of the trend in the healthcare industry of becoming a high-margin business in high-risk areas.[5] Accordingly, in 2000 the Agribusiness was placed in a separate company, Syngenta, created from a merger with AstraZeneca's Agrochemicals.[6]

STRATEGIES

Novartis faces many challenges and opportunities that require a strategic response. The chairman of Novartis AG, Daniel Vasella, cited Heraclitus at the May 2000 Annual General Meeting: 'Everything is in flux, nothing is permanent. No-one can step into the same river twice, for everything is subject to constant change.'[7]

Vasella's message was that the corporate landscape is changing the world over and the pharmaceutical industry is no exception in facing major challenges. These challenges include:

- cost containment in the healthcare industry;
- spiralling costs of R&D and new technology;
- global players dominating the field; and
- more proactive, better-educated patients, who demand cost-effective, quality care.

However, according to Vasella, the most important changes facing the healthcare industry stem from changing demographics, specifically, aging populations and declining birthrates. Age is the most important risk factor in diseases such as cancer and cardiovascular disease.

At the same time, new opportunities and areas are opening up, such as *neutroceuticals*, which is medical nutrition or functional food; the Internet;

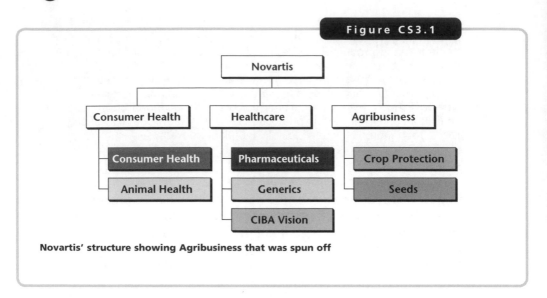

Novartis' structure showing Agribusiness that was spun off

genomics and new global markets. The Internet is a major opportunity, making information easily available and offering the prospect of more direct-to-consumer marketing. Uncovering the human genetic code through genomics has radically altered the healthcare industry through such possibilities as individual genetic identity cards and tailoring therapies to an individual's genetic profile. To capitalize on these prospects, Novartis is expanding globally in every sector where it is active. Despite a preference for organic growth, about 20 acquisitions and collaborations with other organizations occurred in 2000.[8]

However, Novartis regards innovation as even more important strategically than geographical expansion or strengthening its brands.[9] Innovation provides the main basis for long-term profitable growth. Between 1997–99, the proportion of newly launched products averaged 15 per cent, planned to grow to 50 per cent in the following three years.[10] A second strategic goal after innovation is to become the world leader in selected therapeutic areas that generate high revenues and are very profitable, such as organ transplantation.

VALUES AND MISSION

In working with professional intellect in an innovative environment, Novartis is becoming a values-driven organization. Novartis people are committed to improving health and wellbeing through innovative products and services around the globe. The organization aims at fostering a climate in which ambitious goals are set and where the hallmarks are trust and mutual support.[11] A balance is sought between the openness and fairness essential to interpersonal relationships and the business needs of speed and discipline, focus and results.

Novartis' goals are based around four core values[12]:

- *External focus*: on customers, markets, competitors and technologies.
- *Innovation*: to create cutting-edge products and technologies.
- *People*: fostering respect, leadership, teamwork and trust.
- *Performance*: to achieve world class results.

The corporate mission is:

> Our mission is to bring value to patients and customers. We want to have a positive impact on lives and to discover, develop and successfully market innovative products to cure diseases and enhance the quality of life. We also want to provide a shareholder return that reflects outstanding performance and to build a reputation for an exciting workplace where people can realize their professional ambitions and where creativity is encouraged. We also care about our world and society and want to operate sustainably.[13]

Novartis has a code of conduct that covers ethical and legal behaviour, including consideration of stakeholder interests, professionalism, and fair, courteous and respectful treatment of employees.[14]

FINANCIAL INFORMATION

Novartis is a successful and cash-rich, publicly-listed company. In 1999, it reported a net liquidity of CHF (Swiss francs) 12.7 billion, operating income growing by 9 per cent to CHF 6.2 billion,[15] and an operating profit rising by 9 per cent.[16] Sales improved by 10 per cent in 2000 over 1999, increasing to CHF 35.805 billion, and operating income grew to about CHF 7.9 billion.[17] The net income of CHF 7.2 billion represented 8 per cent increase on 1999, a return on sales of 20.1 per cent, and return on average equity of 19.5 per cent. In 2000, sales by sector were:

- **Pharmaceuticals:** 60 per cent;
- **Generics:** 7 per cent;
- **CIBA Vision:** 7 per cent;
- **Consumer Health:** 22 per cent; and
- **Animal Health:** 4 per cent.

Financial highlights (full year 2000)

	2000 CHF millions	1999 CHF millions	Change %
Group sales	35 805	32 465	10
Operating income	7 883	7 343	7
Net income	7 210	6 659	8
Earnings per share (CHF)	110	100	10
Dividend per share (CHF)[1]	34	32	6
Sales from ongoing activities[2]	29 112	25 227	15
Operating income from ongoing activities[2]	6 727	6 321	6
Net income from ongoing activities[2]	6 511	6 041	8

Notes:
[1]2000: Proposal to the shareholders' meeting.
[2]Excluding the divested Consumer Health and Agribusiness activities.
Source: http://www.novartis.com/ accessed 6 December 2001.

In 2000, Novartis possessed sufficient resources to be able to make all the necessary investments in its own R&D, sales and marketing to meet its objectives of remaining globally competitive and expanding.[18] Table CS3.1 summarizes the 2000 results.

Novartis' 1999 sales by region were Europe 36 per cent, the Americas 47 per cent, and Asia/Australia/Africa 17 per cent.[19] In its largest market, the US, Novartis had faced stiff competition in 1999 and sought to strengthen its US presence.[20] The success of this strategy is reflected in the 2000 sales in the three regions, with Europe reducing to 32 per cent, America increasing to 50 per cent, and the rest remaining almost constant at 18 per cent.[21]

ORGANIZATION

The Novartis Board of Directors, consisting of 14 members and chaired by the CEO, is responsible for the ultimate direction, strategy, organization and administration of the entity. The Group Executive Committee consists of nine members who work under the authority of the CEO to develop and implement strategies for the entire Novartis Group, and to procure and allocate the required resources. The legally separate companies operating in the various sectors report to Divisional Heads.[22]

In 2000, Novartis reduced the number of employees from the 1999 level of about 82 000 people to 67 653 workers in 54 countries. Employees come from diverse cultural backgrounds, with different educational qualifications, and are distributed over the regions as follows: Europe 43 per cent, the Americas 40 per cent, and Asia/Australia/Africa 17 per cent.[23]

In selected countries or regions, a Country President represents the Group Executive Committee internally and externally, working to promote the image and attain the objectives of Novartis in that country. In countries without a Country President, this role is assigned to one of that country's Sector Company Heads.

Employees are encouraged to work in teams, and special cross-functional problem-solving focus groups are created to solve particularly challenging problems under the Novartis FAR (Fast Action for Results) process. This process is designed to fast-track innovations and change.

PRODUCTION

Most production is done in Basel, but six other production sites are located in Europe, India, Egypt and the US. Certain plants are equipped with special technologies, and manufacturing is undertaken at the appropriate site. Manufacturing is mostly retained in-house because it guarantees speed and flexibility during development, protects know-how, enables Novartis people to fully understand the products and associated processes, and ensures a competitive price.[24] Novartis manufactures its own key products, that is, those that protect it against competition, but may buy materials for non-strategic brands. Only in introducing a new brand would outsourcing be considered, and even then, only parts of the process would be outsourced to protect the intellectual property.

Novartis calls its employees 'associates'. Associates are responsible for controlling their own quality, although formal audit processes are applied. In addition to the voluntary quality management system derived from ISO 9000, pharmaceutical companies adhere to special guidelines from regulatory quality systems in the interests of public health. This legally-binding system is known as Good Practice (GxP), which prescribes three areas of good practice: Good Manufacturing Practice (GMP), Good Laboratory Practice (GLP) and Good Clinical Practice (GCP). The focus of the GxP regulations is on the product, not the processes and systems considered by ISO 9000.

INNOVATION

Novartis strives for continuous innovation and the development of break-through technologies. Innovation is an articulated strategic goal. Investment in R&D in 1999 was 13.1 per cent of sales.[25] In fostering innovation, Novartis employs the following main strategies:

- balancing internal and external research;
- developing a broad, strong alliance network;
- fostering small entrepreneurial discovery groups; and
- supporting selected and focused investment in new technologies and high risk areas.[26]

Market research among medical experts tends to drive new developments, and it can take about six years from the initial idea to placing a product on the market.[27] Normally the process starts with identifying about 10 000 compounds, only a few dozen of which get to the GMP, GLP and GCP stages of the Good Practices system. From these, only one or two get to market, despite the fact that the discarded products tend to absorb most of the developmental costs.

The company estimated that by 2003, new products would generate about 50 per cent of sales.[28] Through its focus on innovation, Novartis is poised to launch a series of new products with substantial sales potential. Examples include Visudyne for age-related eye degeneration, Starlix for treatment of diabetes and various anti-cancer, asthma and Alzheimer agents. Products in the pipeline are normally planned about three years ahead, and the crop of innovations in 2000 is expected to propel Novartis into significant growth.[29]

Novartis attempts to build on synergies within its pharmaceutical sector and among its nutrition and over-the-counter business units to create product innovations in the nutrition and self-medication fields. The company has also invested heavily in biotechnology/gene technology with a view to developing such applications as:

- gaining insight into the fundamental processes of viruses, bacteria and animal and human cells by basic research;
- elucidating the causes of specific human diseases and their possible link to gene dysfunctions and genetic predispositions;
- personalizing medical treatment by helping to select the most optimally effective therapy for specific patient populations (pharmacogenetics);
- finding solutions to overcome the severe shortage of human organs for donation; and
- correcting genetic processes (somatic gene therapy).[30]

STAKEHOLDER DIALOG

Recognizing that its reputation is a key corporate asset, Novartis uses corporate communications to maintain and enhance its positive image. Communication is regarded as a strategic business tool, with its strategy and priorities defined by the Executive Committee.[31] A designated department encourages employees to engage in innovative communication by providing state-of-the-art tools and services, guidance and feedback. Through open communication, Novartis aims to offer better transparency and responsiveness than its competitors, thus furthering its business goals.[32]

Communication is considered part of management responsibilities at all levels. Direct communication with customers is regarded as the responsibility of the business sectors, but the formal corporate communication department addresses other stakeholders, including customers, employees and shareholders, governments and authorities, local communities, the media and special interest groups.

To further increase dialog with its stakeholders, Novartis has created an interactive Internet resource, the Life Sciences Network, which is an integral part of their website dedicated to providing information for both professionals and consumers. The Network offers a broad range of links to institutions, organizations, industry and news groups active in the biotechnology and life sciences areas, as well as posting news articles on life sciences topics. In addition, Novartis publications dealing with various life sciences can be viewed and ordered online.[33] E-business technology is used to enhance communication, build brands and products, and streamline interactions with vendors, suppliers and distributors.

HUMAN RESOURCES

The role of HR at Novartis is to create and sustain an effective organization that brings into alignment the strategic goals of the business and its people.[34] In building a high-performing company, the goal is to outperform competitors and to anticipate and adapt to the changing business environment. Corporate HR acts to support associates' development, and thus, the future leadership of the company, which is striving to be agile enough to anticipate and respond quickly to its dynamic environment.

The basic principles of the HR policy at Novartis are established centrally. Sector companies then implement the policies, modifying them to suit local requirements. To align business goals with the collective efforts of associates,

HR policies align individual, team and business objectives, supporting the knowledge, skills and behaviours required to meet business targets. This is reinforced by a reward system that recognizes the achievement of stretch goals.

For example, top scientific, sales and marketing people are required in order to achieve Novartis' projected growth. Attracting this talent is a challenge because Novartis is competing directly with universities for the best researchers, and today's universities can offer scientists both academic freedom and commercial opportunities. To compete with universities, Novartis has created smaller, interconnected units and adjusted its incentives system. An alternative strategy involves collaborating with university researchers and institutes directly. Novartis actively recruits from MBA programs, using 'funky' marketing campaigns, and then trains new associates, for example, by rotating them through different departments.

The organization strives for high performance by building a management style of trust, openness and support, and developing a culture that allows individuals to realize their full potential and contribution. Challenge, innovation, collaboration and learning are valued in the culture. Key core capabilities are 'people, innovation, external focus and performance', all of which are covered in the performance management system, which is designed to promote innovation and a working environment characterized by the free flow of ideas and open discussion.[35]

As an innovation-focused company, Novartis' success depends heavily on the creativity and performance of its employees at all levels. The company therefore assigns its people challenging tasks and provides them with opportunities for personal growth and development, for example, through increased responsibility, functional and international job rotation and training. Continuous learning is regarded as crucial to the success of the company. Employees are sponsored into MBA programs to bridge the gap between commercial and scientific worldviews, and an arrangement with Harvard Business School provides customized courses for high-potential managers. Novartis' executive education develops management and leadership skills and provides associates with opportunities to develop and grow through a continuous process of education and learning, including e-learning. These activities also support and reinforce the core values and capabilities.

The company strives to increase its attractiveness as an employer of choice by offering challenging and rewarding career opportunities. Radical changes of direction are possible within Novartis. Career development is viewed as a shared responsibility involving the worker, line manager and HR function. Dual career paths are provided for those pursuing a scientific track and those preferring the business side.[36]

Compensation and benefits are designed to support Novartis' business objectives. The overall remuneration package is aimed at attracting, motivating and retaining employees who share Novartis' values and contribute to high performance. Base salaries are targeted to meet the competitive requirements of the marketplace; short- and long-term incentives reward excellent contributions;

stock options are available to senior associates; benefits programs are designed to provide an appropriate and flexible support for associates. Flexible work programs are in place for those who choose to take them up. Some people work remotely, particularly sales personnel. Various work models allow people to choose to work part-time, such as 50 per cent or 75 per cent rather than 100 per cent of the time.

COMMUNITY OUTREACH

As a multinational enterprise and corporate citizen, Novartis is committed to promoting research, education and development projects all over the world in the environment, health or nutrition areas. As part of this commitment, Novartis has established various initiatives and foundations in many countries, including Switzerland, France, the UK, the US and Japan.

In working towards sustainability, Novartis supports the United Nations' Global Compact initiative, has launched a Foundation for Sustainable Development, cooperates with the World Health Organization by donating all the drugs needed to eradicate leprosy, and is seeking to develop affordable products for the developing world. Sustainable operation is a specific corporate goal.[37]

As part of its corporate citizenry, Novartis promotes health, safety and environmental issues. It seeks to make this part of the Novartis corporate identity, with a company-wide philosophy and commitment to health, safety and the environment. This policy sets forth three key principles:

- to integrate health, safety and environment into line management responsibility;
- to provide and emphasize leadership and active management in health, safety and environment; and
- to care for stakeholders.

Good performance in these areas is intended to enhance corporate credibility and contribute to Novartis' 'license to innovate'.[38]

Health, safety and environment operate on five levels – Site, Sector Company, Country and Corporate – thereby achieving a balance between global and local company priorities. At each level, the Health, Safety and Environment (HSE) function supports the responsible line management and undertakes the tasks that best suit the function's central position. For example, throughout ongoing and planned restructuring projects, measures and systems are put in place to ensure that HSE performance is maintained, even during times of turbulent change.

Each level of the organization defines practices and procedures for good HSE performance, according to its individual scope and concerns. Every sector has also defined an area of HSE performance where it will demonstrate leadership. On the corporate level, internal guidelines establish global standards and operating procedures for important HSE issues. These either meet, or exceed, external standards, and are designed to ensure that the company demonstrates superior HSE performance wherever it operates. Novartis issues an annual report detailing its HSE performance.

KNOWLEDGE MANAGEMENT

The role of the Senior Corporate Knowledge Officer, Dr Joerg Staeheli, is to foster networks to share knowledge, rather than managing knowledge. He believes that everyone has the same access and obligation with respect to knowledge. Dr Staeheli focuses on people networks, which are then supported by electronic networks. People need to be managed to promote knowledge sharing, which is part of organizational learning. Trust is also vital to knowledge sharing, particularly as knowledge sharing is a political process, because of the power knowledge generates. A paradigm shift to wanting to share knowledge is required, and the CEO, Daniel Vasella, strongly supports this shift.[39]

As in many other organizations, the challenge for Novartis is to discover where the knowledge is. This is important to shareholders as well, because intellectual capital makes the difference between the market value and book value of an organization. The financial to intellectual capital ratio at Novartis is estimated to be 1:6–7, showing the vital role that intellectual capital plays in the organization.[40] To achieve its objective of continuous improvement, Novartis protects its intellectual knowledge. Networking the knowledge between the autonomous sectors belonging to the Novartis Group presents a considerable challenge, especially when they are involved in over 400 alliances with universities, are globally distributed, and the knowledge lies in around 82 000 minds in 140 countries at over 400 sites! At Novartis, such knowledge management is viewed as a 'product' that requires resources. 'Knowledge management is expensive, but so is stupidity,' Dr Staeheli quipped.[41]

DISCUSSION ISSUES

1 Where is the leadership at Novartis? What kind(s) of leadership can you identify? Which leadership paradigms are evident?

2 How does Novartis' management view followers? What is the organization doing that would be attractive or unattractive to the self-managing professionals they are seeking to employ and retain?

3 How would you describe Novartis' culture? What are the vision and values of the organization? What would it be like to work there?

4 How are the leaders, followers and organizational systems aligned with each other? With the business strategy? Is this organization well placed for an uncertain, dynamic future? If not, what would you recommend? If yes, why?

5 Which substitutes for leadership can you see operating at Novartis? What role(s) would management play in this organization and how would you recommend a manager behave towards Novartis' staff?

6 Is Novartis a good corporate citizen or is it just exercising effective public relations through the corporate communications department? What role does the HSE program play?

7 How is innovation fostered at Novartis, and why? What could they do better to promote innovation that is so vital to their future?

8 What role does the HR function play in achieving the company's future?

9 Is this a learning organization and why do you say this? What is the purpose of managing knowledge at Novartis?

10 Is Novartis managing its globalization appropriately? Could there be too much focus on Basel at the expense of the US or other foreign markets? If this were so, what could top management do to remedy this?

KEY ISSUES

- Global organization in 140 countries, financially very successful.
- Diverse workforce in national culture, education and professional background.

- Highly innovative, poised for substantial growth with current products already in the pipeline.
- Faces continual change in the healthcare industry.
- Innovation is the key to growth.
- Highly-skilled, professional workforce.
- Seeking to become a values-driven organization.
- Culture of trust and mutual support that values challenge, innovation, collaboration and learning.
- In-house production retained in key areas to protect intellectual property and gain speed to market.
- Engages in proactive communications to relate to stakeholders, with communications regarded as a strategic business tool.
- Focus on open communication, both internally and externally, within the constraints of protecting competitive advantage.
- Recognizes a wide range of stakeholders in addition to customers and employees, such as government, media and special interest groups.
- Established links to a broad range of interest groups via the Internet.
- Challenge of attracting top talent away from universities and competitors.
- To attract talent, has created smaller interconnected units, provided new incentives, offers challenging tasks and opportunities for personal growth and development.
- HR's role is to align people with strategic goals.
- Trains new associates, for example, by rotating them through different departments or sending them on MBA programs.
- Striving to be an agile, responsive organization.
- Wants to be an employer of choice, so encourages personal development and permits people to make radical career changes within the organization.
- Dual career paths for scientists and managers are available.
- Continuous learning is regarded as crucial to the organization's success.
- Offers flexible work models.
- Performance Management System supports business objectives.
- Extensive community outreach programs have been developed.
- Corporate citizen programs focus on promoting health, safety and the environment at all organizational levels within Novartis.
- Sustainable operation is a strategic goal.
- Knowledge management is part of organizational learning, and attempts are being made to shift the culture towards sharing knowledge.
- Some challenges in sharing knowledge, for example, within the organization and with a large workforce distributed across many countries.
- Issues of capturing knowledge from diverse professional intellect.

NOTES

1 The author is indebted to the many senior executives at Novartis who generously gave of their knowledge and time for this project.
2 *Novartis Facts and Figures 1999/2000*. Accessed on-line on 21 September 2001 at http://www.novartis.com/
3 Orr, D. and Kitchens, S. (2001) 'I'll pay yours if you'll pay mine', *Forbes Global, 40*, 3 September, 36–8.
4 *Novartis Facts and Figures 1999/2000*. Accessed on-line on 21 September 2001 at http://www.novartis.com/
5 Hill, M., Novartis Communication, Media Relations, during visit to Novartis, 22 June 2000.
6 *Novartis Operational Review 2000*. Accessed on-line on 21 September 2001 at http://www.novartis.com.investors/financial_reports.shtml
7 Vasella, D. (2000). Address to the Annual General Meeting of Novartis AG, Basel, Switzerland, May.
8 *Novartis Operational Review 2000*. Accessed on-line on 21 September 2001 at http://www.novartis.com/.investors/financial_reports.shtml
9 Vasella, D. (2000). Address to the Annual General Meeting of Novartis AG, Basel, Switzerland, May.
10 Vasella, D. (2000). Address to the Annual General Meeting of Novartis AG, Basel, Switzerland, May.
11 Vasella, D. (2000). Address to the Annual General Meeting of Novartis AG, Basel, Switzerland, May.
12 http://www.novartis.com/about_novartis/company_info.shtml accessed 30 October 2001.
13 http://www.novartis.com/about_novartis/company_info.shtml accessed 30 October 2001.
14 http://www.novartis.com/about_novartis/company_info.shtml accessed 30 October 2001.
15 *Novartis Facts and Figures 1999/2000*. Accessed on-line on 21 September 2001 at http://www.novartis.com/
16 Vasella, D. (2000). Address to the Annual General Meeting of Novartis AG, Basel, Switzerland, May.
17 *Novartis Operational Review 2000*. Accessed on-line on 21 September 2001 at http://www.novartis.com/.investors/financial_reports.shtml
18 Vasella, D. (2000). Address to the Annual General Meeting of Novartis AG, Basel, Switzerland, May.
19 *Novartis Operational Review 2000*. Accessed on-line on 21 September 2001 at http://www.novartis.com/.investors/financial_reports.shtml
20 Vasella, D. (2000). Address to the Annual General Meeting of Novartis AG, Basel, Switzerland, May.
21 *Novartis Operational Review 2000*. Accessed on-line on 21 September 2001 at http://www.novartis.com/.investors/financial_reports.shtml

22   *Novartis Facts and Figures 1999/2000.* Accessed on-line on 21 September 2001 at http://www.novartis.com/

23   *Novartis Operational Review 2000.* Accessed on-line on 21 September 2001 at http://www.novartis.com/.investors/financial_reports.shtml

24   Wetter, H.-J., Head of Pharma Chemical Production, during visit to Novartis, 22 June 2000.

25   *Novartis Facts and Figures 1999/2000.* Accessed on-line on 21 September 2001 at http://www.novartis.com/

26   Staeheli, J., Corporate Knowledge Management, Novartis International, during visit to Novartis, 22 June 2000.

27   Matter, B., Quality System and Quality Management, Notes issued during visit to Novartis, 22 June 2000.

28   Vasella, D. (2000). Address to the Annual General Meeting of Novartis AG, Basel, Switzerland, May.

29   Vasella, D. (2000). Address to the Annual General Meeting of Novartis AG, Basel, Switzerland, May.

30   *Novartis Facts and Figures 1999/2000.* Accessed on-line on 21 September 2001 at http://www.novartis.com/

31   *Novartis Facts and Figures 1999/2000.* Accessed on-line on 21 September 2001 at http://www.novartis.com/

32   *Novartis Facts and Figures 1999/2000.* Accessed on-line on 21 September 2001 at http://www.novartis.com/

33   The website can be viewed at www.life-sciences.novartis.com.

34   *Novartis Facts and Figures 1999/2000.* Accessed on-line on 21 September 2001 at http://www.novartis.com/

35   Seiter, A., Responses to formal questions in a paper distributed during visit to Novartis, 22 June 2000.

36   Himberg, C., HR Manager, Novartis International, during visit to Novartis, 22 June 2000.

37   *Novartis Operational Review 2000.* Accessed on-line on 21 September 2001 at http://www.novartis.com/investors/financial_reports.shtml

38   *Novartis Facts and Figures 1999/2000.* Accessed on-line on 21 September 2001 at http://www.novartis.com/

39   Staeheli, J., Corporate Knowledge Management, Novartis International, during visit to Novartis, 22 June 2000.

40   Staeheli, J., Corporate Knowledge Management, Novartis International, during visit to Novartis, 22 June 2000.

41   Staeheli, J., Corporate Knowledge Management, Novartis International, during visit to Novartis, 22 June 2000.

Four Royal Australian Navy:
Commanding New Leadership[1]

GAYLE C. AVERY AND STUDENT TEAM

Fair play, equality and a can-do attitude ...[2]

Vice Admiral, David J. Shackleton, AO, Chief Of Navy

Although Australia has long been dependent on the seas, her first naval fleet consisted of only two destroyers in 1909. This became the Royal Australian Navy (RAN), an Australian Defence Force Service that has since played major roles in a range of conflicts and peacekeeping efforts. About 12 500 people work in the Royal Australian Navy, in addition to 5 815 reserves whom the Navy can call upon if needed. Approximately one-third of the force serves at sea in 59 fleet units. When figures are totalled for Defence expenditure on navy related activities, more than A$2.7 billion is spent annually and naval assets total more than A$7.6 billion.[3]

Maritime Headquarters (MHQ) is located in Sydney in one purpose-planned building and several annexes.[4] The headquarters is specifically designed to support maritime operations and organized functionally with major divisions for operations planning, command/control communications and intelligence, as well as logistic and administration support. MHQ also possesses facilities for environmental support, tactical development and shares a warfare strategy resource with Navy Headquarters. A 'mirror' headquarters located in Western Australia, which shares all data and information, is designed to facilitate command and control continuity in the event of the destruction of MHQ.

The Royal Australian Navy's operational vessels range from small fleet auxiliaries to large amphibious and support ships. The modern Royal Australian Navy's mission is to be able to fight and win at sea as part of an Australian joint or international combined force. 'Everything we do must recognize that and be

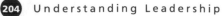

linked to it,' according to the Chief of Navy.[5] Like most modern organizations, the Navy sees achieving its goals and associated strategic priorities as critical to high-level outcomes.

ORGANIZATION AND STRUCTURE

The Royal Australian Navy is a highly-structured Defence organization at the beginning of the twenty-first century, residing in the Department of Defence (DOD) and being dependent on the DOD for functions such as acquisitions (for example, new submarines). The Royal Australian Navy's reporting lines to 14 different DOD sections were to reduce considerably under the envisaged new structure (see Figure CS4.1).[6] Internally, the Royal Australian Navy has its own defined structure that sees ultimate reporting responsibilities resting with the Commander or Chief of the Navy (CN), David Shackleton.

As shown on Figure CS4.1, the Warrant Officer of the Navy (WO-N) is responsible to the CN as the most senior-ranking sailor, and exercises command over all other sailors in the Royal Australian Navy. The WO-N is a member of the personal staff of the CN and as such operates from the office of the CN and is a member of the CN's Senior Advisory Committee. The WO-N's primary duty is to represent to CN and others the solicited and unsolicited views, concerns and opinions of sailors that affect the Navy as a whole. In addition, the WO-N is responsible for assisting in the overall maintenance of discipline and morale of sailors.

Two high-ranking officers support the CN: the Deputy CN (DCN) and the Maritime Commander (MC). Rear Admiral Brian Adams was appointed Deputy Chief of Navy in 1999 and is responsible to the CN for overseeing the day-to-day business and administration of the Navy, and for the development and coordination of the Navy's strategic policies and plans. The CN assigned full command of all Navy combat forces to his Maritime Commander, Rear Admiral Geoff Smith. The Maritime Commander is also responsible, among other things, for the operational training, readiness and effectiveness of units and personnel assigned to the command; naval control of shipping; Royal Australian Navy search and rescue authority; submarine search and rescue; submarine operating authority; and administering Maritime Command assets.[7]

Australian Navy Systems (NAVSYSCOM) is a new command created to exploit the synergy of the Navy's components and introduce a systems approach to management. By bringing together personnel management, training, engineering, operational and logistics support, safety and certification, NAVSYSCOM strives to be a 'one stop shop' to deliver the support and services demanded by a modern Navy, which would focus particularly on Force Element Groups (FEG).

The FEGs are regarded as the Navy's engine room for generating naval combat power. This is because the FEGs pull together and integrate the necessary

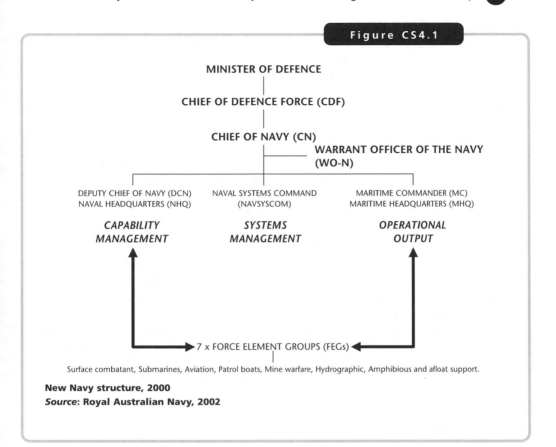

Figure CS4.1

MINISTER OF DEFENCE

CHIEF OF DEFENCE FORCE (CDF)

CHIEF OF NAVY (CN)

WARRANT OFFICER OF THE NAVY (WO-N)

| DEPUTY CHIEF OF NAVY (DCN) | NAVAL SYSTEMS COMMAND | MARITIME COMMANDER (MC) |
| NAVAL HEADQUARTERS (NHQ) | (NAVSYSCOM) | MARITIME HEADQUARTERS (MHQ) |

CAPABILITY MANAGEMENT — *SYSTEMS MANAGEMENT* — *OPERATIONAL OUTPUT*

7 x FORCE ELEMENT GROUPS (FEGs)

Surface combatant, Submarines, Aviation, Patrol boats, Mine warfare, Hydrographic, Amphibious and afloat support.

New Navy structure, 2000
Source: **Royal Australian Navy, 2002**

inputs and convert them into operational outputs such as platforms, weapons systems and people able to conduct the Navy's core business. The FEGs define and articulate their requirements, priorities and expectations from other agencies and service providers within the Navy's planning framework.

The intent of the Navy's new structure is to align accountability and authority. FEGs monitor the delivery of goods and services to achieve goals defined by the Maritime Commander and Deputy CN. Each FEG coordinates and takes overall responsibility for a comprehensive planning process encapsulated in an FEG Master Plan. FEGs also include relevant support centres, facilities and infrastructure, and either own or have direct call upon the necessary integrated, multi-disciplinary staff expertise and resources to encompass all aspects of the responsibilities assigned to it.

The seven FEGs are:

1 Australian Navy Surface Combatants Force (comprising ADELAIDE and ANZAC Class frigates);

2   Australian Navy Submarine Force;
3   Naval Aviation Force;
4   Australian Navy Patrol Boat Force;
5   Mine Warfare and Clearance Diving Forces;
6   Australian Navy Hydrographic Force; and
7   Amphibious Warfare Forces along with the Afloat Support Force (Site Offline).

Both internal and external environments affecting the Royal Australian Navy are changing radically. The CN reported that greater concentration is required on the unchanging core businesses of delivering combat power, helping provide central policy direction, resource priority setting and allocation, while enabling groups to deliver common goods and services to the entire organization.[8]

However, a long-term shift is anticipated from funding current capability to also funding future capability, forcing a greater drive for efficiencies with the Royal Australian Navy. Practices must add value, and everything must be questioned. The Royal Australian Navy has changed the peacetime internal structure from a simple hierarchy to more of a matrix structure, using a circle communications strategy. The new matrix structure is intended to enable people to work together as a close, coordinated team in combat situations, and to enable other team members to cover for the skills of any lost personnel. Therefore, close teamwork and complete flexibility are required in the new naval structure.

PEOPLE

The old belief that people are a cost to be minimized in order to achieve efficiency runs counter to the CN's comment that 'the quality of Navy people still comes through as the Navy's greatest attribute.'[9] The Royal Australian Navy's highest stated priority relates to its people.[10]

Breaking with tradition, the CN explicitly holds both civilian and uniformed members of the Royal Australian Navy as equally important members of the naval team. The following general principles apply to developing and employing people in the Royal Australian Navy[11]:

- Officers are responsible for leading and managing the Navy in conducting operations, and its on-going strategic development and improvement.
- Sailors are responsible for giving management effect to the leadership direction of officers through their technical expertise to operate and maintain the Navy's platforms and systems. Sailors lead and manage in their areas of expertise.

- Civilian members of the Navy complement the roles of the officers and sailors. They provide expertise outside the core competency requirement of uniformed people. They are not normally required to serve at sea. Civilian members lead and manage in their area of expertise.
- Contractors provide expertise that officers, sailors or civilian members of the Navy do not possess. Their tenure and responsibility is limited through contractual mechanisms. Contractors provide supplementary support in niche areas.
- Officers and sailors form the seagoing Navy, and civilian members of the Navy shape and implement the support and maintenance framework that enables the Navy to go to sea. Collectively they are responsible to the CN for the Royal Australian Navy's efficient running.
- In exceptional cases, Navy civilians and contractors may be required to go to sea and serve in a combat zone.
- The Navy's approach to people is to be shaped around these requirements.

The objective is for staff to not only maintain their combat capability through training and exercises, but also to continually develop their operational capability by relying heavily on training, particularly complex technical training.

HUMAN RESOURCE POLICIES

Critical to achieving the people-focus of the new leadership is realigning the traditional 'personnel' departments with the new business direction. Personnel departments need to change from their traditional welfare-focus and seeing their mission as assisting members to work through the formal regulations on allowances, conditions of service, employment transfers or discharge procedures.

The Navy acknowledges that managing people is an important function for managers and supervisors. An on-going issue is managing people to be responsive in a hostile or dangerous situation, using minimal resources while relying on their initiative, taking responsibility, and complying with orders.

Therefore, the Royal Australian Navy is attempting to embrace a range of HR-related strategies aimed at increasing workforce flexibility and organizational performance. The goal is to ensure, amongst other things, that the right people are in the right jobs and that the organization can attract, develop and retain quality people in a more competitive employment environment.[12] Over recent years, this approach has led the Royal Australian Navy to adopt various HR policies already in place in the wider community, such as performance-based pay, flexible work practices and flexible remuneration opportunities.[13] In addition, the CN has called for performance measures and uses 360-degree feedback to complement the formal assessment process, to help identify outstanding performers or underperformers, and to give individuals feedback on their performance.[14]

Providing a work environment that is free of harassment and discrimination is a primary goal, and appropriate strategies are in place. The main objectives of the Royal Australian Navy's equity and diversity policy are to:

- ensure that equity and diversity principles are embedded in workplace practices, leadership and management;
- foster workplace equity and diversity;
- recruit and retain people from diverse backgrounds; and
- enable employees to participate in forming personnel policies.[15]

The Defence equity and diversity program is widely communicated and disseminated, and the policy is constantly monitored and evaluated. It also includes redundancy measures designed to compensate for any particular weakness.

The equity and diversity policies appear to be working. In 1998, only 3.3 per cent of Royal Australian Navy officers and 10.2 per cent of sailors were women.[16] At the time, in 1998, 34 per cent of officers under training were female, as were 15.5 per cent of sailors under training. In 2001, the breakdown between men and women in the Royal Australian Navy showed an increased proportion of females, with about 16 per cent of the total Royal Australian Navy personnel being female. In 2001, 18.5 per cent of officers and 14.9 per cent of the sailors were women, representing increases of about 15 per cent and 4.7 per cent respectively.

Approximately one-third of Royal Australian Navy personnel actually serve at sea, including roughly similar proportions of men and women officers and sailors. For some time in the late 1980s, debate raged about whether women should be allowed to hold combat positions and fight alongside men at sea. Clearly, by limiting women's opportunities, the Royal Australian Navy was in breach of its non-discrimination and equal employment opportunity policies, and this was one area where long-ingrained beliefs had to be challenged.

Succession planning is vital, but the Royal Australian Navy's closed system means that it can only recruit from within for almost all important positions. People are therefore expected to 'train up' their immediate relief staff, ideally having at least two people to choose from for senior positions, without any gaps in the succession pipeline.[17]

LEADERSHIP PHILOSOPHY

The Royal Australian Navy places considerable emphasis on leadership, asserting that strong leadership and managing people effectively at all levels is required to retain its reputation for professionalism and maintain the necessary competencies to achieve the appropriate level of operational efficiency to 'fight and win at sea'. The Royal Australian Navy has long recognized that its ability to deal with change should also be included in its leadership and management culture.[18]

Different kinds of leadership apply within the Royal Australian Navy, depending on the context and nature of the management issue. Lower levels of the Royal Australian Navy operate under a simple hierarchical structure in peacetime, with clear and rigid reporting lines. These reporting lines change in combat situations, where members from different task forces combine together to form fighting teams.

In July 1999, the then new CN issued a report on leadership. In this report, which was intended to start a dialog about leadership, he outlined his leadership philosophy:

> Our successors must be able to thank us for a job well done and take over a better ship, or we will have failed in our duty. Our leadership approach therefore needs to be one with the characteristics of honesty and competency, and be inspirational and forward looking. We all need to lead. I am proud to have the privilege of leading and serving you. I am on watch. I have the ship.[19]

Naval values, as expressed in the CN's own words,[20] are:

> to reinforce that the Defence of our country is a serious responsibility, it is only entrusted to those who are worthy of the task. Earning the trust of Australians, understanding that our country trusts us; and not damaging that trust is a central consideration for all of us. Fair play, equality and a can-do attitude are distinctly Australian qualities, and the Navy will be an organisation that reflects these features of our society. Particular principles we will all be prepared to stand by and demonstrate in our behaviour are:
>
> - our proven world class professionalism;
> - the personal application of physical and moral courage, loyalty, honesty and integrity as individual men and women; and
> - demonstrable dedication and commitment to serving the Navy and country as Australians.
>
> If anyone does not believe that they can live by these values, be they uniformed or non uniformed, men or women; then they have no place in the Navy. It is that fundamental.

According to the CN:

> All officers, sailors and civilians exercise leadership in some form at some level and the success of the Navy is dependent on

the quality of its leadership. However, I look specifically to officers, warrant officers and senior civilian officers to form the leadership team of the Navy. Junior sailors and civilians can of course look forward to becoming a member of this team as they gain experience and advance. As a component of the Australian Defence Force, and like the Army and Air Force, the Navy is one of Australia's enduring institutions. But, like all institutions, if it is to remain relevant to contemporary society and the people it serves, it needs to constantly refresh itself with new ideas and approaches to doing business. But it needs to do this while retaining its focus on its core business – a business that will not always be in vogue in all areas of our society.[21]

LEADERSHIP

Naval and infantry leadership differ in that 'the aim of leadership at sea is the ship's company and their ship as a fighting instrument and the aim on land is the individual as a fighting instrument.'[22] Navy leaders are required to demonstrate flexible leadership styles appropriate to the task and team environment, be committed to Navy values and display leadership characteristics such as appropriate interpersonal skills, high levels of self-discipline and high ethical, moral and personal standards. The Navy has also concluded that leaders who direct their leadership toward the aspirations of their people find that their people perform better, require less supervision and are highly motivated to continuously improve the organization.[23]

Recognizing that leadership will affect the Royal Australian Navy's success in the face of rapid change in the Defence area, the CN wrote:

... strong leadership is required to meet these goals and implement these principles. All members of the Navy are considered leaders, but those officers and sailors at the most senior ranks must set directions for others to follow, and lead from the front. By 'leadership', I mean task oriented and objectively focused direction that uses a wide range of tools and techniques to implement and measure performance. I do not mean 'yell louder until they acquiesce or go deaf'. Leadership is the engine, the glue, the enabling function and the main multiplier. It's a key deliverable of our senior officers as well as being an attribute to which team outcome is highly sensitive. I expect leaders to consistently demonstrate honesty and professional competence, and be able to inspire other people to strive for their vision of the future. In this sense, it is vital that *all* those who lead *have a vision of the future* which, if I am succeeding, will be about the same as mine. CNSAC members are personally and actively to generate and foster an environment that encourages this philosophy to flourish. This is of great importance to me.[24]

Naval personnel have two kinds of behaviour to exhibit.[25] Sometimes they are expected to obey without question, but the key elements of naval discipline are said to be cooperation and teamwork. Further, much of the discipline at sea is self-discipline. Leadership at sea depends vitally on people with professional competence, and risks being shared by everyone on board in times of war. Lord Nelson provides 'the crowning example of naval leadership, whose ability to generate enthusiasm and devotion amongst his subordinates at every level was a basic element of his success in battle.'[26]

Strong symbolism runs through the armed forces, and can be used to create devotion and enthusiasm. Elaborate ceremonies, crisp uniforms decorated with medals, a unique language and reverent observance of authority are proudly displayed within the Naval arenas. The Royal Australian Navy's culture is built upon the British heritage and the core values of courage, loyalty and dedication. Some traditional naval customs are described in Box CS4.1.

Box CS4.1

Some Royal Australian Navy customs, traditions and language[27]

Customs and traditions are regarded as important in growing and maintaining naval *esprit de corps* and identity. Examples of naval ceremonies and phraseology provide a brief insight into this part of naval life:

- *The salute*: Traces of the origin of saluting can be seen in the conventional exchange of this courtesy between officers and sailors today. Saluting with an open hand indicates friendly intentions and can be traced back to times when this form of salute indicated to people that both were unarmed; the hand being raised to indicate that it was clear of any object that could be used to injure the other. The hand carried to the head in salute has descended from the Middle Ages, and is a further indication of friendship between people. The present day salute is a symbol of greeting, of mutual respect, trust and confidence, initiated by the junior in rank, but with no loss of dignity on either side.
- *Ceremonial sunset*: Beat to quarters and ceremonial sunsets are perhaps the oldest and most significant of naval ceremonies. Although steeped in Naval history, they now usually conclude days of special importance. Beat to quarters stems from the 17th Century when a drum roll or beating of drums was carried out in warships to signify a 'Call to Arms', when an enemy ship had been sighted. Today, ships' companies are called to 'action stations' by loud electronic alarms. Ceremonial sunset is traditionally maintained by Navies throughout the world to salute the lowering of the ensign at the close of the day. It was also the custom for Captains of men of war to prove that their gunpowder was dry and ready for the next encounter. This they did by firing an evening gun and having their Marine Detachment fire a fusillade of rifles.

- *Splice the mainbrace*: Many different explanations concern the origin of this expression, but it is generally considered that this operation was one of such rarity and difficulty in the days of sail as to warrant the issue of an additional amount of rum to the ship's company. The main brace, being one of the heaviest pieces of running rigging in the ship, was probably seldom spliced if damaged, but totally renewed instead. Today, the term is used to signify a change of monarch or to congratulate the company of a ship.
- *Port and starboard*: The term 'port' is mentioned as far back as 1580. Legend has it that the name is derived from the ancient practice of placing the left side of the vessel towards the shore when going alongside, because the leeboard side could be easily unrigged to avoid damaging the rigging, while the starboard side would be required to safely navigate the vessel. 'Starboard' is derived from the old Saxon word 'steerboard', which was a paddle situated on the right hand quarter to act as a rudder.
- *Aye aye*: The correct and seaman-like reply on board a ship upon receipt of an order. The literal translation is 'At your service always'.
- *Mess and Messmates*: 'Mess' comes from the Latin word *mensa,* meaning a table, or the Gothic *mesa,* meaning a dish of food. Sailors eating from the same mess or at the same table are 'messmates'. A sailor is always to be loyal and true to messmates.
- *Medals and decorations*: The custom of wearing medals on the left breast can be traced back to the time of the Crusades, when Knights wore their badge of honour near the heart. Also, the left side was the side that was covered by the shield, which was held on the left arm protecting both the heart and the badge of honour.
- *Admiral*: The word 'Admiral' is a corruption of the Arabic *Amir-al-Bahr*, meaning Commander of the Sea.

DISCUSSION ISSUES

1 Who are the current leaders in the Royal Australian Navy, and who will be tomorrow's Naval leaders? Which leadership paradigms can you identify in this case, and who is exercising the various paradigms?

2 Identify the kinds of leadership paradigms that the Royal Australian Navy requires in fulfilling its mission. Where does Visionary leadership fit into the Royal Australian Navy's leadership?

3 Which systems and processes need adjustment and/or aligning? How does the structure fit with the other parts of the system and the past and future leadership styles in the Navy?

4 Do you agree that command and team styles are appropriate for peace and combat conditions respectively? If you do agree, suggest how Royal Australian Navy personnel might develop the flexibility to move between these styles. If you do not agree, should there be any difference in leadership style between peace and war? How could the Royal Australian Navy achieve this?

5 Examine the quotations of the CN and identify his personal leadership style. Where does the CN see leadership in the Navy? What kinds of leadership does he want in the organization and who should be the leaders?

6 The Royal Australian Navy has to change. Identify the extent of the changes necessary and the kinds of leadership required to achieve these changes. Consider the relevance of different leadership paradigms, including Classical, Transactional, Visionary and Organic modes. Can the CN command the necessary changes to happen? Outline how the Royal Australian Navy might go about effecting such change.

7 Can you identify substitutes for leadership in the Royal Australian Navy? Is there evidence for spirituality and emotion in the Royal Australian Navy workplace?

8 What are the vision and values that the CN is espousing, and how could the Royal Australian Navy culture and symbolism be used to support the vision and reinforce the values? How could the traditional culture serve to impede change?

9 Is there evidence that the Royal Australian Navy is a learning and/or teaching organization? How does the Royal Australian Navy manage its knowledge? What role does mentoring play in this organization? How would you recommend the Royal Australian Navy goes about developing its future leadership?

10 Who are the stakeholders in the Royal Australian Navy, and how are their interests being addressed? What evidence is there that the leadership is concerned about the organization's sustainability?

KEY ISSUES

- Special naval language, culture and tradition provide a strong context.
- Use of strong symbolism to unite people and culture.
- Royal Australian Navy is answerable to a range of stakeholders including naval and civilian staff, government departments, government of the day, media, Australian taxpayers, at times to other Navies.
- Vision and values espoused by the CN.
- Teamwork at various levels within a matrix structure.
- New matrix structure with multiskilled personnel working in teams is aimed at increasing flexibility.
- All personnel are required to exhibit leadership of some sort.
- Striving for more distributed leadership.
- Distinguish between leadership and management at officer and sailor levels.
- Sailors lead and manage in areas of their expertise.
- Civilian members of Royal Australian Navy lead and manage in areas of their expertise.
- Collectively, civilian and naval members are responsible for the efficient running of the Navy.
- Need to realign central defence personnel departments with the new business direction of the Navy.
- Increasing numbers of women officers but still a relatively male-dominated organization.
- Navy leaders need flexible leadership styles: commitment to values, alignment with follower aspirations.
- Leadership is task-oriented and goal-oriented, but simultaneously expected to be inspirational and guided by a vision.
- CN requires all leaders to have a vision of the future, which is aligned to the CN's overall vision.
- Mixed leadership styles, sometimes command and control, at others self-disciplining and self-directing.
- Manage knowledge via training, mentoring and developing others, and through formal records.
- Succession planning and mentoring evident, with people developing their immediate reliefs.
- Incremental change required (continuous improvement).
- Central control, power diffused to teams at various levels.
- Substitutes for leadership: teams, training, systems and procedures, professionalism.
- Potential clash of strong culture with more flexible new leadership.

- In/out groups may form among ship's crew or back at base, making LMX theory applicable.

NOTES

1 The Royal Australian Navy (RAN) is undergoing major change in its direction and leadership development. This case study expands on research undertaken for an assignment by Kerri Gill, Louise Hands, Andrew Hosking, Frank Luksic, David Scott and Bridget Stafford at Macquarie Graduate School of Management and refers to the period 1999–2001.

2 Shackleton, D.J. (1999) *Leadership Issues for the Navy*, 26 July, 1999, accessed December 2001 at http://www.navy.gov.au

3 *Defence Annual Report, 1997–1998*. Defence Publishing Service, Canberra.

4 http://www.navy.gov.au/ accessed 10 December 2001.

5 Shackleton, D.J. (1999) *op. cit.*

6 Within the Department these sections are called Programs and have equivalent standing with the commonly known sections, Army, Navy and Air Force.

7 http://www.navy.gov.au/ accessed 10 December 2001.

8 Shackleton, D.J. (1999), op. cit.

9 Shackleton, D.J. (1999), op. cit.

10 Australian Maritime Doctrine. Accessed on-line on 23 May 2001 at http://www.navy.gov.au/6_facts/factsandfigures.html

11 Shackleton, D.J. (1999). op. cit.

12 Department of Defence *Defence and People and How We Work*, Canberra: Department of Defence, June 1999.

13 http://www.defence.gov.au/dpe/

14 Shackleton, D.J. (1999), op. cit.

15 *Defence Workplace Equity and Diversity Plan – 1998–2001*. Defence Publishing Service, Canberra.

16 *Defence Annual Report 1997–1998*. Defence Publishing Service, Canberra.

17 Shackleton, D.J. (1999), op. cit.

18 Defence Instruction (Navy) – *Personnel 18–1*, 27 May 1996.

19 Shackleton, D.J. (1999), op. cit.

20 Shackleton, D.J. (1999), op. cit.

21 Shackleton, D.J. (1999), op. cit.

22 Australian Maritime Doctrine. Accessed on-line on 23 May 2001 at http://www.navy.gov.au/6_facts/factsandfigures.html, p. 77.

23 *Navy Publication ABR 2010* (1996).

24 Shackleton, D.J. (1999), op. cit.

25 Australian Maritime Doctrine. Accessed on-line on 23 May 2001 at http://www.navy.gov.au/6_facts/factsandfigures.html

26 Australian Maritime Doctrine. Accessed on-line on 23 May 2001 at http://www.navy.gov.au/6_facts/factsandfigures.html, pp. 77–78.

27 http://www.navy.gov.au/6_facts/1_tradition.htm

Five **SAP: Leader of the Internet Pack**[1]

GAYLE C. AVERY

I'm a Berliner – fast, loud, obnoxious, industrious, brutally open.[2]

Attributed to Hasso Plattner, former co-CEO and co-Founder.

Almost by chance in 1972, five former IBM systems engineers founded SAP (Systems, Applications, and Products in Data Processing) in Germany. The founders' vision was to develop and provide standard software solutions to business problems – revolutionary at the time because their competitors were developing only expensive, customized software for businesses. Given the emerging technological revolution, the time was ripe for an organization like SAP to differentiate itself and carve out new directions in computer technology and data processing.

Today, SAP is the world's largest inter-enterprise software company, providing a range of software packages that can integrate internal and external parts of an organization. SAP provides software that helps businesses integrate their far-flung departments and systems, such as HR, finance and sales. SAP's mission is to 'lead the industry by providing complete, industry vertical solutions enabling our customers to harness the power of the Internet and exploit e-business opportunities'.[3]

The SAP vision is 'to be the market leader in the definition and delivery of software solutions for rapid and sustainable customer value.' Externally, SAP has a vision of how businesses can and will succeed today – and tomorrow in what they call the new, new economy. 'The New, New Economy ... will help put e-business and its importance to overall business growth in perspective for visitors, whether they are current SAP users or are exploring the benefits of technology solutions for their businesses for the first time,' says Marty Homlish, SAP Executive Vice President and Global Chief Marketing Officer.[4]

Although criticized for sometimes treating customers poorly and some quality assurance problems,[5] SAP soon won 80 per cent of the German market.

Despite on-going technical problems with the software, big corporations the world over adopted SAP products because of promised efficiency gains.[6]

SAP came to dominate in enterprise resource planning (ERP) software, with approximately 25 per cent of that market.[7] SAP has experienced rapid organic growth, rather than growing through acquisition. In 2001, Forbes Global ranked the company as the 38th largest (by market capitalization) company outside the US.[8] As the third-largest independent software company in the world, SAP counts more than half the world's 500 top companies among its 13 500 users in 120 countries.[9] Forming a partnership with Microsoft in 1993 to define industry standards for conducting business on the Internet accelerated SAP's global expansion. However, less than 10 years on, this partnership had started to turn into a battleground for software for business processes in small and medium enterprises (SMEs).[10]

STRATEGIES

To survive, SAP needs to be agile in addressing changing situations. SAP is under constant pressure from many sources, including globalization, the expanding technological industry, diversification, mergers and acquisitions, and the Internet. These pressures also provide opportunities to innovate and offer consumers new business solutions.[11] In the second half of the 1990s, SAP appears to have been caught off guard by the staggering increase in competition and its customers' sudden interest in e-business.[12] The potential of the World Wide Web (the web), particularly for delivering enterprise software systems, had largely escaped the attention of the European SAP executive leadership team, possibly because the US market was the key driver in the e-commerce revolution. The company was losing ground in the US market, particularly to close competitor Oracle, and needed strategies for stemming the tide.

One response resulted in the rapid development of mySAP.com™, a product that provides a platform for e-business. MySAP.com™ enables companies of all sizes and industries to fully engage their employees, customers and partners in capitalizing on the Internet's capabilities.[13] In the first year, one million people signed up for mySAP.com™, representing about 10 per cent of e-business at the time. However, the product ran into some problems, probably because of the haste with which it was developed and marketed.[14]

At the 1998 'Enterprise 98' conference, Co-CEO Plattner stated that SAP needed to reframe its business strategies. The focus would be on using the web as a vehicle for delivering SAP's ERP business solutions. Plattner was reported as wanting to grow the company's existing 10 million users to 100 million, primarily via the release of mySAP.com™ This represented a brave vision in a competitive world, as the dot.com revolution demonstrated.

Ironically, rapid changes in technology pose a threat to SAP, which not only needs to provide leading products and services, but also to stay ahead of the competition in this fast-paced industry. SAP's business is moving away from being a mere product vendor to becoming a solutions provider concerned with the business side of a customer's needs. A customer could stipulate an increase of, say, 25 per cent required in its business, and SAP would take responsibility for delivering this increased success. This change of focus created special leadership challenges at SAP, as the company has been forced to re-invent itself to stay competitive. For example, the company had originally been structured to support ERP sales. By 1999, ERP vendors were no longer the driving force behind a SAP focused on the Internet, and ERP sales staff needed to change direction and be retrained to become knowledgeable about the Internet.

More recently, SAP is evolving further from being a solutions provider into becoming a service provider. This strategy is based on the assumption that by selling solutions, people also sell hardware and software. This requires a new kind of sales force, where understanding what is being sold is very important. The product is much more intangible, as the present customer wants painless e-business.

FINANCIALS

Since going public on the German stock exchange in 1988, SAP is now listed on several international stock exchanges. However, three of the founders of the company and their families retain the bulk of the ordinary shares (63 per cent); the remaining shares are held primarily by institutional investors in Germany, Europe and North America.[15]

From 1991–95, growth in the US market overtook the revenue generated in Germany, and the US-generated revenue stream continued to grow at more than 85 per cent per year, compared with Germany's 22 per cent. Customers pay monthly or yearly fees, depending on which software programs they have purchased and how many employees use them.

R&D is the highest growth area at SAP, registering the second highest expense on the balance sheet. Survival depends, however, on the firm's being able to finance the implementation of the many innovations emerging from this area.[16]

In 2000, the firm hit rocky financial times.[17] SAP announced a 45 per cent reduction in pre-tax profit for the first quarter of 2000, despite a reported 10 per cent increase in revenue. The organization attributed this reduction in profitability to a decrease in consulting following the Y2K problem, and lower income from software sales brought about by fierce competition among web-based products.[18] The company's financial performance improved throughout the 2000 fiscal year, exceeding expectations to conclude with total revenues of €6266 million.[19] Revenues from mySAP.com™ continued to grow throughout the year. As the joint CEOs put it,' … after a turbulent and challenging year, we are in a strong position and we look forward to the future with great confidence.'[20] However, in 2001, SAP's share price decreased substantially and remained volatile well after the technology bubble burst.

ORGANIZATION

With head office located in Walldorf, Germany, SAP has offices spread around the globe including Europe, the Americas and Asia Pacific. An Executive Board and an Extended Management Board, comprising six and 12 members respectively, manage the company. In 2000, the Executive Board was reconstituted, with five new members being appointed.

SAP is a highly global organization with just under 80 per cent of sales and over 50 per cent of employees worldwide (see Figure CS5.1).[21] Being dispersed around the world, with suppliers and customers all over the globe, SAP is itself a virtual organization and, internally, the company works as far as possible in a paperless way, relying heavily on e-mail. SAP uses some of its own technologies in organizing the business. For example, Product Lifecycle Management software links SAP's business planning and product configuration applications, as well as providing web-based tools that facilitate collaboration with customers, suppliers and contractors on product design changes.

Originally, SAP did not believe that it needed managers, but as the firm grew, the unwanted hierarchies appeared.[22] After reaching 8000 employees, SAP could no longer cope without managers. Large numbers of managers were hired to 'manage' the organization's rapid growth. In 2000, SAP had seven layers of management, making it very hierarchical.

One of the consequences of this focus on management was that people may be located with their manager rather than being co-located with those they actually work with. This impacted badly on collaboration, a serious issue for SAP. Since restructuring to become more Internet-oriented, work at SAP is organized largely through teams, which are typically composed of consulting staff, sales people, solutions architects and training staff. These teams form Quality Circles, are attuned to customers' needs, and are committed to bringing competitive advantage to SAP. Thus the hierarchy appears to be hindering collaboration, communication and teamwork.

SAP's operations consist of two main areas: a *front end* developing the business application software, with sales and pre-sales service; and a *back end* consisting of implementation services, training and life cycle support.

Implementation services cover four major activities, starting with advising on appropriate software that makes cost and efficiency sense for a particular customer. A second implementation service customizes the software. SAP's specialized templates and methodology assist customers with the flow of business processes needed to make the SAP software work efficiently for

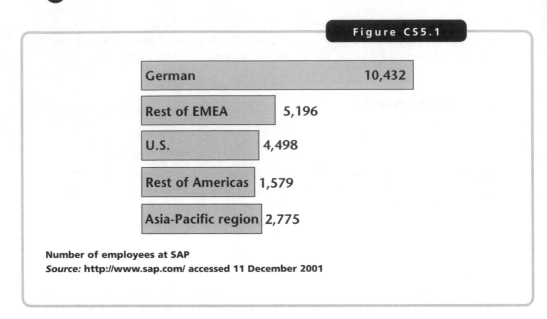

Figure CS5.1

German	10,432
Rest of EMEA	5,196
U.S.	4,498
Rest of Americas	1,579
Asia-Pacific region	2,775

Number of employees at SAP
Source: http://www.sap.com/ accessed 11 December 2001

industries such as automotive, consumer goods, higher education and media. The technical management service is concerned with upgrading technology and methods to minimize business disruption to the client, system maintenance and advice on appropriate hardware. Finally, the development area enables information to flow appropriately between SAP and other software applications.

By combining or bundling their front-end and back-end capabilities, SAP gains additional competitive advantage. Each new capability added to the bundle makes the combination more difficult for competitors to copy.[23] It is also less likely that a single individual can command all these capabilities.

PARTNERS

Once, SAP claimed that it did not need any partners. Today, SAP is a global network of networks.[24] This is very evident in SAP's partnership arrangements. Through extensive strategic partnering with customers, competitors and suppliers, SAP aims to grow further because forming relationships is seen as an opportunity to extend the business, rather than as a cost. This spirit of cooperation and partnering is critical to SAP's competitive advantage. For example, in compensating for its own weakness in the HR area, SAP draws on PeopleSoft's HR expertise through a strategic partnership.

Customers are key to SAP's networks, and its 6000 primary customers come from manufacturing, retailing, banking, telecommunications, utilities and the public sector. Of SAP's approximately 10 million secondary customers, around half generate over US$200 million revenue per year.[25] Plattner's vision was to grow the customer base, and SAP developed strategies to address the customer dissatisfaction the company once ignored.[26]

SAP systematically channels customer feedback into product development, and engages in projects with individual customers to speed up development and ensure that new applications meet customer needs. Customers benefit by helping shape the software and using it before competitors. In-depth dialog with customers and formal meetings with user groups enable SAP to convert its customers' specialist knowledge into industry-specific solutions. Even the relationship between two key customers is recognized and maximized.

By partnering with expert developers, SAP improves its speed to market, and also improves the customer service experience. The SAP Strategic Network leverages the strong relationships built with customers. SAP forms relationships when improving a customer's business efficiency, which may be reactivated when future software improvements are being designed and tested.

An organization that once claimed it did not need alliances, SAP even forms strategic partnerships with suppliers, particularly those experts who accelerate the speed of supplying the customer.[27] For most supply partners, their exclusive contract with SAP precludes them from building partnerships with other vendors, creating a significant barrier to entry for SAP's competitors. In 2000, SAP announced the establishment of a mySAP.com™ Partner Network, designed to assist customers with faster implementations and greater product support. Partners certified as e-business solution providers in the mySAP.com™ Partner Network can use their e-business expertise to provide a bridge between people and technology for SAP customers worldwide. Members of the mySAP.com™ Partner Network include major consulting firms and information technology (IT) companies such as Compaq Computer Corp., Hewlett-Packard Company, IBM Corp., Sun Microsystems Inc. and Unisys Corp.

Each partner is fully capable of supporting the requirements of SAP customers in implementing mySAP.com™ solutions, and brings significant experience providing e-commerce-related services across multiple industries.

LEADERSHIP

The combined approaches of the dual CEOs have had an enduring influence on the company, particularly in achieving its success in Germany. Although there is no formal hierarchy among the top management, in an informal one, Kagermann and Plattner, were the most visible. Box CS5.1 provides an insight into these two very different men. Essentially, SAP was led by the visionary but temperamental Plattner, and managed by the more pragmatic, calm and efficient Kagermann. Interestingly Kagermann himself refers to 'managing the unmanageable' in reference to globally distributed organizations such as SAP.[28] It is to address this complexity that SAP developed much of its software.

Box CS5.1

Contrasting Co-CEOs and Co-Chairs

Hasso Plattner

According to the German press, Hasso Plattner has had a 'dream career'[29] This energetic sportsman was born in Berlin in 1944, with his father a doctor and mother a teacher. He attended a strict military style school in Bavaria after his parents divorced, where he developed a street-fighter mentality.[30] The young Plattner greatly admired J.F. Kennedy for his vision of getting to the moon.[31]

After graduating in telecommunications engineering from Karlsruhe University in 1968, he worked at IBM in Germany. Four years later, in 1972, he and four IBM colleagues founded a software development business, after being rebuffed by IBM when they wanted to create an off-the-shelf financial package for businesses. Their small business was incorporated in 1976, having reached 20 employees and a turnover of around €2 million. Today, Plattner is ranked number 22 among the 100 richest people in Germany, with an estimated private fortune from his 10 per cent share of SAP now worth about €4.2 billion. Golf, skiing and other sports help Plattner relax. In particular, he is a keen yachting man, willing to race against Larry Ellison, Chairman of Oracle, a major SAP competitor, at sea as well as in business.[32]

The media are not always flattering, describing Plattner as SAP's 'red-meat-for-breakfast co-CEO', and 'a pit-bull of a man with a squared-off jaw'.[33] The dark side of Plattner has even been referred to as 'the sludge that clogs up its engine'.[34] He adopts a confrontational style, claiming that 'he doesn't care how much he irritates people along the way' in obtaining consensus among his people.[35] Others in the organization describe Plattner's style as provocative, rigid, rude, stressful … but point out that he gets people to be creative.

Plattner is also referred to as SAP's 'spark plug', cheerleader and visionary,[36] and said to be very hands-on in solving problems. He is credited with having quickly developed the mySAP.com™ concept in response to news that SAP was seriously behind in the Internet area in 1999.

Henning Kagermann

Born in 1947, Henning Kagermann grew up in a relatively simple family. His father died when he was seven years old. Kagermann went on to study experimental physics at Munich University, then to do his doctorate in theoretical physics at the University of Braunschweig. A researcher and academic, he joined SAP in Germany in 1982. Originally employed in developing financial software for SAP, this acknowledged expert in finance and accounting rose to top management in 1991. Kagermann's appointment to the top management board was the first such appointment outside the founders and major shareholders of SAP. In September 2000, Henning Kagermann was appointed to the Supervisory Board of Deutsche Bank.

He is respected as a matter-of-fact, efficient analyst, and a calm and communicative person.[37] Shy and less confident and comfortable than his more flamboyant co-CEO in public speaking, Kagermann uses the polished rhetoric of the professor that he is at heart.[38] Some employees at SAP regard Kagermann as so unspectacular that they play on his name to create the nickname 'Stingy man'. A story doing the rounds in the media is that he prefers to buy Christmas presents in January because they are cheaper then.[39]

Kagermann relaxes at the weekend with mathematical problems. Despite his wealth, he does not show off, has no chauffeur, and does not like to raise people's expectations. He appears to embody classical German engineering virtues: solidity, technical and mathematical understanding, and reliability. These characteristics appeal to the finance markets that seem to trust him.[40] He is said to plan thoroughly and be systematic, and is conservative in giving estimates and information to people outside the organization. While this strategy works in building trust, it is not foolproof even for Kagermann. In 2000, the rapidly changing peaks and troughs at SAP led to an unexpected loss in the first quarter. Analysts deserted the company, only to return in 2001.[41]

SAP PEOPLE

In the e-business environment, SAP has to rely on its employees, particularly on self-managing, professional employees who create opportunities to fulfil their potential and maximize their value to the organization. In harnessing the power of the Internet and exploiting e-business opportunities, this global organization places significant trust and responsibility in management and employees at all levels and in all locations. The 2000 annual report describes SAP culture as innovative and entrepreneurial, but with the stability of a successful global company. Part of this stability comes from retaining its people. At the end of 2000, SAP employed 24 178 worldwide.[42]

Plattner did not welcome people leaving SAP, and the company does not release people just because their skills and knowledge have become out of date.[43] Considerable efforts are made to retain employees. For example, career paths are tailored to individuals as they develop, and employees can fairly easily move outside their area of expertise if they are able to match their skills to another area within the organization. SAP also attempts to promote employees from within the organization before looking externally.

Despite these efforts, retaining people was a major challenge at SAP. People were leaving SAP partly because the organization could not legally offer stock options, which were particularly important to US executive management.

Some employees left to work for competitor firms that did provide stock options, while others joined dot.com startups. Others left because of the organizational culture, as indicated below.

To stem the loss of staff, SAP battled German laws that prohibited public companies from issuing employee stock options. This resulted in SAP introducing a US-style stock option scheme in 2000.[44] In addition, the company encouraged flexible working hours, casual dress and an informal, relaxed work atmosphere. Management was encouraged to be accessible to staff at all levels through an open door policy. Opportunities were created to enhance communication and share a common vision throughout the organization. For instance, staff and management mingle in the cafeteria, where people are expected to spend about two hours daily to meet others and exchange information. To support an employee-oriented management culture, SAP introduced a management development program for high-level executives, in collaboration with major international business schools.[45]

SAP also attempted to arrest staff attrition by offering its people developmental opportunities, paying above-market salaries and bonuses of up to 30 per cent of salary, plus a discretionary profit-sharing bonus to all staff. Some employees receive a company car. Other benefits include superannuation paid above statutory level and a fringe benefit tax for managers. A child referral service is available to all parents, and an employee assistance program provides confidential counselling. These initiatives were introduced in recognition of the stresses that employees encounter in SAP's hyper-competitive, challenging environment, and that burnout is an issue at SAP. To reflect SAP's commitment to open communication and continual improvement in its people management, staff satisfaction is surveyed every two years.

However, when leaders are perceived as ineffective or their actions work against the vision and mission, courageous followers know that it is time to leave.[46] In 2000, SAP people were calling for leadership that they could trust, and that made sufficient sense for them to follow. Too few people at SAP were able to make decisions within the seven-layer hierarchy, keeping SAP far from its goal of a self-managing workforce. It needed to become much flatter and more decentralized, with power devolved to the employees. Although the managers also brought in some Taylorist efficiency principles, SAP was learning that in a global, entrepreneurial organization, commanding people no longer works.[47] They have to be convinced.

SAP CULTURE

Some people argue that Plattner had built SAP's corporate culture after his own image, that of being engineering-focused, headstrong and determined to succeed alone. In the IT industry, change is especially ubiquitous, but SAP is said to resist change. One of the stories at SAP is that some upset people literally ran out of an early meeting at which mySAP.com™ was introduced. However, after the launch, people's enthusiasm grew and they supported mySAP.com™ and the idea that SAP should become the 'leader of the Internet pack'.[48]

Resistance to change tends to come from both older and new employees. The key driver of change at SAP is Hasso Plattner's personal engagement, which then influences the Board, executives and others in the process, creating top-down momentum.[49]

Being global and embracing multiple cultures is a challenge for the leadership of any organization. Plattner constantly travels, visiting customers. He spends considerable time in the US. Despite being a global organization, there is some resistance at SAP to globalizing people by sending them on international postings.[50] Some observers argue that while SAP needed to let go of the German language, it needs to simultaneously make the US culture less dominant when using English as the official SAP language.

In 2000, a culture of fear reigned in many countries, particularly where people had to break SAP's bureaucratic rules in order to be able to do their innovative, entrepreneurial work.[51] Fear was also engendered by manager behaviours. For example, a previous managing director in Switzerland used to videotape people in meetings, thereby stimulating fear. In the US, the prevailing culture tended to centre on fear, driven by incidents such as firing an entire layer of management, including valuable employees. Not surprisingly, some people at SAP feared for their jobs.

SAP's reputation as a leading software company should attract dynamic, innovative, technical/professional employees, and some are even recruited on the recommendation of current employees.[52] On the other hand, people are leaving the organization of their own accord because of dissatisfaction with the current culture, claiming that 'this culture doesn't work any more'. The challenge for SAP is how to keep the workplace small and nonbureaucratic (to foster innovation and teamwork) in a large global company.

Change was inevitable, given the loss of SAP people, product problems and falling revenues in 2000. SAP endeavoured to become more flexible, able to adapt to new situations, and exhibit intelligent behaviour. The engineering culture was being turned inside out.

SWISS SAP: A MODEL FOR THE FUTURE?

An ideal spirit for SAP may have emerged in Switzerland, when a Belgian managing director, Erwin Gunst, was brought in to turn the flagging Swiss operation around. His background is in HR. Within one year he had developed Swiss SAP into the number one in Europe, underpinned by winning a major contract with Nestlé for 250 000 users. Since then, the German operation has admired Gunst's HR philosophy, which has four components: best practice, best frame, best team and best people.

- **Best practice**: SAP wants to excel in recruitment; assessment via goals, feedback and change; and development through training and learning. Recruitment growth has slowed, possibly because the 50 000–60 000 SAP consultants are required to sell products and services where the price is high but the quality is sometimes weak. Profitability is the key for these people, who are also measured on growth, sales and costs. Consultants are expected to sell a minimum of 120 days consulting per year, although some choose to maximize their income by selling 250–260 days. Development through learning is promoted through the SAP University, which also aims at increasing retention rates by providing continuous learning opportunities.

- **Best frame**: This component refers to the overall working conditions and environment at SAP. It is based on the view that facilities, equipment, services and compensation need to meet employees' requirements wherever they work. This includes the workspace at home or in the office, and the office-in-the-machine, for example, the laptop computer. Providing appropriate equipment and keeping employees well supplied with logistical, administration and communication support are normally achieved. Other motivations include providing fun, although parts of the company are still considered somewhat dour.

- **Best team**: SAP Switzerland set its teams a goal of CHF 150 million and promised its people that when they reached the goal, the entire company would go away to an island for three days. After 80 per cent had reached the goal, all 300 employees went away to the island to have fun. Despite this, the attrition rate in Switzerland remains around 20 per cent.[53] To stem the attrition, one strategy has been to create smaller units so that people can network well. A challenge in moving to this structure is that it conflicts with the bureaucracy in place under SAP's management-heavy pyramidal structure.

- **Best people**: SAP people need to be self-organizing, self-managing, self-motivating and willing to work in a fun, innovative and enthusiastic culture. People are expected to have at least three SAP 'hobby projects'. If one works, they become heroes. Employability is also important, in that everyone has to earn their keep. 'Cover your base' is another important part of SAP culture, meaning that one needs to find the right people to contact on an issue, that is, employees must be pro-active in connecting with others. SAP people are also expected to give and receive appreciation, which works well among the 300 people in Switzerland.[54] People are encouraged to 'explore, discover, act' and to take their chances. They should try to be successful without damaging others or being arrogant.

Despite these Swiss successes, there is some room for improvement in the HR area at SAP, particularly in using HR strategically. For example, until recently there was no formal set of capabilities for selecting new staff, nor a process for inducting new recruits into the SAP culture.

MANAGING KNOWLEDGE

Knowledge transfer is the real challenge for SAP, given the fast pace of introducing new products. The half-life of knowledge is decreasing to one year or less in this industry.[55] SAP's famous ERP product took eight years to develop, followed by one release each year. For the next generation of Inter-enterprise Cooperation software, the development time was down to two years. This time is reducing further for the e-community collaboration products.

Fostering innovation is a key challenge. SAP provides an opportunity for all employees to grow and develop, is proactive in providing training, and is committed to empowering employees through knowledge, via courses in products, and in leadership, negotiation and assertiveness skills. SAP has numerous options for transferring knowledge, including classroom training, the SAP University, and self-taught training using both on-line and web-based tutorials. Life cycle support, involving rectifying bugs and problems, takes high priority at SAP. Support can be web-based, via telephone or personal contact with regional or national SAP support centers.

The company has established the SAP University with advanced multi-media capabilities to house its training operations. The Director of the Global Institute of Higher Learning at SAP is responsible for liaising with over 450 universities and business schools and 100 000 students. In addition, SAP sponsors university chairs and research.

In developing its knowledge management, SAP links technology, people practices and a customer focus in order to deliver a quality service. The circle has come fully round, as SAP's own knowledge finds its way into its new products and services. From remote data centres, customers can access SAP applications via the Internet and significantly reduce the cost of operating their own computer systems.

DISCUSSION ISSUES

1 Which leadership paradigm(s) have driven SAP? Where is the leadership at SAP? Can you see substitutes for leadership operating? How appropriate is having seven layers of management for achieving SAP's strategic goals?

2 What sort of followers does SAP say it wants? How can it stem the huge attrition rate and retain good staff? Are the current HR and other measures likely to be sufficient?

3 What comments can you make about the structure at SAP? Would you recommend any changes in the light of the competitive industry and SAP's own strategic goals?

4 If people are asking for different leadership at SAP, what does this suggest about the paradigms of leadership in the heads of the leaders and followers at SAP? Are the ideas of leadership held by management and by the SAP staff aligned with each other, and with the systems and processes in the organization? Is there a mismatch, and if so, where? What can be done about it?

5 Is SAP becoming a learning organization? How is it managing its knowledge? What role do partnerships with customers and suppliers play in knowledge management?

6 Is SAP poised to become a truly global organization as opposed to remaining a German company that has gone international? What does it still need to do to become global, if anything?

7 What would SAP need to do to become an Organic organization with self-managing teams? Would this be a useful goal to aim for, and if so, how far is SAP from achieving self-leading teams?

8 What would you advise top management to do in addition to what it is already doing to ensure the organization's sustainability?

9 Describe the organizational culture at SAP. Is this appropriate for the organization? Why/why not? Do you see evidence of emotion and spirituality at SAP? Should either of these be enhanced, and if so, how could one go about it?

10 Could the HR success factors employed in SAP Switzerland be adopted in SAP Germany and SAP US? If so, how would you advise the leadership to manage this major change?

KEY ISSUES

- Global, fast-growing organization in a fast-paced industry.
- Highly successful in revenue terms, with mostly continual growth.
- US market dipped at the end of 1990s.
- Stock still strongly held by the founders, despite being publicly listed on stock exchanges around the world.
- One entrepreneur-founder is involved in management as co-CEO and co-Chairman.
- Leadership duo takes complementary roles – visionary versus management.
- SAP needed to reinvent its products, and did so with mySAP.com™ and an Internet focus.
- Changing from a product focus to service, solutions and knowledge.
- Needs high knowledge employees and vendors.
- Highly educated, professional workforce.
- Very bureaucratic, top-down management, with seven layers of management.
- Bureaucracy stifles change to self-leading teams and impedes communication and collaboration.
- Training lags behind innovation.
- Innovation times are shortening.
- Competitive advantage is derived from bundling its components, making the result hard to copy.
- Strong emphasis on strategic partnering with customers, experts and suppliers.
- Uses customer feedback and complaints in new product development.
- Management by area of competence means that it can be difficult to get top executives to focus on management rather than on technical matters.
- Swiss subsidiary very successfully turned around, especially in the HR area.
- Visionary leadership, but a specific vision and consistent set of values do not seem to predominate.
- Problems with attracting and retaining staff.
- No stock options were available to staff until recently.
- Offers above-average pay and conditions, internal promotion, bonuses, personal growth opportunities.
- Employees can change career radically within the organization.
- CEO does not like people to leave the company.
- Suggestion that leadership and management styles are not appropriate for the employees the organization is seeking to attract, especially the fear culture, bureaucracy, firing one entire layer of managers in the US.

- Difficult to let go of the German language and culture to become a truly global organization, as opposed to a German company operating abroad.
- Likes to develop a fun culture.
- HR practices need revising, for example, set of capabilities, aligning leadership and followership with business goals.
- Change resistant culture is a challenge in SAP's industry.
- Managing knowledge is done in a variety of ways, for example, University, communication in cafeteria, networking and through technology.
- R&D is the second highest expense and highest growth area at SAP because innovation is essential to SAP's survival.
- No evidence of any great focus on sustainability except for funding research and learning.
- Spirituality in the SAP workplace is probably low because of the fear culture, bureaucracy, and rule-governed culture.

NOTES

1   The author is indebted to the many senior executives at SAP who generously gave of their knowledge and time for this project, in particular Dr K.-D. Gronwald. Mr Plattner stepped down as CEO in 2002.
2   Hamm, S. (2001) 'Meet the new Hasso Plattner', *Business Week*, 9 July.
3   Provided by SAP Sydney, April 2000.
4   Accessed on-line on 27 September 2001 at http://www.sap.com/company/events/nnet/pressoverview.asp
5   Hamm, S. (2001) 'Meet the new Hasso Plattner', *Business Week*, 9 July.
6   Fox, J. (2000) 'Lumbering towards B2B', *Fortune*, 18 January.
7   Bartholomew, D. (1998) 'Hasso Plattner: Growing software's quiet giant', *Industry Week*, 21 December.
8   Orr, D. and Kitchens, S. (2001) 'I'll pay yours if you'll pay mine', *Forbes Global*, 40, 3 September, 36–8.
9   Accessed on-line on 9 August 2001 at http://www.sap.com/company/profile_long.htm
10 Zepelin, J. (2001) 'Microsoft gräbt SAP die Kunden ab', *Financial Times Deutschland*, 18 September. Accessed on-line on 27 September 2001 at http://www.ftd.de/sap
11 SAP 2000 *Annual Report* Accessed on-line on 9 August 2001 at http://www.sap.com/company/
12 Mullin, R. (2000) 'SAP's new role-playing catch-up', *Chemical Week Associates*, 29 March, p. 39.

13 Accessed on-line on 9 August 2001 at http://www.sap.com/company/ profile_long.htm

14 Hamm, S. (2001) 'Meet the new Hasso Plattner', *Business Week*, 9 July.

15 SAP 2000 *Annual Report*. Accessed on-line on 9 August 2001 at http://www.sap.com/company/

16 Gronwald, K.-D. (2000). Presentation made during visit to SAP in Walldorf, 21 June.

17 Kagermann, H. (2001) *Solutions for the New, New Economy*. Paper presented at CSFB Technology Conference, Barcelona, 21 May. Accessed on-line on 23 September 2001 at http://www.sap.com/company/

18 Anonymous (2000) *Information Week*, 19 April.

19 SAP 2000 *Annual Report*. Accessed on-line on 9 August 2001 at http://www.sap.com/company/

20 SAP 2000 *Annual Report*. Accessed on-line on 9 August 2001 at http://www.sap.com/company/

21 SAP Investor Conference, July 2001. Accessed on-line on 23 September 2001 at http://www.sap.com/company/

22 Gronwald, K.-D. (2000) Presentation made during visit to SAP in Walldorf, 21 June.

23 Collis, D.J. and Montgomery, C.A. (1995) 'Competing on resources: Strategy in the 1990s', *Harvard Business Review*, 73(4): 118–28.

24 SAP 2000 *Annual Report*. Accessed on-line on 9 August 2001 at http://www.sap.com/company/

25 Scott, R. (2000) 'SAP rubs shoulders with the low end', *Accounting Technology*, January–February, p. 60.

26 Hamm, S. (2001) 'Meet the new Hasso Plattner', *Business Week*, 9 July.

27 Hamm, S. (2001) 'Meet the new Hasso Plattner', *Business Week*, 9 July.

28 Kagermann, H. (2001) *Solutions for the New, New Economy*. Paper presented at CSFB Technology Conference, Barcelona, 21 May. Accessed on-line on 23 September 2001 at http://www.sap.com/company/

29 Stuhr, A. (2001) 'Der siegelnde Professor', *Manager Magazin*. Accessed on-line on 23 September 2001 at http://www.manager-magazin.de/ unternehmer/boersenbarometer/0,2828,126590,00.html

30 Hamm, S. (2001) 'Meet the new Hasso Plattner', *Business Week*, 9 July.

31 Hamm, S. (2001) 'Meet the new Hasso Plattner', *Business Week*, 9 July.

32 Stuhr, A. (2001) 'Der siegelnde Professor', *Manager Magazin*. Accessed on-line on 23 September 2001 at http://www.manager-magazin.de/ unternehmer/boersenbarometer/0,2828,126590,00.html

33 Hamm, S. (2001) 'Meet the new Hasso Plattner', *Business Week*, 9 July.

34 Hamm, S. (2001) 'Meet the new Hasso Plattner', *Business Week*, 9 July.

35 Hamm, S. (2001) 'Meet the new Hasso Plattner', *Business Week*, 9 July.

36 Hamm, S. (2001) 'Meet the new Hasso Plattner', *Business Week*, 9 July.

37 *Financial Times* Deutschland Portrait: Henning Kagermann, 20 July 2001. Accessed on-line on 27 September 2001 at http://www.ftd.de/db/mu/FTDWW08IDPC.html?nv=se

38   Enzweiler, T. (2001) 'Henning Kagermann: Der Asket aus Walldorf', *Financial Times Deutschland*, 20 July. Accessed on-line on 27 September 2001 at http://www.ftd.de/leute

39   Enzweiler, T. (2001) 'Henning Kagermann: Der Asket aus Walldorf', *Financial Times Deutschland*, 20 July. Accessed on-line on 27 September 2001 at http://www.ftd.de/leute

40   Enzweiler, T. (2001) 'Henning Kagermann: Der Asket aus Walldorf', *Financial Times Deutschland*, 20 July. Accessed on-line on 27 September 2001 at http://www.ftd.de/leute

41   Enzweiler, T. (2001) 'Henning Kagermann: Der Asket aus Walldorf', *Financial Times Deutschland*, 20 July. Accessed on-line on 27 September 2001 at http://www.ftd.de/leute

42   SAP Investor Conference, July 2001. Accessed on-line on 23 September 2001 at http://www.sap.com/company/

43   Gronwald, K.-D. (2000). Presentation made during visit to SAP in Walldorf, 21 June.

44   Stedman, C. (2000) 'SAP execs to get options', *Computerworld*, 24 January.

45   SAP 2000 *Annual Report*. Accessed on-line on 9 August 2001 at http://www.sap.com/company/

46   Chaleff, I. (1995) 'The courageous follower', *World Executive Digest*, November, pp. 68–9.

47   Gronwald, K.-D. (2000) Presentation made during visit to SAP in Walldorf, 21 June.

48   Gronwald, K.-D. (2000) Presentation made during visit to SAP in Walldorf, 21 June.

49   Hamm, S. (2001) 'Meet the new Hasso Plattner', *Business Week*, 9 July.

50   Gronwald, K.-D. (2000) Presentation made during visit to SAP in Walldorf, 21 June.

51   Gronwald, K.-D. (2000) Presentation made during visit to SAP in Walldorf, 21 June.

52   Boudette, N. (2000) 'USA: SAP to set up camp in Silicon Valley', *Wall Street Journal*, 23 March.

53   Gronwald, K.-D. (2000). Presentation made during visit to SAP in Walldorf, 21 June.

54   Gronwald, K.-D. (2000) Presentation made during visit to SAP in Walldorf, 21 June.

55   Gronwald, K.-D. (2000) Presentation made during visit to SAP in Walldorf, 21 June.

Six Bonduelle: Leadership,
French Style[1]

ANNE E. WITTE

All kinds of vegetables, in all sizes, at any time, and for all budgets.

Christophe Bonduelle, Chairman of the Board of Directors

Bonduelle, headquartered at Villeneuve d'Ascq near Lille, France, specializes in producing canned, frozen and fresh vegetables, and their prompt and competitive delivery to consumer and other markets. In 2002, the company employed around 4705 permanent staff in 19 countries and had 24 production sites, whereas in 1999 the company had employed 4300 permanent staff in 20 production locations.[2] Bonduelle's highly successful business is associated with a product development strategy focused on producing as many different varieties of vegetables as possible, to a high quality and using the latest available technologies.

The European vegetable industry is a €50-billion business, with market segments spanning canned/jarred, frozen and fresh vegetables. Bonduelle represents 30 per cent of the canned/jarred vegetable segment in Europe, and is the leading brand in France, Germany, Belgium, Luxembourg, Poland and the Czech Republic. Bonduelle is the number two leader in the European frozen vegetable segment, securing 12 per cent of the market. Traditional canning operations still provide the majority of the firm's business, representing 53 per cent of turnover, but frozen foods have increased, accounting for 29.5 per cent of turnover. The newest segment, fresh vegetables, covers the remaining 17.5 per cent of turnover and is growing rapidly in all European markets. This has been attributed to a more sophisticated consumer demand for fresh and nutritious vegetables, changes in demographics, improvements in transportation, lifestyle, patterns of eating and the combined role of men and women in providing family meals.

Group Bonduelle and its penetration of European vegetable markets over 150 years reflects the major sociological eating trends of the twentieth century, as the company's product portfolio and business strategy adapted to a growing middle class and more discerning consumer.

FINANCIALS

In 1998, Bonduelle listed for the first time on the Paris stock market. Its turnover in 2001 was €1.25 billion, generating a healthy cash flow, substantial market growth and sparking investment interest. Profits and cash flow from operations and investment have continually increased between 1997 and 1999 (see Figure CS6.1). Price/earnings ratio is 9:5, with the market value of the company reported as less than its net assets.[3]

COMPANY HISTORY

The two founding members of Bonduelle were born into northern French farming families. Louis Bonduelle-Dalle and Louis Lesaffre-Roussel founded the initial business in 1853, when they created and developed a farm and juniper distillery in a small town outside the Flemish city of Lille. The two men married each other's sister and by a surprising twist of fate, both men died on the same night in 1901. The widows divided the seven existing factories between three family branches: Bonduelle, Lesaffre and Lemaître. The Lesaffre industry went on to become a world leader in malt production. In 1926, canning machinery was added to the family farm in Woestyne to can the peas they cultivated. The first production line provided 120 000 cans of peas in one year. These canning activities set the groundwork for the craftsmanship that would later make the company famous. Today, billions of units are sold annually.

In 1947, Bonduelle established a distribution network allowing for commercializing its canned products and creating a brand name. Soon, demand exceeded supply and the company recruited local farmers to provide additional production resources. Following a governmental incentive to convert distilleries into agro-business and anticipating a change in consumer eating and drinking habits, the company experimented briefly with canned fish and prepared dinners, but eventually Bonduelle directed its entire operations towards canned vegetables. By the end of the 1950s, this decision marked all of its future product policy. Bonduelle distilleries were productive throughout the early twentieth century, but it was only after the Second World War that the company began to introduce major changes in its business strategy.

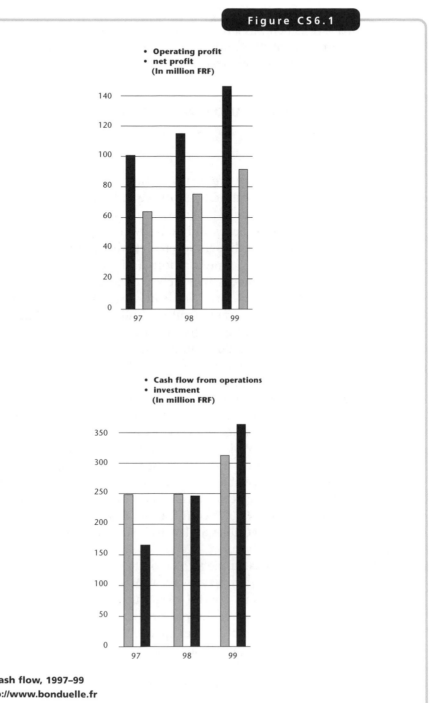

• **Operating profit**
• **net profit**
  (In million FRF)

• **Cash flow from operations**
• **investment**
  (In million FRF)

Profit and cash flow, 1997–99
Source: **http://www.bonduelle.fr**

In 1957, Bonduelle introduced customers to the innovative peas and carrots in a can, which was a resounding commercial success. As the company grew, concerns for quality and changing consumer patterns were constant influences on the company's strategy.

PRODUCT FOCUS AND INNOVATION

Bonduelle continued to face product innovation challenges, particularly as it internationalized. Being a culturally-sensitive industry, vegetables require local adaptation to consumer tastes – even within France. Vegetables such as peas, carrots, mushrooms, string beans and cauliflower are prepared differently in different European regions. Although vegetables were in growing demand everywhere in Europe, the variety of preparations and presentations commanded the attention of product engineers. Bonduelle's early product policy consisted of adapting vegetables to local tastes, an early example of thinking global but acting local. Attention to consumer culture and aptly responding to changing tastes, particularly important in France, contributed to establishing Bonduelle's competitive advantage and unique product niche. Product innovation allowing for a large portfolio of vegetable products reflecting a wide range of cultural taste buds has continually driven managerial strategy, pricing policy and the vertical integration pattern that has marked the company's recent history.

Between 1963 and 1974, production capacity increased. The company acquired new fields to allow for the very best quality agriculture, and its brand name became associated with quality by French consumers – who are reputed to be particularly critical on the subject of food. In 1968, new freezing technology allowed frozen vegetables to be significantly developed, and a new consumer trend grew enthusiastically as freezers became common household items all over Europe. The ISO 90023 certification was obtained in 1986 and new technologies in frozen vegetables and factory standards allowed for innovation with quality food products.

Today, more than 5500 farmers collaborate with Bonduelle. Bonduelle outsources its production to farms through annual contracts, thereby providing the company with rigorous control over outputs and standards. Company agro-engineers select grains on the basis of taste, texture and colour and all seeds are currently free from any genetically modified organisms. The company's engineers also monitor the farming, taking special environmental measures during fertilization and irrigation. Bonduelle researchers monitor product quality from beginning to end, advising farmers and improving industry standards. Currently, the delay between harvesting the vegetables and transforming them at the factory is no longer than four hours. This allows the company to offer fresh vegetables of a highly nutritious value.

Over 3400 products are now available within the three Bonduelle brands: Bonduelle (Europe and Latin America), Frudesa (Spain) and Cassegrain (France). The former Belgian brand, Marie-Thumas, is being completely integrated into the Bonduelle brand (general public and restaurants in Belgium). This spectacular product portfolio reflects a concern with consumer diversity, varying preparation habits and price.

GOING INTERNATIONAL

Internationalization began in 1969 with the first exports to Germany, which has remained the most important foreign export recipient for Bonduelle products. Subsidiaries were created in Italy in 1972 and England in 1973. By 1973, half of Bonduelle's turnover was made in exports and currently annual sales are increasing in Spain and Italy by about 15 per cent. From 1975–84, Bonduelle enhanced production in other parts of Europe, allowing the company to expand operations and invest in corn and mushrooms. In 1980, the company acquired Marie-Thumas. By 1983, the company was producing 350 000 tons of canned vegetables and 90 000 tons of frozen vegetables, establishing its reputation as a European leader. Between 1985 and 1993, Bonduelle increased its strategy of internationalization and growth in Spain in 1986 and Portugal in 1988. Bonduelle products were sold in East Germany, the Czech Republic and Poland by 1992. A distribution network in Brazil followed in 1994 and in Argentina in 1996. By 1997, Bonduelle was exploring fresh vegetables and a concept allowing for consumers to have a ready-to-use vegetable such as the 'one minute salad'.

COMPANY ORGANIZATION

In 1999, the company launched its five-year plan, with a new internal structure and close focus on the customer. Divisions were removed between marketing and production, and five autonomous subsidiaries were created, served by six centralized functions: Finance, HR and Communication, Management Information Systems, R&D, Corporate Marketing and Purchasing.[4] The five subsidiaries are:

- *Bonduelle Frais* is the creative arm, fast growing and innovative. It employs 900 people. Products are fresh greens, and produce brought to market and consumed within 8–15 days.

- *Bonduelle Grand Public* assures production, distribution and marketing of frozen and canned goods directly to consumers.
- *Bonduelle Food Service* sells vegetables business-to-business throughout Europe.
- *BPL Private Label* assures the sale of vegetables to secondary distributors.
- *Bonduelle Development* manages Central and Eastern Europe, South America and North America.

The directors of each subsidiary are on the Group's Operational Management Board. At least five members of the founding families are on the Supervisory Board, which is presided over by Daniel Bracquart. Christophe Bonduelle chairs the Bonduelle Board of Directors, which includes nine directors who monitor the different brand names and the overall management of the company. They help implement development strategies in the subsidiaries, each of the latter run by a local director. A central office in France (with about 100 employees) maintains the administrative control and management over the entire group Three main executive directors consolidate decision making from the Lille offices.

Bonduelle's French headquarters originally exercised strong centralized control over the group's expansion. Decisions were traditionally made by the highest executives, and operations throughout Europe were run from France using French managers assigned to oversee production, marketing and the general management of foreign subsidiaries. The structure has changed from the former vertical structure of power and command towards a matrix type organization, which although still directed by the French headquarters allows for both national and divisional expertise to cross over the different brands. Changes were introduced in 1998 to decentralize decision-making and delegate greater autonomy to foreign subsidiaries. The director of each subsidiary became responsible for all the mainstream activities within his area, including logistics, HR, production and marketing. A state-of-the-art information management system was introduced in 2000.

PEOPLE

Diversity is an issue being addressed at Bonduelle. About 200 of the 800 managerial positions are currently assigned to foreign personnel. Although the executive board is still entirely male, middle-aged and French (except for one Italian), new HR policies are being implemented to inject diversity into the workforce to stimulate creativity at all levels of company operations, and to encourage a flatter hierarchy within the firm's international base. Recruiters are also diversifying their employment criteria by encouraging university degree holders to integrate management tracks in addition to the traditional holders of the *grande école* diplomas, which are the traditional educational criteria for business leaders in France. International experience, language proficiency and the ability to 'think outside the box' also move line managers into more strategic managerial posts.

Leadership still relies heavily on product creativity, and so the creative agro-engineer holds the symbolic and charismatic power within the organization. This concurs with predictable French industrial patterns that assign the greatest power to those possessing mathematical and chemical expertise.

Appointment to the highest managerial positions is made by internal review, using a process of internal and external recruitment for senior posts. Access to these positions remains highly guarded from public scrutiny.

LEADERSHIP

At present, at least four directors proudly carry the name 'Bonduelle', demonstrating the strong family identity within this multinational corporation. The paternalistic, family-style pattern of power reflects Classical leadership. The new pattern of decentralization and a focus on local expertise introduced by Christophe Bonduelle in 2000 was created to flatten the tall, vertical structure that had typically been adopted by the previous administrations. Efforts are being made to diversify the workforce, to integrate different nationalities and women into key decision-making positions, and to decentralize decision-making processes further by empowering local subsidiaries to make autonomous decisions on price, advertising and distribution.

Over 50 per cent of Bonduelle French employees have taken stock in the company, which is probably a strong indication that employees are confident in the industry's health and are also enjoying the products they manufacture! Although one could not describe the management procedures at the factory or farm level as truly participative, they are not autocratic either. Employees seem to appreciate the family-style ownership within a traditional French company with French-style values. Followership, therefore, draws strongly on the power and reputation of the Bonduelle family and the 150 years of tradition that have given the company its international acclaim. The relative stability (only one factory closing within recent history) and even growth within the organization compared to the car, textile and high-technology industries, is also greatly appreciated by the French workforce, which values job stability and long-term employment over higher salaries and stock options. These factors have also spurred investors to take a second look at the food industry in their stock portfolios.

FUTURE STRATEGIES

Bonduelle's corporate culture and leadership style have been shaped by the strong conviction that people will always need to eat, and that eating is a pleasure and a privilege. The company's challenges lie in providing quality foods at competitive prices to markets far away from the initial geographic areas where certain vegetables were originally grown. Hence, Bonduelle's strategy is focused on setting up production units closer to its markets, penetrating local distribution channels for better transportation prices, monitoring competitors and decentralizing decision making so that foreign subsidiaries can make decisions autonomously. The company has also experienced tremendous organizational challenges through its different mergers, acquisitions and vertical takeovers.

Bonduelle's major challenges over the next 20 years will be ensuring rapid response to expanding markets, changing eating trends, and scientific breakthroughs in the food industry. Other challenges in the vegetable industry include the instability of weather patterns and natural disasters, which can disrupt steady distribution flows to markets. Preventing product shortages often entails a highly technical mastery of distribution channels, of electronic communication with rural and urban supermarkets, and of sales, production, packaging and transportation personnel issues, among others. The competition in the mass distribution sector also requires technical marketing expertise to remain competitive worldwide. These challenges affecting success in the food industry are mostly hidden from the consumer, but are expressed in prices, which are a strong factor in purchasing decisions.

COMPANY VALUES

The core values relating to Bonduelle's products are quality foods and the respect for nature, health[5], technology and innovation. Values associated with the corporate culture include tradition, quality and creativity.

The company relies on the consumer's desire to have personalized and imaginative mixtures of vegetables and preparation styles. All packages of vegetables give nutritional information and remind consumers about the importance of a balanced diet. A few recipes and suggestions about the ways in which the product can best be prepared are mentioned. Marketing tends to capitalize on family values and tradition, values for which the Bonduelle brand name stands.

The company owes part of its success to anticipating sociological trends. When opting to leave the distillery business to focus on canned vegetables in the 1950s, the company exhibited a forward-looking vision for the French and European consumer who was looking for easy-to-prepare nutritious foods without sacrificing taste and tradition. In developing the concept of frozen and ready-to-eat fresh vegetables, Bonduelle captured a growing market of double-income families with less time for food preparation. They also captured the upper middle-class and university-educated consumer who has been switching to vegetable-based meals and moving away from the traditional meats and cheeses. Finally, Bonduelle's company history reflects the changing needs of the female buyer who considers ease in preparation along with nutrition as equal purchasing decision factors to price. Additionally, the growing use of the microwave oven, the concern over contaminated beef, a growing segment of vegetarians throughout the Western world, and a strong concern with vitamins through good eating habits equally assure future markets for vegetable producers. By adapting products to local tastes throughout Europe and making the entire European range available in Europe, Bonduelle has also demonstrated good international strategy by improving the product line while decentralizing production facilities and distribution networks, thereby keeping prices down.

Box CS6.1

Christophe Bonduelle

Christophe Bonduelle is 44 years old and native to the north of France. He is the sixth generation removed from the company's founder. Graduating from EDHEC Business School, Lille in 1982, after two years of marketing assignments in various organizations he began working at Group Bonduelle. Here he was first a production manager, then a factory director, next Managing Director of the Spanish subsidiary, then he headed a project management activity focused on frozen vegetables in Europe. From 1993 to 2001 he was the Managing Director for Group Bonduelle, and since 2001 Chairman of the Board of Directors. He believes in adapting products to local tastes, is passionate about finding new international markets where Bonduelle products will be appreciated by consumers, believes that his product line has helped to liberate women by facilitating the preparation of fresh vegetables so that all members of the family can prepare them, and has the strong personal conviction that Group Bonduelle's products and their adherence to industry standards have introduced better eating habits in Europe.

DISCUSSION ISSUES

1   Which leadership paradigm(s) have driven Bonduelle? Are they trying to change this/these paradigm(s), and if so, how?

2   Where is the leadership and power at Bonduelle? How appropriate is it to have so many family members managing the company? Can you identify Bonduelle's stakeholders?

3   Can you see any substitutes for leadership operating? How do the followers and their expectations align with the leadership at Bonduelle?

4   Describe the organizational culture as you see it at Bonduelle, including its values. Are the culture and values appropriate for the organization? Why/why not? Do you see evidence of emotion and spirituality there? Should either of these be enhanced, and if so, how could one go about it?

5   Bonduelle does not seem to have explicit HR measures for recruitment, developing their people or managing the culture. Is this a problem in a hierarchical, Classical, relatively stable organization? Do you think this may need to change in the future? If so, why?

6   What comments can you make about the structure at Bonduelle? Would you recommend any changes in the light of Bonduelle's strategic goals and the French workers' apparent satisfaction?

7   Is Bonduelle a learning organization? How does it manage its knowledge? What role do partnerships with farmers and knowledge of customers play in knowledge management at Bonduelle?

8   Could Bonduelle become a truly global organization, as opposed to remaining a European company? Would it need to change its leadership and people management practices to manage production outside Europe?

9   What would you advise top management to do in addition to what it is already doing to ensure the organization's sustainability? What does it do for the environment and society? What more could the company do?

10   Diversity appears to be an issue at Bonduelle, particularly regarding gender and nationality in management. How would you advise Bonduelle to introduce more diversity into the organization, particularly given the current strong national culture? Would you recommend any particular support services or systems to help the outsiders adjust?

KEY ISSUES

- Global, fast-growing, innovative French company in the European vegetable business.
- Largely family-run for 150 years, includes some outside and local management.
- Strong customer focus, continually adapting product range to customer trends.
- Highly successful in revenue terms, with mostly continual growth in profits and sales in recent years.
- Publicly listed on Paris stock exchange in 1998.
- Stock still strongly held by the founders and many staff.
- Vertically integrated processes from field (production) to consumer (marketing/sales).
- Strong brand, associated with quality, family values and tradition.
- Core values: tradition, quality, creativity.
- Production values: quality foods, respect for nature, technology, innovation, health.
- Classical leadership endeavouring to empower management and operations at local levels.
- Control was strongly based in Lille, although autonomous subsidiaries have been created to spread decision making.
- Hierarchical, mostly male, French, middle-aged board.
- Traditional French management seems to align with workers' expectations, particularly of long-term employment and stability.
- Organization has been relatively stable over its lifetime, with some recent downsizing and only one closure in recent times.
- Workers are proud of the organization, its tradition and family associations.
- Engineering/science backgrounds are valued.
- Outsources production to 5500 farmers, contracts renewed annually, constant monitoring by company.
- Philosophy: eating is a pleasure.
- Challenges created by the many mergers and acquisitions as the company grew.
- Aiming for a flatter structure by moving to a matrix structure.
- Seeing diversity in the workforce.
- Broadening the recruitment base for new managers beyond traditional *grandes écoles*.
- Promote employees who can think creatively into management.
- Power is based on position (authority) and expertise (for example, agro-engineers).

- Uses customer feedback in product development.
- Knowledge management – through MIS system, specialist employees and farmer partners.
- HR practices are not clearly articulated, for example, set of capabilities, strategically aligning leadership and followership with business goals, and management development strategies.
- Chairman of the Board of Directors has a typical background for a French business leader, and brings extensive local and international knowledge of the business to the position.
- Chairman of the Board of Directors is passionate about the business.

NOTES

1 The author is grateful to the Managing Director and others at Bonduelle for their support of this case study. She is Professor, Centre for Culture and Society at EDHEC Business School, France (Lille and Nice).
2 http://www.bonduelle.fr/htm/corporate/financial/financialdata/
3 *Annual Report*, 1999.
4 http://www.bonduelle.fr/htm/corporate/financial/index.htm
5 See their website for recipes and advice for growing your own vegetables at http://bonduelle.com

Seven EKATO Rühr-und Mischtechnik GmbH: Mixing People and Innovation[1]

GAYLE C. AVERY

You have to allow people to make mistakes and learn from them.[2]

Gerhard Zeiler, co-CEO

EKATO, a family-owned enterprise, was established in 1933. Located in Schopfheim, a small town in the south-western part of Germany near Basel, EKATO's 600 employees produce approximately 2500 industrial mixing machines each year. The second largest company in its field with an annual turnover of about €35 million, EKATO is the market leader in Europe. It has about 40 subsidiaries, including EKATO USA established in Ramsey, New Jersey, in 1985.[3] From the 1990s, the company grew consistently by around 5–7 per cent per annum.[4]

EKATO received its name from the founder, Eric Karl Todtenhaupt, who ran it until the late 1970s. Although originally very technically oriented, EKATO prospered initially because of Todtenhaupt's excellent relationships with his workers and with people in the chemical industry. However, times changed and these relationships are no longer key to EKATO's success.

The founder's sons took over the firm after acquiring doctorates in chemical engineering, and ran the company until the 1980s. At this time, they brought in an outsider as the third CEO/President. In 1999, one of the sons left and sold his share in the company. Then Eric Todtenhaupt Junior continued to manage EKATO jointly with Gerhard Zeiler.

PRODUCTION AND SERVICE

The firm specializes in making customized mixing machines for the chemical and food industries – agitators, drive shafts and impellers, as well as developing mechanical seals for mixers. They make sterility machines for the cosmetics and pharmaceutical industries, and about 85 per cent of Germany's atomic reactor agitators. Time horizons are relatively long because a typical product takes about nine months to develop and deliver.

Although EKATO manufactures exclusively in Germany, a relatively expensive location, it once tried operating in Louisiana, where labour was cheaper but less skilled. Apart from the availability of a more skilled workforce in Germany, an unforeseen complication stemmed from differing traditions in producing drawings in the US and Germany. Differences in standard symbols created errors and misunderstandings. EKATO has therefore concluded that the cost of doing business using somewhat less skilled people in the US was not low after all.

EKATO's production is highly oriented to the specific needs of individual customers, with about 75 per cent of all orders being designed for a particular use. Impeller parts and gearboxes, for example, are all individually designed for customers. Around 7000 working drawings are customized and about 2000 new designs produced each year.[5] This requires employees to be highly innovative.

Technology, such as expert systems, helps the organization manage and share solutions and knowledge, thereby reducing duplication. However, in an environment of high customization, and hence relatively few repetitive components, production is not greatly automated. Machine centres are used where they can add value, but computer simulation is not regarded as a substitute for direct testing, because computers cannot yet simulate the turbulence generated by mixers.

Increasingly, EKATO sees itself as a service organization, providing solutions for mixing problems, rather than just designing and manufacturing agitators, impellers or drive shafts. One of the barriers to EKATO becoming a service provider is that large customers tend to employ their own engineers to provide these services. This is partly out of concern about know-how leaking to competitors via an outside firm. In a similar desire to protect its intellectual property, EKATO avoids engaging in joint ventures.

The complexity and uniqueness of EKATO's products complicates customer service. Usually sales people are either engineers themselves or they take qualified engineers with them on service visits. By using people from production or assembly in service roles, EKATO ensures that service personnel have sufficient knowledge and experience to fix agitator problems. The supplier firm that manufactured gearboxes, motors or other externally sourced components rectifies faults with them.

About 60–70 per cent of EKATO's business is international, and EKATO operates abroad with local sales and service people. The process is often complicated, involving more than one sales area. An example is an American engineering company's Japanese operations. Here, sets of sales people from three countries are involved.

FACILITIES

In the early 1990s, EKATO developed a new production plant to mirror a new organizational structure.[6] In an acclaimed project, workers and architects jointly developed plans for the new plant, taking account of technology, people, society and the environment. The objective was to design a flexible and optimized production facility at a realistic cost, while creating an attractive environment to foster innovation.[7] The different 'languages' spoken by the developer, architects, factory planners and affected workers complicated collaboration on the new design, as did the differing values and priorities of the parties. The result of this complex planning process was an award-winning facility.

The facility is divided into three halls, linked by covered roadways. A courtyard serves as a communications centre. Office and production areas are integrated, and island production units, or cells, have been provided with distinctive building layouts. The modern, light and airy factory is designed around cells, with people in each cell being responsible for a whole component, that is, drive, shaft or impeller.

Provision has been made for a fourth building, intended to house assembly, painting and other processes. At present, EKATO is not planning to extend the plant, enduring extra logistical complications in driving between different sites and delivering components within the present facility. Management's stated preference is to invest in new markets, such as South America, rather than enhancing production facilities.

DEVELOPING SELF-MANAGING TEAMS

The new building was designed to support a cell-based, self-managing culture, which was a radical departure from EKATO's former bureaucratic ways.[8] However, employees were well prepared for the change. An extensive consultation and participation program preceded the change, which was based around people, process, technological and architectural strategies. All changes affecting employees were discussed in planning groups consisting of both workers and representatives of the workers' council.[9] Moderated employee focus groups discussed future problems and issues likely to affect daily work, and groups began to develop the necessary capacity to think in terms of the overall system.

Team skills were enhanced through training both before and after the move to the cell-structure, with workers also becoming multi-skilled and so able to rotate roles to some extent. Coaching assisted individuals in personally adapting to working in teams on a day-to-day basis. Group members were trained in conflict resolution, problem solving, interpersonal relationship skills, team roles, group dynamics and decision making, as well as setting group goals and priorities. Team development was treated as an on-going process, with support continuing beyond the actual move to the new facility.

Wide-ranging internal information was made available to employees to support the new self-managing, self-optimizing approach. In addition, the reward system was adjusted to include an individual bonus for workers' contributions, a bonus based on the productivity of the group, and an annual profit-sharing bonus.

The new arrangements brought almost instant results:[10]

- the new decentralized system amortized itself within the first two years of operation;
- throughput times were reduced by over 50 per cent;
- inventories fell by about 50 per cent;
- spare part stores were reduced by one-third;
- machine costs fell;
- changes to plans were reduced by about 40 per cent;
- information was more efficiently available and communication was easier, halving previous costs of obtaining information and passing it on;
- doubling up on work, a former cause of considerable wastage, was virtually eliminated; and
- a group identity among the production islands began to develop, fostered by on-going team development courses and regular group meetings within and across islands.

However, over time EKATO has reduced its emphasis on self-managing manufacturing cells. In 1991–92, EKATO had twice as many cells and groups as in 2000. The original three-person groups were considered too many for the relatively small size of the company, generating more coordination effort than was considered appropriate, with too many meetings involved in coordinating the groups.[11] EKATO subsequently re-formed the cells into eight to nine member groups, allocated to the three major manufacturing areas responsible for drives, shafts and impellers. Each of the three new areas now has a clear leader responsible for that group's part of the production.

EKATO management conceded that some people want to be involved in the workplace, but not necessarily to take responsibility. While workers like to have leaders, not all employees are born leaders and coordinators. The company is now striving to make its people more self-managing than they currently are, recognizing that some people are resisting and need further training in self-managing and group processes.[12] The basic philosophy is: 'Entrusting employees with responsibility assures highest quality standards and low costs, to the customer's advantage'.[13]

Effective coordination across the three production areas is also vital. For example, delivery time problems due to late shipments arose when changing from SAP's R2 to R3 software. This meant that EKATO had to start the year 2000 without data, and the company was unprepared for this eventuality. One solution was to make the assembly group responsible for the timely delivery of all components, replacing a system where delivery was part of a chain. The group acting as coordinator makes sure that all the components are there, managing across all three manufacturing areas.

INNOVATION AND CREATIVITY

Creativity is fundamental to EKATO's customized business, and the new facility and culture were designed with this in mind. EKATO engineers strive to innovate, even with fairly conventional mixing machines, to generate savings. For example, if they can create lower forces using innovative agitators, this will mean a need for smaller gears, bearings and motors, and less energy will be consumed. This efficiency in turn should make the company more competitive.

Overall, EKATO's preference is to innovate in small steps, rather than radically. However, one ambition is to develop mixing solutions that do not rely on agitators. Although EKATO's only serious competitor sells slightly different mixing solutions, such as chemical reactors, it employs EKATO agitators.

A major challenge for EKATO is how to protect and exploit its core know-how. The company has developed its own expertise in its highly specialized production steps, and therefore keeps production in-house. Investing about 4 per cent of its turnover in applied research, EKATO often sells its R&D capacity, for example, working on research projects relating to specific applications with large customers. In selling its innovation and expertise, EKATO aims to achieve higher profits to generate a return on its investment. However, some client companies require their purchasing departments to obtain the lowest possible price, making these purchasing departments uninterested in paying for innovation. Engineers or other end-users who do their own purchasing directly are more likely to value innovation. While expertise and manufacturing both generate income for EKATO, one does not necessarily lead to the other. In other words, receiving fees for their creative R&D work provides no guarantee that EKATO will be commissioned to manufacture the resulting hardware.

COMMUNICATION

Communication and sharing information are important at EKATO. As part of preventing classical labour problems, open discussion on numbers, problems and goals takes place within the firm. By law, EKATO must stage two annual meetings, organized by unions, between management and employees. At these meetings, the workers' council and the CEO report to the staff.

Top managers meet weekly, and senior managers engage in cross-functional weekly problem-solving meetings. Following an annual senior management retreat, EKATO issues its yearly plan, setting goals for the company, as well as for individual departments. These goals are communicated and discussed within the departments at special meetings, which are held every one to two weeks. Cross-functional groups of senior managers meet quarterly to discuss direction, strategy and areas of innovation within their departments. At this meeting, the managers are required to present results, costs and feasibilities on innovations. The results of these meetings are fed back into regular update meetings with broader groups.

MANAGING PEOPLE

The CEO, Gerhard Zeiler, believes that leadership has to do with the style of the person in a particular leadership role. In the 1980s, EKATO's then CEO tended to concentrate on company internal matters. Zeiler, with a sales background, changed this to a people focus. He is trying to delegate responsibility to people and empower skilled employees, re-creating a self-managing environment. Trust underpins this approach, which must include allowing people to learn from mistakes.[14] However, non-performance also needs to be addressed.

HR is decentralized and devolved to line management. EKATO employs a combined central finance/HR person, making department managers responsible for most HR matters and staff training. Managers take responsibility for appraisal and performance management, and their style can determine the amount of feedback given and received in their area. For example, the head of one area does not foster open discussion, in contrast to another senior manager who encourages people to discuss, generating excellent communication. This latter leader manages the service areas and debriefs all service calls with the people responsible so that they can avoid repeating mistakes. Team social pressure forces people to resolve localized problems, such as coming to work late.

All new employees are rotated through different areas for a few months. This includes assembly, to give them hands-on experience in the entire organization. Hiring decisions are vital to an innovative organization, since staff composition determines whether the firm has the necessary creativity skills and attitudes. Fruitful sources of future employees for EKATO lie in connections to universities and customers. Although the firm has no fixed alliances with universities, it maintains relationships with universities that specialize in processes and engages this expertise on specific assignments.

An important way EKATO retains its people is by providing them with interesting work.[15] Working at EKATO is relatively challenging for many employees – they have to keep up with new developments, attend seminars and read to stay current. EKATO supports its people in doing this, providing many opportunities to continue learning and to feel challenged.

Retaining people in less interesting roles is a challenge. For example, it is easier to make the job interesting for R&D people than for sales people. Conventional bonuses are not applicable to EKATO's sales force because much of what the field sales people achieve is outside their control. It is difficult for the sales force to generate its own markets, and salespeople depend on serendipity, relationships and persistence, rather than science and analysis. Mixer sales occur infrequently – agitator equipment typically lasts over 30 years and is normally only replaced when it stops operating.

DISCUSSION ISSUES

1   Where is leadership at EKATO? Which leadership paradigms can you identify at which points in time? Are leaders and followers aligned in their ideas of leadership? Where is the decision making? Are EKATO's systems and processes aligned with these ideas of leadership/followership?

2   Do you find evidence of vision and values driving EKATO today or in the past? Can you identify substitutes for leadership at EKATO?

3   Are there differences in leadership discernible at different times? Why might the self-managing teams have initially worked so well (compared with the former bureaucratic approach), and then ceased to serve the company's needs? Could anything have been done to prevent this change?

4   How does the organization attract, and try to motivate and retain its staff? Are mentoring and personal development opportunities evident at EKATO? What is the role of training?

5   How does EKATO foster creativity and manage its innovation? What evidence is there that EKATO is a learning organization? How does it manage its knowledge and intellectual property? Could the organization manage its knowledge better?

6   How might the long tradition, culture and symbolism at EKATO support and/or impede cultural change?

7   What would it take to make EKATO a global organization rather than a German company operating abroad? Do you agree that its core competency is so specialized that EKATO needs to remain based in Germany?

8   What are the constraints and challenges ahead for EKATO?

9   Can you see evidence of spirituality and emotion at the EKATO workplace? Are these elements important in the EKATO context?

10   Who are the stakeholders in EKATO, particularly since it operates in a rural part of Germany? What evidence do you see for the company managing its sustainability?

KEY ISSUES

- Small town pressures on employer/employee relationships.
- Family-owned organization, brought in some external management.
- Originally the business relied on personal connections, but this has changed today in a global organization.
- Trying to change from a product focus to a solutions and knowledge orientation.
- Manage knowledge via expert systems, central depot for designs, regular internal meetings at all levels, links to universities, training, educating and updating workers.
- New facilities support cell-based manufacturing in autonomous teams.
- Management went from bureaucratic to fractal, highly self-managing teams, then reverted back to somewhat larger groups with designated leaders.
- Self-managing teams received extensive training.
- Total self-management was too costly in coordination and time, not all employees wanted this much responsibility.
- New facility led to improved financial results, as well as reduced inventory, and other process improvements.
- Introduced coordination across the drive, shaft and impeller divisions to ensure more timely delivery.
- High level of innovation required, as well as a customer focus.
- Reinvests 4 per cent of turnover in R&D.
- Sharing information between groups is given high priority.
- Core know-how and intellectual property are recognized as valuable, and are used in consulting and customizing designs.
- Retain production in-house to protect intellectual property.
- Unsuccessful foray into cheaper US labour market led to returning to skilled, German production.
- Extensive management responsibilities are pushed to line management.
- Very small central HR function, HR is decentralized.
- CEO is trying to strengthen the empowered, self-managing employee culture.
- Motivation is largely through providing interesting work wherever possible in an effort to retain people.
- The infrequent and complex nature of sales makes it difficult to reward the sales employees via commissions.

- Spirituality and emotion are evident through personal development, concern for interesting work and using workers' brains and creativity.
- Two-thirds of EKATO's business is international, they are trying to increase international markets.

NOTES

1   The author expresses her appreciation to Hr Zeiler and Dr Krebs for sharing their knowledge and experience during her visit to EKATO.
2   Zeiler, G. (1999) Personal communication.
3   http://www.ekato.de/ekatojavae/menue.php3 accessed 5 December 2001.
4   Zeiler, G. (1999) Personal communication.
5   Hallwachs, U., Kummle, H., Schroedter, C., Steiner, G. and Todtenhaupt, P. (1991). 'Integrierte Fabrik- und Industrieplanung: Rahmen für Wertewandel und Produktionskompetenz', *Industriebau*, 6, Sonderdruck.
6   Hallwachs et al. (1991), ibid.
7   ibid.
8   Hallwachs, U., Todtenhaupt, P. and Schlund, M. (1995) *Mehr Effizienz durch dezentrale Verantwortungsbereiche: Eine praxisnahe Anleitung für die Reorganisation mittelständischer Betriebe*. Renningen-Malmsheim: Expert Verlag.
9   Schlund, M. (1995) 'Dezentrale Organisationsstrukturen mit Teamarbeit'. Paper presented to the AIC Conference, 29 June.
10 Schlund, M. (1995), ibid.
11 Zeiler, G. (1999) Personal communication.
12 Houry, R. (1999) Personal communication.
13 http://www.ekato.de/ekatojavae/menue.php3 accessed 5 December 2001.
14 Zeiler, G. (1999) Personal communication.
15 ibid.

Eight Schering-Plough: Mentoring
Presidents

MARTIN HILB[1]

Give and take

Max von Dach, former CEO of Schering-Plough[2]

Max von Dach began his business education in Bern and Neuenberg in Switzerland, followed by further study at Harvard Business School. His career started at the former Swiss chemical giant, Ciba Geigy. During part of his time there, he took a management role in India. He then moved to what became known as the Schering-Plough Corporation, a major US-based pharmaceutical concern. As CEO of Schering-Plough for Europe, Africa and the Middle East over a 20-year period, he was regarded as a top intrapreneur because of his achievements in developing over 20 companies in these regions, creating success for Schering's shareholders, employees and customers alike.

Schering-Plough is a worldwide pharmaceutical company committed to discovering, developing and marketing new therapies and treatment programs that can improve people's health and extend lives. The company is a recognized leader in biotechnology, genomics and gene therapy. Its core products are grouped into the following areas: allergy and respiratory, anti-infective and anticancer, cardiovascular and dermatological products. Schering-Plough has a global animal health business, as well as leading consumer brands of foot care, over-the-counter and sun care products. Innovative research, effective marketing and solid financial management have enabled the company to grow and deliver attractive financial results.[3]

Sales continue to grow at Schering-Plough. Consolidated net sales increased 14 per cent from 1998 to 1999 (US$9.1 billion in 1999), and increased 8 per cent from 1999 to 2000 (US $9.8 billion in 2000).[4] In 2000, the company enjoyed its 15th consecutive year of double-digit growth in earnings per share.

While head of Schering-Plough in Europe, Max von Dach liked to hire promising young graduates as his personal assistants, and then mentor them. The results of his mentoring can be seen in the success of six of his mentees, who are now high-flying leaders of industry. This is the story of how six of the mentored assistants, from diverse backgrounds, went on to distinguished careers as heads of prominent organizations.

THE MENTEES

1   Dr Jean-Pierre Garnier (French and US citizen, born 1947) has been Chief Executive Officer of GlaxoSmithKline[5] since December 2000.[6] Prior to that, from 1995 he was Chief Operating Officer of the then SmithKline Beecham, where he had been Chief-Executive-Officer-elect since December 1999, and on the Board of Directors since 1992. Holding a Doctor of Pharmacology plus an MBA from Stanford University, US (which he attended as a Fullbright Scholar), Garnier rose to become President of Schering-Plough's US business. During his 15 years at Schering, Garnier reported indirectly to Max von Dach while in various general management roles in France, Switzerland, Belgium, Denmark and Portugal. He was awarded the French Legion of Honour from President Chirac in 1997.

2   Dr Franz Humer (Swiss and Austrian citizen, born 1946) is currently Chief Executive Officer, and since 2001 Chairman of the Board of Directors,[7] at F. Hoffmann La Roche.[8] He held a series of senior positions in various European, African and Middle Eastern countries with Glaxo Holdings before joining Roche in 1995. In 1996, he became Chief Operating Officer, and two years later was appointed Chief Executive Officer of Hoffmann La Roche. He holds a Doctor of Jurisprudence from Innsbruck University, Austria and an MBA from Insead in Fontainebleu. Humer worked directly with Max von Dach as his assistant, and indirectly while heading the British and Portuguese subsidiaries.

3   John A. Kenward (British, born 1951) became Chairman and Chief Executive Officer of US-based Zarix, Inc., which he founded.[9] His biography emphasizes that he has focused on the challenges of European operations for most of his career, which has been characterized by outstanding business performance. Kenwood was trained as an organic chemist and holds a master's degree in chemistry from Oxford University, England. After a time at SmithKline Beecham he moved to Schering, where he worked directly with Max von Dach as his assistant. He reported indirectly to Max von Dach in various general management roles in Schering subsidiaries in

Sweden, Holland, Belgium and France. Kenward's last position at Schering was that of Senior Vice President for marketing, medical and scientific operations for all products and markets outside the US. He left Schering to found the bio-high-tech IXSYS in San Diego.

4   Hans-Jörg Kummer (Swiss, born 1941) is currently President for Europe, the Middle East and Canada of Schering-Plough. He graduated from the Business Faculty at the University of Zurich, Switzerland. Hans-Jörg Kummer reported directly to Max von Dach as his first assistant, and indirectly in other roles, including as general manager for subsidiaries in South Africa, Spain and France. Kummer is the only one of the six mentees still with Schering-Plough, and holds a position similar to that of his former mentor.

5   Peter Simon (Swiss, born 1945) is co-founder and Chairman of Impetus AG, an international management consulting firm based in Basel.[10] In 1999, Impetus established Innovens as an independent, virtual, project management and licensing organization in the health care business. Educated at the University of Basel, Switzerland, Simon holds a degree in business. Prior to a role as senior executive of Hoffmann La Roche, he joined Schering-Plough to work as assistant to Max von Dach and then became Marketing Director for Europe, Africa and the Middle East. In these roles, he reported directly to Max von Dach. In between these assignments, Simon reported indirectly to Max von Dach when heading the South African subsidiary.

6   Dr Anthony H. Wild (British, born 1948) is on the Board of Directors of Variagenics after three decades of pharmaceutical experience at the senior executive level.[11] He is founder, partner and Chief Executive Officer of MedPointe Capital Partners, Inc., and most recently served as President of Warner Lambert's Global Pharmaceuticals sector until May, 2000. From February 1995 until May 1996, Wild was President of Parke-Davis North America. Prior to this appointment, he held various management, marketing and operating positions at Schering-Plough, including President of Schering-Plough in Osaka, Japan, the largest Schering division outside the US. He took his PhD in physical chemistry at the University of Cambridge, England. At Schering-Plough, he reported indirectly to Max von Dach in various general management capacities, including while in the Swedish, South African and Dutch subsidiaries. Wild reported directly to Max von Dach while Director of Organizational Planning and Development for Europe, Africa and the Middle East.

Noteworthy is that when the mentees joined Max von Dach, they were somewhat older and more experienced than many young trainees. While their education was different – some had MBAs, others had doctorates – the most common characteristic appears to be prior work experience, which allowed

Max von Dach to quickly assign these mentees tasks with real responsibilities from the beginning of their employment. This seniority and experience also allowed mentees to be sent out as general managers fairly quickly. Max von Dach describes them as agile, ambitious young people, hungry for knowledge.

SUCCESSFUL MENTORING

How did Max von Dach's mentees come to achieve these successes? What is it about the situation surrounding von Dach and his six mentees that influenced this success? The results of interviews conducted with the mentees provide some insights.[12]

- *Most important learning experience*: When asked about their most important learning experiences, mentees responded in different ways. Many experiences originated from their student times and included interfacing with major decision-makers in the industry, taking on significant responsibilities for the first time, learning to put the company ahead of one's own interests, learning to work with people, engaging in international experiences, and working in a stimulating and fun environment.
- *The mentoring experience:* Overall, the mentoring time with Max von Dach was regarded as an invaluable experience by the mentees. Broad exposure to the top of the organization through the mentoring program, and seeing first-hand how senior managers operate was valued in comparison with taking on a narrow functional role. Mentees said that this provided an opportunity to learn the business from many perspectives, to network and to learn how to navigate through the organization. From Max von Dach, mentees gained a multicultural perspective, for example, one mentee (Kenward) learned how to blend the European's strategic vision with the American need for results and change. Von Dach provided mentees with considerable freedom and a wide range of tasks, stimulating interest in his mentees. Others learned trust in, and empowerment of, people from their mentor, and how to blend analytical skills with entrepreneurial flair.
- *Mentor's influence on career:* Garnier learned from von Dach that one cannot learn the management craft without going international. The mentor was preoccupied with global business and thus expanded the horizons of some of the mentees, particularly as they realized that global experience was something that few have and most need or want. Several dreamt of succeeding their mentor and taking over his position. For those who held specific career ambitions, Max von Dach provided opportunities and counsel.

- *What to avoid:* Roles that have lost their excitement or opportunities for learning and personal development would be avoided by several mentees. Others said that they would prefer to avoid roles that compromized them for the sake of expediency, or where they were not able to affect the situation they found themselves in (for example, realize their visions, lead and develop people).

- *Ethical influences:* The most frequently used word when asked which ethical values the mentees considered important for their professional career was 'integrity'. Mentees perceived Max von Dach as a consistent living example of integrity, on a daily basis. Garnier defined integrity in the following terms: 'If a decision I just made was published on the front page of the *New York Times*, would I feel at peace with myself? If the answer is no, then the decision should not be made.'[13] Another common ethical theme was the need for respect for each individual, and Max von Dach was seen as having high moral commitment to his employees. Wild pointed out that Max von Dach's greatest value was trusting his people and giving them the freedom to do their jobs.

- *Refusing promotions:* With the exception of Franz Humer, all mentees had refused at least two opportunities for promotion. Sometimes family or other personal reasons were given, but often the reasons for rejecting promotions involved not feeling ready or being willing to break off a current project, or because of their feelings about Schering-Plough.

- *Assisting young graduates:* The mentees offered recommendations for assisting young graduates in reaching their full potential. On-the-job experience, with mentoring early in the career, was regarded as highly important in developing a young graduate. Mentoring was considered critical because the mentor could make the company transparent, point out the opportunities and invisible rules, as well as highlight the young graduate's flaws. However, the mentees warned young people against being too ambitious, thinking of the next job instead of doing the best possible job in their current role. Mentees should quickly become mentors themselves as a way of contributing to the organization, and ideally mentoring should be firmly anchored in the organizational culture.

MENTORING PROGRAM

The interviews revealed that Max von Dach's mentoring program was characterized by two main factors:

- The most senior person in the organization engaged in mentoring, acting as role model for other mentors in the organization, and particularly for the mentees themselves. Others in the organization saw a humane entrepreneur, with his focus on people, trust and integrity.
- A simple concept of mentoring was used, based on teaching through consultation and affection rather than on judgement and constriction.

The mentor claimed that he learned as much from the mentees as they may have from him in a give-and-take relationship, characterized by trust and respect – essential components in mentoring. He regarded respect for the individual and providing flexibility in a non-political context as critical to guiding well-educated young people along the path of success. The mentee needed to be introduced to the organizational philosophy and management culture as soon as the mentee's capabilities allowed. By providing real projects that could add value to the business and lead to an experience of success, the mentee's management skills were challenged and stretched. This also fostered the required loyalty in the new management generation, and so enabled these people to be put into responsible management roles. It was also important that the salaries of the mentees remained within the established framework of the organization, because money does not buy loyalty.

Max von Dach also recognized the inevitability that some of the mentees would be attracted away from the organization and regarded this as not particularly tragic if they had already served the organization well. Mentees were frequently searching for greater challenges than the organization could offer them.

DISCUSSION ISSUES

1 What can you conclude about Max von Dach's mentoring process? What are the key factors in developing successful presidents?

2 What are the characteristics of a successful mentor, judging by this case? Do successful mentees need special traits or qualifications?

3 Can you identify the leadership paradigm(s) behind Max von Dach's approach? Does he possess special leadership traits? How did his leadership style fit the leadership ideas and needs of his followers?

4 Which parts of the system was Max von Dach trying to align with his mentoring program? Are substitutes for leadership evident in this case? Was the mentoring likely to stop after von Dach left or was it anchored in the culture, as far as the case study indicates?

5 Does the mentoring style identified in this case study suit global organizations? Does the mentor need to be physically present for the mentoring to work? Why? Why not?

6 Do you think the mentor's primary motivation was succession planning? Should a mentor worry that mentees might leave the organization and benefit competitors?

7 Could one consider Schering-Plough a learning or teaching organization under Max von Dach? What factors could have induced the organization to continue with the mentoring program with one of the original mentees as president? How would Max von Dach's retirement have impacted the production of presidents in the organization?

8 What is required to create a mentoring culture? Could some of the lessons from this case study be transferred to other organizations, or is the Schering-Plough case unique?

KEY ISSUES

- Mentoring international and global players.
- High potential mentees.
- Strong, active role for followers.
- Mentor role-modelled personal qualities of ethics, integrity.

- Provided developmental opportunities and experiences, stretch tasks, global assignments.
- Gave freedom and autonomy, trusted people to do their jobs.
- Provided intellectual stimulation to mentees.
- Applied individualized consideration to mentees' needs.
- Could have formed in- and out-groups, so that LMX theory could apply.
- Enabled mentees to pursue their dreams and visions.
- Sought to apply commitment leadership (Visionary).
- Mentees were expected to become mentors in turn, anchoring mentoring in the organizational culture.
- Strong focus on people.
- Mentoring is viewed as a two-way learning experience for mentor and mentee.
- Teaching from the top down, possibly early cascading of learning throughout the organization.
- Focus on positive emotion.
- Belief that loyalty is not bought with money.
- Align followers with organizational culture to create loyalty.
- Evidence of spirituality in the workplace in the availability of personal growth and development opportunities, and intellectual contribution required from mentees.

NOTES

1   Professor Martin Hilb is Director, Institute for Leadership and Human Resource Management, University of St Gallen, Switzerland.
2   Hilb, M. (1997) *Management by Mentoring – How to develop Presidents*. Neuwied: Luchterhand verlag.
3   Accessed on-line on 10 July 2001 at http://www.schering-pough.com/finance/
4   Accessed on-line on 10 July 2001 at http://www.schering-plough.com/finance/
5   Ranked number two among the world's 50 largest (by market capitalization) companies outside the US by *Forbes Global*, 3 September 2001, p. 40.
6   Accessed on-line on 11 May 2001 at http://corp.gsk.com/bios/bio_garnier.htm
7   Accessed on-line on 16 May 2001 at http://www.roche.com/
8   Ranked number 24 among the world's 50 largest (by market capitalization) companies outside the US by *Forbes Global*, 3 September 2001, p. 40.
9   Accessed on-line on 16 May 2001 at Zarix web site at http://206.137.122.101/
10 Accessed on-line on 16 May 2001 at http://www.innovens.com/
11 Accessed on-line on 16 May 2001 at http://www.variagenics.com/
12 Hilb, M. (1997), ibid.
13 Hilb, M. (1997), ibid. p. 76.

Nine Swatch: Leading
Through Emotion[1]

GAYLE C. AVERY

... if we could add genuine emotion ...[2]

Nicolas G. Hayek, President and Founder

A key to understanding the nearly two-decade success story of the Swatch Group is emotion – Swatch aims to continually engage the emotions of buyers. Before Swatch was created, analysts had assumed that consumers buy one or two watches in their lifetime. Analysts reasoned that the European watch industry had to decline because nearly everyone owned a couple of watches and did not *need* more and, in particular, the Swiss watch industry would fail because Switzerland was too expensive a production location.

It seems that the analysts were wrong. By 2000, the President of the Swatch Group, Nicolas G. Hayek, could write: 'The Swatch craze has relented a little but the brand is still here ... is growing steadily and with all the innovations ... is attracting more and more buyers.'[3] What analysts did not take into account was the emotion that could be associated with buying a highly-personal item like a watch. Thanks to innovative design and marketing at Swatch, the public has just kept on buying watches, and the entire Swiss watch industry has flourished once again. The Swatch Group has become the world's largest manufacturer of finished watches, representing about 22–25 per cent of the world's watch sales.[4]

Not only the success of the Swatch Group, but much of the resurgence in the entire Swiss watch industry can be attributed to the vision of the Swatch Group's President and Chief Executive Officer, Nicolas G. Hayek. In 1993, Hayek claimed that buyers flocked to Swatches, because Swatch emotionalized the high quality but traditionally rather austere Swiss watch. Hayek told the *Harvard Business Review* that watches are emotional products, not commodities – as much of the Swiss industry used to position them.

To Hayek, watches are important facets of self-image.[5] 'I thought if we could add genuine emotion ... and attack the low end of the market (Asian quartz watches) we could succeed,' he said. In the 1996 Annual Report, Hayek noted that the company's unique culture is made up of emotionalism and realism, of humanism and 'combativity in the face of formidable competitors'. Not only are the pragmatic elements of low cost, high quality and good design important to the Swatch concept, crucial to their success is Swatch laying its culture on the line. That is the most difficult element for others to copy, Hayek claimed.

SWISS WATCH INDUSTRY

From the early 1970s, the Swiss watch industry had been slowly losing market share to cheap Asian quartz watches, especially from Hong Kong and Japan, but also from Taiwan, China and South Korea. Switzerland's share of the global market dropped from 43 to 15 per cent between 1977 and 1983, and jobs in the watch industry fell by more than 50 per cent, from 90 000 to fewer than 40 000.[6]

By the early 1980s, the Swiss share of the low price watch market, representing annual sales of about 450 million watches up to CHF 75 each, had become practically zero. Barely better was the Swiss share of the middle segment of about 42 million units selling up to CHF 400 each, at about 3 per cent. However, in the top layer of about eight million units, Switzerland had about 97 per cent of the market. Overall, the Swiss watch industry had slipped from a 30 per cent share of the world watch market to 9 per cent.[7]

The decline has largely been attributed to the Swiss watch industry remaining loyal to its tradition of mechanical watch movements and not adjusting to changing consumer habits. The banks, becoming increasingly concerned, called on Hayek Engineering AG, Hayek's consulting firm, to assess the future for the then two flagship companies of Switzerland's watch industry, SSIH (Société Suisse pour l'Industrie Horlogère SA) and ASUAG (Allgemeine Schweizerische Uhrenindustrie AG). Hayek's report described a 'chaotic jungle' in both companies: SSIH appeared to lack discipline and strategy, while Switzerland's largest watch group, AUSAG, was struggling to accommodate more than 100 Swiss watch companies that were acquired to face the Asian competition. In late 1983, the two major players in the Swiss watch industry were amalgamated into one entity. These and other acquisitions within the watch industry form the production arm of the Swatch Group.[8]

Hayek recommended maintaining a presence in each market segment. However, the banks were nervous about the report's suggestion that Switzerland tackle the Asian challenge head on, and recommended that Hayek buy 51 per cent of SSIH and ASUAG, which he did. This became the foundation of the Swatch Group.

Many of the independent watch manufacturers have since been amalgamated into one major producer, ETA SA Fabriques d'Ebauches (ETA). Since its origins in 1793, the ETA group has continued to innovate and win awards for its production. For example, the Swiss-based EEM (Ebauches Electronique Marin), now part of ETA, had made the first quartz movements with digital and analog displays in 1970. In 1979, spurred on by Japanese achievements of a 2.5 mm-thick watch, revolutionary technology enabled the Swiss to produce the Delirium watch, the thinnest in the world with a thickness of 1.98 mm. The Delirium's success inspired the creation of a less expensive quality watch made out of plastic. In the late summer of 1981, the Swatch watch was born – a Swiss-made watch using synthetic material, which is shockproof, accurate, suited for mass production, inexpensive and available in a range of colours.

SWATCH SUCCESS

In 1982, the thin plastic Swatch fashion watch was launched in the US with 27 unisex models in the first collection, and March 1983 saw the launch in Switzerland.[9] The Swatch went on to achieve high success in both the US and European markets, as well as in other places, including Japan, with the one-millionth watch produced in the next year.[10] By 1988, 50 million watches had been manufactured, doubling to 100 million by 1992.

Swatches involve major technological innovations. For example, the watch looks like it is made in a single casting, and with just 51 parts has far fewer parts than any other quartz analog watch. Second, the Swatch sold for between US$25–35, reflecting the company philosophy of high quality at the best possible price. Through continuing innovation in multifunctionality, watches that dive, alarms that play music, watches with smart chips, beeping pagers, solar-powered watches and watches incorporating ski passes were developed. *Swatch Talk*, a telephone in a watch, was presented at the CeBIT '98 World Telecommunications exhibition in Hannover (Germany). In that year, *Swatch Access* was unveiled at the Expo '98 in Lisbon (Portugal), a multifunctional, interactive watch with built-in memory. Equipped with a microchip, *Access* can store ski passes or other information and can be used to provide access at cultural and athletic events. In 1997, the new *Swatch Skin* became the then thinnest Swatch of all time. In 1998, *Swatch.beat* heralded a 1000-unit time system for measuring Internet time from a new meridian at the Swatch Headquarters in Biel.

Financially, the Swatch Group continues to perform well, outpacing the watchmaking sector as a whole. Gross consolidated sales of all watches, movements and stepping motors reached CHF 3.269 billion in 1998, increasing to CHF 3.626 billion in 1999, and over CHF 4 billion in 2000.[11]

The fourth quarter of 1999 and the whole of 2000 broke all records since 1993 in turnover, with sales generally increasing in all markets. The overall value of sales of components and watches to the various geographic regions in 2000 were: Europe 55 per cent, Asia 29 per cent, America 14 per cent and Oceania 2 per cent.[12] The ongoing group expansion has led to production sites opening in Asia (for example, Thailand and China) and other parts of Europe. The Swiss share of the global watch market has recovered to 51 per cent, with Swatch the world's largest watchmaker at the beginning of the twenty-first century.

GROWTH STRATEGY

Swatch continues to enjoy considerable growth. Since the fusion of ASUAG and SSIH in 1983, Hayek identified four major phases in Swatch's development.[13] First came the survival phase, which was achieved largely because of the Swatch watch and an effective international wholesale distribution system. The second phase involved reviving the luxury sector Omega, Rado and Longine brands, plus acquiring additional luxury brands. At the same time, the Swatch Group expanded its production of movements and mechanical components through ETA and other companies.

The third phase was the worldwide distribution phase, when the Swatch Group created a dynamic, international distribution network with branches in many countries around the world. At this stage, they also focused on the middle-price-range segment of the market with brands such as Tissot. Swatch established a new brand – cK Watch Co Ltd – using a young team of managers.

Finally, the current phase involves rapid global expansion while keeping the know-how inside the organization – from production to R&D. The Internet is a key part of this strategy, with over 50 million people visiting the Swatch Watch Internet site every month. The site itself has won numerous international multimedia prizes.

Continued growth is vital to Swatch: 'Growth is and always has been the motto of the Swatch Group, but a growth that is progressive and conscious. It must be based on solid foundations such as expanding customer acceptance of our products, continual and permanent improvement of quality, stringent unit cost controls, and the development and launch of innovative products.'[14] Hayek added that growth 'must be based on improving the qualifications and motivation of our staff, as well as our management's desires to be met by a sea of smiling faces on a Monday morning, belonging to people who are happy to come to work.'

SWATCH ORGANIZATION

ASUAG and SSIH joined forces to form the *SMH Swiss Corporation for Microelectronics and Watchmaking Industries Ltd*, headquartered in Biel, Switzerland. SMH became known as *The Swatch Group Ltd* in 1998. As at 1 January 2001, the Swatch Group Management Board consisted of nine core members, and an extended Board contains another 15 members from operations around the world.[15]

Outside Switzerland, the Swatch Group has subsidiaries in some 11 European countries, with European agencies in 19 countries. The global Swatch Group is represented by subsidiaries and agencies in North, Central and South America, Australasia, Asia-Pacific, the Middle and Far East, and Africa. Swatch has some 50 production centres, mainly in Switzerland, plus others in the US, other European countries and Asia.

The Swatch Group produces major brands of watches, from luxury and private labels to basic watches. Brands include Omega, Breguet, Blancpain, Rado, Longines, Tissot, ckWatch, Hamilton, Certina, Mido, Pierre Balmain, Flik Flak (for children) and Endura. The group also operates Swatch retail stores, produces watch movements and components, manufactures electronic systems for cars and other products, plus provides a range of general services.

Each part of the Group generally has its own organization, management and often their own buildings. The Group is strongly decentralized, with well over 200 profit centres facing demanding budgets. Profit centres provide monthly sales figures by the sixth day of the following month, and profit and loss statements 10 to 15 days later.

Project teams are very common. In planning a new product, Swatch assembles a project team as soon as agreement is reached on product performance specifications. Then the team is presented with parameters for its performance. Hayek said, 'We present the team with target economics: this is how much the product can sell for … this is the margin we need to support advertising, promotion and so on. Thus these are the costs we can afford. Now go and design a product and a production system that allows us to build it at these costs in Switzerland.'[16] Creative people tackle an issue and then move on to the next one.

Although many parts of the Swatch Group are in fact highly organized, the aim is to minimize bureaucracy in the Group. Hayek has stated that organizational structure is 'the most inhuman thing ever invented. It goes against our nature as people.'[17] Instead, Swatch works by using clear-but-flexible boundaries and targets, encouraging conflicting targets between different units within the Group. The brands have complete autonomy over design, marketing and communications, but still need to resolve conflicts with ETA, the Group's manufacturer, when it comes to production. This means negotiating over factors like quality, style, speed of production and cost. Such differences are resolved with the minimum of bureaucracy, without a formal intermediary in the organization, and as directly and quickly as possible. While each unit has its own delineated responsibilities and rules, each unit is required to interact with others in order to get its job done.

It is rare for major companies that market complex products to be as vertically integrated as Swatch. Swatch owns the factories, research laboratories and other facilities involved in watchmaking, and owns and operates every process, from manufacturing to retailing.[18]

STRATEGIC INDEPENDENCE

Hayek Senior believes that vertical integration is the only way Swatch can maintain its strategic independence. For example, unlike three- and five-volt chips used in computers, televisions, and video-cassette recorders, only three major manufacturers in the world make 1.5 volt semiconductor chips needed for watches. One is the Swatch Group, and the other two are in Japan. Hayek argues that if Swatch did not make its own chips, it would be at the mercy of the two Japanese manufacturers. Market research has indicated that Swatch could have to pay three times as much for these chips as it costs Swatch to manufacture their own.[19]

To manufacture the chips economically, Swatch had to invest heavily and produce in large volumes. Thus Swatch chips are not only used in its own watches, but also in other brands' hearing aids, pacemakers, mobile telephones and even in the monitor switches for anti-lock brakes on cars and other vehicles. Over two-thirds of the revenue from 0.9–1.5 volt chips comes from these external markets in 35 countries.[20]

ETA often makes its own tools using in-house resources. This is necessary because off-the-shelf equipment is often of inferior quality, and at times the highly specialized tools needed are not available from outside. The company claims that custom-built tools and constantly upgraded production lines are key to steady development and manufacture of innovative new products. An example is the development of a new CHF 47 million[21] metal injection-molding machine for the *Swatch Irony* range of 63 metal watches, including the Swagman, Penrith, Uluru, Tholos and Rushcutters in the *Olympics 2000* range. The payoff from the metal injection molding machine was substantial: a 90 per cent reduction in the cost of watchcases from CHF 40 to CHF 4. Making its own tools also protects Swatch's know-how.

Swatch competes on price by automating aggressively, thereby keeping labour costs down. For the Swatch Group, it is imperative that direct labour accounts for less than 10 per cent of total manufacturing costs. The ETA factory at Grenchen, making 35 000 Swatch watches and millions of components a day, runs practically unattended from midnight to 8 am every day. 'Innovation, creativity, imagination, vision and control mean that from Switzerland, one of the most expensive countries in the world in terms of labour costs, over 80 per cent of our products can be exported to the rest of the world, despite fierce competition from other countries, particularly in Asia,' Hayek said in 1998.[22]

Swatch uses its own distribution network, paying as much attention to the look of its points-of-sale as to the products themselves. By 2001, nearly 600 Swatch stores had been opened around the world.[23] Increasingly, the witty, fresh Swatch megastores in New York, London, Tokyo and Paris provide a special Swatch experience. In Paris, the gleaming mosaics and mirrors lend the spacious interior a special feel, while interactive games and exhibits, an unusual piano and various other attractions entice visitors to spend time in the megastore. The megastores reflect the Swatch philosophy that adults should always continue to enjoy the unrestrained, colourful world of children.[24]

MARKETING

Much of the Swatch success can be attributed to clever marketing, creating a product with trend-setting colourful design and unconventional appearance. The products' presentation mirrors the Swatch message of 'always new, always different'. Swatch is *fashion that ticks*, each product having its own emotive name and two collections appearing each year. According to Hayek, 'Swatch is provocation, innovation, and fun – forever.' [25]

The Swatch Group places great emphasis on public relations and capitalizing on public events. The Group has long been involved in the Olympics and space missions, and continues to form creative alliances, including with Time Warner and the International Olympic Committee.

Global campaigns and unconventional presentations enhance the Swatch brand. Swatch is present at a range of events around the world from sporting to musical, from environmental to United Nations' activities. A flamboyant marketing venture was achieved by using the Grauholz railway tunnel near Berne, Switzerland, to show Swatch's 1998 30-second 'Time is what you make of it' slogan. As trains passed through the tunnel, a series of images on the tunnel wall flashed by like staccato frames from a movie, presenting passengers with a television commercial about Swatch and reminding them to make the most of their time.[26]

Creativity abounds at Swatch, which executes many of its 'extreme' ideas. For example, hanging a 150 m-high, 13-tonne working Swatch from Frankfurt's tallest building successfully launched Swatch in Germany. The only words on the face were 'Swatch. Swiss. DM 60'. That marketing idea was repeated successfully in Tokyo's Ginza, although with a smaller display, and at the 1998 Goodwill Games in New York a huge Swatch clock informed people about the latest news and results.

The Swatch Club brings together tens of thousands of fans from all over the world.[27] According to the 1999 Annual Report, the club's objective is to promote communication among like-minded people, across the barriers of country, language and race, for people of any age. Members are identified through their club watches.

Since 1985, when Swatch entered the world of art with the first *Swatch Art Special* designed by Kiki Picasso, Swatch has been promoted as a form of wearable art. Many well-known artists have been engaged to design Swatches, and some of their creations can fetch high prices among collectors. For example, in 1986 Swatch commissioned graffiti artist Keith Haring, famous for work in New York subways, to design a series of four Swatches. Subsequently Haring's watches have sold at auction for more than US$5000. In 1989, Swatch asked Italian artist Mimmo Paladino to design a watch, and produced only 120 of Paladino's designs. One was auctioned two years later for US$24 000.[28]

INNOVATION

Innovation is at the core of Swatch's activities. Hayek Senior and his son, G. Nicolas Hayek Junior, have been the driving force in terms of innovation, although new ideas come from all levels of the company. Formal research and development is not a major feature at Swatch; very often the President's intuition, or that of other employees, is developed to see if it is marketable. Both Hayeks are available 24 hours a day, seven days a week to provide 'very hands on' assistance on many levels.

If an idea fails, people move on to the next idea 'without blame', as is evident in the Swatch attitude to mistakes: 'Just move on to the next thing'. Discontinued ideas include *Swatch Eyes* (spectacles with interchangeable mountings launched in 1991) and the smart car.

Hayek Senior was behind designing and manufacturing the smart car, via Micro Compact Car (MCC) AG based in Hambach, France.[29] The Swatch Group became involved in this joint venture with Daimler-Chrysler as part of Hayek's vision of revolutionizing the transport system. Part of this revolution involved developing a small dual petrol/electric car to minimize toxic emissions and parking problems. As well, because Swatch manufactures and markets electronic components to most car manufacturers, it made business sense to use these Swatch Group components in the smart car. With production commencing in 1994, the smart car concept evolved into a sophisticated, 2.5 m-long two-seater vehicle with airbags and ABS braking. For the first time in the car industry, a vehicle had moulded, coloured plastic panels, which could be changed. This last feature was a natural flow-on from the Swatch culture of having a watch for every occasion, because owners could exchange the car panels for different coloured panels in less than one hour. After exiting the smart car joint venture, the Swatch Group founded SMH Automobile to experiment with developing its own environmentally-friendly car with a hybrid drive system.[30]

However, Hayek is highly innovative in various fields, including being involved in designing and building the radically different MCC factory in Hambach. The patented factory design enables car parts to be delivered in 4.5 hours – which must be the epitome of the just-in-time concept. Major suppliers facilitated this by having built plants adjacent to the cross-shaped assembly area where the cars are assembled.

Many innovations, particularly in the areas of public relations and marketing at Swatch, come out of ordinary meetings or brainstorming sessions. Swatch seeks to enhance creativity by fostering a relaxed, chaotic workplace in which people can change jobs easily. It starts with a totally relaxed attitude to dress: Hayek Senior dresses in a unique 'casual' style. Hayek Junior wears jeans, although that is not totally unusual in Swiss business. Most others take their cue from these leaders, and those wearing formal work suits and ties stand out.

The Hayeks do not believe that there is an ideal company structure. They prefer to encourage creativity in employees by emphasizing that employees should be themselves, have fun and not mind what others in the company think or say. As Hayek Senior put it, 'We kill too many good ideas by rejecting them without thinking about them, by laughing at them.' His strength as a businessman is that he has retained the 'fantasy of a six-year-old. If you can keep and use the curiosity of a child, you can only improve everything around you'.[31]

Hayek Senior describes his talent as being able to spot new ways of selling emotional products. Designer of the limited edition *Swatch Roboboy*, Steven Guarnaccia, was reported as saying that Swatch owes its success to 'finding people who have an interesting way of looking at an object'. One of Swatch's creative team, Tom Webster, said that one way Swatch dominated the watch industry was by 'creating brand experiences that successfully promote the object: an exciting ski weekend where your watch serves as a ski tow pass.'[32]

Individuals exhibiting eccentric behaviour can thrive at Swatch, as long as the Hayeks are happy with their creative output. However, some jobs require intense concentration for long periods, leading to early burnout and hence a high turnover in employees.

LEADERSHIP

Hayek Senior provided the vision, cash and style to make Swatch successful. Variously described by the media as egocentric, idiosyncratic, passionate, a business celebrity and an engaging presence, Nicolas G. Hayek was born in

1928 in Beirut, Lebanon, with an American father (George N. Hayek) and a Lebanese mother. After primary and secondary education in Beirut, he moved to Switzerland with his family, where he became a citizen in 1964.

In 1963, Hayek Senior formed Hayek Engineering in Zurich, which became famous for finding waste and mismanagement in everything from the Swiss Army to the Swiss state radio. By 1994, Hayek's company was the biggest management consulting firm in Switzerland, a US$1 billion business.

In recognition of his achievements, France made Hayek Senior President of its Innovation Council for Economic Strategies; Germany appointed him a member of its 17-member Council for Research, Technology and Innovation; and Italy's University of Bologna and Switzerland's University of Neuchâtel awarded him honorary doctorates of law and economics. (Neuchâtel was the site for ETA's first watch movement factory.) *Forbes Magazine* listed Hayek Senior among the world's richest people in 1999, with a net worth of about US$1.4 billion. This is double his estimated worth in 1973.

To secure the future leadership of the Swatch Group, Hayek Senior has placed members of his family in significant positions in the Group. Son, G. Nicolas is head of Swatch marketing/communications, and by 2001 he was also the Swatch brand's delegate to the Swatch Group Management Board as well as carrying responsibility for Swatch operations in Germany, Italy and Spain.[33] Hayek's daughter, Nayla, became administrator of the company and sits on the board of directors. Hayek's wife, Marianne, was appointed an administrator of Hayek Engineering, of which its founder remains Chairman and CEO.

Hayek Senior's philosophy is that he 'injects himself directly and visibly throughout' Swatch, especially where strategy and new products are concerned.[34] He works constantly to cut red tape. Most people seem to be aware of the strong influence that both Hayeks exert on the company, and it could be difficult not to let the owners' moods affect company performance, particularly in Biel. This is not only due to the family members holding significant positions of power, but also to the hands-on approach of both senior and junior Hayeks. If the Hayeks dislike a product or idea, company morale is said to decline; morale is high if the Hayeks are behind an idea.

Despite the strong influence of the owners over most major decisions – and there is no doubt who is running the organization – leadership seems to be widely distributed at Swatch. A small number of positions exist to 'head' different sections, but basically there is little formal hierarchy at Swatch. The head positions are predominantly liaison roles between staff and senior management, according to Swatch employees in Biel. Creative young people with good ideas lead project teams, which form around specific ideas. Creativity develops through the informal interactions of the people in Biel, and temporary leaders emerge as projects arise. Communication is spontaneous with no strongly enforced formal communication lines. While there are rules and procedures, people can contact others spontaneously and take the associated risks of 'going around the system'.

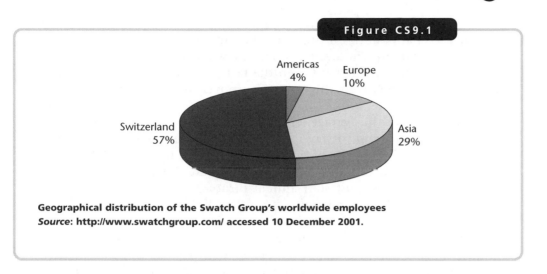

Figure CS9.1

Geographical distribution of the Swatch Group's worldwide employees
Source: http://www.swatchgroup.com/ accessed 10 December 2001.

Employees describe the Swatch culture using words such as 'spontaneous', 'chaotic', 'cool' (no tie), 'casual' (no business suit), 'simple' (no glamour) and 'unsophisticated' (no company cars!). The culture is full of emotion, dancing, music, ski-boarding, laughing and tolerates no rigidity. Offices are open space. Cultures in some parts of the Swatch Group may be quite different, presenting interesting challenges when Swatch marketing employees interact with staff from manufacturing or other less flamboyant divisions of the Group.

PEOPLE

In 1999, Swatch employed an average of 17 751 employees, 57 per cent of whom were employed under a Swiss contract (see Figure CS9.1).[35] In 2000, of the 19 284 employees, 56 per cent were employed in Switzerland. The remainder worked abroad, with around 10 per cent elsewhere in Europe, 29 per cent in Asia and 4 per cent in the US.

The Swatch Group consistently employs more women than men. In 1999, 8065 men and 9654 women were on the payroll, compared with 7676 men and 10 139 women in 1998. The feminization of the staff continued in 2000, with 8704 men and 11 044 women employees. Women represented approximately 56 per cent of the Swatch Group workforce in 2000.[36] Over 400 senior managers are responsible for the more than 440 reporting units around the world.

People at Swatch in Biel are young (average age 30 years), and in 2000 included 27 nationalities using 3–4 common languages (English, French, German and Italian). The Swatch Group as a whole claims to employ people from over 50 nationalities.[37] Given the fast pace at Swatch and the need for new ideas, relatively high staff turnover is tolerated. Some new employees leave after a three-month trial period because the culture does not suit them, but the average length of stay is about three years. Finance and logistics staff tend to stay longer than their colleagues in marketing and the more creative parts of the company, according to the HR manager in Biel. While high turnover is accepted in Swatch's exciting culture, the 1999 peak of 45 per cent staff annual turnover was unacceptably high, even at Swatch. The company is trying to reduce annual turnover to around 20 per cent.

Staff are paid a performance bonus on top of their fixed payment, and the Swatch Group strives to reward their people well. The performance management system focuses on goals, objectives and developing the necessary skills to achieve them. While careers probably cannot be planned within Swatch's turbulent environment, many opportunities arise for people to progress.

In recruiting new staff, Swatch seeks people with special backgrounds, which the Biel HR manager describes as 'practical, globe-trotting, sporting, with language skills and university qualifications'. In addition, particular social skills are highly valued, including having a 'Swatchy personality', being committed, open-minded, customer-oriented, flexible, market-oriented, mobile, and a doer rather than a thinker. Swatch employees should communicate well, think globally in systems terms, and be prepared to act fast.

DISCUSSION ISSUES

1 The Swatch Group is an exciting, creative organization. Which leadership paradigms can you see operating there? Where is the leadership at Swatch? How dependent is the company on the energy and influence of the Hayeks? Is the Group developing leaders elsewhere in the organization?

2 Can you identify substitutes for leadership in the organization? Where are decisions made and which kinds of decisions can you see?

3 How would you describe the culture at Swatch? What would it be like to work there, as far as you can tell from the case study?

4 How are the following leadership contradictions resolved? Bureaucracy, vision, emotion, chaos, automated production, decentralized versus hands-on availability of the founders?

5 The company has some succession plans in place, but does it have the appropriate style of leaders for the future? If future markets lie in Asia, how can Swatch adapt its leadership style to meet Asian expectations, without losing its creativity? How is diversity currently used?

6 There is evidence of extensive teamwork, but how do teams seem to operate in Swatch's chaotic environment? If more designing in the future will revolve around virtual and distributed teams, how well equipped is Swatch's culture to adapt to this style of operation?

7 What is the core business at Swatch and where is the unique difference from other organizations? Can you describe the Swatch experience provided to customers and staff?

8 Is Swatch a learning or teaching organization? How can mentoring work in a climate of rapid staff turnover? How is knowledge shared and managed through the organization, or is this not an issue for Swatch? What happens to mistakes?

9 Does Swatch offer spirituality in the workplace? What would attract people to work there, and why would they leave on average after three years? Is this attrition a problem in Swatch's culture? If so, how could it be fixed?

10 Who are the stakeholders in Swatch and how are their needs addressed by the organization? How is Swatch addressing the issue of its future sustainability?

KEY ISSUES

- World's largest watch manufacturer.
- Growth is vital to its success.
- Vision-driven, passionate.
- Heroic leader, who rescued the Swiss watch industry.
- Financially well performing.
- Values – fun, quality, fashion, design, low cost.
- Core competency is the Swatch culture.
- Decentralized hands-off management, yet hands-on Hayeks are always available.
- Hayek hates bureaucracy.
- Flamboyant and creative culture.
- Team-based culture, especially in marketing and innovation.
- R&D teams are given parameters within which to work and then autonomy to come up with the solution.
- Highly-integrated vertically, ensures that Swatch can retain its strategic independence.
- Produces not only its own products, but also tools, components, chips and machines.
- Competes on price by automating aggressively and keeping labour costs down.
- Can operate in expensive Switzerland because of its level of automation, but has about 50 production centres worldwide.
- Has its own distribution network, for example, megastores, Swatch stores.
- Brands have considerable autonomy but must collaborate, for example, with production at ETA.
- Automation controls production processes, marketing is uncontrolled and chaotic.
- Highly innovative in technology.
- Pressure to produce two fashion catalogues annually.
- The Swatch 'experience' affects design of their megastores, employees and customers.
- Tries to relate marketing to current events, with Swatch poking fun or taking a position.
- Hayeks are the driving force in innovation, together with employee teams.
- Mistakes – just move on to the next thing, no scapegoating.
- Fractal workplace, chaotic, change jobs easily, creative.
- Leader can spot new ways of selling emotional products.

- Heroic, much decorated visionary leader injects self visibly and directly throughout the organization.
- If the leader disapproves, the project is dropped.
- Distributed leadership, with team leaders providing a buffer between staff and senior management.
- Global and highly diverse workforce.
- High staff turnover (45 per cent in 1999), average length of stay is three years.
- Staff burnout is common.
- Swatch people are young, cool, global, practical, sporting and university-qualified.
- Performance bonus is paid on top of salary.
- Women represented over 56 per cent of the workforce in 2000.

NOTES

1 The author is indebted to the many executives at Swatch who generously gave of their knowledge and time for this project, and the assistance of David Palmer in earlier drafts of this case study.
2 Taylor, W. (1993) 'Message and muscle: An interview with Swatch titan Nicolas Hayek', *Harvard Business Review*, March/April, 99–110.
3 Swatch Group 1999 *Annual Report*. Biel.
4 Accessed on-line on 17 May 2001 at http://www.swatchgroup.com/group/present.asp
5 Taylor, W. (1993), ibid.
6 Swatch Group (undated) *Swatch Basics: Facts and Figures from the World of Swatch*, Biel.
7 Taylor, W. (1993), ibid.
8 *Historique d'ETA 1793–1998*. ETA SA Fabriques d'Ebauches Marketing-Sales, Grenchen, Switzerland.
9 Swatch Group 1999 *Annual Report*. Biel.
10 ETA SA (undated) *The Time Maker*. 28pp ETA brochure.
11 Swatch Group 1999 *Annual Report*. Biel.
12 Accessed on-line on 16 May 2001 at http://www.swatchgroup.com/
13 Swatch Group 1999 *Annual Report*. Biel.
14 Swatch Group 1999 *Annual Report*. Biel.
15 Swatch Group 1999 *Annual Report*. Biel.
16 Taylor, W. (1993), ibid.
17 Taylor, W. (1993), ibid.
18 Swatch Group 1999 *Annual Report*. Biel, p. 3.
19 SMH 1997 *Annual Report*. Biel.

20 Taylor, W. (1993), ibid.
21 Taylor, W. (1993), ibid.
22 SMH 1997 *Annual Report*. Biel.
23 Personal communication, Swatch PR Department, 17 May 2001.
24 SMH 1997 *Annual Report*. Biel.
25 Swatch Group (undated) *Swatch Basics: Facts and Figures from the World of Swatch*, Biel.
26 Swatch Group 1998 *Annual Report*. Biel.
27 Swatch Group(undated) *Swatch Basics: Facts and Figures from the World of Swatch*, Biel.
28 Guinness (1998) *1999 Book of Records*. London: Guinness Publishing. p. 246.
29 Swatch Group 1999 *Annual Report*. Biel.
30 Swatch Group (undated) *Swatch Basics: Facts and Figures from the World of Swatch*, Biel.
31 Time Inc. (1994) 'A car, a watch? Swatchmobile!' *Time Magazine,* 28 March 1994.
32 Potlach Corporation (1999) *Swatch Recap*. Accessed on-line on 24 September 2001 at http//www.aigaphilly.org/events/swatch
33 Swatch Group 2000 *Annual Report*. Biel.
34 Taylor, W. (1993), ibid.
35 Swatch Group 1999. *Annual Report*. Biel.
36 Swatch Financial Statements. Accessed on-line on 16 May 2001 at http//www.swatchgroup.com
37 Accessed on-line on 16 May 2001 at http//www.swatchgroup.com

Ten Rodenstock: Working
with Vision[1]

GAYLE C. AVERY

We strive for visualisation. Visualisation resolves the imprecise, the uncertain.[2]

Randolf Rodenstock, CEO

Randolf Rodenstock personally guarantees his company's products. As Germany's leading spectacle maker, the Rodenstock Group has a proud tradition to uphold – in developing, manufacturing and distributing spectacle lenses and frames, as well as precision mechanical instruments, optical machines and workshop equipment, ophthalmic computer services and industrial and photo optics.

This family-owned company was founded in 1877 in Würzburg by the present CEO's great-grandfather, Josef Rodenstock.[3] Contrary to the then prevailing belief that blurred vision was a disease, Josef Rodenstock introduced the idea of correcting blurred vision using lenses. He introduced eye examinations for customers that allowed spectacles to be made up using ready-made lenses, but with high precision. He extended the range of lenses to include popular yellowish-green sun lenses, as well as ophthalmic and photographic lenses.

Josef's oldest son, Alexander Rodenstock, began working in the company in 1905, and commenced serial production of ophthalmic lenses. In 1935, Rodenstock lenses were exported worldwide, and the innovative binoculars, which could be adjusted to any distance between the eyes, were patented.

During the Second World War, Hitler's German State intervened in the Rodenstock organization, requiring processes to be automated to keep up with production. Alexander strove to minimize expansion for military purposes and managed to retain some production capacity for civilian requirements. Josef's grandson, Professor Rolf Rodenstock, joined the company in 1944, took over the reins in 1953, and began to develop Rodenstock into a major company. Rolf

Rodenstock added frames to the highly successful lens business, and soon built Rodenstock into a leading frame manufacturer. Expansion to Italy, the US and other countries followed, and companies were acquired to expand the group.

The present CEO, Randolf Rodenstock, graduate physicist and MBA, joined the company in 1976. Randolf Rodenstock has grown the organization further, expanding international production and subsidiaries in Europe, the US and Asia. Rodenstock's sales offices are represented in 110 countries. Employee numbers reached 6712 in 1999, with over half of Rodenstock's people employed in Germany.

SALES

Sales are around €500 million (see Figure CS10.1)[4]. In 1999, sales were divided into 48 per cent in Germany and about 37 per cent in other parts of Europe, with the remainder in the US and Oceania/Asia. In 2000, the Rodenstock Group achieved 11 per cent of their sales in the US market and 4 per cent in Asia/Oceania.

Most sales are to opticians, although understanding the end-consumer's preferences is critical to Rodenstock's success. The trade within Germany consists of 9400 optician shops, with typically four to five employees per shop, each averaging about €375 000 turnover annually. Shops sell an average of four spectacles per day. Rodenstock sales tend to come from independent opticians (34 per cent), purchasing and marketing groups (35 per cent), optician chains (25 per cent) and department store opticians (6 per cent).

MARKETING

Rodenstock is renowned for its quality lenses and frames, and is the only major player in the industry to supply both frames and lenses. Rodenstock's strengths come from its well-recognized range, design, quality of products and on-time delivery. These qualities are widely acknowledged, with the company receiving the 1997 Bavarian Quality Award and 1998 Federal Product Design Award. Its nearest competitor, Zeiss, is hot on its heels.

Much of Rodenstock's capital lies in its name, which enjoys wide recognition in the German market. A 1999 survey showed that Rodenstock's brand awareness is high in Germany, with recognition among 55 per cent of the

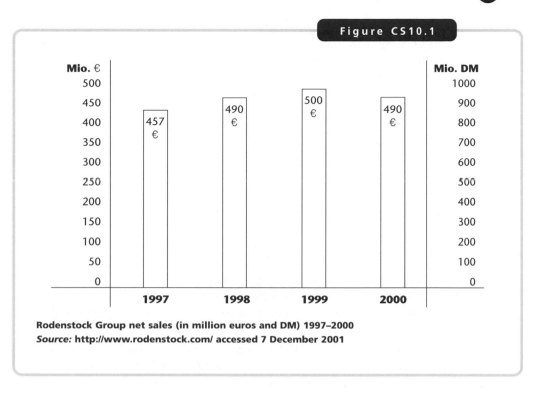

Rodenstock Group net sales (in million euros and DM) 1997–2000
Source: http://www.rodenstock.com/ accessed 7 December 2001

general public, 68 per cent of spectacle wearers and 90 per cent of progressive (for example, bifocal) lens wearers. The Rodenstock brand suggests confidence, trust and friendliness.

Rodenstock uses both direct and indirect marketing. Direct marketing techniques include not only conventional media such as advertisements, attending international fairs, trade marketing and point-of-sale, but also new technologies such as the Internet and their own Extranet. Direct selling is done through five of Rodenstock's regional agencies, which are now showrooms, and 40 sales representatives who go into the market. In addition, 20 product specialists advise opticians by phone. About 100 customer service people take Internet and phone orders and communicate with the customer. The Rodenstock Extranet, linking opticians and the company, allows frames and lenses to be ordered 24 hours a day, 7 days a week.

More subtle marketing is done through the Rodenstock Academy, a company profit centre.[5] The Academy provides training for universities and colleges, Rodenstock employees, opticians and ophthalmologists in technical areas. The Rodenstock Academy also offers a large range of business management courses to help the customer enhance his or her business. The philosophy behind the Academy is that Rodenstock employees and customers should learn from each other, and employees now join in the optician seminars. The hope is that one day doctors will also mix with the employees and opticians at these seminars, creating seamless learning that complements what each group is doing. People at Rodenstock say 'we are in the relationship business', as they try to create an open, reliable relationship with customers.[6]

STRATEGIES

In looking to the future, three key areas offer opportunities:

*   *International growth* would allow Rodenstock to tap into larger markets outside Germany. For example, in the US, the normal wearer has heavy, thick lenses with no anti-reflection coating, leaving a niche for Rodenstock with its thinner, lighter and coated products. In 2000, Rodenstock had an 11 per cent share in the US market, anticipated to grow to 15–17 per cent within five years.
*   *Faster replacement* and encouraging people in existing markets to replace their spectacles earlier is another growth strategy. Nearly 60 per cent of the population in Germany wears glasses, with 11.3 million pairs being sold annually there. However, the average replacement time for spectacles is 4.3 years. Rodenstock is trying to understand why people do not replace their spectacles more often and usually possess only one pair of glasses. A result of this reluctance to replace their glasses is that about 25 per cent of the population wears the wrong lenses.
*   *To reduce optician markups* is a further strategy. The reluctance to change spectacles more frequently can be partly attributed to the high cost of spectacles in Germany, where opticians charge 200–300 per cent markup. This is expected to change. Discount optician, Fielmann, cleverly advertises spectacles at a discount to attract customers, but his staff then upsell customers to pay an average of €200 for spectacles. This is still lower than the regular €275–300 elsewhere.

To opticians, receiving deliveries on time is critical because customers need their prescription lenses supplied quickly. Rodenstock people say 'we are in the speed business', and so increasing speed to market is a key objective.[7]

Another key strategy, integrated into the overall strategic plan, is innovation through R&D (see Box CS10.1 for examples of Rodenstock's innovations). 'All parts of the Rodenstock Group work together in their total commitment to realize and implement innovations to redefine the future.'[8]

Lens innovations

Rodenstock's reputation as an innovator of lens-making techniques continues. For example, plastic lenses were introduced in 1978 and then improved with high-index plastic lenses in 1988. In 1990, photochromics were incorporated into plastic lenses, creating the 'self-tinting' lens. Solitaire, the integral hard, anti-reflex coating for plastic lenses, emerged in 1994.

Rodenstock has revolutionized the making of spectacles. Traditionally, standard lenses were cast, but more complicated products such as bifocals had to be made using semi-finished lenses, ground in special laboratories to opticians' prescriptions. This was a slow process and meant that Rodenstock, like its competitors, needed to have a stock of semi-finished and blank lenses on hand to be able to fill opticians' orders quickly. In 1999, Rodenstock brought in a new technique that allowed almost instant direct casting of spectacle lenses – employing the innovative 2C optics technique. Using ultraviolet light, production time was reduced from one day to a few seconds, while also allowing prescription lenses to be perfectly fitted to each wearer for the first time.

A year later, in mid-2000, Rodenstock unveiled its new individual lens technology, which enables even greater customization than in the past. Before this, lens-makers used to have to assume that the lens sat in a particular position on the wearer's head, which did not provide perfect solutions for the wearer when he or she or the spectacles moved about. Rodenstock mathematicians modelled the complex 3D free-form surfaces used in making so-called progressive lenses with multiple focal points. This allowed Rodenstock to provide a perfect viewing field, where both eyes match automatically, using computers. The new process is much easier and faster. With this major innovation, Rodenstock can make the perfect progressive lens, providing benefits to the end consumer through a highly customized product. In addition, the process reduces production time, saves costs and eliminates the need for keeping stock. This innovation arms Rodenstock with the necessary speed and cost advantages for entering the lower-priced spectacle market should it decide to do so as part of its strategy.

RESEARCH AND DEVELOPMENT

The R&D process is closely linked to marketing, design and production. At Rodenstock, innovation is a managed process and involves five formal stages:

1 *Preliminary proposal stage*: following approval from the business team, a cross-functional project team is set up, including sales, marketing, production and design people.
2 *Feasibility stage*: economic, marketing and time are prime considerations.

3 *Proposal*: specifications, marketing and business plans are required at this stage.

4 *Development*: project reviews, milestones and a special steering committee to oversee projects are established. Here, various approval steps include product managers and monitoring to ensure that initial intentions are actually being realized by marketing and others.

5 *Pilot run*: at the pilot or prototype stage, Rodenstock's own production people and manufacturing facilities are used.

Investment in new products occurs at different stages for different projects. For a new coating product, the company invests heavily at the feasibility stage. For an optical product requiring faster lead-time, more investment goes into the development phase. For the new customized lenses, Randolf Rodenstock's formal approval was sought, because €15 million was needed to establish a new production plant.

Rodenstock's R&D department conducts wide-ranging research, resulting in 15–20 patents each year. R&D is kept in-house to protect this valuable know-how, although close links are maintained with universities and professional institutes as part of the R&D process. Research projects cover optics (design of lenses), materials, product and manufacturing development. The design section works at the cutting edge of technology and has developed its own measuring technology. Coatings research resulted in special dyes capable of tinting glass in different lights. In addition, the R&D department provides technical product management and product information.

Benchmarking is important to the R&D team, but they find it difficult getting information from competitors. Some information comes from industry association meetings and patent data, and Rodenstock people also benchmark themselves against similar non-optics businesses.

Vision 20/20

The dynamic R&D department has developed its own Vision 20/20 campaign, which includes an explicit set of values and goals for the team.[9] In addition to enhancing its acknowledged technical and organizational capabilities, the R&D team values customer orientation, taking responsibility, teamwork, productivity (both effectiveness and efficiency) and innovation in processes and products. The team aims at understanding lenses in their entirety, taking all lens functions into account (aesthetics, optics, longevity) and all lens components (for example, material, tinting, optical design, lacquer and anti-reflection coatings).

R&D goals are to:

- develop new market-oriented products;
- focus on innovative products that solve problems for the customer ('honest and full of quality');

- engage in 'time competition' rather than 'performance competition' (because time to market is crucial);
- design to cost; and
- reach break-even within a short time.

STRUCTURE

Underneath the four-member Executive Board, the Rodenstock company is organized into three main groups: Capital Goods, Spectacles and Central groups (see Figure CS10.2).

The Spectacles group forms the core group in the organization. Marketing, market research, design, R&D, HR, production and international distribution all are represented within this group. In addition, the group contains product divisions of e-commerce, precision optics and lenses, of which lenses are the largest component, generating 60 per cent of turnover. Marketing, operations and sales are assigned to frames, lenses and ideas so that people can focus on the entire process.

The Capital Goods group maintains expertise in IT and is responsible for the optical business web, e-commerce and website. Also in this group are smaller divisions such as Doctor Optics.

Finally, the Central group manages cross-group functions such as parts of HR, finances and controlling, quality management, corporate communications and purchasing.

Basically, Rodenstock designs the frames and outsources production – all over Europe, as well as in places like Thailand, the US and Chile. Increasingly, production is being done in Asian countries, with lower-priced frames made in China and titanium frames made in Japan. Serial production is strong in Thailand for finished and semi-finished lenses.

Rodenstock's need for speed in delivering prescription lenses still requires laboratory production to be based in a range of countries. The company is reducing the number of countries where it produces as logistics improve to enable it to deliver finished frames faster. The organization expects to have more centralized laboratory production sites within Europe, in addition to the existing central laboratory plant in the Czech Republic.

LEADERSHIP

There is no doubt that the Rodenstocks are 'heroic' leaders at the company. The family is featured on the website along with its history and profiled on

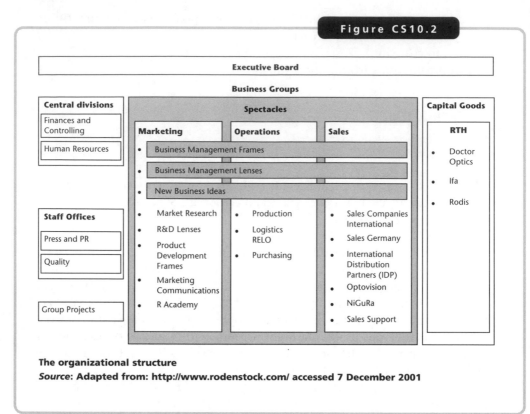

Figure CS10.2

The organizational structure
Source: Adapted from: http://www.rodenstock.com/ accessed 7 December 2001

brochures, advertisements and in other ways.[10] Stories of high employee commitment to the firm and the Rodenstocks abound within the organization, such as Randolf Rodenstock's touching speech to celebrate an employee's 25th year with the company.

However, the firm's philosophy revolves around success being a joint effort, rather than due to the top leaders.[11] The firm 'stands for joint effort which gives life a common spirit; one which transcends all the differences between the individual divisions and departments and which is borne by the personal commitment and individuality of each employee.'[12]

Rodenstock sees itself as:[13]

- a brand company, known internationally as the best problem-solver for spectacle wearers;
- among the global market leaders, not necessarily the largest, but the high-profit pearl of the industry; and
- a home base for expert and empowered employees.

Mission and values

The stated mission is to supply products that 'improve the quality of life within the world of vision.'[14] Rodenstock's articulated values include:

- *Quality aspiration*: maintaining the tradition of high quality in meeting requirements agreed with internal and external customers, suppliers and partners reliably, each and every time.
- *Customer orientation*: customers should feel secure in Rodenstock hands, achieved by remaining sensitive and responsive to the needs of those served to continue to justify their trust. Rodenstock wants to continue to serve the needs of the ophthalmologist, optometrist and dispensing optician with technical competence and dedication that enrich the partnership.
- *Commitment to society*: Rodenstock takes seriously and endeavours to fulfil its responsibility towards society, including protecting the environment, and remaining open to diversity. This provides strategic advantage because by doing so the organization can detect changes in their international markets without ever losing sight of local and national markets, thereby identifying market opportunities and changes rapidly.

In addition, after involving employees from all sectors of the business, both in Germany and abroad, the company developed a values framework to guide all Rodenstock people's actions. The goal is to make these values a living reality within the organization and evident in responsible management actions. The values framework lists:

- seeing the company as a learning community;
- corporate success requires participatory management;
- expertise and responsibility belong in one pair of hands – 'with responsibility comes accountability';
- promoting corporate thinking at all levels to ensure employees act in the interests of the corporation, and can weigh up risks and grasp initiatives using balanced judgement; and
- the benefit to the whole organization takes priority over individual or sub-group interests.

The company personality is shown as a star in Figure CS10.3. The points represent attitude, interests, needs, constitution, its origin, expertise/performance or temperament. Everything from Rodenstock is expected to be meaningful, independent, aggressive to the market, understandable, reliable, quality and to show initiative.[15]

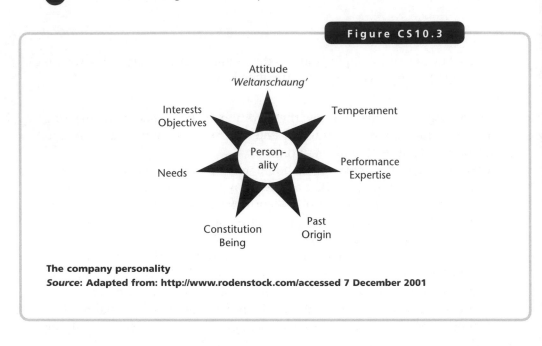

Figure CS10.3

The company personality
Source: Adapted from: http://www.rodenstock.com/accessed 7 December 2001

MANAGING CHANGE

The Vice-President of HR played a major role in helping the company change from essentially Classical/Transactional leadership to Visionary and Organic. In this process, HR was linked closely with business strategy.

HR managed company-wide changes aimed at meeting the following objectives: increasing speed, emotion and price pressure in the marketplace, developing mass customisation (that is, meeting individual customer's needs), rapid changes to trade structures, and the Internet's generating borderless markets. To stay ahead, Rodenstock needed to continually learn. This meant changing from a technology-driven company to a customer-focused and marketing-driven organization. The leadership style needed to change from Classical 'patriarchal' to 'participatory' and from seniority to merit based. People at Rodenstock needed to recognize that speed, branding, adding value and forming relationships are vital for future growth.

Rodenstock's strategic goals include:[16]

- continue to be a brand with a core competence in 'spectacles';
- retain a strong customer and end-user focus;
- grow to be number three in the world in the industry;

- continue providing adequate profitability;
- maintain modern management and attractive HR management; and
- realize employee potential through a high degree of individual responsibility.

To reach these goals, the company needed to reinvent itself dramatically, particularly as it aspired to becoming publicly listed. Randolf Rodenstock and top management were strongly behind this huge shift to enabling employees in Germany and elsewhere to become self-managing, self-responsible and empowered. This meant making major changes to the corporate culture. Processes needed redesigning to increase effectiveness and efficiency. A culture of professionalism and sense of community needed to be fostered. The former divisionalized organization needed to be changed into a function-based structure. In doing so, lenses and frames were amalgamated into one department, a new market research function was introduced, and R&D was put into marketing to support the new market-driven culture. To get people to focus on achieving these goals, the 'Think Spectacles' change project was started in February 1999.

Think Spectacles

The change program needed to be completed quickly, within six months, placing all employees under high pressure. A small core change-management team was established. It reported to the executive board, and worked with external consultants in planning and implementing the change. The executive team became the Steering Committee, which set objectives, commissioned the project team and accepted results. The core team was responsible for overall coordination, detailed planning and ensuring consistency in procedures and results. Various implementation teams were responsible for subgoals, details and documentation of the new organization, and setting up new teams and departments. The initial intention was to devolve implementation throughout the organization, but this turned out to require some monitoring and centralization.

Broad, on-going communication was a prime focus, including via bulletin boards, question-and-answer boards, newsletters and the Intranet. The firm's Intranet provided a forum for informing people about the change, future career opportunities and available services, while also enabling them to talk about issues. People had access to the Steering Committee minutes along the way.

The new 'Think Spectacles' culture was welcomed using considerable symbolism, including a special change logo and extensive celebrations. The program began with corporate theatre. The process involved considerable visible management support. People recounted how the CEO perched in the bar and rallied everyone to support the changes to move the company forward. 'As valued employees, you can choose your own role in our future company', was the message. No one was made redundant via downsizing in this campaign, and so the process sent mainly positive signals about the changes.

As the new culture was introduced, most employees lost their jobs but reapplied for new roles under the new structure. Project leaders were nominated and allowed to recruit their own team members. A special employee fair was held to facilitate this, at which display stands were set up where the employees talked with one another to decide on their new jobs. For some people, it was not all that difficult to find jobs similar to the ones they had held in the old structure, but for others this was either a welcome or unwelcome opportunity to apply for a different role. Some employees left the organization, but the spill of roles was basically done with little 'bloodshed', attributed to the positive involvement of the staff from the beginning of the change process.[17]

Of course, not everyone saw the changes positively. People began to lose their way, particularly those who were used to the old seniority-counts system. A move to merit-based promotion and compensation was threatening to some people. Surprisingly, union representatives were supportive, partly out of long-held respect for the Rodenstock family, but also because few employees were lost as part of the change process. Employees having to apply for new jobs unsettled the union somewhat, especially when the initial euphoria died down and people realized how much they had to learn in their new jobs. This could have been addressed by more attention to training needs, particularly after the event, to consolidate the change.

Another issue arising from the change was a culture clash between the lenses and frames divisions that now needed to work together. Lenses had a culture of technology, based on maths and physics, and this culture clashed with the style, fashion and design culture of frames. 'It's unrealistic to expect a large company to have only one culture, and different cultures need to learn to coexist.'[18] Perspectives held by the 'old Rodenstock' versus the 'new Rodenstock' employees also led to clashes. The longer-serving employees tended to believe that they could stay with the company for life, and to them, the more recent employees appeared to be 'trying to change everything'. The two groups fell to arguing and were suspicious of each other.

The short time-frame for change was considered advantageous in many ways, in that people knew where they were going, particularly when all jobs and employment contracts were dissolved. However, the fast change also led to problems, especially in changing processes. Changes to structure were easier to deal with and communicate than process changes. Process change often needs more time and such changes initially did not work well, for example, the ordering and sales planning processes. If people had taken more time to find what did not run well, these processes could have been improved and optimized. Perhaps Rodenstock should have looked at processes first, then restructured, instead of the other way around. Here, the concern for people overruled structure and process issues. The company wanted to address the change quickly, and be able to give people answers to 'Where am I?'.[19]

Manager incentives

Significant changes were made at the manager level. The Management Incentive Plan (MIP) was introduced, embodying the principle of manager responsibility.[20] The number of executive levels was reduced to two: Manager and Senior Manager. An internal audit/assessment of all managers was conducted, and new contract regulations were introduced for every manager. Executives agree on one to three goals with their boss in annual dialogs, setting goals and targets for returns and sales growth three years ahead. New contracts included variable remuneration, based 50/50 on corporate factors, and the team's performance as measured by the Rodenstock Balanced Scorecard, which covers financials, customers, internal processes, and innovation and learning.

The organizational changes and the incentive plan were introduced in parallel, creating major changes at Rodenstock. Executives were now to be evaluated in terms of their 'inputs' (intellectual potential, social potential, focus on action and focus on values). 'Outputs' also became important, particularly goal achievement, contribution to business success and corporate identity, and feedback from cooperation partners.

The old level of trust at Rodenstock fell when they changed people's jobs and traditions. However, it helped to have an inspiring, respected leader who was willing to speak to the people during the change process. In addition, it was useful to have Rodenstock Project Managers reinforce changes in behaviour.[21]

DISCUSSION ISSUES

1 Which leadership paradigms can you identify at Rodenstock? Who and where are the leaders in today's new organization? What part do symbolism, vision and values play in the new leadership?

2 How are followers regarded at Rodenstock? Is the organization really people-focused? What does Rodenstock expect from its employees?

3 How is Rodenstock positioned for its future leadership, and where is it going? How do the organization's leadership style, vision and values suit a multicultural, global world?

4 What is the role of Rodenstock's HR strategy? How do managers and the performance management system support the new leadership ideas? What is the role of emotion at Rodenstock? Would you regard Rodenstock as offering spirituality in the workplace?

5 Can you identify substitutes for leadership in the Rodenstock case?

6 How was the change process managed at Rodenstock? What were the strengths and what could have been done to improve the change process? What elements of leadership were involved in the changes?

7 Is Rodenstock a learning organization, and if so, what is the evidence? How does it develop its employees and other stakeholders?

8 How does Rodenstock manage knowledge and intellectual property? What is Rodenstock's core competence that competitors cannot copy? How is creativity fostered? Is managing innovation as a process effective at Rodenstock?

9 Who are the stakeholders at Rodenstock? How are customers treated? How is the organization trying to ensure its future sustainability? Does it have effective strategic alliances and partnerships?

10 What would it be like to work at Rodenstock judging by this case study?

KEY ISSUES

- Global organization, growth potential in both domestic and foreign markets.
- Classical leadership based on respect – even the unions respect the Rodenstock family.
- Heroic leadership from the family, Classical/patriarchal style originally.
- Leadership moved from patriarchal to participative.
- Form alliances with trade, medics, universities and colleges.
- Customers are partners.

- Learning organization: customers and employees learn from one another, leading to seamless learning.
- The aim is to develop a deep understanding of lenses.
- Knowledge management: patents, Rodenstock Academy, seminars with opticians and employees, Intra/Extranet, close customer contact to the organization via the sales representatives and customer service people, links to universities and professional institutes.
- Focus on quality and innovation.
- Brand is a major marketing tool.
- Innovation is a managed process (five stages), for example, Vision 20/20 in the R&D department, 15–20 patents annually.
- Values framework should become a living reality.
- Core values include honesty, quality, customer focus and commitment to society.
- Philosophy of 'joint effort' in successes, rather than attribution to top leadership.
- Empowered expert employees.
- Performance management system supports the changes.
- Changed from seniority to merit-based system.
- Role-modelling the values is expected.
- Academy is a profit centre, used for learning and forming alliances.
- Responsibility and accountability pushed to the lowest level.
- With responsibility comes accountability.
- HR is strongly aligned to the business strategy.
- Change management was well executed, bloodless, radical, fast.
- Communication was a central focus during change.
- Speed of change process impacted some processes adversely.
- Trying to move to self-managing, self-responsible, empowered employees (that is, elements of Visionary and Organic leadership).
- Substitutes for leadership: professionals, teams, vision, values, processes.
- Culture of professionalism introduced (possible substitute for leadership).
- Symbolism is widespread: for example, campaign names, theatre to kick off 'Think Spectacles', history, job market, stories of high employee commitment, working for the social good.
- Sustainability via service to society, protecting the environment and remaining open to diversity.
- Use of emotion evident, for example, in products, marketing, attachment to Rodenstock family, used extensively in change program.
- Spirituality arises from the expectation that everything at Rodenstock should be meaningful, challenging work, choosing own new roles, opportunities for personal growth and continuous learning.
- Rodenstock is in the speed business.
- Considerable use of e-technology, for example, Intranet (used in change process), Extranet for customer care and relationships.

- Rodenstock's balanced scorecard includes financials, customers, internal processes, innovation and learning.

NOTES

1 The author expresses her gratitude to senior Rodenstock executives who hosted a visit to the group in Munich in June 2000.
2 http://www.rodenstock.com/2000/company/company_features/company_views.htm
3 http://www.rodenstock.com/.
4 http://www.rodenstock.com/2000/company/company_features/company_views.htm
5 Leusmann, M. (2000). Note on *Customer Relation*, 27 June, Rodenstock, Munich.
6 Von Pappenheim, J. (2000). Notes on *Strategic Alignment – HR Systems and Change Management*, 27 June, Rodenstock, Munich.
7 Von Pappenheim, J. (2000). Notes on *Strategic Alignment – HR Systems and Change Management*, 27 June, Rodenstock, Munich.
8 http://www.rodenstock.com/2000/company/company_features/company_innovation.htm.
9 Rodenstock (2000). Notes on *Research and Development: Ophthalmic Lenses: Innovative Products for Spectacle Wearers*, 27 June, Munich.
10 http://www.rodenstock.com/2000/tradition/.
11 http://www.rodenstock.com/2000/company/company_features/company_men.htm/.
12 http://www.rodenstock.com/2000/company/company_features/company_men.htm/.
13 *Rodenstock – The Company*. Document issued during visit to Rodenstock, June 2000.
14 *Rodenstock Corporate Guidelines*, July 1995.
15 Von Pappenheim, J. (2000). Notes on *Strategic Alignment – HR Systems and Change Management*, 27 June, Rodenstock, Munich.
16 Von Pappenheim, J. (2000). Notes on *Strategic Alignment – HR Systems and Change Management*, 27 June, Rodenstock, Munich.
17 Von Pappenheim, J. (2000). Notes on *Strategic Alignment – HR Systems and Change Management*, 27 June, Rodenstock, Munich.
18 Von Pappenheim, J. (2000). Personal communication during visit, 27 June, Rodenstock, Munich.
19 Von Pappenheim, J. (2000). Personal communication during visit, 27 June, Rodenstock, Munich.
20 Von Pappenheim, J. (2000). Notes on *Strategic Alignment – HR Systems and Change Management*, 27 June, Rodenstock, Munich.
21 Von Pappenheim, J. (2000). Personal communication during visit, 27 June, Rodenstock, Munich.

References

Abell, A. (2000) 'Skills for knowledge environments', *Information Management Journal*, 34(3): 33–41.

Albert, M. (1992) 'The Rhine model of capitalism: An investigation', *European Business Journal*, 4(3): 8–22.

Alvesson, M. (2002) *Understanding Organizational Culture*. London: Sage.

Andrews, J.P. and Field, R.H.G. (1998) 'Regrounding the concept of leadership', *Leadership and Organization Development*, 19(3): 128–36.

Aryee, S., Chay, Y.W. and Chew, J. (1996) 'The motivation to mentor among managerial employees: An interactionalist approach', *Group and Organization Management*, 21(3): 261–77.

Ashkanasy, N.M. and Weierter, S.J.M. (1996) 'Modeling the leader–member relationship: The role of value congruence and charisma', in K.W. Parry (ed.), *Leadership Research and Practice: Emerging Themes and New Challenges*. Melbourne: Pitman. pp. 91–103.

Atwater, D.C. and Bass, B.M. (1994) 'Transformational leadership in teams', in B.M. Bass and B.J. Avolio (eds), *Improving Organizational Effectiveness Through Transformational Leadership*. Thousand Oaks, CA: Sage. pp. 48–83.

Atwater, L.E. and Yammarino, F.J. (1996) 'Bases of power in relation to leader behavior: A field investigation', *Journal of Business and Psychology*, 11(1): 3–22.

Australian Bureau of Statistics (2001) '*Employment arrangements and superannuation, Australia*', Report 6361.0. Canberra: Government Printer.

Avery, G.C. (2001) 'Situational leadership in Australia: Congruity, flexibility and effectiveness', *Leadership and Organization Development Journal*, 22(1): 11–21.

Avery, G.C. (2003) 'Weathering the Storm: Towards Sustainable Leadership'. Unpublished paper. Sydney: Macquarie Graduate School of Management.

Avery, G.C. and Ryan, J. (2002) 'Applying situational leadership in Australia', *Journal of Management Development*, 21(4): 242–62.

Avolio, B.J. (1996) 'What's all the Karping about Down Under? Transforming Australia's leadership systems for the twenty-first century', in K.W. Parry (ed.), *Leadership Research and Practice: Emerging Themes and New Challenges*. Melbourne: Pitman. pp. 3–15.

Avolio, B.J. and Bass, B.M. (1988) 'Transformational leadership, charisma and beyond', in, J.G. Hunt, B.R. Baliga, H.P. Dachler and C.A. Schreisheim (eds), *Emerging Leadership Vistas*. Lexington, MA: Lexington Books. pp. 29–49.

Avolio, B.J. and Bass, B.M. (1991) *The Full Range Leadership Development Program*. Binghamton, NY: Bass Avolio.

Avolio, B.J. and Bass, B.M. (1994) 'Conclusions and implications', in B.M. Bass and B.J. Avolio (eds), *Improving Organizational Effectiveness Through Transformational Leadership*. Thousand Oaks, CA: Sage. pp. 202–17.

Ayman, R., Chemers, M.M. and Fiedler, F.E. (1995) 'The contingency model of leadership effectiveness: Its level of analysis', *Leadership Quarterly*, 6(2): 147–67.

Ball, G.A., Trevino, L.K. and Sims, H.P., Jr. (1992) 'Understanding subordinate reactions to punishment incidents: Perspectives from justice and social affect', *Leadership Quarterly*, 3: 307–34.

Bass, B.M. (1985) *Leadership and Performance Beyond Expectations*. New York, NY: Free Press.

Bass, B.M. (1988) 'The inspirational process of leadership', *Journal of Management Development*, 7(5): 21–31.

Bass, B.M. (1990a) *Bass and Stogdill's Handbook of Leadership: Theory, Research, and Managerial Applications*, 3rd edn. New York, NY: Free Press.

Bass, B.M. (1990b) 'From transactional to transformational leadership: Learning to share the vision', *Organizational Dynamics*, 18(3): 19–31.

Bass, B.M. and Avolio, B.J. (1990) 'Developing transformational leadership: 1992 and beyond', *Journal of European Industrial Training*, 14(5): 21–7.

Bass, B.M. and Avolio, B.J. (eds) (1994) *Improving Organizational Effectiveness Through Transformational Leadership*. Thousand Oaks, CA: Sage.

Bass, B.M., Valenzi, E.R., Farrow, D.L. and Solomon, R.J. (1975) 'Management styles associated with organizational, task, and interpersonal contingencies', *Journal of Applied Psychology*, 60(6): 720–9.

Baum, J.R., Locke, E.A. and Kirkpatrick, S.A. (1998) 'A longitudinal study of the relation of vision and vision communication to venture growth in entrepreneurial firms', *Journal of Applied Psychology*, 83(1): 43–54.

Bechtold, B.L. (2000) 'Evolving to organizational learning', *Hospital Materiel Management Quarterly*, 21(30): 11–25.

Bennis, W. (1983) 'The artform of leadership', in S. Srivastva and Associates (eds), *The Executive Mind: New Insights on Managerial Thought and Action*. San Francisco, CA: Jossey-Bass.

Bennis, W. (1989) *Why Leaders Can't Lead: The Unconscious Conspiracy Continues*. San Francisco, CA: Jossey-Bass.

Bennis, W. (1998) 'Rethinking leadership', *Executive Excellence*, 15(2): 7–8.

Bennis, W. and Nanus, B. (1985) *Leaders: The Strategies for Taking Charge*. New York, NY: Harper and Row.

Bergsteiner, H. and Avery, G.C. (2003) 'Responsibility and accountability: Towards an integrative process model', *International Business and Economics Research Journal*, 2(2): 31–40.

Bernardin, H.J. and Russell, J.E.A. (1993) *Human Resource Management: An Experiential Approach*. New York, NY: McGraw-Hill.

Berstein, B.J. and Kaye, B.L. (1986) 'Teacher, tutor, colleague, coach', *Personnel Journal*, 65(11): 44–51.

Blanchard, K.H. and Nelson, R. (1997) 'Recognition and reward', *Executive Excellence*, 14(4): 15.

Blanchard, K.H., Zigarmi, D. and Nelson, R.B. (1993) 'Situational leadership after 25 years: A retrospective', *Journal of Leadership Studies*, 1(1): 22–36.

Blanchard, K.H., Zigarmi, P. and Zigarmi, D. (1985) *Leadership and the One Minute Manager*. New York, NY: Morrow.

Blank, W., Weitzel, J.R. and Green, S.G. (1990) 'A test of situational leadership theory', *Personnel Psychology*, 43(3): 579–97.

Boal, K.B. and Hooijberg, R. (2001) 'Strategic leadership research: Moving on', *Leadership Quarterly*, 11(4): 515–49.

Bolman, L.G. and Deal, T.E. (1997) *Reframing Organizations: Artistry, Choice, and Leadership.* San Francisco, CA: Jossey-Bass.

Bradford, D.L. and Cohen, A.R. (1984) *Managing for Excellence: The Guide to Developing High Performance Organizations.* New York, NY: Wiley.

Briscoe, J.P. and Hall, D.T. (1998) 'Grooming and picking leaders using competency frameworks: Do they work? An alternative approach and new guidelines for practice', *Organizational Dynamics,* 28(2): 37–52.

Britt, D.W. (1997) *A Conceptual Introduction to Modeling: Qualitative and Quantitative Perspectives.* Mahwah, NJ: Erlbaum.

Brodbeck, P.W. (2002) 'Implications for organization design: Teams as pockets of excellence', *Team Performance Management: An International Journal,* 8(1/2): 21–38.

Brown, A.D. (1994) 'Transformational leadership in tackling change', *Journal of General Management,* 19(4): 1–12.

Brown, S.L. and Eisenhardt, K.M. (1997) 'The art of continuous change: Linking complexity theory and time-paced evolution in relentlessly shifting organizations', *Administrative Science Quarterly,* 42(1): 1–34.

Burke, R.J. and McKeen, C.A. (1997) 'Benefits of mentoring relationships among managerial and professional women: A cautionary tale', *Journal of Vocational Behavior,* 51(1): 43–57.

Burla, S., Alioth, A., Frei, F. and Müller,W.R. (1994) *Die Erfindung von Führung: Vom Mythos der Machbarkeit in der Führungsausbildung.* Zurich: vdf Verlag der Fachvereine an den schweizerischen Hochsculen und Techniken AG.

Burns, J.M. (1978) *Leadership.* New York, NY: Harper and Row.

Bussel, R. (1997) 'Business without a boss: The Columbia Conserve Company and workers' control, 1917–1943', *Business History Review,* 71(3): 417–43.

Cacioppe, R. (1997) 'Leadership moment by moment!', *Leadership and Organization Development Journal,* 18(7): 335–45.

Cacioppe, R. (1998) 'Leaders developing leaders: An effective way to enhance leadership development programs', *Leadership and Organization Development Journal,* 19(4): 194–8.

Cairncross, F. (1997) *The Death of Distance: How the Communications Revolution will Change our Lives.* London: Orion Business Books.

Cairns, T.D., Hollenback, J., Preziosi, R.C. and Snow, W.A. (1998) 'Technical note: A study of Hersey and Blanchard's situational leadership theory', *Leadership and Organization Development Journal,* 19(2): 113–16.

Cameron, K.S., Whetten, D.A. and Kim, M.U. (1987) 'Organizational dysfunctions of decline', *Academy of Management Journal,* 30(1): 126–38.

Campbell, J.P. (1977) 'The cutting edge of leadership: An overview', in J.G. Hunt and L.L. Larson (eds), *Leadership: The Cutting Edge.* Carbondale, IL: Southern Illinois Press. pp. 221–34.

Cannella, A.A., Pettigrew, A. and Hambrick, D. (2001) 'Upper echelons: Donald Hambrick on executives and strategy', *Academy of Management Executive,* 15(3): 36–42.

Carless, S.A., Mann, L. and Wearing, A.J. (1996) 'Transformational leadership and teams: An examination of the Bass and Kouzes-Posner models', in K.W. Parry (ed.), *Leadership Research and Practice: Emerging Themes and New Challenges.* Melbourne: Pitman. pp. 77–90.

Carroll, P.J. (1999) 'A letter to the people of Shell Oil Company' at URL: http://learning.mit.edu/pra/pro/shell/people_of_shell/full.htm accessed on 3 March 1999.

Chaleff, I. (1995) 'The courageous follower', *World Executive's Digest,* November: 68–9.

Chao, G.T. (1997) 'Mentoring phases and outcomes', *Journal of Vocational Behavior*, 51(1): 15–28.

Chao, G.T., Walz, P.M. and Gardner, P.D. (1992) 'Formal and informal mentorships: A comparison on mentoring functions and contrast with nonmentored counterparts', *Personnel Psychology*, 45(3): 619–36.

Clegg, S.R. and Gray, J.T. (1996) 'Leadership research and embryonic industry: Harvesting competitive advantage', in K.W. Parry (1996) (ed.), *Leadership Research and Practice: Emerging Themes and New Challenges*. Melbourne: Pitman. pp. 29–40.

Cohen, E. and Tichy, N. (1997) 'How leaders develop leaders', *Training and Development*, 51(5): 58–73.

Colins, C. and Chippendale, P. (1991) *New Wisdom II: Values-Based Development*. Brisbane: Acorn.

Collins, J. (1999) 'And the walls came tumbling down', in F. Hesselbein, M. Goldsmith and I. Somerville (eds), *Leading Beyond the Walls*. San Francisco, CA: Jossey-Bass. pp. 19–28.

Collins, J. (2001) 'Level 5 leadership: The triumph of humility and fierce resolve', *Harvard Business Review*, 79(1): 67–76.

Collins, J. and Porras, J. (1994) *Built to Last*. New York: HarperCollins.

Communal, C. and Senior, B. (1999) 'National culture and management: Messages conveyed by British, French and German advertisements for managerial appointments', *Leadership and Organization Development Journal*, 20(1): 26–35.

Complexity and Management Centre (2000) 'Survey of complexity science and how it is being used in organisations and their management'. University of Hertfordshire. URL: http://www.herts.ac.uk/business/centres/cmc/pub8.htm, accessed August.

Conger, J.A. (1989) *The Charismatic Leader: Behind the Mystique of Exceptional Leadership*. San Francisco, CA: Jossey-Bass.

Conger, J.A. and Kanungo, R.N. (1987) 'Toward a behavioral theory of charismatic leadership in organizational settings', *Academy of Management Review*, 12(4): 637–47.

Conger, J.A. and Kanungo, R.N. (1988) 'Behavioral dimensions of charismatic leadership', in J.A. Conger and R.N. Kanungo (eds), *Charismatic Leadership: The Elusive Factor in Organizational Effectiveness*. San Francisco, CA: Jossey-Bass. pp. 78–97.

Conger, J.A. and Kanungo, R.N. (1994) 'Charismatic leadership in organizations: Perceived behavioral attributes and their measurement', *Journal of Organizational Behavior*, 15(4): 439–52.

Coulson-Thomas, C. (1992) 'Strategic vision or strategic con? Rhetoric or reality?', *Long Range Planning*, 25(1): 81–9.

Cross, R. and Baird, L. (2000) 'Technology is not enough: Improving performance by building organizational memory', *Sloan Management Review*, 41(3): 69–78.

Dansereau, F., Graen, G. and Haga, W.J. (1975) 'A vertical dyad linkage approach to leadership within formal organizations: A longitudinal investigation of the role making process', *Organizational Behavior and Human Performance*, 13: 46–78.

de Vries, R.E., Roe, R.A. and Taillieu, T.C.B. (1998) 'Need for supervision: Its impact on leadership effectiveness', *Journal of Applied Behavioral Science*, 34(4): 486–501.

Deming, W.E. (1993) *The New Economics for Industry, Government, Education*. Cambridge, MA: Massachusetts Institute of Technology.

den Hartog, D.N., House, R.J., Hanges, P.J., Ruiz-Quintanilla, S.A. and Dorfman, P.W. (1999) 'Culture specific and cross-culturally generalizable implicit leadership theories: Are attributes of charismatic/transformational leadership universally endorsed?', *Leadership Quarterly*, 10(2): 219–56.

Donaldson, T. (1999) 'Making stakeholder theory whole', *Academy of Management Review*, 24(2): 237–41.

Donaldson, T. and Preston, L.E. (1995) 'The stakeholder theory of the corporation: Concepts, evidence, and implications', *Academy of Management Review*, 20(1): 65–91.

Douglas, C.A. and McCauley, C.D. (1999) 'Formal developmental relationships: A survey of organizational practices', *Human Resource Development Quarterly*, 10(3): 203–20.

Drago, W.A. (1998) 'Mintzberg's "pentagon" and organizational positioning', *Management Research News*, 21(4/5): 30–40.

Drath, W.H. (1998) 'Approaching the future of leadership development', in C.D. McCauley, R.S. Moxley, and E. van Velsor (eds), *The Center for Creative Leadership Handbook of Leadership Development*. San Francisco, CA: Jossey-Bass. pp. 403–39.

Drath, W.H. (2001) *The Deep Blue Sea: Rethinking the Source of Leadership*. San Francisco, CA: Jossey-Bass.

Dreher, G.F. and Ash, R.A. (1990) 'A comparative study of mentoring among men and women in managerial, professional, and technological positions', *Journal of Applied Psychology*, 75(5): 539–46.

DuBrin, A.J. (1998) *Leadership: Research Findings, Practice and Skills*, 2nd edn. Boston, MA: Houghton Mifflin.

Duchon, D., Green, S. and Tabor, T. (1986) 'Vertical dyad linkage: A longitudinal assessment of attitudes, measures and consequences', *Journal of Applied Psychology*, 71(1): 56–60.

Duerst-Lahti, G. and Kelly, R.M. (eds) (1995) *Gender Power, Leadership and Governance*. Ann Arbor, MI: University of Michigan Press.

Dunphy, D. and Stace, D. (1988) 'Transformational and coercive strategies for planned organizational change', *Organization Studies*, 9(3): 317–34.

Dunphy, D. and Stace, D. (1990) *Under New Management: Australian Organisations in Transition*. Sydney: McGraw-Hill.

Dyer, J.H. and Nobeoka, K. (2000) 'Creating and managing a high-performance knowledge-sharing network: The Toyota case', *Strategic Management Journal*, 21(3): 345–67.

Emery, F.E. and Trist, E.L. (1973) *Toward a Social Ecology*. New York, NY: Plenum.

Emrich, C.G. (1999) 'Context effects in leadership and perception', *Personality and Social Psychology Bulletin*, 25(8): 991–1006.

Estes, R. (1996) *The Tyranny of the Bottom Line: Why Corporations Make Good People Do Bad Things*. San Francisco, CA: Berrett-Koehler.

Fagenson, E.A. (1989) 'The mentor advantage: Perceived career/job experience of protégé vs. non-protégé', *Journal of Organizational Behavior*, 10(4): 309–20.

Fairholm, G.W. (1998a) *Perspectives on Leadership*. London: Quorum.

Fairholm, G.W. (1998b) *Values Leadership: Toward a New Philosophy of Leadership*. New York, NY: Praeger.

Farnham, A. (1993) 'Mary Kay's lessons in leadership', *Fortune*, 20(58): 60–4.

Fayol, H. (1949) *General and Industrial Management*. London: Pitman.

Fiedler, F.E. (1967) *A Theory of Leadership Effectiveness*. New York, NY: McGraw-Hill.

Fiedler, F.E. (1997) 'Situational control and a dynamic theory of leadership', in K. Grint (ed.), *Leadership: Classical, Contemporary, and Critical Approaches*. Oxford: Oxford University Press. pp. 211–23.

Fleischman, E.A. and Harris, E.F. (1962) 'Patterns of leadership behavior related to employee grievances and turnover', *Personnel Psychology*, 15: 43–56.

Fondas, N. (1997) 'Feminization unveiled: Management qualities in contemporary writings', *Academy of Management Review*, 22(1): 257–82.

Freeman, R.E. (1984) *Strategic Management: A Stakeholder Approach*. Englewood Cliffs, NJ: Prentice-Hall.

French, J. and Raven, B.H. (1959) 'The bases of social power', in D. Cartwright (ed.), *Studies of Social Power.* Ann Arbor, MI: Institute for Social Research. pp. 150–67.

Frink, D.D. and Klimoski, R.J. (1998) 'Toward a theory of accountability in organizations and human resources management', *Research in Personnel and Human Resources Management*, 16: 1–51.

Geletkanycz, M.A. and Hambrick, D.C. (1997) 'The external ties of top executives: Implications for strategic choice and performance', *Administrative Science Quarterly,* 42(4): 654–81.

Gemmill, G. and Oakley, J. (1992) 'Leadership: An alienating social myth?', *Human Relations*, 45(2): 113–29.

Gergen, K.J. (1997) 'Social psychology as social construction: The emerging vision', in C. McGarty and A. Haslam (eds), *The Message of Social Psychology: Perspectives on Mind in Society.* Oxford: Blackwell.

Ghoshal, S. and Bartlett, C.A. (1998) *The Individualized Corporation*, London: Heinemann.

Gilmore, T.N. and Shea, G.P. (1997) 'Organizational learning and the leadership skill of time travel', *Journal of Management Development*, 16(4): 302–311.

Gleick, J. (1987) *Chaos: Making a New Science.* London: Cardinal.

Goleman, D. (1995) *Emotional Intelligence.* New York, NY: Bantam.

Goodson, J.R., McGee, G.W. and Cashman, J.F. (1989) 'Situational leadership theory: A test of leadership prescriptions', *Group and Organizational Studies*, 13(4): 446–61.

Graeff, C. (1983) 'The situational leadership theory: A critical review', *Academy of Management Review*, 8(2): 285–91.

Graeff, C. (1997) 'Evolution of situational leadership theory – A critical review', *Leadership Quarterly,* 8(2): 153–70.

Graen, G. and Cashman, J.F. (1975) 'A role-making model of leadership in formal organizations: A developmental approach', in J.G. Hunt and L.L. Larson (eds), *Leadership Frontiers.* Kent, OH: Kent State University. pp. 143–65.

Greenleaf, R.K. (1977) *Servant Leadership: A Journey into the Nature of Legitimate Power and Greatness.* New York, NY: Paulist.

Gregersen, H.B., Morrison, A.J. and Black, J.S. (1998) 'Developing leaders for the global frontier', *Sloan Management Review*, 40(1): 21–32.

Grendstad, G. and Strand, T. (1999) 'Organizational types and leadership roles', *Scandinavian Journal of Management,* 15(4): 385–403.

Grensing-Pophal, L. (1998) 'Plays well with others', *Credit Union Management*, May, 52–4.

Gronn, P. (1995) 'Greatness re-visited: The current obsession with transformational leadership', *Leading and Managing*, 1(1): 14–27.

Hambrick, D.C. and Mason, P.A. (1984) 'Upper echelons: The organization as a reflection of its top managers', *Academy of Management Review*, 9(2): 193–206.

Hamel, G. and Prahalad, C.K. (1989) 'Strategic intent', *Harvard Business Review*, 89(3): 63–76.

Hay-McBer (1995) 'Mastering Global Leadership: Hay/McBer International CEO Leadership Study'. Report issued by the Hay Group, McBer and Company Inc., Baston.

Hede, A. and Wear, R. (1996) 'Dimensions of political and organizational leadership', in K.W. Parry (ed.), *Leadership Research and Practice: Emerging Themes and New Challenges.* Melbourne: Pitman. pp. 65–75.

Heifetz, R.A. (1994) *Leadership Without Easy Answers.* Cambridge, MA: Harvard University Press.

Helgesen, S. (1990) *The Female Advantage: Women's Way of Leadership.* New York, NY: Double Day/Currency.

Henriques, I. and Sadorsky, P. (1999) 'The relationship between environmental commitment and managerial perceptions of stakeholder importance', *Academy of Management Journal*, 42(1): 87–99.

Herbert, I. (2000) 'Knowledge is a noun, learning is a verb', *Management Accounting*, 78(2): 68–9.

Hersey, P. and Blanchard, K. (1969) 'Life-cycle theory of leadership', *Training and Development Journal*, 2(May): 6–34.

Hersey, P. and Blanchard, K. (1982) *Management of Organizational Behavior*. 4th edn. Englewood Cliffs, NJ: Prentice-Hall.

Hersey, P. and Blanchard, K. (1996) 'Great ideas revisited: Revisiting the life-cycle theory of leadership', *Training and Development*, 50(1): 42–7.

Hesselbein, F., Goldsmith, M. and Somerville, I. (eds) (1997) *The Organization of the Future*: *The Drucker Foundation*. San Francisco, CA: Jossey-Bass.

Hesselbein, F., Goldsmith, M. and Somerville, I. (eds) (1999) *Leading Beyond the Walls*. San Francisco, CA: Jossey-Bass.

Hilb, M. (1997) *Management by Mentoring: How to Develop Presidents*. Neuwied: Luchterhand.

Hilb, M. (1999) *Integriertes Personal-Management: Ziele, Strategien, Instrumente*, 7th edn. Neuwied: Luchterhand.

Hillman, A.J. and Hitt, M.A. (1999) 'Corporate political strategy formulation: A model of approach, participation, and strategy decisions', *Academy of Management Review*, 24(4): 825–42.

Hirschhorn, L. (1988) *The Workplace Within*. Cambridge, MA: MIT.

Hirschhorn, L. (1997) *Reworking Authority: Leading and Following in the Post-Modern Organization*. Cambridge, MA: MIT.

Hochschild, A. (1997) *Timebind: When Work Becomes Home and Home Becomes Work*. New York, NY: Metropolitan.

Hofstede, G.H. (1984) *Culture's Consequences, International Differences in Work-Related Values*. Thousand Oaks, CA: Sage.

Hofstede, G.H. (1991) *Cultures and Organizations: Software of the Mind*. London: McGraw-Hill.

Hofstede, G.H. (1996) 'An American in Paris: The influence of nationality on organization theories', *Organizational Studies*, 17(3): 525–37.

Hollander, E.P. (1979) 'Leadership and social exchange processes', in K. Gergen, M.S. Greenberg and R.H. Willis (eds), *Social Change: Advances in Theory and Research*. New York, NY: Wiley.

Holt, K. (1999) 'Management and organization through 100 years', *Technovation*, 19(3): 135–40.

House, R.J. (1971) 'A goal-path theory of leader effectiveness', *Administrative Science Quarterly*, 16: 321–39.

House, R.J. (1977) 'A 1976 theory of charismatic leadership', in J.G. Hunt and L.L. Larson (eds), *Leadership: The Cutting Edge*. Carbondale, IL: Southern Illinois Press. pp. 189–207.

House, R.J. and Dessler, G. (1974) 'The goal-path theory of leadership: Some post hoc and a priori tests', in J.G. Hunt and L.L. Larson (eds), *Contingency Approaches to Leadership*. Carbondale, IL: Southern Illinois Press.

House, R.J. and Mitchell, T.R. (1974) 'Path-goal theory of leadership', *Contemporary Business*, 3(4): 81–98.

House, R.J. and Shamir, B. (1993) 'Towards the integration of transformational, charismatic and visionary theories', in M.M. Chemers and R. Ayman (eds), *Leadership Theory and Research*. San Diego, CA: Academic Press.

Howard, A. and Bray, D.W. (1988) *Managerial Lives in Transition: Advancing Age and Changing Times.* New York, NY: Guilford Press.

Howell, J.P., Bowen, D.E., Dorfman, P.W., Kerr, S. and Podsakoff, P.M. (1990) 'Substitutes for leadership: Effective alternatives to ineffective leadership', *Organizational Dynamics*, 19(1): 21–38.

Hunt, D.M. and Michael, C. (1983) 'Mentorships: A career training and development tool', *Academy of Management Review*, 8(3): 475–85.

Hunt, J.G. (1991) *Leadership: A New Synthesis.* Thousand Oaks, CA: Sage.

Ichikawa, A. (1996) 'Leadership as a form of culture: Its present and future states in Japan', in R.M. Steers, L.W. Porter and G.A. Bigley (eds), *Motivation and Leadership at Work.* 6th edn. New York, NY: McGraw-Hill. pp. 455–68.

Intagliata, J., Ulrich, D. and Smallwood, N. (2000) 'Leveraging leadership competencies to produce leadership brand: Creating distinctiveness by focusing on strategy and results', *Human Resource Planning,* 23(3): 12–23.

Jacobs, D. and Singell, L. (1993) 'Leadership and organizational performance: Isolating links between managers and collective success', *Social Science Research,* 22(2): 165–89.

Jacobs, T.O. and Jaques, E. (1990) 'Military executive leadership', in K.E. Clark and M.B. Clark (eds), *Measures of Leadership.* West Orange, NJ: Leadership Library of America. pp. 281–95.

Johns, G. (1978) 'Task moderators of the relationship between leadership style and subordinate responses', *Academy of Management Journal,* 21(2): 319–25

Jones, T.M. (1995) 'Instrumental stakeholder theory: A synthesis of ethics and economics', *Academy of Management Review,* 20(2): 404–437.

Judge, W.Q. (1999) *The Leader's Shadow: Exploring and Developing Executive Character.* Thousand Oaks, CA: Sage.

Kantabutra, S. (2003) 'An empirical examination of relationships between vision components, and customer and staff satisfaction in retail apparel stores in Sydney, Australia'. Unpublished PhD thesis, Macquarie University, Sydney, Australia.

Kantabutra, S. and Avery, G.C. (2002a) 'Proposed model for investigating relationships between vision components and business unit performance', *Journal of Australian and New Zealand Academy of Management,* 8(2): 22–39.

Kantabutra, S. and Avery, G.C. (2002b) 'Effective visions: Components and realization factors', *SASIN Journal of Management,* 8(1): 33–49.

Kaplan, R. and Norton, D. (1992) 'The balanced scorecard – Measures that drive performance', *Harvard Business Review,* 70(1): 71–9.

Kerr, S., Schriesheim, C.A., Murphy, C.J. and Stogdill, R.M. (1974) 'Toward a contingency theory of leadership based upon the consideration and initiating structure literature', *Organizational Behavior and Human Performance,* 12: 62–82.

Kets de Vries, M.F.R. (1994) 'The leadership mystique', *The Academy of Management Executive*, 8(3): 73–93.

Kets de Vries, M.F.R. with Florent-Treacy, E. (1999) *The New Global Leaders: Richard Branson, Percy Barnevik, David Simon and the Remaking of International Business.* San Francisco, CA: Jossey-Bass.

Kezar, A. (2000) 'Pluralistic leadership: Incorporating diverse voices', *Journal of Higher Education,* 71(6): 722–43.

King, A.B. and Fine, G.A. (2000) 'Ford on the line: Business leader reputation and the multiple-audience problem', *Journal of Management Inquiry,* 9(1): 71–86.

Kirkpatrick, S.A. and Locke, E.A. (1991) 'Leadership: Do traits matter?', *Academy of Management Executive,* 5(2): 48–60.

Klimecki, R. and Lassleben, H. (1998) 'Models of organizational learning: Indications from an empirical study', *Management Learning,* 29(4): 405–30.

Kotter, J.P. (1985) *Power and Influence: Beyond Formal Authority.* New York, NY: Free Press.

Kotter, J.P. (1990) *A Force for Change: How Leadership Differs from Management.* New York, NY: Free Press.

Kotter, J.P. and Heskett, J.L. (1992) *Corporate Culture and Performance.* New York, NY: Free Press.

Kotter, J.P., Schlesinger, L.A. and Sathe, V. (1979) *Organization: Text, Cases and Readings on the Management of Organizational Design and Change.* Homewood, IL: Richard D. Irwin.

Kouzes, J.M. and Posner, B.Z. (1987) *The Leadership Challenge: How to Get Extraordinary Things Done in Organizations.* San Francisco, CA: Jossey-Bass.

Kouzes, J.M. and Posner, B.Z. (1995) *The Leadership Challenge.* San Francisco, CA: Jossey-Bass.

Kraatz, M.S. (1998) 'Learning by association? Interorganizational networks and adaptation to environmental change', *Academy of Management Journal,* 41(6): 621–43.

Kram, K.E. (1983) 'Phases of the mentor relationship', *Academy of Management Journal,* 26(4): 608–25.

Kram, K.E. (1985) 'Improving the mentoring process', *Training and Development Journal,* 39: 40–3.

Krantz, J. (1990) 'Lessons from the field: An essay on the crisis of leadership in contemporary organizations', *Journal of Applied Behavioral Science,* 26(1): 49–64.

Kuhnert, K.W. (1994) 'Transforming leadership: Developing people through delegation', in B.M. Bass and B.J. Avolio (eds), *Improving Organizational Effectiveness Through Transformational Leadership.* Thousand Oaks, CA: Sage. pp. 10–25.

Lam, A. (2000) 'Tacit knowledge, organizational learning and societal institutions: An integrated framework', *Organization Studies,* 21(3): 487–513.

Lambert, L. (1995) *The Constructivist Leader.* New York, NY: Teachers College Press.

Larwood, L., Falbe, C.M., Kriger, M.R. and Miesling, P. (1995) 'Structure and meaning of organizational vision', *Academy of Management Journal,* 38(3): 740–69.

Lawler, E.E., III and Mohrman, S.A. (1989) 'With HR help, all managers can practice high-involvement management', *Personnel,* 66(4): 26–31.

Lawrence, P.R. and Lorsch, J.W. (1967) *Organization and Environment: Managing Differentiation and Integration.* Boston, MA: Harvard Business Press.

Leavitt, H.J. (2003) 'Why hierarchies thrive', *Harvard Business Review,* 81(3): 96–102.

Lewis, D. (1996) 'New perspectives on transformational leadership', in K.W. Parry (ed.), *Leadership Research and Practice: Emerging Themes and New Challenges.* Melbourne: Pitman. pp. 17–28.

Lieberson, S. and O'Connor, J.F. (1972) 'Leadership and organizational performance: A study of large corporations', *American Sociological Review,* 37(2): 117–30.

Lim, B. (1997) 'Transformational leadership in the UK management culture', *Leadership and Organization Development Journal,* 18(6): 283–9.

Locke, E.A., Kirkpatrick, S., Wheeler, J.K., Schneider, J., Niles, K., Goldstein, H., Welsh, K. and Chah, D.O. (1991) *The Essence of Leadership.* New York, NY: Lexington Books.

Lord, R.G. (1985) 'An information processing approach to social perceptions, leadership and behavioral measurement in organizations', *Research in Organizational Behavior,* 7: 87–128.

Lord, R.G. and Maher, K.J. (1991) 'Leadership and Information Processing: Linking Perceptions and Performance', *People and Organizations*, Vol. 1. Boston, MA: Unwin and Hyman.

Maccobry, M. (2000) 'Narcissistic leaders: The incredible pros, the inevitable cons', *Harvard Business Review*, 78(1): 68–77.

Mann, S. (1997) 'Emotional labor in organizations', *Leadership and Organization Development Journal*, 18(1): 4–12.

Manz, C.C. (1986) 'Self-leadership: Toward an expanded theory of self-influence in organizations', *Academy of Management Review*, 11(3): 585–600.

Manz, C.C. (1990) 'Beyond self-managing work teams: Toward self-leading teams in the workplace' in R. Woodman and W. Pasmore (eds), *Research in Organizational Change and Development*. Greenwich, CN: JAI Press.

Manz, C.C. (1996) 'Self-leading work teams: Moving beyond self-management myths', in R.M. Steers, L.W. Porter and G.A. Bigley (eds), *Motivation and Leadership at Work*. 6th edn. New York, NY: McGraw-Hill. pp. 581–99.

Manz, C.C. and Sims, H.P. (1989) *SuperLeadership: Leading others to lead themselves*. New York, NY: Prentice-Hall.

Manz, C.C. and Sims, H.P., Jr. (1991) 'Superleadership: Beyond the myth of heroic leadership', *Organizational Dynamics*, 19(4): 18ff.

Masi, R.J. and Cooke, R.A. (2000) 'Effects of transformational leadership on subordinate motivation, empowering norms, and organizational productivity', *International Journal of Organizational Analysis*, 8(1): 16–47.

Mayrhofer, W. (1997) 'Of dice and men: High-flyers in German-speaking countries', *Career Development International*, 2(7): 331–40.

McCauley, C.D. and Lombardo, M.M. (1990) 'Benchmarks: An instrument for diagnosing managerial strengths and weaknesses', in K.E. Clark and M.B. Clark (eds), *Measures of Leadership*. West Orange, NJ: Leadership Library of America. pp. 535–45.

McCauley, C.D. and Young, D.P. (1993) 'Creating developmental relationships: Roles and strategies', *Human Resource Management Review*, 3(?): 219–30.

McClelland, D. (1973) 'Testing for competence rather than intelligence', *American Psychologist*, 28: 1–14.

McCullough, C. (1998a) *The Song of Troy*. London: Orion.

McCullough, C. (1998b) *Caesar*. London: Arrow.

McKinley, W., Mone, M.A. and Moon, G. (1999) 'Determinants and development of schools in organizational theory', *Academy of Management Review*, 24(4): 634–48.

Meindl, J.R. (1998) 'Invited reaction: Enabling visionary leadership', *Human Resource Development Quarterly*, 9(1): 21–4.

Meindl, J.R. and Ehrlich, S.B. (1987) 'The romance of leadership and the evaluation of organizational performance', *Academy of Management Journal*, 30(1): 90–109.

Meindl, J.R., Ehrlich, S.B. and Dukerich, J.M. (1985) 'The romance of leadership', *Administrative Science Quarterly*, 30(1): 78–102.

Merry, U. (1995) *Coping with Uncertainty: Insights from the New Sciences of Chaos, Self-Organization, and Complexity*. Westport, CT: Praeger.

Merry, U. (1999) 'Nonlinear organizational dynamics', URL: http://pw2.netcom.com/~nmerry/art2.htm accessed August 2000.

Miles, R. and Snow, C. (1978) *Organizational Strategy, Structure, and Process*. New York, NY: McGraw-Hill.

Miller, D. (1990) 'Organizational configurations: Cohesion, change, and prediction', *Human, Relations*, 43(8): 771–89.

Miller, D. and Droge, C. (1986) 'Psychological and traditional determinants of structure', *Administrative Science Quarterly,* 31(4): 539–60.

Miller, D. and Friesen, P.H. (1980) 'Momentum and revolution in organizational adaptation', *Academy of Management Journal,* 23(4): 591–614.

Mintzberg, H. (1973a) *The Nature of Managerial Work.* New York, NY: Harper and Row.

Mintzberg, H. (1973b) 'Strategy-making in three modes', *California Management Review,* 16(2): 44–53.

Mintzberg, H. (1979) *The Structuring of Organizations: A Synthesis of Research.* Englewood Cliffs, NJ: Prentice-Hall.

Mintzberg, H. (1993) *Structure in Fives: Designing Effective Organizations.* Englewood Cliffs, NJ: Prentice-Hall.

Mintzberg, H. (1994) *The Rise and Fall of Strategic Planning.* New York, NY: Free Press.

Mintzberg, H. (1998) 'Covert leadership: notes on managing professionals', *Harvard Business Review,* 76(6): 140–7.

Mintzberg, H. and van der Heyden, L. (1999) 'Organigraphs: Drawing how companies really work', *Harvard Business Review,* 77(5): 87–94.

Mitchell, T.R., Agle, B.R. and Wood, D.J. (1997) 'Toward a theory of stakeholder identification and salience: Defining the principle of who and what really counts', *Academy of Management Review,* 22(4), 853–86.

Mitroff, I.I. and Denton, E.A. (1999) 'A study of spirituality in the workplace', *Sloan Management Review,* 40(4): 83–92.

Mitroff, I.I. and Pondy, L.R. (1978) 'Afterthoughts on the leadership conference', in M.W. McCall, Jr. and M.M. Lombardo (eds), *Leadership: Where Else Can We Go?* Dunbar, NC: Duke University Press. pp. 145–50.

Moss Kanter, R. (1989) *When Giants Learn to Dance – Mastering the Challenges of Strategy, Management and Careers in the 1990s.* New York, NY: Simon and Schuster.

Nadler, D. and Tushman, M. (1990) 'Beyond the charismatic leader: Leadership and organizational change', *California Management Review,* 32(2): 77–97.

Nahavandi, A. (1997) *The Art and Science of Leadership.* Englewood Cliffs, NJ: Prentice-Hall.

Nanus, B. (1992) *Visionary Leadership: Creating a Compelling Sense of Direction for Your Organization.* San Francisco, CA: Jossey-Bass.

Noe, R.A. (1991) 'Mentoring relationships for employee development', in J.W. Jones, B.D. Steffy and D.W. Bray (eds), *Applying Psychology in Business: The Handbook for Managers and Human Resource Professionals.* Lexington, MA: Heath. pp. 475–82.

Noe, R.A. (1988) 'An investigation of the determinants of successful assigned mentoring relationships', *Personnel Psychology,* 41(3): 257–81.

Norburn, D. and Birley, S. (1988) 'The top management team and corporate performance', *Strategic Management Journal,* 9(6): 225–37.

O'Hara-Devereaux, M. and Johansen, R. (1994) *Global Work: Bridging Distance, Culture and Time.* San Francisco, CA: Jossey-Bass.

O'Reilly, C. (1996) 'Corporations, culture and commitment: Motivation and social control in organizations', in in R.M. Steers, L.W. Porter and G.A. Bigley (eds), *Motivation and Leadership at Work.* 6th edn. New York, NY: McGraw-Hill. pp. 370–82.

O'Shannassy, T. (2003) 'Modern strategic management: Balancing strategic thinking and strategic planning for internal and external stakeholders', *Singapore Management Review,* 25(1): 53ff.

Ogden, S. and Watson, R. (1999) 'Corporate performance and stakeholder management: Balancing shareholder and customer interests in the UK privatized water industry', *Academy of Management Journal,* 42(5): 526–38.

Oswald, S., Mossholder, K. and Harris, S. (1994) 'Vision salience and strategic involvement: Implications for psychological attachment to organization and job', *Strategic Management Journal,* 15(6): 477–89.

Oswald, S., Stanwick, P. and LaTour, M. (1997) 'The effect of vision, strategic planning, and cultural relationships on organizational performance: A structural approach', *International Journal of Management,* 14(3): 521–9.

Parry, K.W. and Sarros, J.C. (1996) 'An Australasian perspective on transformational leadership', in K.W. Parry (ed.), *Leadership Research and Practice: Emerging Themes and New Challenges.* Melbourne: Pitman. pp. 105–11.

Pearson, A.E. (1989) 'Six basics for general managers', *Harvard Business Review,* 67(4): 94–101.

Perlow, L.A. (1999) 'The time famine: Toward a sociology of work time', *Administrative Science Quarterly,* 44(1): 57–82.

Peters, L.H., Hartke, D.D. and Pohlmann, J.T. (1985) 'Fiedler's contingency theory of leadership: An application of the meta-analysis procedure of Schmitt and Hunter', *Psychological Bulletin,* 97(2): 274–85.

Pfeffer, J. (1978) 'The ambiguity of leadership', in M.W. McClelland, Jr. and M.M. Lombardo (eds), *Leadership: Where Else Can We Go?* Dunbar, NC: Duke University Press. pp. 13–34.

Pfeffer, J. (1992) 'Understanding power in organizations', reprinted in R.M. Steers, L.W. Porter and G.A. Bigley (eds), *Motivation and Leadership at Work.* 6th edn. New York, NY: McGraw-Hill. pp. 280–99.

Pfeffer, J. (1998) 'The ambiguity of leadership', in M.W. McClelland, Jr. and M.M. Lombardo (eds), *Leadership: Where Else Can We Go?* Dunbar, NC: Duke University Press. pp. 13–34.

Pfeffer, J. and Sutton, R.I. (1999) 'Knowing "what" to do is not enough: Turning knowledge into action', *California Management Review,* 42(1): 83–108.

Phillips, R.L. and Hunt, J.G. (1992) 'Strategic leadership: an introduction', in R.L. Phillips and J.G. Hunt (eds), *Strategic Leadership: A Multiorganizational-level Perspective.* Westport, CT: Quarum.

Pierce, C. (1994) 'Executive competencies: Research issues, activities and responses', *Executive Development,* 7(4): 18–24.

Porter, L.W. and Lawler, E.E. (1968) *Managerial Attitudes and Performance.* Homewood, IL: Irwin-Dorsey.

Raelin, J. (2003) *Creating Leadership Organizations: How to Bring out Leadership in Everyone.* San Francisco, CA: Berrett-Koehler.

Ragins, B.R. (1997) 'Diversified mentoring relationships in organizations: A power perspective', *Academy of Management Review,* 22(2): 482–521.

Ragins, B.R. and Scandura, T.A. (1994) 'Gender and the termination of mentoring relationships', in *1994 Academy of Management Best Paper Proceedings.* Dallas, TX: Academy of Management. pp. 361–65.

Roberts, N. (1985) 'Transforming leadership: A process of collective action', *Human Relations,* 38(11): 1023–46.

Roethlisberger, E.J. and Dickson, W.J. (1939) *Management and the Worker.* Boston, MA: Harvard University Press.

Rokeach, M. (1973) *The Nature of Human Values.* New York, NY: Free Press.

Rosenbach, W.E. (1993) 'Mentoring: Empowering followers to be leaders', in W.E. Rosenbach and R.L. Taylor (eds), *Contemporary Issues in Leadership.* Boulder, CO: Westview Press. pp. 141–51.

Rost, J.C. (1991) *Leadership for the Twenty-first Century.* New York, NY: Praeger.

Rothschild, J. and Whitt, J.A. (1986) *The Cooperative Workplace: Potentials and Dilemmas of Organizational Democracy and Participation,* Cambridge: Cambridge University Press.

Rousseau, D. (1997) 'Organizational behavior in the new organizational era', *Annual Review of Psychology,* 48: 515–46.

Salancik, G.R. and Pfeffer, J. (1977) 'Constraints on administrator discretion: The limited influence of mayors in city budgets', *Urban Affairs Quarterly,* 12(4): 475–96.

Salovey, P. and Mayer, J.D. (1990) 'Emotional intelligence', *Imagination, Cognition and Personality,* 9(3): 185–211.

Sashkin, M. (1988) 'The visionary leader', in J.A. Conger and R.N. Kanungo (eds), *Charismatic Leadership: The Elusive Factor in Organizational Effectiveness.* San Francisco, CA: Jossey-Bass. pp. 122–60.

Scandura, T.A. and Viator, R. (1994) 'Mentoring in public accounting firms: An analysis of mentor-protégé relationships, mentoring functions, and protégé turnover intentions', *Accounting, Organizations and Society,* 19(8): 717–34.

Schein, E.H. (1985) *Organizational Culture and Leadership.* San Francisco, CA: Jossey-Bass.

Schein, E.H. (1992) *Organizational Culture and Leadership.* 2nd edn. San Francisco, CA: Jossey-Bass.

Schermerhorn, J.R. and Bond, M.H. (1997) 'Cross-cultural leadership dynamics in collectivism and high power distance settings', *Leadership and Organization Development Journal,* 18(4): 187–93.

Schriesheim, C.A. and Kerr, S. (1977) 'Theories and measures of leadership: A critical appraisal of current and future directions', in J.G. Hunt and L.L. Larson (eds), *Leadership: The Cutting Edge.* Carbondale, IL: Southern Illinois Press. pp. 51–6.

Schriesheim, C.A. and Neider, L.L. (1989) 'Leadership theory and development: The coming "new phase"', *Leadership and Organization Development Journal,* 10(6): 17–26.

Scott, S.G. and Lane, V.R. (2000) 'A stakeholder approach to organizational identity', *Academy of Management Review,* 25(1): 43–62.

Senge, P.M. (1990a) *The Fifth Discipline: The Art and Practice of the Learning Organization.* New York, NY: Double Day/Currency.

Senge, P.M. (1990b) 'The leader's new work: Building learning organizations', *Sloan Management Review,* 31(1): 7–23.

Senge, P.M., Kleiner, A., Roberts, C., Ross, R.B. and Smith, B.J. (1994) *The Fifth Discipline Fieldbook: Strategies and Tools for Building a Learning Organization.* London: Nicholas Brealey.

Shamir, B. (1991) 'The charismatic relationship: Alternative explanations and predictions', *Leadership Quarterly,* 2: 81–104.

Shamir, B., House, R.J. and Arthur, M.B. (1993) 'The motivational effects of charismatic leadership: A self-concept based theory', *Organization Science,* 4(4): 577–94.

Silverhart, T.A. (1994) 'It works: Mentoring drives productivity higher', *Managers,* October: 14–5.

Sims, H.P., Jr. and Lorenzi, P. (1992) *The New Leadership Paradigm: Social Learning and Cognition in Organizations.* Thousand Oaks, CA: Sage.

Sinclair, A. (1998) *Doing Leadership Differently: Gender, Power and Sexuality in a Changing Business Culture.* Melbourne: Melbourne University Press.

Spillane, R. and Spillane, L. (1998) 'The two faces of authority: A critique', *Journal of the Australian and New Zealand Academy of Management,* 5(2): 1–11.

Stacey, R. (2000) *'Excitement and tension at the edge of chaos',* University of Hertfordshire, Complexity and Management Centre, UK. URL: http://www.herts.ac.uk/business/centres/cmc/pub6.htm, accessed August.

Steers, R.M., Porter, L.W. and Bigley, G.A. (eds) (1996) *Motivation and Leadership at Work.* 6th edn. New York, NY: McGraw-Hill.

Steiner, D.D. (1988) 'Value perceptions in leader-member exchange', *Journal of Social Psychology,* 128: 611–18.

Stewart, G.L. and Manz, C.C. (1995) 'Leadership for self-managing work teams: A typology and integrative model', *Human Relations,* 48(7): 747–70.

Stogdill, R.M. (1948) 'Personal factors associated with leadership: A survey of the literature', *Journal of Psychology,* 25: 35–71.

Strube, M.J. and Garcia, J.E. (1981) 'A meta-analytical investigation of Fiedler's contingency model of leadership effectiveness', *Psychological Bulletin,* 90(2): 307–21.

Sveiby, K. (2000) 'The knowledge-focussed manager', URL: http://www.sveiby.com.au/KnowledgeManagement.html accessed October.

Takala, T. (1998) 'Plato on leadership', *Journal of Business Ethics,* 17(7): 785–98.

Tan, J. (2000) 'Knowledge management – Just more buzz words?' *The British Journal of Administrative Management,* 19 (March/April): 10–11.

Tannenbaum, R. and Schmidt, W.H. (1973) 'How to choose a leadership pattern', *Harvard Business Review,* 51(3): 162–4, 166–8.

Taylor, F.W. (1911) *Principles of Scientific Management.* New York, NY: Harper.

Thomas, A.B. (1988) 'Does leadership make a difference to organizational performance?' *Administrative Science Quarterly,* 33(3): 388–400.

Tichy, N.M. and Cohen, E. (1997) *The Leadership Engine: How Winning Companies Create Leaders at All Levels.* New York, NY: Harper Collins. pp. 57–81.

Tichy, N.M. and Devanna, M.A. (1986) *The Transformational Leader.* New York, NY: Wiley.

Tracey, J.B. and Hinkin, T.R. (1998) 'Transformational leadership or effective managerial practice?' *Group and Organization Management,* 23(3): 220–36.

Trice, H.M. and Beyer, J.M. (1993) *The Cultures of Work Organizations.* Englewood Cliffs, NJ: Prentice-Hall.

Truskie, S. (1990) *The President/CEO Study: Leadership Behaviors, Skills, and Attributes of Executives Who Lead Corporate 1000 Companies.* Pittsburgh, PA: Management Science and Development.

Turner, J. (1999) 'Spirituality in the workplace', *CA Magazine,* 132(10): 41–2.

Tvorik, S.J. and McGivern, M.H. (1997) 'Determinants of organizational performance', *Management Decision,* 35(6): 417–35.

Vaill, P.B. (1989) *Managing as a Performing Art.* San Francisco, CA: Jossey-Bass.

Vecchio, R.P. (1987) 'Situational Leadership Theory: An examination of a prescriptive theory', *Journal of Applied Psychology,* 72(3): 444–51.

Vroom, V. (1964) *Work and Motivation.* New York, NY: Wiley.

Vroom, V. and Jago, A.G. (1988) *The New Leadership: Managing Participation in Organizations.* Englewood Cliffs, NJ: Prentice-Hall.

Vroom, V. and Yetton, P.W. (1973) *Leadership and Decision Making.* Pittsburgh, PA: University of Pittsburgh Press.

Waldman, D.A. and Yammarino, F.J. (1999) 'CEO charismatic leadership: Levels-of-management and levels-of-analysis effects', *Academy of Management Review,* 24(2): 266–85.

Warnecke, H.-J. (1993) *Revolution der Unternehmenskultur – das Fraktale Unternehmen.* Berlin: Springer.

Wasielewski, P. (1985) 'The emotional basis of charisma', *Symbolic Interaction,* 8(2): 207–22.

Weber, M. (1947) *The Theory of Social and Economic Organization,* (T. Parsons, trans.). New York, NY: Free Press.

Weber, M. (1978) *Economy and Society.* Berkeley, CA: University of California Press.

Weick, K. (1991) 'The vulnerable system: An analysis of the Teneriffe air disaster', in P.J. Frost, L.F. Moore, M.R. Louis, C.C. Lundberg and J. Martin (eds), *Reframing Organizational Culture.* Thousand Oaks, CA: Sage.

Weick, K.E. (1995) *Sense-making in Organizations.* Thousand Oaks, CA: Sage.

Westley, F. and Mintzberg, H. (1989) 'Visionary leadership and strategic management', *Strategic Management Journal,* 10 (Summer): 17–32.

Wexley, K.N., Alexander, R.A., Greenwalt, J.P. and Couch, M.A. (1980) 'Attitudinal congruence and similarity as related to interpersonal evaluations in manager-subordinate dyads', *Academy of Management Journal,* 23(2): 320–30.

Wheatley, M.J. (1992) *Leadership and the New Science.* San Francisco, CA: Berrett-Koehler.

Wheatley, M.J. (1999) *Leadership and the New Science: Discovering Order in a Chaotic World,* 2nd edn. San Francisco, CA: Berrett-Koehler.

Wilson, D.D. and Collier, D.A. (2000) 'An empirical investigation of the Malcolm Baldrige National Quality Award causal model', *Decision Sciences,* 31(2): 361–90.

Wilson, J.A. and Elman, N.S. (1990) 'Organizational benefits of mentoring', *Academy of Management Executive,* 4(4): 88–93.

Wolff, M.F. (1999) 'In the organization of the future, competitive advantage will lie with inspired employees', *Research Technology Management,* 42(4): 2–4.

Worrall, L. and Cooper, G.L. (1999) 'Working patterns and working hours: Their impact on UK managers', *Leadership and Organization Development Journal,* 20(1): 6–10.

Yammarino, F.J. (1997) 'Models of leadership for sales management', *The Journal of Personal Selling and Sales Management,* 17(2): 43–56.

Yammarino, F.J. and Dubinsky, A.J. (1994) 'Transformational leadership theory: Using levels of analysis to determine boundary conditions', *Personnel Psychology,* 47(4): 787–810.

Yammarino, F.J., Spangler, W.D. and Bass, B.M. (1993) 'Transformational leadership and performance: A longitudinal investigation', *Leadership Quarterly,* 4(1): 81–102.

Yukl, G. (1981) *Leadership in Organizations.* Englewood Cliffs, NJ: Prentice-Hall,.

Yukl, G. (1994) *Leadership in Organizations,* 3rd edn. Englewood Cliffs, NJ: Prentice-Hall.

Yukl, G. (1998) *Leadership in Organizations,* 4th edn. Englewood Cliffs, NJ: Prentice-Hall.

Yukl. G., Kim, H. and Falbe, C. (1996) 'Antecedents of influence outcomes', *Journal of Applied Psychology,* 81(3): 309–17.

Zaheer, S., Albert, S. and Zaheer, A. (1999) 'Time scales and organizational theory', *Academy of Management Review,* 24(4): 725–41.

Zaleznik, A. (1989) *The Managerial Mystique: Restoring Leadership in Business.* New York, NY: Harper and Row.

Zey, M. (1991) *The Mentor Connection: Strategic Alliances in Corporate Life.* New Brunswick, NJ: Transaction.

Index